FILM EDITING
Theory and Practice

Christopher Llewellyn Reed

MERCURY LEARNING AND INFORMATION
Dulles, Virginia
Boston, Massachusetts
New Delhi

Publisher: David Pallai
Mercury Learning and Information
22841 Quicksilver Drive
Dulles, VA 20166
info@merclearning.com
www.merclearning.com
1-800-758-3756

This book is printed on acid-free paper.

Christopher Llewellyn Reed. *Film Editing:Theory and Practice.*
ISBN: 978-1-9364201-0-0

Library of Congress Control Number: 2011931637

121314321

Printed in Canada

Our titles are available for adoption, license, or bulk purchase by institutions, corporations, etc. For additional information, please contact the Customer Service Dept. at 1-800-758-3756 (toll free).

FILM EDITING
Theory and Practice

To Martine Billet Reed, my mother,
who rented a 16mm film projector for my 12th birthday
so we could watch a print of High Noon,
and created a lifelong cinephile

CONTENTS

WHY AWARD-WINNING ACTORS SHOULD ALWAYS THANK THEIR EDITORS!

OVERVIEW AND LEARNING OBJECTIVES

In this introduction, you will:

- Understand the role of the film editor
- Understand how this book is organized
- Understand how this book can work with other books in this series on different aspects of filmmaking

What Does an Editor Do?

Quick. Name a film editor. Any film editor. Can't name one? OK – let's try your favorite director. Do you immediately think of Alfred Hitchcock, Billy Wilder, John Ford, or someone more contemporary like Steven Spielberg, Spike Lee, Guy Ritchie, Kathryn Bigelow, Jason Reitman, Catherine Hardwicke, or Judd Apatow? If you like foreign films, maybe you're a François Truffaut, Agnieszka Holland, Akira Kurosawa, Zhang Yimou, Abbas Kiorastami, or Pedro Almodóvar fan.

For those of you who don't recognize anyone from either list, perhaps you could name your favorite actor or actress (or one of your many favorites). Do you like old films and are a Humphrey Bogart and/or Katharine Hepburn fan? Or are you more into Kal Penn and/or Zoe Saldana? Perhaps you prefer slightly younger actors, such as Shia LaBeouf and Ellen Page, or slightly older actors, such as Denzel Washington and Meryl Streep. Maybe you're a big fan of late 1960s and early 1970s cinema, so you think of Dustin Hoffman, Al Pacino, Robert De Niro, Faye Dunaway, Diane Keaton, and Sissy Spacek, for example.

Now think about the performance of an actor that you especially admire. Perhaps you like the Oscar™-winning performances, as Best Actor, of Sean Penn in *Milk* or Forest Whitaker in *The Last King of Scotland*. Maybe you appreciate the Best Actress winners Kate Winslet (*The Reader*) and Hilary Swank (either for *Boys Don't Cry* or *Million Dollar Baby*). Let's not forget the Best Supporting Actor and Actress winners, either: Benicio del Toro in *Traffic* and Alan Arkin in *Little Miss Sunshine*, or Jennifer Hudson in *Dreamgirls* and Penélope Cruz in *Vicky Cristina Barcelona*.

What do all of these actors have in common with each other? They should all, in their Oscar acceptance speeches, have thanked their editors. They may have thanked – in fact, most of them did – their directors, but who thinks of the editor as an important part of the filmmaking process? After all, thanks to a small group of French film critics writing in the 1950s for an influential film magazine called *Les Cahiers du Cinéma*, a certain theory about filmmaking – called the *auteur theory* – has become almost the standard way of thinking about how movies are made. The theory claims a film's director is the sole creator of the work. And while that theory served its purpose by focusing attention on certain film directors as important major artists (Roberto Rossellini, Orson Welles, Alfred Hitchcock), it also taught many people to neglect the vast contributions the rest of the crew makes to a film.

Most of us understand, on some level, that it takes many people to create a successful film, but most of us don't think about this when we're watching the film. Even though, occasionally, we might pay attention to the name at the beginning and/or end of a film, under the heading "A Film by," "Directed by," etc.

Let's pause and think about how an actor's performance differs from the stage and the screen. Theatre is an actor's medium, while film is an editor's medium. Who most controls the pacing of the production when you sit in a darkened theatre on Broadway? The actor. Who most controls the pacing of the film you watch at the multiplex? The editor. This is a gross oversimplification of the process, for sure, but it is essentially true.

The shape of an actor's performance, and the shape of the overall movie, is controlled by the people in charge of cutting the raw footage. Sometimes it is the editor, and sometimes it is the editor and director both. Sometimes the director and the editor are the same person. Regardless of who is doing the actual cutting, the concept is the same: you take the raw footage of the actor's performance (different takes, or versions, of the same shots) and shape it to fit the evolving movie.

Not every bit of captured film performance is brilliant and not every bit of brilliance fits the required moment. Occasionally, performances that were considered bad on set end up being used in the finished film because it is possible to take certain parts and insert them into a scene so they work for the story. It is true that a bad performance by an actor is almost impossible to salvage, but it is also true that a good performance by an actor can be cut so badly that it is impossible to appreciate it for what it could have been.

So next time you watch an acceptance speech on Oscar night, look up the film's editor and listen for his or her name. Most of the time you won't hear it. But at least Hollywood, as a whole, recognizes the importance of all members of a creative crew by making sure that most important positions are honored with a separate Oscar category.

Why a Good Director Helps the Editor

As we will see in Chapter 1, the very first filmmakers put the camera down in a chosen spot and gave us one particular visual vantage point of a scene, hoping to show us all of the action in a way that would best allow us to appreciate a story. Relatively quickly, however, some intrepid and inventive young filmmakers realized the importance of showing different details within a scene at different moments, for dramatic effect. Good directors began to understand how camera placement and shot choice could help them tell their stories effectively.

In other words, if a character enters a room with the intention of killing another character, you might choose, as a director, to have your cinematographer shoot the scene from a location that shows the whole room (what we call a long, or wide, shot), then shoot a closer shot of the gun in the character's hand, and then shoot another close shot of the other character's reaction as he or she sees the gun. With just these three shots, you - the editor - suddenly have a potentially cinematic scene, as you can then cut between them, heightening tension. By pre-editing the film through an intelligent choice of shots, the director has made the task of the editor that much easier.

About This Book

This book is part of the *Digital Filmmaker* series of titles about different aspects of filmmaking, and some of the other books in this series deal with those subjects, such as cinematography, distribution, production, storyboarding, and scriptwriting.

In this book, however, we will deal primarily with the art and craft of editing, but that doesn't mean we won't touch on some of the other disciplines. The best way to edit well, for example, is to shoot well, and gather all of the "coverage" (the footage you need to tell your story) ahead of time. A well-prepared director provides enough raw material for the editor to edit well (whether or not the director and editor are the same person). A good editor can certainly do more with bad footage than a bad editor can, but even a brilliant editor has limitations. So direct your actors well, shoot beautiful compositions, and you have a chance, as an editor, at making a decent movie.

Here are some names of film editors, linked to some of the movies they have cut:

Dede Allen (*The Hustler, Dog Day Afternoon, The Breakfast Club*)

William Chang (most of the films of Wong Kar-Wai)

Verna Fields (*Medium Cool, American Graffiti, Jaws*)

Michael Kahn (most big Steven Spielberg films since *Close Encounters*)

Stephen Mirrione (*Traffic*, the *Ocean's* films, *21 Grams*, *Babel*)

Walter Murch (*Apocalypse Now*, *The English Patient*, *Jarhead*)

Sam Pollard (*Jungle Fever*, *Juice*, *Clockers*, *4 Little Girls*)

Thelma Schoonmaker (every Martin Scorsese film since *Raging Bull*)

George Tomasini (*Rear Window*, *Psycho*, *Cape Fear*)

In this book, you will learn about the history of film editing and how it developed from the single-shot movies of the 1890s to the crazy split-second montages of today. You will also learn the different editing aesthetics – the when, how, and why of cutting, as well as the proper terms for different shots – so you can start to develop your own style. You will study some in-depth, shot-by-shot breakdowns of various film scenes, and explore the different editing concerns of narrative (fiction) films vs. documentaries and full-length features vs. shorts. You will learn about non-linear editing systems, such as AVID and Final Cut Pro, and how they have affected the film industry and editing styles. You will study the basic interface of Apple's legacy non-linear editing system – Final Cut Express – as well as LiveType.

Since the release of *Final Cut Pro X*, Apple has touted its newer program as the answer to all of your editing issues, but *Final Cut Express* might be a more viable and more versatile option – for now – for the low-budget filmmaker.

You will also learn about formats and compression. Finally, you will work with the accompanying video footage, included on the DVD that comes with this text, in a variety of ways to put theory into practice and strengthen your understanding of the lessons in the book.

This book, as well as the other books in this series, give you a firm foundation in the basics of craft, grounded in the history of the medium, and teach you how to apply this craft with the technology of today.

How This Book is Organized

This book has 15 chapters. Each chapter builds on the lessons of its predecessor, and takes you one step farther to an understanding of the why, how, and how-to of editing. What follows is an overview of what each chapter teaches you.

Chapter 1 - A Brief History of Film Editing

In this chapter, we go through an overview of the major milestones and movements of narrative (fiction) film history. We pay specific attention to how these movements affected the art and craft of editing. We study montage, continuity, and everything technique in between and beyond.

Chapter 2 - To Cut or Not to Cut

In this chapter, we study film language in greater depth. We learn about shot sizes, shot angles, camera movement, and scene construction. We also study the why and the when of editing, and how the choice to cut, or not to cut, affects the meaning of the story.

Chapter 3 - How Genre Affects Editing

In this chapter, we cover genre, and how it affects the style and editing of a particular film. We focus primarily on the three genres we will emulate in later chapters - drama, comedy and suspense - when we practice actual editing, but we also learn about the many other genre names and styles. Finally, we analyze - in great detail - scenes from three different feature-length films, to see how each film treats the conventions of its genre through its editing.

Chapter 4 - Documentary vs. Narrative

In this chapter, we go through an overview of the major milestones and movements of documentary film history. We also look at the various techniques that are used to shoot and edit documentaries, as they have evolved over time. Finally, we study the different documentary genres, and how they affect the style of a particular film.

Chapter 5 - Features vs. Shorts

In this chapter, we discuss the differences between features films and shorts. We also introduce ourselves to the short film, *Nail Polish*, which we will dissect and recut in later chapters. We study that film's script and watch it on this book's companion DVD. We also analyze some professionally made shorts, and discuss how the issues of time and format affect the editing choices one might make in a short vs. a feature.

Chapter 6 - The NLE Editing Revolution

In this chapter, we go through the history of non-linear digital editing systems, and how those systems have changed the way we edit. We also discuss some important terms, such as *online, offline,* and *timecode.* Finally, although this book focuses on Final Cut Express, we analyze the tools and methods that all digital editing systems share.

Chapter 7 - Final Cut Express: Basic Interface

In this chapter, we discuss how to navigate the basic interface of Final Cut Express (FCE). We learn the names of the various windows and tools, and learn some simple keyboard shortcuts, as well. We then begin to use the program by importing footage from the DVD. Finally, we manipulate this footage in very simple ways, to make us comfortable with the tools and menus.

Chapter 8 - Beyond the Basics: Understanding the Tools of Final Cut Express

In this chapter, we begin to edit by taking footage from the first scene of the short film *Nail Polish,* and attempting to recreate that first scene, ourselves. As we perform these functions, we learn more complex tools than we used in Chapter 7. These tools include the Razor Blade, speed controls, and clip overlays. We also discover simple transitions and how to apply them.

Chapter 9 - Effects and Advanced Techniques

This is the chapter where we complete our training on the FCE interface. We study each dropdown menu in depth. We also study each tool on the *Tool Palette,* in depth. We learn how to customize the *Browser* and *Timeline,* and how to create title cards. We learn the difference between *insert* and *overwrite* edits, as well as *replace* and *fit to fill* edits. We study and use the *Trim Edit Window,* and learn how to copy and paste *clip attributes.* While we practice these new tools, we simultaneously continue to work on recutting the first scene of the movie *Nail Polish.*

Chapter 10 - All About Formats: Capturing, Importing and Exporting

In this chapter, we study video and audio formats, and why it is important to understand the different kinds of compression used in editing and post-production. We also learn how to capture and import footage from a variety of different devices, both tape and flash-based. Finally, we practice exporting video clips, both to tape and as self-contained digital QuickTime files.

Chapter 11 - LiveType: Advanced Titling

In this chapter, we learn a new program - LiveType - that comes bundled with FCE. This program allows for more the creation of more advanced and complex title cards and motion graphics. We study each of the menus and tools, and practice making titles, ourselves. Finally, we discuss the many different ways to export these titles to FCE.

Chapter 12 - The Kuleshov Effect

In this chapter, we apply the lessons of the early Russian film pioneer, Lev Kuleshov, to an editing exercise of our own. Using footage from the DVD, we cut a short film in which the same repeating shot of a man staring off-camera is meant to look different each time we see it, based on its juxtaposition with other shots. Upon recreating the original Kuleshov experiment, we add a modern addition of our own - music - to see how this affects the piece.

Chapter 13 - Nail Polish - Cutting for Comedy

In this chapter, we take all of the footage used to cut the original short film *Nail Polish*, and use it to cut a brand new version of the film, as a comedy. We break down each step, in turn, and compare and contrast the process with that used to edit the first film. As we do so, we discuss the nature of comedy, and how to choose a pace - and the appropriate footage - to maximize the laughs.

Chapter 14 - Nail Polish - Cutting for Drama

In this chapter, we follow the same process as the one we used in Chapter 13, except that this time we are cutting a drama. Again, we break down each step, in turn, but this time we not only compare and contrast the process with that used to edit the original film, but also with that used to edit the comedy. As we do so, we discuss the nature of drama, and how to choose a pace - and the appropriate footage - to maximize the emotional content of the story.

Chapter 15 - Nail Polish - Cutting for Suspense

In this, our final chapter, we follow the same process as the one we used in Chapters 13 and 14, except that this time we are cutting a thriller. We quickly discover, however, that the footage from the original film does not work as well in this genre as it did in a comedy or drama. We therefore spend some time creating a title sequence, using LiveType and sound files found on the DVD, to build suspense before the first shot ever appears. Again, we break down each step, in turn, but this time we not only compare and contrast the process with that used to edit the original film, but also with that used to edit the comedy and drama, both. As we do so, we discuss the nature of thrillers, and how to choose a pace - and the appropriate footage - to maximize the suspense.

The Video and Audio Files on the DVD

This book comes with a companion DVD, on which you will find all of the files you will need to perform all of the exercises in all of the chapters. Most of the video files come from the short film *Nail Polish*, made by the author of this book. The footage for Chapter 12 - *The Kuleshov Effect* - was generated specifically for this text and for that chapter. The audio files used in Chapters 13–15 are all taken from the loops included in Apple's GarageBand software.

Spoiler Alert

As in all books about filmmaking, we will discuss scenes from various films, in depth. Just in case you haven't seen a given movie, you should keep in mind that we have to give enough plot summary for the analysis to make sense and you might read something you don't want to yet know. So – here is the official *spoiler alert*! You have been warned.

CHAPTER 1

A BRIEF HISTORY OF FILM EDITING

OVERVIEW AND LEARNING OBJECTIVES

In this chapter, you will:

- Understand how and where filmmaking began
- Take a short journey through the history of film editing
- Understand the basic unit of filmmaking – the shot
- Become familiar with some major figures and movements in editing history
- Start to think like an editor

The First Films

Depending on your country of origin, you may claim that Thomas Alva Edison (1847–1931) is the "father of cinema," or that August (1862–1954) and Louis (1864–1948) Lumière are, jointly, the "fathers of cinema." Like most human innovation, and like the cinema itself, the invention of the medium was a collaborative effort. Each person working to create the technology necessary to shoot and project moving pictures did their work standing firmly on the shoulders of the people who came before. It is, however, a matter of historical record that the first public commercial projection of a moving picture occurred on the evening of December 28, 1895, in Paris, and so the Lumière brothers can therefore claim some verifiable credit as the inventors of movies.

For an in-depth analysis of film history as it developed in the United States, read Robert Sklar's Movie-Made America.[1]

Still, Thomas Edison, the American inventor, had patented a device called the Kinetoscope in 1891, which allowed individual users to view short strips of film as they leaned into a screen, or peephole, on top of a large chamber, or cabinet. It was an individual viewing experience, which is why the Lumière brothers get the official credit for the first *public* projection of movies. Their device, the Cinématographe, which doubled as both camera and projector, was able to throw the moving images on a wall, or large screen, thus creating, for the first time, the film-going experience that would come to dominate much of 20ᵗʰ century culture. Interestingly enough, with the recent invention of small portable devices, like iPods®, iPhones®, iPads®, and other small video-playing units, we are returning, in some way, to the original film experience of Edison's Kinetoscope.

Both Edison and the Lumière brothers were building on the work of previous scientists and inventors who had done so much to invent photography in the first half of the 19ᵗʰ century. The popularity of "series photography" (basically the making of a "flip book," but with photos) in the 1880s was the direct precursor of the first movie cameras and projectors. Since this is a book on editing, however, let us leave the more detailed history of camera invention to the text on cinematography in this series, and focus instead on what these early films of the 1890s were like.

To begin with, the early films were short. Both the Edison and Lumière films, whether projected using a Kinetoscope, Cinématographe, or Edison's

1896 answer to the Cinématographe, the Vitascope, were all under a minute in length. The Lumières' films tended to be primarily documentary in nature, while Edison's were more staged, but both productions were limited by the technology of the time to films of a certain length, because longer films would have caused the tension on the feed or take-up reels to snap the filmstrip. As we exit – most likely permanently – a world where many of us have touched or seen physical film, be it for photography or cinematography, this concept may become harder for future generations to visualize.

It's fairly simple, though. The physical film strip, whether in a camera or on a projector, is coiled on a metal feed reel. It is then wound through the mechanism of either the camera or the projector and attached to a take-up reel. This physical film, treated with chemicals to react to light and fix an image to itself, though flexible enough to be coiled and wound, has a certain brittle quality to it. If there is too much weight on either end of the camera or projector – that is, if the film is too long, making the feed or take-up reels too heavy – the filmstrip cannot withstand the tension applied to it and snaps.

So what's a young inventive filmmaker in the 1890s to do? Well, the original solution was to just make short films. And then, if you wanted to create a longer screening program, you would show several of these short films in a row. And that's how it worked, at first.

It was, in spite of the Lumières' belief that their invention had no real future, a success. Audiences in New York flocked to short movies showing people and places in Egypt, Moscow, Paris, etc., and audiences in those places likewise flocked to short films showing the residents in New York.

In addition to being short, these films were also all made up of a single shot each.

Defining a *Shot*

Let's make sure we understand the first important term. In the Introduction, we noted that the word is to the sentence as the shot is to the scene. Even if you didn't know exactly what a *shot* was, you could still tell from that context that it is the building block of a movie scene: a sequence of shots makes up a scene.

To better understand this term, let's leave behind our current digital age for a moment and imagine we are holding a strip of actual, 35 mm film from the middle of the 20th century. On either side of this filmstrip are little sprocket holes for engaging with sprockets in the camera and projector. These metal sprockets, running through the sprocket holes, are what pull the film through the camera, one *frame* at a time.

What is a *frame*? Well, picture a pre-digital still photography camera with a coil of 35 mm film inside (in fact, this film strip is almost identical to the kind of film strip used to make motion pictures, only much shorter). Every time you press the button on top of the camera to take a photograph, a single frame is exposed to light, fixing an image on the filmstrip in that exact spot. Then, the camera either advances the filmstrip to the next frame automatically, or you have to manually advance the filmstrip, yourself. That, then, is a single frame, which is the unit with which you work, in still motion photography.

In cinematography, however, you need many of these frames exposed per second, with each frame having an image that is slightly different than the one preceding it and following it. When these images are played back, the viewer sees a reasonable approximation of smooth and uninterrupted motion (like a flip book). There's a little more to it than that, involving the shutter of the camera/projector, and concepts known as the *phi phenomenon* and *persistence of vision*, but we will leave the in-depth discussion of the science of that to the book on cinematography in this series.

So how many of these frames-per-second (fps) are exposed and then played back to mimic normal motion? 24. Like the number of hours in a day. The French New Wave filmmaker Jean-Luc Godard once said, "The cinema is truth 24 frames per second."

In the silent era of filmmaking (1895–1927), there was no absolute fps number that everyone followed – some shot at 18 fps, some at 20 fps, some at 22 fps, etc. It didn't matter that much, because there was no sound to synchronize with the picture. Plus, many cameras were hand-cranked, which made consistency difficult. But once sound synchronization technology started being widely used (following the phenomenal success of the first feature-length talking picture, *The Jazz Singer*, in 1927), it was important to finally pick a number that everyone could stick to, and that number was 24 fps. It's a good number, as it turns out that motion is well served by that many frames-per-second. Fewer than that, and the projection might look a little jerky; more than that, and you're wasting film.

So what is a *shot*?

A **shot** is an unbroken series of frames, recording everything that passes in front of the camera's lens from the time you turn the camera on until the time you turn the camera off, or from the time you start recording until the time you stop recording.

Imagine yourself looking out at a room full of people, with your eyes as the lens and your brain as the filmstrip. If you look from one corner of the room to the other, without closing your eyes, you have just recorded a single shot of that space. If, however, you do close your eyes, or blink, then you have broken up your recording of the room into separate shots.

This is why Walter Murch calls his classic book on editing In the Blink of an Eye *(Silman-James Press, 2001).*[2]

NOTE

This definition holds true in the video realm as well. Whatever the frame rate of capture, be it 24, 25, 29.97, 30, 60, or any other rate, a shot is a series of unbroken frames. Even in this brave new world of ours, where we might be recording to flash memory cards or hard drives, there is still some sort of facsimile of that original film strip, exposing separate little frames to light, thereby capturing and fixing one image per frame.

Once you have captured your shots, whether on film or video, tape or flash memory, you can break up the shots into smaller bits, use parts of one shot here, other parts there, and keep some of them whole while chopping up others. Whatever serves your story.

This is called *editing*.

The Films Grow Longer

At first, Edison, the Lumière brothers, and their contemporaries made short films of approximately 50 seconds to a minute in length. This format suited the documentary style of some of their respective work – for a quick glance at a foreign city – but it quickly became extremely limited for telling a fictional story.

Before long, Woodville Latham patented a technique for creating a loop (now known as the Latham Loop), which diffused the tension on the filmstrip with some slack just after the feed reel and just before the take-up reel. This allowed for longer films to exist in the camera and on the projector.

Once it was possible to have more film on a reel without the film snapping, it was only a matter of time before someone figured out that you didn't just have to film reality, or a staged scene. After all, as Walter Murch describes in his book *In the Blink of an Eye*, we humans have always dreamed cinematically. In our deepest slumber, we conjure up crazy collages of moving images that jump from one scene to the next. In other words, visual editing should come naturally to us.

One of the first great editing innovators in this new age was the Frenchman Georges Méliès (1861–1938). Méliès was a practicing magician, and he had the idea that this new invention called "le cinéma" could, in fact, be used for magic tricks. Imagine it. There stands the incredible magician, with nothing in his hat. Then, there is a cut – and presto, voilà! – there is now a rabbit. Fortunately, Méliès had far better ideas than just making a rabbit appear, or we wouldn't still be remembering him, and we recommend that you watch as many of his early films as possible. His most famous one was *A Trip to the Moon* (1902). It is incredibly clunky and corny by today's standards, but you can see how innovative it must have been at the time, with the magic of the cuts within it. At slightly longer than 10 minutes, it was a definite step up from the films of just a few years before.

Another great early innovator was Edwin S. Porter (1870–1941), who worked for Edison. His best-known contribution to the annals of film history is *The Great Train Robbery* (1903). This is not to be confused with the 1979 film by the novelist Michael Crichton (also called *The First Great Train Robbery*). Porter's film is another *one-reeler*; that is, at just over 10 minutes, it fit on one large projection reel. Films a little longer than this would require two reels, and therefore be called *two-reelers*.

The Great Train Robbery, like *A Trip to the Moon*, is made up of a number of different scenes, all of which, for the most part, are staged in single "wide" shots; the camera is placed far enough away from the action to show everything that transpires in the scene. Within each scene, there is no real editing. The scene unfolds as would a staged play in a theatre. Our vantage point never really changes.

The only slightly "cinematic" aspect of these movies, from a modern point of view, is the use of cuts for certain special effects. Méliès uses cuts to make the alien creatures on the moon dissolve into puffs of smoke; Porter, at one point, in the middle of a fight on top of a moving train, uses a cut to transform an actor into a dummy that can be thrown from the train. In terms of the language of editing, as we now know it – incorporating multiple shot sizes and angles to vary the point of view and heighten dramatic tension – there is nothing.

Still, these films represent a huge leap forward, both technically and artistically, from the first films of the 1890s. They both tell real stories, with a beginning, middle, and end, and use the new medium in other innovative ways: Méliès with his "magic tricks" and Porter with the use of hand-colored frames for explosions and puffs of gun smoke. The groundwork was laid for other filmmakers to build the foundations of editing.

Shot Sizes

In Chapter 2, we will go through all of the different kinds of shots – and how to describe them – that make up the modern filmmaker's vocabulary. But for now, let's pause to discuss the basics.

All filmmakers tell their stories using a variety of three basic shots: far away from the action, closer to the action, and extremely close. We call these three basic divisions *wide* (as shown in Figure 1.1), *medium* (as shown in Figure 1.2), and *close* (as shown in Figure 1.3). All other shot names flow from this simple breakdown. Sometimes you need to see things from a distance. Sometimes you want to be close, but not too close. And, finally, sometimes you really want to see that eye-popping detail right up close and personal.

FIGURE 1.1 Wide shot of man.

All figures appear in color on the companion DVD.

FIGURE 1.2 Medium shot of man.

The following figure shows a close shot.

FIGURE 1.3 Close shot of man.

This is what ultimately makes filmmaking a director's and editor's medium, rather than an actor's, as in the theater. You control the audience's reaction to your story by focusing the gaze on specific moments. The audience member has no choice but to see what you show them. We will discuss shot sizes in even greater detail in Chapter 2.

Film Language Develops

Have you heard of United Artists®? It's a film studio, which produced, among many other films, the James Bond series. It was originally founded in 1919 by D.W. Griffith, Charles Chaplin, Mary Pickford, and Douglas Fairbanks. You may not have heard of Pickford and Fairbanks, but you probably know Chaplin (the most famous character he played was the funny little tramp with the moustache, cane, and bowler hat). And right now, let's meet Griffith.

So what about David Wark Griffith (1875–1948)? Well, as with much of human innovation, it is rarely just one person who invents something or single-handedly pioneers a technique. Often, the people who get the historical credit are the ones who filed the patent first, or whose work best exemplifies the technique then being pioneered. The latter reason is why D.W. Griffith gets the title of "father of the close-up."

Griffith was originally an actor, who then became a director, and who demonstrated an intuitive grasp of the possibilities of the new medium. It may seem obvious to us now to use a variety of different shot sizes, but if you watch films prior to the Griffith era they feel very much like filmed stage plays. After Griffith, they feel like movies.

If, because of Griffith's racist views,[3] you don't want to watch all of his film, The Birth of a Nation, *you should at least see the sequence of Lincoln's assassination. It goes back to the "man with a gun" scenario we discussed in the introduction. Using a variety of shots of different sizes, and cutting back and forth from character to character, Griffith builds a sequence of high dramatic tension as we watch John Wilkes Booth in the wings of the theater as he prepares for, and then executes, his terrible crime. We see close-ups of various faces and details, and we cut away from a shot just as we want to see what's about to happen. It's very well shot and edited for its time.*

And what is a *feature*? Well, a few pages ago, when we discussed film length, we were still dealing with one-reelers and two-reelers. Theaters of the first two decades of the 20th century would project an evening's worth of entertainment by combining a variety of these short films into a length that would rival a night out at the theater (but for less money, maybe a . . . nickel, which is where the term *nickelodeon* comes from). Eventually, filmmakers around the world became increasingly ambitious and started making longer and longer movies, until a single film could potentially be the sole *featured* entertainment of a given projection.

One especially noteworthy example of an early feature is the Italian master-piece *Cabiria*, made in 1914 by Giovanni Pastrone, which, at close to 150 minutes, is a sweeping historical epic set in the 3ʳᵈ century B.C. *The Birth of a Nation*, at a little over three hours, was made as an American response to the international success of Pastrone's film.

Griffith's film used other techniques as well. This was still the age of black & white, but filmmakers would often choose to color their films in some way. Edwin S. Porter hand-colored individual frames in *The Great Train Robbery*, as previously mentioned. Griffith dipped entire scenes in dye (blue for night, yellow for day, red for some battle scenes, etc.) for special effect. He also used a technique known as *irising*, in addition to playing with shot sizes.

KEY TERM:

Irising is where you apply a black matte around the edges of the frame, sometimes making the matte grow or shrink in the frame (imagine a black circle closing in on the subject).

As people became more used to sudden changes in perspective with the increasing use of shots of different sizes, irising as a technique was used less and less. You will sometimes see modern filmmakers use it in homage to an older style.

The Kuleshov Effect

Most of you, if you have read anything about the Soviet filmmakers of the 1920s, have heard of Sergei Eisenstein (1898–1948) and his film *The Battle-ship Potemkin*, made in 1925.

NOTE

Eisenstein also wrote an important book on film editing called Film Form, *but nothing beats watching the actual art speak for itself, and* Battleship Potemkin *is stunning, even today.*

But before Eisenstein became the innovative filmmaker he became, he was part of a collective of young theatre and film artists loosely headed up by Lev

Kuleshov (1899–1970). Together, Kuleshov, Eisenstein, and their contemporaries developed theories that would revolutionize how the rest of the world thought about editing.

Russia, known from 1917–1991 as the Union of Soviet Socialist Republics (the Soviet Union, for short), was recovering from both World War I and the subsequent extremely violent revolution and civil war that followed. The centuries-old system of the Tsars (Russia's monarchs) was overthrown in favor of a State run by the Communist Party. After the end of the Civil War between the Tsarists and the Communists, there was real hope and optimism, particularly among young artists, that this new State would be a paradise of equal opportunity for all. It is in this context that Kuleshov and Eisenstein did their best work.

Kuleshov and company, university students and artists, found themselves in the unique position of needing to reinvent the Russian film industry. After the Tsar abdicated, and the provisional government was then overthrown by the Communists in October, 1917, life in Moscow settled down a bit while the battle for control of the country moved elsewhere. The war had taken a toll on Russia, and most non-essential industries had ceased to function. In addition, in the aftermath of the revolution, most of the aristocrats and middle-class businessmen fled, and it was the latter that had controlled film production. There was, in short, no one to make movies.

But Kuleshov discovered a print of Griffith's film, *Intolerance*, and he and his cohorts watched that print over and over, took it apart, and edited it in a multitude of ways before the print started to disintegrate. As these young Russians played with Griffith's movie, certain ideas about how the cinema functions – or could function, with some new ideas – arose in their minds.

Conveniently, while he was reshaping *Intolerance*, Kuleshov also came across some pre-revolutionary footage of a Russian actor, Ivan Mozzhukhin, and decided to try an experiment to put his ideas to the test. He took some of this footage – about 10 seconds of it – and decided to *splice* different shots of unrelated items before and after the shot. These three items were: a bowl of soup, a child in a coffin, and a woman lounging on a sofa. Kuleshov then screened this compilation of shots for an audience, asking them afterwards what they thought of the actor's performance in each case. What he didn't tell them was that the shot of the actor was exactly the same, no matter what came before or after. Amazingly, the audience read different emotions into Mozzukhin's performance, depending on what had preceded the shot.

NOTE

Splice, in the days before digital editing, meant to tape or glue two shots of film to each other; it's how all films were edited until the invention of the Avid® – more on that in Chapter 6.

This has since been given the name the "Kuleshov Effect." It's the root of the ideas behind the movement known as "Soviet Montage." It's also the single most important concept behind all editing.

So what does this experiment really tell us? It tells us, yet again, that film-making is an editor's medium. The effect of a film is controlled by the juxtaposition of shots. How we react to actors' performances depends on the context in which we see them. That makes sense now, but someone had to figure it out first.

NOTE

Eisenstein actually called this editing style the montage of film attractions. *The word* montage, *as used by Eisenstein here, is not to be confused with the modern meaning of the word as a way to conflate multiple scenes and quickly show a passage of time (think 2004's* Team America *and the song "You Need a Montage"). The Soviets took the term from the French word for editing, which is* monter. *Eisenstein's* montage of film attractions, *then, meant throwing all sorts of images together in unconventional ways, not always motivated by strict plot concerns, to affect the audience's perception of the story on the screen.*

In Eisenstein's film *Strike*, made the year before *Battleship Potemkin*, about a factory uprising that is brutally suppressed by the evil capitalist bosses, he cuts back and forth between images of the workers being chased down by guards and images of real cows being slaughtered, with their throats slit open. This was a very effective way of illustrating what Eisenstein saw as the evils of Capitalism.

In *Battleship Potemkin*, about a mutiny on a Russian Navy ship that took place in 1905 (based on a true story), Eisenstein was a little more subtle. In one of the most famous scenes in all of movie history – the Odessa steps sequence – he uses fast cuts and sudden jarring switches between characters to unsettle and excite the audience. We see a baby carriage crash at the bottom of the stairs, then cut between a beaten student, a woman shot in the eye, and a Cossack swinging his sword.

These films were made as propaganda, but art is often created when people are trying to affect audiences through powerful manipulation of emotions.

Think of *Casablanca* (1942). On some level it's really just trying to make us want to join the war effort and fight the Nazis.

Mise-en-Scène and Montage

When you make a film, you often face a choice as to whether or not you want to shoot a scene with lots of *coverage* (that is, many different shots with which you can edit for proper dramatic effect, and show different elements of the scene in detail), or shoot a scene where you edit *in camera*. The latter concept means that you have people walk into the frame, come closer or move away, or you move the camera around, without cutting, to show all of the action. This kind of staging or blocking within the camera frame is called *mise-en-scène*. In French, this literally means *putting in the scene*, which is the French idiom for *directing*.

Eisenstein, though the father of Soviet Montage, was also a master of mise-en-scène. There are scenes of crowds moving through Odessa, in *Battleship Potemkin*, that are breathtaking.

We often think of mastery of mise-en-scène as being reflected in long single shots. Some notable examples of this are the opening shot of Orson Welles's *Touch of Evil* (1957); the opening shot of Paul Thomas Anderson's *Boogie Nights* (1997); the opening shot of Brian De Palma's 1998 *Snake Eyes*; and, thanks to video technology, the entire 90-plus minutes of Aleksandr Sokurov's 2002 *Russian Ark*. You probably have your own personal favorites.

The Hollywood Studio System and Continuity

What we have described, so far, were the real breakthroughs, as far as editing goes. In 1927, there was one more important innovation: the arrival of synchronized sound. This was also an extremely revolutionary development, which affected the development of continuity editing (as well as a universalizing of frame rates). Editing with sound is something we will touch upon in some detail in later chapters.

Do you recognize the name Irving G. Thalberg? You may have heard it in the context of award given at the Oscars™ to "creative producers whose bodies of work reflect a consistently high quality of motion picture production."[3]

It's a kind of lifetime achievement award for producers. The person after whom the award is named played an important part in the development of Hollywood as we know it. He was also the model for the main character in F. Scott Fitzgerald's final novel, *The Last Tycoon*.

Irving G. Thalberg (1899–1936), first as head of production at Universal®, and then at the just-created MGM Studios®, did more than almost anyone else to create the heavily compartmentalized world of the Hollywood Studio System, which lasted from the late 1920s through the mid-1950s. There are still studios in Hollywood, but some of them are owned by foreign corporations, and none of them function as a world unto themselves the way they did in the days of the Thalberg model.

Basically, Thalberg created a system where everything resided under a single roof – the studio – so that everything was done in-house. Whether you were a screenwriter, director, producer, cinematographer, composer, actor, editor, etc., you were under contract to a particular studio, and that is where you did the bulk of your work. The singing and dancing star Gene Kelly (1912–1996) worked at MGM; the director Frank Capra (1897–1991) worked at Columbia®. The actress Katharine Hepburn (1907–2003) started out at RKO. Oscar-winning editor Barbara McLean (1903–1996) worked at 20th Century Fox®, where she cut 62 films, among them the brilliant *All About Eve* (1950). Some people – particularly stars – could be loaned out to other studios, but as long as you were under contract to a studio, they owned you, more or less.

Under this system, many films were made quickly and efficiently. But instead of the director playing the main role, it was really the studio, or the producer at the studio, who put the film together, and every studio had its own style. In order to maximize efficiency within each studio, however, there had to be certain rules in place, which allowed trained craftspeople to work without constant supervision from the director or producer. So the footage from a film in production might be developed, then watched by the director, producer, and editor, and then the editor would go off, with notes, to make a *rough cut* of a scene. The scene would have been shot, for maximum efficiency, with particular *coverage*, and the editor would know what to do with that footage. The director, producer, and editor might then sit down again, watch it, and if all the rules had been followed, there might be some minor tweaks before moving to the fine cut. Since Thalberg also pioneered the use of preview audience screenings to test out works-in-progress, nothing would be finalized until after those screenings.

ROUGH CUT VS. FINAL CUT

When you make a film, you shoot a lot of film or video – the raw *footage* – not all of which will be used. In order to stay productive, you need to organize that footage, and start discarding what you don't think you'll need. Here is a simplified list of the steps, or *cuts*, you'll most likely go through:

1. **First assembly** – a compilation of all of the shots you think you'll use in your film, in rough story order. No attempt is made to make the shots work with each other – you've just thrown them all together as a starting point.

2. **Rough cut** – an early version of the film, with shots running longer than they will in the final cut of the movie. This, unlike the assembly, can actually be watched as a story, but cuts between shots may be very clunky, and sound levels may not match well.

3. **Fine cut** – most, if not all, of the sound and picture issues have been fine-tuned, and the film has the shape it will have when it is finished. Perhaps the soundtrack will change, but this cut presents the movie in an almost-completed state.

4. **Final cut** – this is it – the movie as you intend it to be!

The rules of film editing as they developed during this period – many of which we still follow, because they make sense – became known as *continuity editing*. The term implies that, even if a single scene has been shot over many days, perhaps out of order, once it is assembled, the story and action flow in a continuous manner that creates the illusion of everything having been shot in absolute chronological order. The artifice is invisible, ideally, so that we do not see the editor's hand at work.

So what are the rules? Well, first of all, you need to remember that the only reality that matters is the reality up on the screen. Filmmakers often cheat, moving props and sets around to match shots, and it can look funny to the untrained observer. But if it works on-screen, that's what matters. In order to cut in a continuity style, however, you have to be given footage that was shot to be cut that way. And shooting is not in your job description as an editor. That's the job of the production crew.

Assuming that the director and cinematographer knew what they were doing, and that the script supervisor, who supervises *continuity*, kept everything together, you, as the editor, would be handed a variety of shots – all the *coverage* you need to tell the story – and then you would put them together in a way that makes the story make sense.

 Basic Continuity Coverage

In order to help you better understand coverage, here are some kinds of shots you might have for a classic two-person dialogue scene:

KEY TERM:

Master Shot This is a wide shot of the whole scene. It establishes screen space so that you know who is on what side of the screen. All of the action in the scene should be visible in this shot. In Figure 1.4 we see Person A on the left of the frame and Person B on the right. They are standing a few feet apart.

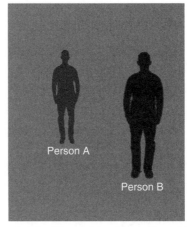

FIGURE 1.4 Person A stands to the left of Person B in a Master Shot of the scene.

KEY TERM:

OTS on Person A An OTS is an *over-the-shoulder shot*. In Figure 1.5 you can see the subject of the shot – in this case, Person A – framed in a medium close shot, with part of the other person – Person B – in the foreground. It doesn't always have to be the *shoulder* of Person B that we see; it could be the side of the face, the nose, etc.

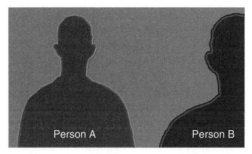

FIGURE 1.5 OTS on Person A, over Person B's shoulder.

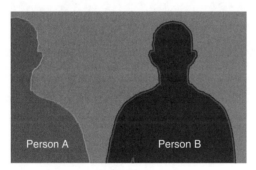

FIGURE 1.6 OTS on Person B, over Person A's shoulder.

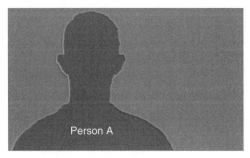

FIGURE 1.7 Close-Up (CU) on Person A.

KEY TERM:

Reverse CU on Person B In Figure 1.8 we see the exact same framing as in Figure 1.8, but now with no Person A in the shot at all. There is just Person B, positioned to the right of the frame, looking left.

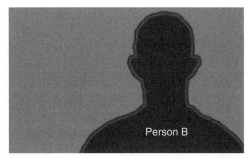

FIGURE 1.8 Close-Up (CU) on Person B.

With these five shots, you can cut a very good dialogue scene. Do you see why it is so important that Person A always be photographed on the left, while Person B always be photographed on the right? If you stick to the initial geography of the Master Shot, then no one watching the film will be confused about who is where. Instead, they'll watch your film and listen to your dialogue.

If you shoot your Master first, and then shoot everything else so that the geography of the scene matches the master, you don't have to show the Master first when you put the scene together (though that is the convention). Everything will match, anyway, because sightlines (which means where people are looking) and body positions will always be the same.

The way directors and cinematographers and script supervisors make sure to shoot in a way that matches the necessary spatial relationships is by drawing an imaginary *180° line* through the middle of the scene. In Figure 1.9, you can see an overhead diagram of such an imaginary line, drawn through a scene where two people stand around a small table. As long as the camera stays on one side of that line, no matter where the director or cinematographer positions it, then Person A and Person B each remain on the same side of the frame. If the camera crosses the line, then those spatial relationships flip.

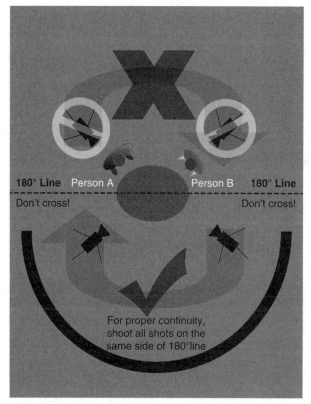

FIGURE 1.9 This is an overhead diagram of a scene where two people stand around a small table, through the middle of which there is an imaginary line drawn. The camera can move anywhere on one side of the line – in a 180° arc – but cannot cross the line, or the positions of Person A and Person B will flip in the frame.

Speaking of movement, however, the 180° line is only part of continuity editing. Another important part is the *match on action*.

KEY TERM:

A match on action is a shot in which an action started in one shot – such as raising a glass of water to drink – is then completed in another shot.

In Chapters 6–8, when we work with the basic interface of Final Cut Express™, you will get a chance to practice this kind of *match cutting*.

Finally, in order to insure continuity, you have to make sure that all kinds of other things are consistent from shot to shot. If someone is walking left to right in one shot, they need to be walking left to right in the next shot. Is the lighting consistent throughout the scene? That's not your job, either, but if it's not consistent, then you need to think about what to do to fix it in the editing. Are there grave continuity mistakes, like props missing from the table from shot to shot?

All of this factors into the style of editing that flourished in the Hollywood Studio era. If you watch numerous films several times, you will see errors in continuity, but for the most part the films of the Studio Era feel very smooth and well crafted. Watch *Casablanca* (1942), and you'll see what we mean.

From the Studio Era to Today: Beyond Continuity

After World War II, in 1948, the United States Supreme Court ruled, in the Paramount Decision, that Hollywood Studios did not have the right to own their own distribution centers (a.k.a. movie theaters), as that constituted a monopoly. This meant that each studio would have to compete in the marketplace of box office receipts to have their films shown. This decision, plus the growing middle class in America that started buying up a certain new appliance – the television – threatened Hollywood's cultural dominance, and most likely set the stage for the eventual demise of the Studio System.

At the same time, other countries began to bounce back from the horrors of World War II and provided an alternate way of making movies. A sleek commercial product is appealing, and we all enjoy it, but sometimes gritty rough dramas are inspiring, as well.

Some of the first post-World War II European filmmakers were the Italians, with a movement called Neo-Realism, led by Roberto Rossellini (1906–1977) and Vittorio De Sica (1901–1974). This style of filmmaking eschewed studio sets and professional actors, bringing the camera into the war-ravaged streets of Rome and other cities. Two films stand out, in particular, *Rome, Open City* (1945, Rossellini), and *The Bicycle Thief* (1948). Both deal with ordinary people – not glamorous stars – dealing with real problems, and the rough camera work and non-continuity-obsessed editing style reflect this. Both films were international successes and helped audiences appreciate a different approach to filmmaking.

Other countries produced post-war filmmakers as well. The Japanese gave us Kenji Mizoguchi (1898–1956), Yasujiro Ozu (1903–1963), and Akira Kurosawa (1910–1998). The situation in Japan after the war was somewhat similar to that of the Italians, and the Japanese had to make do with some similarly reduced circumstances. But Mizoguchi and Kurosawa still managed to make compelling historical dramas, such as *Ugetsu Monogatari* (1953, Mizoguchi) and *The Seven Samurai* (1954, Kurosawa). Ozu focused more on the alienation of modern life, with films like *Tokyo Story* (1953).

Perhaps the most influential movement of the 20 years after World War II, however, came from France. This was *La Nouvelle Vague*, or *The New Wave*. This self-named movement was founded by a group of young film critics who had spent the 1950s writing for a magazine called *Les Cahiers du Cinéma*, which loosely translated means *Cinema Notebooks*. The two most famous members of this group were Jean-Luc Godard (1930–) and François Truffaut (1932–1984).

> *Truffaut is responsible for the* auteur theory, *which claims that a good film director is the most important author – if not the sole author – of a movie.*

NOTE

Godard, Truffaut, and their peers greatly admired both Hollywood Studio films and Italian Neo-Realism. They wanted to revitalize the French film industry, which they found dull and stale, by taking the best storytelling techniques of Hollywood and combining them with the freshness of the cameras-in-the-streets style of Neo-Realism. They loved American gangster films, which they called *film noir*, or *black film*, because of the pools of dark shadows in almost every shot. Finally, at the end of the 1950s, they launched themselves into the fray, becoming directors themselves.

Truffaut was first, with *The 400 Blows* (1959), the sensation at the Cannes Film Festival that year, and Godard followed, with *Breathless* (1960).

Both films were international successes and ended up having a significant influence on American filmmaking of the late 1960s and early 1970s, especially as Hollywood tried to rebuild itself after the collapse of its studios in the late 1950s and early 1960s.

This movement left a multifaceted legacy. These filmmakers were really not concerned with continuity – especially Godard – and left the filmgoer to figure out what was going on. Truffaut was more traditional in his editing style, but incorporated many handheld camera moves into his shooting. Godard loved the *jump cut*, which is an editing technique where you simply remove frames from within a shot, jumping ahead without any regard to continuity. As we will see in the next chapter, this can be a very useful technique, but at the time it was quite striking.

Just as the New Wave was gaining ground, so was documentary filmmaking. Because you don't usually stage action for a documentary film, you are forced to gather footage as it comes, and traditional continuity is impossible to maintain. The story becomes the important part. If the story is compelling, the audience will watch. The French style of documentary that rose to prominence in the 1960s, where there are no commentaries and no interviews, is called *Cinéma Vérité*, or *Cinema Truth*. A useful example of this kind of film is *Don't Look Back* (1967) by D.A. Pennebaker (1925–) about Bob Dylan's tour of England in 1965.

Over the last 40 plus years, since the 1960s, we have seen a confluence of all of these different kinds of styles. The boundaries between continuity-style filmmaking and documentary-style filmmaking, for example, have blurred, a fact that films such as *Cloverfield* (2008) and *District 9* (2009) exploit. The jump cut is no longer so radical. Just watch the opening of the remake of *Assault on Precinct 13* (2005), with Ethan Hawke's opening monologue, and you'll see many jump cuts.

In the early 1980s, the rise of music videos, thanks to the popularity of MTV®, made us accustomed to faster and faster cutting styles. Since the late 1980s, when the Avid – the first non-linear digital editing system – was invented, we have been able to cut more easily, and faster, in whatever style we want.

It is far less expensive and easier to practice editing now than it used to be, which means you can try, fail, and try again. Imagine that you are part of Kuleshov's collective, dissecting Griffith's *Intolerance*. Cut and re-cut!

The purpose of this chapter was to help you understand the state of film editing today by understanding how we got here. We covered a number of topics in film history and film aesthetics.

We began with the very first films of the 1890s, made by the Lumière Brothers, in France, and Thomas Alva Edison, in the United States. Then we paused to cover the terms *shot* and *frame*. We then went from *one-reelers* and *two-reelers* to *features*, and discussed the controversial epic, *Birth of a Nation*.

We also learned the differences between wide shots, medium shots, and close-ups. We'll learn more about shots in our next chapter, but this basic breakdown of three sizes is a great starting point. In the early part of the 20th century, filmmakers began to use these kinds of shots in more and more sophisticated ways.

After D.W. Griffith, we looked at the films of the young Soviet Union, and of Kuleshov and Eisenstein, in particular. Eisenstein's and Kuleshov's ideas on film editing became known as *Soviet Montage* and centered around the concept of creating new meanings from the juxtaposition of seemingly unrelated shots. Some film editing can happen in camera, however, when the director of a film practices innovative *mise-en-scène*.

We also discussed the birth of the Studio System, largely the creation of Irving Thalberg. Under this system, the studios operated as large movie factories and began to codify the language of filmmaking, creating the *continuity* style that we still employ today. Using a series of carefully composed and staged shots, a filmmaker can create the illusion of continuous action, even though he may have filmed a scene over days, weeks, or months.

After learning the roots of this continuity style, we studied a simple scene breakdown and learned the basics of *coverage*. We also read about the progression, in the editing process, from *first assembly* to *rough cut* to *final cut*.

SUMMARY

Finally, we wrapped up the chapter with a quick discussion on the history of filmmaking, post-World War II, as the Hollywood Studios collapsed and filmmakers explored the influences of other film industries and techniques.

In the chapters ahead, we will explore the basics of actual editing in far more detail.

REVIEW QUESTIONS: CHAPTER 1

1. Name the major figures in the invention of cinema. When was the first public projection of a motion picture?

2. What is a shot? What are the three basic shot sizes?

3. Why is D.W. Griffith an important figure?

4. What is the Kuleshov Effect? What is Soviet Montage?

5. What is the 180° line?

6. What are some important post-World War II film movements? Why are they important, and what is their legacy?

1. Explain what a shot is, and how you can differentiate one shot from another in an edited film.

2. What do you think is the most important innovation in the history of film editing, and why?

3. As an editor, in which historical time period would you most like to find yourself, and why?

4. Discuss a favorite film of yours, and the editing techniques in it that you like.

Further Research

Here is a short list of films mentioned, plus a few others, to help you study the material in this chapter:

- Early films by Thomas Edison

- Early films by Auguste and Louis Lumière

- Early films by Georges Méliès, including *A Trip to the Moon* (1902)

- *The Great Train Robbery* (Edwin S. Porter, 1903)

- *The Birth of a Nation* (D.W. Griffith, 1915) – CAUTION! you might be offended by the racist views in this film.

All of the above films, and many more, can be watched on the five DVD set, entitled The Movies Begin, *released by Kino Video.*

NOTE

- *Cabiria* (Giovanni Pastrone, 1914)

- *Intolerance* (D.W. Griffith, 1916)

- *Strike* (Sergei Eisenstein, 1925)

- *Battleship Potemkin* (Sergei Eisenstein, 1925)

- *It Happened One Night* (Frank Capra, 1934)
- *Bringing Up Baby* (Howard Hawks, 1938)
- *The Wizard of Oz* (Victor Fleming, 1939)
- *Casablanca* (Michael Curtiz, 1942)
- *Rome, Open City* (Roberto Rossellini, 1945)
- *The Bicycle Thief* (Vittorio De Sic, 1948)
- *All About Eve* (Joseph L. Mankiewicz, 1950)
- *Singin' in the Rain* (Gene Kelly & Stanley Donen, 1952)
- *Ugetsu Monogatari* (Kenji Mizoguchi, 1953)
- *Tokyo Story* (Yasujiro Ooze, 1953)
- *The Seven Samurai* (Akira Kurosawa, 1954)
- *Touch of Evil* (Orson Welles, 1957)
- *The 400 Blows* (François Truffaut, 1959)
- *Breathless* (Jean-Luc Godard, 1960)
- *Don't Look Back* (D.A. Pennebaker, 1967)
- *Boogie Nights* (Paul Thomas Anderson, 1997)
- *Snake Eyes* (Brian De Palma, 1998)
- *Russian Ark* (Aleksandr Sokurov, 2002)
- *Assault on Precinct 13* (Jean-François Richet, 2005)
- *Cloverfield* (Matt Reeves, 2008)
- *District 9* (Neill Blomkamp, 2009)

References

1. Sklar, Robert. *Movie-Made America: A Cultural History of American Movies*. New York: Vintage Books, 1994.

This is a comprehensive survey of the history of filmmaking in the United States. The advantage of this book is that it is supremely readable. The disadvantage is that it barely mentions non-American films.

2. Murch, Walter. *In the Blink of an Eye*, Rev. Ed. Beverly Hills, CA: Silman-James Press, 2001.

Walter Murch, one of America's best editors (*Apocalypse Now*, *The Unbearable Lightness of Being*, *The English Patient*, *Jarhead*, and many more) wrote one of the best books on the art of editing post-Eisenstein.

3. Rausch, Andrew J. *Turning Points in Film History*. New York: Citadel Press, 2004, pp. 32–33.

4. www.oscars.org – the quoted text is taken straight from the official description of the Thalberg Award.

CHAPTER 2

TO CUT OR NOT TO CUT

OVERVIEW AND LEARNING OBJECTIVES

In this chapter, you will:

- Learn the basic terminology of shot sizes, angles, and movement
- Review continuity editing and scene construction
- Learn when and why to make a cut
- Explore how rhythm and pacing affect story
- Discuss editing aesthetics of a few key films

Shot Language

Cinema is a language, so in this chapter we will master the terminology that will help us speak that language. It is time to learn the specifics of shot sizes, angles, and camera movements.

As we discuss these terms, however, you should know that some of the names and descriptions are often relative to each other, so that what might be a *long shot* in one scene could be described as an *extreme long shot* when used in conjunction with other, closer shots in other scenes. After each shot, you will see its accepted abbreviation. The word *subject* means the main focus of the shot, be it a person, other live being, or an inanimate object.

NOTE

To demonstrate these shot sizes, we are using a version of Leonardo da Vinci's Vitruvian Man drawing,[1] since it represents the "proportions of man."

Shot Sizes

KEY TERM:

Long Shot (LS) As shown in Figure 2.1, this is a shot framed from far enough away from a subject so that you see all of that subject and all of the action that might take place around that subject. An absolute synonym for a *long shot* is a **Wide Shot (WS)**.

FIGURE 2.1 Long shot of man.

 All figures appear in color on the companion DVD.

FIGURE 2.2 Extreme long shot of man. We are even farther away from the same subject.

FIGURE 2.3 Full shot. We see the full subject in the frame, and little else.

KEY TERM:

Medium Full (or 3/4) Shot (MFS) As shown in Figure 2.4, this is a tighter, or closer, version of a *full shot*, cutting the subject off at the knees. If you are framing a non-human subject, then this shot would include approximately three-fourths, or 75%, of that subject.

FIGURE 2.4 Medium full shot. We see the human subject cut off at the knees.

KEY TERM:

Medium Shot (MS) As shown in Figure 2.5, this is a shot that cuts the subject off at the waist, or shows half of a non-human subject.

FIGURE 2.5 Medium shot. We see the human subject cut off at the waist.

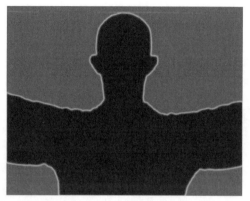

FIGURE 2.6 Medium close-up. We see the human subject cut off at the chest.

FIGURE 2.7 Close-up. We see the face, and little else.

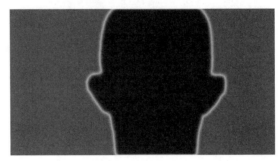

FIGURE 2.8 Extreme close-up. We are too close to the face for all of it to fit in the frame.

The word *tighter* describes shots that are closer to the subject than the previous one. *Wider* can be used in the reverse sense, as you move further away from the subject. This is particularly useful if you are the editor of a movie and find yourself discussing different *takes* of a shot. Perhaps the camera frame was changed slightly between takes, for some reason, and you want to let your director know that you favor the shot where the camera is closer. You would refer to it as the *tighter close-up* (or *tighter medium shot*, or *tighter full shot*, etc.). Of course, if the production crew did its job, labeling every shot properly, you should also be able to refer to a shot by its scene number, shot letter, and take number, such as "Shot 15C, Take 5" (but saying "the tighter close-up" might be easier). A common language can be very useful.

And now, very quickly, let's discuss *shot angles*. A director may choose to film a scene where the camera changes vantage points. In addition to shot size, the *angle*, or vertical position relative to the subject, changes how we, the audience, perceive the scene. Here are the four basic kinds of *shot angles*:

Shot Angles

KEY TERMS:

Straight on This is the most neutral kind of angle, where the camera is on an even plane with the subject. If you are filming a person, then the camera would be at that person's eye level.

Low Angle This is a shot in which the camera is below the subject, pointing up. If you are filming a movie like *Twins* (1988), with a short Danny DeVito and a much taller Arnold Schwarzenegger, then this would be good for Danny DeVito's point of view of Schwarzenegger. You could also use it in Spike Jonze's *Where the Wild Things Are* (2009), for the point of view of Max, the boy, looking up at the monsters.

High Angle This is the reverse concept, with the camera above the subject. This would be good for Schwarzenegger looking down on Danny DeVito, or for the monsters looking down on Max. If you get high enough, we call it a *bird's-eye-view angle*. Hitchcock used this, quite literally, in *The Birds* (1963), when the gas station of the town explodes, lighting up the place like a beacon for the marauding avian hordes.

Dutch Angle This is a skewed, canted, or tilted angle, where the camera is not level with anything. This name most likely comes from confusion over the word *Deutsch*, which means German in the German language, and Dutch. This angle was used in many German Expressionist films of the 1920s.[2] Dutch filmmakers used it, too, so it is possible that the name is not a mistake, after all. This shot angle was used in Carol Reed's *The Third Man* (1949) and Spike Lee's *Do the Right Thing* (1989).

Since the camera is rarely static, and moves about a lot, it is not impossible for a single shot to be both a close-up and a wide shot, a high angle and a low angle, etc. In the last chapter, we discussed a few notable opening shots that are masterpieces of mise-en-scène. One of them was from Orson Welles's *Touch of Evil* (1957). This shot was filmed on a film crane, which has a long flexible arm, and the camera is attached at the end. The whole structure rests on a movable platform (known as a *dolly*).

In this opening shot, the camera moves throughout a Mexican border town in a dizzying display of staging and blocking virtuosity. We begin on a close-up of a timer, as a hand turns it, and then the camera pulls back and cranes up, turning into a high angle shot of the man with the timer as he puts his object – a bomb – into the back of a car. We then follow this car as it moves through the town over the course of three minutes, before the bomb inside explodes. It is an example of well-orchestrated mise-en-scène, and it brings us to a discussion on camera movement.

Camera Movement Terminology

KEY TERMS:

Pan This is a horizontal movement back and forth, right to left or left to right, while the camera remains fixed to a tripod or other immovable support.

Tilt This is a vertical movement up and down, down and up, while the camera remains fixed to a tripod or some such support.

Dolly A dolly is any platform, with wheels attached, on which you place the camera and tripod. If it's a fancy dolly, it might have its own *jib arm*, which is like a mini-crane, allowing you to smoothly move the body of the camera up and down while you dolly forwards or backwards. A dolly can operate with rubber wheels – with no track – or with train-like wheels – on a track – for smoother movement. A dolly doesn't have to be fancy: you can sit in a wheelchair holding a camera while a friend pushes you, and technically you are operating a "dolly." A shot that includes dolly movement is referred to as either a *dolly shot* or a *tracking shot*.

Zoom This is not really a camera movement, but a movement within the lens. Lenses have different properties, based on focal length. A wide – or short – lens sees much of the world, and makes objects that are far away look very far away, and objects that are close look very close. A telephoto – or long – lens has a very narrow field of view, and makes objects that are far away look much closer than they are. A zoom lens is a lens that lets you transition from one focal length to another within a single shot. You can appear to bring a subject closer, or push it away, without moving the camera. A zoom looks and feels very different than a dolly, however, and should not be used as a substitute. It is its own thing.

Crane A crane is similar to a dolly, only bigger. It has a very long crane arm – like a super giraffe neck – and a moving platform on wheels, which lets directors swoop the camera from very high to very low while also moving across the set. It can also be used for more subtle movements. In the opening of *Do the Right Thing* (1989), the shot begins on an ECU of Samuel Jackson's mouth. The camera begins to pull back, then slowly cranes up and pans left into the street, continuing to rise as it does so.

Steadicam Invented in the mid-1970s, this is basically a harness with a gyro-scope and balancing system attached. This setup allows a designated *steadi-cam operator* to keep the camera steady while she walks carefully through the set. A steadicam movement looks different than a dolly shot because of the way the camera appears to glide through the air. The opening shots of *Boogie Nights* (1997) and *Snake Eyes* (1998) both use steadicams. Stanley Kubrick used a steadicam throughout his classic horror film *The Shining* (1980).

Handheld Finally, there is the simple use of handheld camera movements. With the popularity of the French New Wave and the documentary *Cinéma Vérité* movements of the 1960s, the use of handheld cameras became much more acceptable to mainstream audiences. If done right, these movements don't have to be that shaky (unless you want them to be). Jean-Luc Godard has a remarkable handheld movement at the opening of his *Alphaville* film (1965), as Eddie Constantine walks through a hotel corridor. Lars von Trier, in his *Breaking the Waves* film (1996), used handheld cameras throughout (and made them shaky).

Many of the above movements can be combined. You can pan and dolly, tilt and crane, zoom while you pan and dolly, etc., as you see fit. Do what you need to do to serve your story.

Scene Construction and Coverage

We can now put a scene together. Or, at least, learn how to describe it being done. We will repeat some terms we saw in Chapter 1, just for review. We discussed, if you remember, the importance of *coverage*, because getting all of the shots you need to tell your story is how you ensure that you will be able to edit your film properly. In other words, shoot well to cut well. Here, then, are some more words you need to know.

Establishing Shot This is any shot that sets the scene by showing us where we are: New York (show us the skyline); Paris (show us the Eiffel Tower); Los Angeles (show us the Hollywood sign). John Carpenter opened his 1982 Sci-Fi masterpiece, *The Thing*, post-credits, with a shot of a foreboding mountain range covered with snow and ice, because that film takes place in Antarctica. Not every establishing shot needs to be so wide. Maybe you just show a house, or a yard, or something to set the location of the scene. Many sitcoms use establishing shots of locations as transitions between scenes. In the 1990s, we would always get an exterior shot of a New York apartment building in shows like *Seinfeld* and *Friends*.

Master Shot This is a wide shot of your scene, in which all of the action can be seen, and it is usually shot first, so that the geography of the space is defined, after which you match all other shots to the master.

OTS This means "over the shoulder," and is a useful shot that allows us to see both people in a conversation while focusing on one particular person at a time. The person in the foreground does not have to be framed with their shoulder, despite the name of the shot; it could be their cheek, their nose, their entire face, their arm. Any upper body part in the foreground makes this an OTS. The TV show *Lost* used OTS shots all the time (as do most film-makers). Watch any scene from that show, and you will see an OTS shot (or two). Close-ups are good if you want to see a person's face, but an OTS includes both protagonists, or a protagonist and an antagonist, and can therefore be even more gripping.

Reverse Angle or Shot The term "reverse" is used to describe one shot in relationship to another shot we have just seen or used. In the movie *Casablanca*, Humphrey Bogart (Rick) and Claude Rains (Louis) spend a lot of time in verbal sparring matches with each other. When we see an OTS on Louis as he tells Rick how much he secretly dislikes the Nazis, too, we might then cut to the reverse OTS as Rick smiles in response. Anytime you cutaway from a shot of a particular frame size to a shot of another subject in the same frame size this is called a "reverse angle." They don't have to be OTS shots. You can have a shot-reverse shot pattern with any kind of frame size.

Reaction Shot This is any shot – usually an MCU or a CU – in which we see a *reaction* on the actor's face – which might be used in a scene to sell a joke or a scary or emotional moment. In a comedy or drama, you want to give your audience permission to laugh or cry, and cutting to another actor at the right moment can really help with that. In *Singin' in the Rain* (1952), during the "Make 'Em Laugh" number, we cut to Gene Kelly at a few points, laughing, to remind us how funny Donald O'Connor is being at that moment. In Eli Roth's film *Hostel* (2005), we frequently cut to the faces of people being dismembered to let us know how much it hurts to have one's fingers cut off.

Single These are, as the name indicates, shots in which we see just a single person – in FS, MS, MCU (usually in MS) – and the term is used, as so many of these are, in a relative fashion. You're talking to the director, or your assistant editor, and you say, "So we have the Master, and then I'm going to cut to the Single of the main actor."

2-Shot, 3-Shot, etc. Then there are shots with more than one person in them, and you name them accordingly. Usually, given the constraints of framing, a 2-shot is an MS or MFS. A 3-shot? It depends. The idea is that these are shots that show that specific number of characters, and not much else. If they're really wide, with many other things in the frame, they're not referred to by the number of people in them. A 2-shot or 3-shot can also be the Master, if it's your widest shot.

Insert An insert is any shot of a detail within a scene. It could be an ashtray on a table, or a glass on which the murderer has just left his or her fingerprints. It's a close-up of some important detail that you want the audience to see. Eisenstein used a famous insert of maggots on rotting meat in *Battleship Potemkin* to sell the audience on the evil of aristocrats.

> *If you show smoking in films these days, however, you will automatically receive an R rating, so be careful!*

NOTE

Cutaway This is a shot of a detail or person or location *outside* of the immediate scene we are watching. The John Landis film *American Werewolf in London* (1981), made long before CGI and other digital effects, relied on many inserts during the one werewolf transformation scene we witness. But there is one cutaway, to a doll of Mickey Mouse. It's a funny shot, which relieves the tension, and it's a cutaway, and not an insert, because the doll is not a part of the transformation. It's in the room, however, so it's not a completely random cut.

> *About inserts and cutaways – These are an editor's best friend. They allow you to control the pacing of the scene and help you get out of shots with bad performances, bad continuity, or bad writing. They allow you to shorten sequences that need shortening, or lengthen sequences that need lengthening. They allow you to increase tension or heighten comedy. If you're not the director, make sure to insist that he give you lots of both.*

! TIP

POV This is our last term in this section, and it is short for "point of view." This is a shot in which the director has tried to capture, visually, what the world actually looks like from a particular character's perspective. A POV shot can be very effective when used well. Think how scary it is to see the dangling legs of shark bait in *Jaws* (1975) through the eyes of the Great White. At the end of Elia Kazan's *On the Waterfront* (1954), Marlon Brando, who has just had a nasty fight with Lee J. Cobb, walks unsteadily towards the factory doors, as the image, from his POV, goes in and out of focus.

Remember that all of these different kinds of shots are what constitute *coverage*. Without good coverage, you have no movie. Unless, of course, you're making a single-shot film, but then you'll edit "in camera" with brilliant blocking (a.k.a., mise-en-scène), which takes a lot of work. So, remember: shoot well to edit well.

Most scenes are put together with a combination of all the shots we just discussed. Just watch any movie or TV show, regardless of era, made post-D.W. Griffith, and you'll see a wide variety of shots. Usually a director and editor start wide and move closer as the scene progresses. But not always. Sometimes they start close and then go wide, as they do in the scene we are about to analyze.

How to Put a Simple Scene Together

If you read Chapter 1 of this book, you will remember the scene we described in the section on continuity editing. It was a two-person dialogue scene, with five shots as coverage. There is a scene exactly like this from the Todd Solondz film *Happiness* (1998).

NOTE   *CAUTION! This film has disturbing subject matter dealing with pedophilia and might offend some viewers.*

In the opening of the film, which is about 5½ minutes long, we watch an end-of-meal conversation between a man named Andy and a woman named Joy. This is a second, or third, or fourth date dinner, and Joy wants to end their not-quite relationship. Andy doesn't take it well, and begins crying, at which point Joy attempts to comfort him. He seems to recover, and hands her a gift he bought for her. She opens it – it's a pewter ashtray (she doesn't smoke, but is flattered by the gift, which has her name engraved on it). Just as she is thanking Andy for such a thoughtful gesture, clearly moved, he yanks it out of her hands, telling her, "This is for the girl who loves me." The scene ends with the two of them still seated at the table, awkwardly side-by-side.

There are six shots used in the scene. Let's look at them and attach a possible numbering configuration that would make sense for such a setup. A shot list, prepared by the director, assistant director, and cinematographer ahead of time, might have looked like this:

2A – Master 2-shot of Andy and Joy, seated at table

2B – OTS on Joy

2C – OTS on Andy

2D – CU Joy

2E – CU Andy

2F – Insert ashtray

In production, you would shoot **2A**, the Master, first. After the Master, it is the director's call whether you shoot Andy's or Joy's OTS. But whether or not you shoot **2B** or **2C** after the Master, it would make sense, after that OTS, to shoot the CU of the same person before doing the reverse OTS and CU. Right? Switching to the other side of the set would involve a change of setup, which takes time. Better to stay on one side of the scene – the same *axis* – until you have shot all of the coverage from that angle, and only then move to the other side of the scene – a new *axis*.

> *Even though this is the first scene in the final film, it was the second scene in the shooting script, which is why we are using the number 2, and not 1. Scene 1 was an exterior shot of the restaurant, which was never used.*

NOTE

After you shoot your OTS and CU shots, you would do the insert last. A good director will always do these kinds of shots at the end, as they do not require any performance from the actors. In fact, the hand holding the ashtray doesn't even have to belong to Jane Adams (the actress playing Joy); as long as it looks like her hand, it works.

Now don't forget about the 180° line. Hopefully the director and crew got it right and stayed on one side of the line. If you watch this scene, you see that they did. Andy is always on the left of the scene, looking right, and Joy is always on the right, looking left. Even when we cut to the insert of the ashtray, her body is on the right side of the frame, with the ashtray extended to the left side of the frame.

This is especially important in this scene, because of how the director and editor decided to cut it. Although they shot the scene in a very traditional way, from wide to medium to close, they edited it in the exact opposite way.

The very first shot we see in the final film is not the Master: it's **2D** – CU Joy. The very next shot is **2E** – CU Andy. There is no other context. And it's a pregnant pause. Something has just happened. Both people look awkward and distressed, as if something has just been said prior to the beginning of the film. Joy looks right to left; Andy looks left to right. Their *eyelines* match, because the 180° line was respected. The logical conclusion of the viewer, then, is that Andy and Joy are looking at each other.

If you hadn't shot the Master first, and been sloppy with the 180° line, you might have ended up with shots where Joy is looking left, and Andy is looking left. Cut them together, and they both look like they're looking off-screen, *at the same thing*, not at each other. The savvy digital editor among you who is reading this might think, however, that you could easily fix a mistake like that in the editing, flipping the image in Final Cut Express. That wouldn't necessarily look right, however, since things like recognizable facial asymmetry, hair parts, etc., could make that a tricky sell in a CU. In *Happiness*, fortunately, that issue is moot, as everyone appears to have known what they were doing, and all is good in the world of continuity.

A final note about this scene, as it touches upon an issue we will discuss throughout the book: rhythm. As the scene starts, we are treated to back and forth cutting between Joy's and Andy's CU's, holding on each for about 4½ seconds, as both characters struggle to talk. We feel uncomfortable, because they look uncomfortable, and 4½ seconds feels very long in a close-up. The pacing of the editing serves the story very well, as it should in a good movie.

When to Cut

Knowing when to cut or not to cut is always the key question in film editing. Now that we have learned the terms of scene construction, we need to know how to actually cut a scene together. Many beginning filmmakers get very excited as they start editing, focusing on things like *match cutting*, or *matching on action*. This is where you cut in the middle of a motion or an action – such as someone moving through a room, or moving a body part – to go from a wide to a medium or a close shot. That is certainly important. Even more important, however, is making sure your cuts serve the movie's story.

In Woody Allen's film *Annie Hall* (1977), there is a funny scene on the balcony of a New York apartment between Alvy Singer (Allen) and Annie Hall (Diane Keaton). These two people have just met, and are attracted to each other, but are still a little nervous. As they stand, a few feet apart from each other, Diane Keaton blurts out, "You're what Grammy Hall would call a real Jew." In the very next moment, we cut to a close-up of Woody Allen, as he begins to bring his head up. It's a logical cut, since we want to see his reaction (how do you respond to that?), and it's made even more dynamic by cutting into the shot as he begins his motion.

Woody Allen and his editor have performed a *match on action*, but they have also served the story. That is an ideal editing situation. The cut is smooth, and it fulfills a story need. In the opening to *Happiness*, however, there is not much action in the frame, and yet the cuts still work. That is because we want to know what is happening, and so the cuts and the story function well together.

Another important consideration in editing is the question of how long you should hold your shots. The late Russian filmmaker Andrei Tarkovsky (1932–1986), who made such masterpieces as *Andrei Rublev* (1964), *Stalker* (1979), and *The Sacrifice* (1986), believed that film is the art of time.[3] The images enter our brains in real time, and as long as you, the editor, choose to hold on a single shot, and we see an uninterrupted series of frames, we understand these images as happening in "real time." As soon as you cut, the relationship to time is changed, and we understand, intuitively, that any amount of time possible can have transpired between cuts. Let's look at two examples, both from the 1950s.

Let's start with that opening shot from *Touch of Evil*. In it, we watch, as previously described, the progress of a bomb from its planting on a car to its explosion. To be more precise, sometimes we watch it, and sometimes we don't, since Orson Welles (1915–1985), the director, has planned a single shot in which the car, at times, leaves the frame. We are also introduced to the two main characters, played by Charlton Heston and Janet Leigh, who also come in and out of frame. Because this is a single shot, its relationship to time is on a 1:1 ratio. We watch in "real time," with no escape. We have seen the bomb, and we know it is ticking. The brilliant mise-en-scène of the shot heightens the tension, and there is no cutting away from it. This is a scene that is best served as a single shot.

Now let's look at a moment from Alfred Hitchcock's film *Strangers on a Train* (1951). Hitchcock (1899–1980), known as the "master of suspense," had a real grasp of the when and how of cutting. His wife, Alma Reville (1899–1982), was an editor, which may have helped him.

In *Strangers on a Train*, there is a truly chilling scene where the main evil character, Bruno (Robert Walker), tracks down the woman he is trying to kill, Miriam (Kasey Rogers), and strangles her in an amusement park.

Especially horrible is when Bruno manages to catch Miriam alone. The entire chase through the fairgrounds has been staged as a seduction of sorts. Miriam thinks Bruno is flirting with her – and she likes him – so she's not scared when he finally manages to talk to her in a secluded spot. She thinks he is going to say something nice, but he strangles her instead.

The part of the film that relates directly to our discussion of editing and time starts at 26:30.

NOTE

Throughout this book, we will list the times within films with the notation 00:00, with the first two digits representing minutes, and the second two digits representing seconds. If we go over 99 minutes, then we will simply expand those first two digits to three digits.

At this point, Miriam bumps into Bruno, away from her companions. She is in close-up. Bruno is out of frame, but we can tell he's there. It's dark; he raises his lighter into the frame, flicks it on, and asks, off camera, "Is your name Miriam?" She replies, "Why yes, how did you . . ." Before she can finish, Bruno's gloved hands come into the frame and grab her by the throat, at 26:38. As he strangles her, Bruno moves into the frame in a ghoulish OTS, his back blocking her from us as he moves from right to left across the screen. At 26:42, when he, back to us, is on the left, and she, facing us, is on the right, Miriam's glasses fall off her face. And we cut. There's the key to making this scene work: that cut.

NOTE

In our discussion of Strangers on a Train, *we use the 101-minute release version of the film. Please note that there are a few versions of the movie floating out there on DVD.*

The very next shot, which lasts barely 2 seconds, is of the glasses hitting the ground, between their feet. Please note that this shot lasts no more than 2 seconds. Then, in the very next shot, we see what is happening as reflected in one of the frames of Miriam's glasses. The glass lens acts as a giant mirror, with Bruno on the left (as he was when the glasses fell) and Miriam on the right. Even though this is a reflection, and the world should be flipped, it is less confusing to the audience if the actors are in the same positions on the screen. What we call the *eye trace* of the audience is critical. Unless you're trying to kick people out of your movie momentarily, your audience should always be able to locate characters in the same spot on the screen where they were before.

This shot of the reflection begins at 26:44. We watch as Bruno, strangling Miriam, slowly lowers her to the ground. At 27:01, his deed done, he lays her down, dead. The whole murder has taken only 23 seconds. This may or may not be long enough to kill someone by manual strangulation, since estimates vary, and a lot of different factors affect the outcome. But even if the death comes quickly, in your mind, when we break it down like this, most viewers buy it. Why? Because of that cut to the glasses falling. Or, rather, because of the cutaway from the beginning of the action. That simple cut breaks our 1:1 ratio of screen time to actual time. In other words, by chopping it up, Hitchcock no longer has to worry about how realistic it is to strangle someone in just 23 seconds. Once you cut, we understand that the action on-screen is taking more time than it takes to watch it. If it were all a single shot, however, we would expect it to be realistic, and take as long as it should.

As you grow as an editor, think about this concept of film as the art of time. Sometimes you should cut, and sometimes you shouldn't. Whatever you do, your story should guide you.

When not to Cut

If you haven't seen Frank Capra's film *It's a Wonderful Life* (1946), you've probably at least heard of it, since it has become a holiday classic. Capra (1897–1991) was a master filmmaker, and also made *It Happened One Night* (1934) and *Mr. Smith Goes to Washington* (1939), among many others. He was especially skilled with the camera, and also in the editing.

The movie stars James Stewart as George Bailey, a man who has dreamed of leaving the stifling environment of his home town, Bedford Falls, his entire life. But fate has conspired to keep him there, as he is blessed/cursed with a deeply held sense of responsibility. No one but he seems to have the personality and will to stand up to the evil Mr. Potter, played by Lionel Barrymore. In the scene we will analyze right now, George Bailey has been waiting for 4 years for his younger brother, Harry – to whom he gave his college money – to finish school and come back and run the family business. This business – the Bailey Brothers Building & Loan – keeps the evil Mr. Potter off the backs of the local residents.

But Harry, it appears, has other plans. He steps off the train and announces to George and their hapless Uncle Billy that he has gotten married. His new wife then announces that her father has offered Harry a job. This leaves George feeling confused, hurt, and angry. Instead of shouting and yelling, however, he decides to remain gracious and calm, since he recognizes the opportunity for his brother.

Frank Capra was very smart as a filmmaker. In the script, once the bombshell has been dropped by Harry on George, everyone walks away, chatting about this and that. We hear their dialogue in the background. But the camera stays on George as he slowly walks over to rejoin the group. At 36:55, we cut from an MS of George to an MCU, right after Harry has run off to pick up luggage. George is turned away from us, watching his brother. But then he turns back, and his face is hard. At 37:01, he starts moving right, the camera panning with him. He comes towards us, moving into a tight CU. At 37:08, a passing couple bumps into him. At 37:11, his face, which has been a mess of warring emotions, begins to settle into a smile, now that he has almost reached his family again. At 37:14, he is back with Ruth, and animatedly starts talking to her – the George Bailey that everybody counts on to run things and keep the town safe has returned. The shot ends at 37:42 as a *screen wipe* takes us into the next scene (that's one of those transitions where the next shot literally "wipes" away the previous shot in a horizontal move across the screen).

Why is this such good filmmaking? Because it's so simple and serves the story so well. We need to stay on George, without cutting away, while he deals with the terrible conflict. He probably wants to scream – a valid reaction to what has just happened – but the mature side of him takes over, after a short struggle. We, however, must see that struggle in order for what happens later in the film to make sense, when George takes drastic action to change his life after some money goes missing. If we hadn't been made to watch his earlier conflict, we wouldn't care as much.

As an editor, then, do not be afraid to hold, if the performance is good enough. As a director, know this and consider staging and shooting a scene with enough options for a decision like this one to be made in the editing room. The success of this scene is a triumph of both mise-en-scène (a lot goes on in under 50 seconds) and editing (the choice not to cut).

There is one other directing choice Capra makes that is powerful (and also simple). He has Jimmy Stewart come *towards* the camera during the shot, so that he walks from that initial MCU into the CU. Kuleshov and Eisenstein had discovered that an audience will read into a performance emotions that may or may not be there, based on the context in which they see the shot (what comes before and what comes after). Similarly, if an actor moves closer to us, we read emotions into the performance as well. Physical proximity equals psychological proximity, in other words. As an experienced screen actor, Stewart understood this, which is why his performance is restrained (on the outside – you can tell he is in turmoil on the inside). And so did Capra. And so, now, do you.

Jane Campion (1954–), the New Zealand-born and Australian-educated director, made a film in 1993, *The Piano*, in which she demonstrated an equal understanding of these principles, as did her star, actress Holly Hunter (who won an Oscar for her performance). Hunter plays Ada, a mute young Scottish widow who has been sold as a mail-order bride to a bachelor settler, played by Sam Neill, in New Zealand, in the mid-19th century. She is deposited on a beach by the crew of the ship that takes her down there, along with her young daughter, played by Anna Paquin (who also won an Oscar for this performance). The largest item she has brought with her is her grand piano, through which she communicates with the world using music. It is her anchor and security blanket, both, a talisman of her former life that she needs in order to feel grounded in this new and strange world.

But her new husband-to-be decides it is too heavy to carry through "the bush," and so his crew of indigenous workmen and he leave it behind. In a very moving moment, we see Ada's longing for the piano expressed in two shots. The first is a gentle zoom in to the piano from the cliff above; the second is a tracking shot around Ada's face, in CU, recording the emotions she feels as she realizes her piano will stay on the beach.

The sequence begins at 14:42, in an OTS on the piano, with the blurry back of Ada's head on the left side of the frame, in the foreground, and the tiny piano in the background on the right side of the frame. It is clear that we are in position above the beach. Right as the shot starts, it is already zooming in from a wide lens setting, bringing the piano closer to us. The zoom stops at 14:54, and we hold on the piano until the next shot begins at 14:59. A particularly nice aspect of this last hold is that Ada's scarf continues to occasionally blow across the frame, out of focus, reminding us that she is very much still there, longing.

The second shot lasts until 15:21, and is a slow circular dolly move, with Holly Hunter in a tight CU, probably on the same platform as the camera, as the mountains of the wild shoreline move right to left across the frame as we move left to right with Hunter. The cinematographer is using a telephoto lens, so everything but Holly Hunter is out of focus, isolating her from the background so we focus on the intensity of her emotion. And we stay with her for 22 seconds, without cutting.

Holly Hunter, like Jimmy Stewart, is another intuitive film actor, who is not afraid to let the director do her work and trust in the mechanics of camera placement and editing. Here, although we are convinced that we feel how strongly she feels, if you look at the shot objectively, you may be reminded of Kuleshov and his experiment. We have just seen the zoom in to the piano (and the rest of the prior 14 minutes as well), so we know how much this piano means to her. And for 22 seconds, we feel her pain, while Hunter actually gives very little external signs of distress. But since physical proximity equals psychological proximity, and we see Hunter's face in CU, this is a very powerful moment, with or without any emoting from the actor. In fact, it is even more powerful for us precisely because we supply our own ideas of what she is feeling.

By choosing *not* to cut for 22 seconds (a decision rooted in the actual shooting, since the shot lasts long enough so that the director can make that choice), Campion leaves us thinking for a substantial amount of screen time about the power of the piano, and the ruthlessness of Ada's husband-to-be in leaving it on the beach. Without this moment, the tragic events that unfold later make no sense. The editing choice serves the story well, just as Capra's and Hornbeck's served *It's a Wonderful Life* equally well.

SUMMARY

The purpose of this chapter was to help you understand shot terminology and scene construction, as well as to give you a basic sense of when and why to cut. In future chapters, we will discuss rhythm and pacing in greater depth but, for now, you should have an understanding of the importance of that initial decision you take to make a cut (or not) in the first place. Remember that you need a reason to cut rather than to hold, and that reason should be rooted in the emotion and story of your film.

We started with the language of shots and went through all of the different shot sizes that are generally used in filmmaking. We then looked at terms related to shot angles and then at terms relating to shot movement. Our goal was to make sure that we are all speaking the same cinematic language.

SUMMARY

After focusing on shots, we looked at scene construction, picking up where we left off in Chapter 1. We illustrated our terms with examples from movies, breaking down the scenes in ways that illustrated what each kind of shot can accomplish. While doing so, we reviewed the art of continuity and coverage, and once more demonstrated the importance of the 180° line.

We next discussed the reasons that editors and directors make their cutting decisions, examining match cuts and mise-en-scène. We analyzed, in depth, why one might wish to hold on a shot, rather than cut. We explored cinema's relationship to time and how the illusion of real time is affected by editing.

We ended the chapter by looking at more examples from more films and discovering how pacing and rhythm are controlled by the timing of the cuts. Throughout our analysis of the art of editing, however, we stressed the absolute importance of shooting well to edit well. Without good coverage, it is hard to cut a film.

REVIEW QUESTIONS: CHAPTER 2

1. List all of the different frame sizes of shots you can remember.

2. What are the four basic shot angles?

3. How many different camera movements can you name?

4. What kinds of shots do we use to put a scene together?

5. What are the main issues you should consider before making a cut?

6. What is a match on action, or match cut?

7. How does mise-en-scène affect editing?

1. Choose a simple scene from a favorite film of yours and break down the shots used to make it, and study the way they are cut together.

2. What do you think is the most important consideration in editing a film?

3. What editing techniques from recent films do you especially like?

4. Write a short scene and break it down into shots. How would you cut it together, and why?

Further Research

Here is a short list of films mentioned in this chapter. Have fun watching some of them, and be sure to analyze how they were shot and edited:

- *Casablanca* (Michael Curtiz, 1942)
- *It's a Wonderful Life* (Frank Capra, 1946)
- *The Third Man* (Carol Reed, 1949)
- *Strangers on a Train* (Alfred Hitchcock, 1951)
- *Singin' in the Rain* (Gene Kelly and Stanley Donen, 1952)
- *On the Waterfront* (Elia Kazan, 1954)
- *Touch of Evil* (Orson Welles, 1957)
- *The Birds* (Alfred Hitchcock, 1963)
- *Alphaville* (Jean-Luc Godard, 1965)
- *Jaws* (Steven Spielberg, 1975)
- *Annie Hall* (Woody Allen, 1977)
- *The Shining* (Stanley Kubrick, 1980)
- *American Werewolf in London* (John Landis, 1981)

- *The Thing* (John Carpenter, 1982)
- *Twins* (Ivan Reitman, 1988)
- *Do the Right Thing* (Spike Lee, 1989)
- *The Piano* (Jane Campion, 1993)
- *Breaking the Waves* (Lars von Trier, 1996)
- *Boogie Nights* (Paul Thomas Anderson, 1997)
- *Happiness* (Todd Solondz, 1998)
- *Snake Eyes* (Brian De Palma, 1998)
- *Hostel* (Eli Roth, 2005)
- *Where the Wild Things Are* (Spike Jonze, 2009)

References

1. Leonardo da Vinci (1452–1519) drew a now-famous drawing of a man inside both a square and a circle, with his arms and legs outstretched within each figure, inspired by the work of the ancient Roman architect Vitruvius.

2. The German Expressionists made films in post-World War I Germany, where life was rough, that focused on horror and gothic themes, and they expressed their view of the world by tilting the camera to its side, to unsettle the audience.

3. Tarkovsky, Andrei. *Sculpting in Time: Tarkovsky The Great Russian Filmmaker Discusses His Art*. Trans. Kitty Hunter-Blair. Austin, Texas: University of Texas Press, 1989.

The title of this book says it all, but you should read the whole thing, anyway.

CHAPTER 3

HOW GENRE AFFECTS EDITING

OVERVIEW AND LEARNING OBJECTIVES

In this chapter, you will:

- Learn the meaning of the word *genre*
- Explore the different kinds of genres in the world of cinema
- Analyze how different films apply and interpret genre
- Discover how to edit in three basic film genre styles

What is Genre?

The word *genre* is more than just a film term. It can be applied to many different artistic and literary endeavors. *Genre* is French for "gender" and comes from an Old French word, "gendre," which later evolved into "genre." It means "kind" or "sort" (hence, "gender"). It is pronounced, in English, like the French male first name Jean ("Zhan") plus "ruh": zhan-ruh.

As used in film or literature, genre describes a particular kind of story with certain pre-determined rules and expectations. When you write or direct a film in a particular genre, you want to respect those rules and expectations. If you don't, you might lose your audience.

As an editor, you want to keep these conventions in mind as you edit. If, for example, you are making a comedy, then you want to cut the story in a way that maximizes the humor of situations that call for it. If you are making a horror film, you want to similarly make people scream when they are supposed to scream.

Genre sets the tone and tells the audience what to expect. We like to know if we're supposed to laugh, cry, or scream. A filmmaker can play with these expectations, to be sure – and some of the best films have elements of different genres in them – but if you play with genre expectations too much, you can end up confusing your viewers who might laugh when you want them to scream, or scream when you want them to laugh.

Basic Film Genres

There are really just three main genres: drama, comedy, and thriller (or suspense). All other genres can fit, to some extent, within these three headings, or some hybrid of them.

Most stories involve a main character living through a period of conflict in his or her life. We, the audience, watch this character as he struggles to defeat forces internal or external, thereby surmounting the conflict (or succumbing to defeat). We yearn for conflict and resolution, in other words. That's how we're wired. A given genre might affect the details of how a story unfolds, and its tone, but not the fact that there will be conflict and some kind of resolution.

Drama

Defined most simply, a drama is a film that tells a story in a predominantly serious and sincere way, usually involving a character overcoming (or succumbing to) serious obstacles in his life. A drama is meant to move us towards serious emotional reactions, and if it succeeds, the resulting tears (or just deeply felt emotions) can be very cathartic. It is the most straightforward kind of filmmaking, with the emphasis on the plot and performances of the actors. Some examples of dramas are:

- *Sunrise* (F.W. Murnau, 1927) – edited by Harold D. Schuster

- *The Grapes of Wrath* (John Ford, 1940) – edited by Robert Simpson

- *The Cranes Are Flying* (Mikhail Kalatozov, 1957) – edited by Maria Timofeyeva

- *The Last Picture Show* (Peter Bogdanovich, 1971) – edited by Donn Cambern

- *Tender Mercies* (Bruce Beresford, 1983) – edited by William Anderson

- *Ratcatcher* (Lynne Ramsay, 1999) – edited by Lucia Zucchetti

- *The Edge of Heaven* (Fatih Akin, 2007) – edited by Andrew Bird

Comedy

A comedy makes us laugh. That's its main purpose. That doesn't mean that a comedy cannot take on serious issues, but if so, it is going to do so in a way that plays up the humor. Here, the cathartic release is through laughter. Making a comedy can be a trickier proposition than making a drama, if only because the rhythm of how you tell your jokes or present your gags (how you edit, in other words), can make or break the film. Some examples of comedies are:

- *The Kid* (Charles Chaplin, 1921) – edited by Chaplin

- *Duck Soup* (Leo McCarey, 1933) – edited by LeRoy Stone

- *The Lady Eve* (Preston Sturges, 1941) – edited by Stuart Gilmore

- *Some Like It Hot* (Billy Wilder, 1959) – edited by Arthur P. Schmidt

- *La Cage aux Folles* (Edouard Molinaro, 1978) – edited by Monique and Robert Isnardon

- *Coming to America* (John Landis, 1988) – edited by Malcolm Campbell and George Fossey, Jr.

- *A League of Their Own* (Penny Marshall, 1992) – edited by Adam Bernardi and George Bowers

- *Harold and Kumar Escape from Guantanamo Bay* (Jon Hurwitz/Hayden Schlossberg, 2008) – edited by Jeff Freeman

Thriller/Suspense

A thriller/suspense film exists to scare the pants off of us, or raise our heart rate in some way as we watch the main protagonist fight his or her way out of some extreme circumstances. This is the genre in which the conflict is most concretely portrayed, since someone or something is trying to kill, capture, maim, or destroy someone or something else. It could also be a film in which a crime is being perpetrated, or a special mission is being undertaken. Whatever the plot may be, there exists a problem that needs to be solved, which makes for a suspenseful story. That's the point of the movie. Some examples of thriller films include:

- *The Cabinet of Dr. Caligari* (Robert Wiene, 1919) – no editor credited

- *The 39 Steps* (Alfred Hitchcock, 1935) – edited by D.N. Twist

- *Stray Dog* (Akira Kurosawa, 1949) – edited by Toshio Goto and Yoshi Sugihara

- *The Hitch-Hiker* (Ida Lupino, 1953) – edited by Douglas Stewart

- *Blow-Up* (Michelangelo Antonioni, 1966) – edited by Frank Clarke

- *The Conversation* (Francis Ford Coppola, 1974) – edited by Richard Chew and Walter Murch

- *Blue Velvet* (David Lynch, 1986) – edited by Duwayne Dunham

- *Face/Off* (John Woo, 1997) – edited by Stephen Kempner and Christian Wagner

- *Signs* (M. Night Shyamalan, 2002) – edited by Barbara Tulliver

These are very simple definitions of genres, but they are a good place for us to start. Many films combine elements of all three genres. We can have comedies with strong elements of drama in them, or dramas with their fair share of laughs. We've even coined a term for this: *dramedy*. *Juno* (Jason Reitman, 2007) is a good example of this kind of film. It's funny, but it's also serious.

There are also thrillers with strong and moving characters going through trauma beyond the fact that they are being chased by bad guys. The French film *Tell No One* (Guillaume Canet, 2006) is this kind of film. The hero's wife was abducted 8 years before the film begins, and he has been an emotional wreck since then. Suddenly, he gets an e-mail from her . . . and the suspense begins. It's thrilling, but also emotionally devastating.

Finally, there are plenty of films with a lot of humor to go with the thrill ride. One such film is *Raiders of the Lost Ark* (Steven Spielberg, 1981). Even while Indiana Jones is fighting Nazis, he's cracking jokes. Now that's a hero you can believe in!

More Specific Genre Names

In Chapters 13–15, you will take video footage from the accompanying DVD, and cut it in the style of each of these three genres – drama, comedy, and thriller/suspense – in turn. Your goals will be to make your audience cry, laugh, or scream.

But within these three major headings – we can call them *super* genres – there are many other genre names that we should know. These genres often denote basic plot and character types, and deal in *archetypes*. This means that the people in the film come pre-packaged with a certain mode of behavior, and that the story has a certain kind of plot audiences expect to see.

> *Archetype is Latin (adapted from the original Greek) and means, quite simply, "a model."*

NOTE

Keep in mind, however, that these genre descriptions are merely guides. If you're not careful, you can get too specific in your terms and end up with a mouthful as you pitch your movie. For example, if you find yourself describing a film as a Sci-Fi Western Action/Adventure Children's Thriller . . . relax and pick the one or two main genres that make the most sense. In any case, here are some of these more specific kinds of genres, with a few examples after each heading.

Western

In most Westerns, the stories seem relatively simple. There is a good guy and a bad guy. The good guy is often someone who has previously led a life of violence, left that life behind, and is now trying to lead a peaceful existence without violence (which is a nice internal conflict). But then the bad guys show up (a big external conflict) and force him to fight. It is this duality of conflict – internal and external – that makes Westerns resonate with audiences. As simple as the actual plot elements might be, the story can become complex as the main character battles the demons within and without.

Not all Westerns fit this paradigm, but this seems to be the most common. There are also Westerns of the Cowboys vs. Indians variety, but these have not aged that well, since societal attitudes towards Native Americans have changed.

In a Western, the most important thing is the physical setting. You need vast open spaces, with dispersed populations. It's the tension between the natural world and the civilized world that forms the interesting backdrop to the protagonist's struggles, and you get this tension by plopping a small cluster of civilization in the middle of vast untamed nature. For this reason, you can't really make a Western in New York City, though you could try. A better setting would be a Western in space.

You also need a cowboy or cowgirl – a rugged individualist. This lone gunslinger battles against impossible odds to survive. Law and order triumphs over the seeming chaos of a dog-eat-dog world.

There are also Westerns with bad guys as heroes, but the location and the struggles of the protagonist are the same. It's just that the law and order universe skews in a different direction when the protagonist is a criminal. Here are a few examples:

- *Destry Rides Again* (George Marshall, 1939) – edited by Milton Carruth

- *Shane* (George Stevens, 1953) – edited by William Hornbeck and Tom McAdoo

- *The Man Who Shot Liberty Valance* (John Ford, 1962) – edited by Otho Lovering

- *Unforgiven* (Clint Eastwood, 1992) – edited by Joel Cox

Action/Adventure

Films in this category are really just thrillers directed at a superfast pace. A lot of stuff happens, and it usually happens quickly. Here are some examples:

- *King Kong* (Merian Cooper and Ernest Schoedsack, 1933) – edited by Ted Cheesman

- *Die Hard* (John McTiernan, 1988) – edited by John Link and Frank Urioste

- *Point Break* (Kathryn Bigelow, 1991) – edited by Howard L. Smith

- *Sahara* (Breck Eisner, 2005) – edited by Andrew MacRitchie

Of course, an Action/Adventure film can also be a Western, or a Sci-Fi or Espionage film. This genre heading, then, is less descriptive than others.

Children's/Family

These are the movies that get the G or PG ratings. They're perfect for young children and parents alike. These days, films from studios like Pixar® make sure to include many jokes for the adults, just to be sure. Here are some examples:

- *The Wizard of Oz* (Victor Fleming, 1939) – edited by Blanche Sewell

- *Mary Poppins* (Robert Stevenson, 1964) – edited by Cotton Warburton

- *Babe* (Chris Noonan, 1995) – edited by Marcus D'Arcy and Jay Friedkin

- *Monsters, Inc.* (Pete Docter, David Silverman, and Lee Unkrich, 2001) – edited by Robert Graham Jones and Jim Stewart

Espionage

Espionage is a French word for "spying." So this is a spy movie, or a movie in which spies, or spying, play important roles. James Bond comes to mind right away, but there are plenty of other options, as well:

- *North by Northwest* (Alfred Hitchcock, 1959) – edited by George Tomasini

- *Goldfinger* (Guy Hamilton, 1964) – edited by Peter Hunt

- *Three Days of the Condor* (Sydney Pollack, 1975) – edited by Don Guidice

- *The Russia House* (Fred Schepisi, 1990) – edited by Beth Jochem Besterveld and Peter Honess

Most Espionage films are really just thrillers in exotic locations.

Sci-Fi

Science Fiction, or Sci-Fi, combines, hopefully, somewhat credible scientific principles with fictional situations. Good Sci-Fi is supposed to stretch the boundaries of what we know to be possible, and should make a decent effort to explain how the impossible might actually be possible. Try watching some of these:

- *Metropolis* (Fritz Lang, 1927) – no editor credited

- *The Day the Earth Stood Still* (Robert Wise, 1951) – edited by William Reynolds

- *THX: 1138* (George Lucas, 1970) – edited by George Lucas

- *Sunshine* (Danny Boyle, 2007) – edited by Chris Gill

True Sci-Fi fans really don't like it when this genre is confused with the next genre in the list, Fantasy, since Sci-Fi is supposed to be a speculative art. At some point, at some time, what is on the screen might be able to occur.

Fantasy

Fantasy exists on a different plane than Science Fiction. In this genre, descended from the fairy tales of previous centuries, myth and fantastical situations collide with the world as we know it (unless the entire story, à la *Lord of the Rings*, takes place in a fictional world). There does not need to be any hard science to explain how witches fly or how Harry Potter does magic. As long as the filmmaker explains the world of the movie right away, we accept that the rules are different in this universe. A movie like James Cameron's 2009 *Avatar* manages to mix Sci-Fi (space travel – a possibility) with complete fantasy (blue mammalian aliens living on a planet with floating rocks). Have you seen any of these examples?

- *Ugetsu Monogatari* (Kenji Mizoguchi, 1953) – edited by Mitsuzô Miyata

- *Chitty Chitty Bang Bang* (Ken Hughes, 1968) – edited by John Shirley

- *Edward Scissorhands* (Tim Burton, 1990) – edited by Richard Halsey

- *Elf* (Jon Favreau, 2003) – edited by Dan Lebental

Ghosts, elves, monsters – these are the characters we often meet in this genre, and they are not even remotely speculative. They do not exist. Robots, on the other hand, which we are in the process of inventing right now, are part of the world of Sci-Fi.

Historical

All this genre means is a film that deals with real historical events. That doesn't mean that the filmmakers don't take extensive liberties in the re-telling of these events, but the movie is supposed to be "based on a true story." Here are a few films from this genre:

- *Napoléon* (Abel Gance, 1927) – editing by Abel Gance

- *Ivan the Terrible, Part 1* (Sergei Eisenstein, 1944) – edited by Sergei Eisenstein

- *Andrei Rublev* (Andrei Tarkovsky, 1965-66) – no editor credited

- *Schindler's List* (Steven Spielberg, 1993) – edited by Michael Kahn

Horror

This is the ultimate thriller/suspense genre. These are the movies that are supposed to make you as terrified as possible. In Vincente Minnelli's 1952 *The Bad and the Beautiful*, the producer played by Kirk Douglas gives an insightful explanation of the best way to make a horror film: show only hints of the monster, and let the audience's imagination do the rest. He's actually describing the first film listed below; there are three more, too:

- *Cat People* (Jacques Tourneur, 1942) – edited by Mark Robson

- *The Howling* (Joe Dante, 1981) – edited by Joe Dante and Mark Goldblatt

- *Mimic* (Guillermo del Toro, 1997) – edited by Patrick Lussier

- *Dark Water* (Walter Salles, 2005) – edited by Daniel Rezende

Some horror films show a lot of blood, or focus on a single killer chasing down what are usually young, nubile, and scantily clad young women.

These are called *slashers*, and *Halloween* (John Carpenter, 1978) and *Friday the 13ᵗʰ* (Sean Cunningham, 1980) are prime examples. These days, often credited in part to Eli Roth, the director of *Hostel* (2005), we have discovered a new kind of ultra-splatterfest film now dubbed the "goreno" genre (as in "gore" plus "porno").

Foreign

All this means is that the film was made in a country different than your own. It could be a comedy, drama, or thriller, a Western or a Sci-Fi film. You'll see it used to help you navigate through various DVD and movie filing systems, whether on Netflix®, Amazon®, or elsewhere, but it doesn't tell you anything other than that the film is not American.

Gay & lesbian

This is also a bit of a non-genre genre. You could have a Gay comedy, a Gay drama, a Gay thriller, a Gay Western, etc. All this term tells you is that the subject matter deals with issues of sexual orientation.

Independent

Another term that means very little. All you know from this is that a film was made outside of a major studio. These days, major studios have special art units, like Sony Pictures Classics® or Fox Searchlight®, designed to produce smaller budget, grittier films (which is what this term really implies to most people). When you make your first movie with your friends after reading this book and the rest of the series, it will be an Independent – or Indie – film.

Documentary

Some people call this a distinct genre, but it is really something more than just a genre. In any case, we'll discuss it in the next chapter.

Other possible genre types

The terms abound. Here are some more: African-American, Animation, Asian, Biopic, Blaxploitation, Crime (or Heist), Disaster, Epic, Experimental, Film Noir, Gangster, Martial Arts, Melodramas, Musicals, Romance, Sports, Swashbucklers, Teen Films, Teen Sex Comedies, War, etc. Do an online search for any of these genres, and you'll see how they're described.

How to Edit in Different Genres

That is the question. There is no right way to edit a Western, a Sci-Fi film, or a Gay/Lesbian film, except to cut in a way that lets the story be told as effectively as possible (which you should always do). But there are things you can do that make a comedy funnier, a drama more moving, or a suspense film scarier. To begin, let's look at one example of each genre and see what we discover. Here are the three films we will discuss:

1. Drama: *The Notebook* (Nick Cassavetes, 2004) – edited by Alan Heim

2. Comedy: *Four Weddings and a Funeral* (Mike Newell, 1993) – edited by Jon Gregory

3. Suspense: *Jaws* (Steven Spielberg, 1975) – edited by Verna Fields

The Notebook – a drama

Like all decent films, dramas or otherwise, this film has many elements to it. There are funny moments, there are sad moments, there are intense moments, and there are happy moments. But overall, one would describe the film as a drama because it treats a subject sincerely, and focuses on the seriousness of the central characters' relationship.

The Notebook tells the story of Duke and Allie, two elderly people who live in a nursing home. Allie suffers from Alzheimer's, and does not seem to know Duke, who nonetheless reads to her every day from the notebook of the title. This notebook tells the story of a young man named Noah and a young woman, also named Allie. The film cuts back and forth between the world of the nursing home and the world of the story in the notebook.

Occasionally, Duke implies a certain intimacy with the Allie of the nursing home, and even introduces her to his children, who come to visit. They seem to know her, but she, alas, does not know them. Perhaps you can guess what relationship Duke and the older Allie have to young Noah and young Allie from the notebook.

Let's look at a short scene from the story of the younger couple. Noah is played by Ryan Gosling (1980–) and Allie is played by Rachel McAdams (1978–). Our scene begins at just over 12 minutes into the film and shows us the first date between Noah and Allie. They have just been out, with another couple, to a movie, and have started to feel some real attraction to each other. Allie is beginning to find Noah more interesting than she thought she would. In a previous scene, Noah had jumped on a Ferris wheel and pulled a daring stunt to get Allie to agree to go out with him. She hadn't been impressed, but thanks to the intervention of their friends, they went out on their date, anyway, and now have decided to walk home together.

Before the scene begins, let us ask ourselves, as filmmakers, what this scene should be about. It's always a good question to ask before you shoot, but it doesn't hurt to ask it again before you edit. In this case, this is the moment when you have to establish that these two attractive and appealing lead actors actually have some chemistry, and that the two characters whom they play might actually have enough in common to make a viable couple later on. This must be where we see them fall in love.

At 12:26, the scene begins with Noah and Allie just out of frame. They walk in, Allie first, from camera right, and as soon as they are both in the frame, the camera begins to track left as they walk. This shot lasts until 14:50. That's 2 minutes and 24 seconds without a cut. What happens? They talk, and Noah, being a little more hyperactive than Allie, walks from the right side of the frame to the left at 13:18, and then ends up on the other side of her. They talk about what interests her, how Noah thinks she is more of a free spirit than she is prepared to acknowledge, and they thereby get to know each other. And there is no cut.

NOTE

As you have probably noticed, the time notation we use in this book is MINUTES:SECONDS, or 00:00. Since there are many ways for you to watch these films, whether online, on an iPhone or iPad, or on a DVD, giving you the exact time of the place in the film seems to make the most sense.

Now, if you remember, in the previous chapter we talked about the power of *not* cutting, and how a cut can represent a break in time, short or long. When you don't cut, the audience experiences the scene in real time. In this scene, for 2 minutes and 24 seconds, we watch Noah and Allie interact and live through their conversation as they do. You will find, if you look at similar kinds of films, and other dramas, that the pacing of the cutting is slower, and the number of actual cuts is less than it is in a comedy or thriller.

So what happens next? Noah walks away from Allie at 14:50, and we cut. Noah wants to demonstrate to Allie the excitement of living without restrictions, and does so by lying down in the middle of the street. Until Allie joins him on the asphalt, it makes sense to show the two of them separately, which is what the director and editor now do. They cut back and forth between them, from wide overhead to medium, using quick switches in angles.

And then, at 15:39, Allie lies down next to Noah on the street. As she lies down, notice the seamless *match on action* from the wide shot, which completes the motion in the OTS on the pavement. That's a perfect example of how to do a *match cut*.

KEY TERM:

A **match on action** is a cut between two shots where an action – sitting down, picking up a cup – is begun in one shot and completed in the next. When you shoot, you have the actor begin and end the action in both shots. When you edit, you find the moment in the middle of the motion where the cut makes the most sense for the smoothest, most invisible, cut.

Noah and Allie remain on the street, together, until 16:38, with occasional cuts from a wide overhead shot to the OTS and back. At 16:38, a car approaches, and they jump and run, separated again. But not for long.

From 16:42, when they make it safely back to sidewalk, to 17:14, when Noah invites Allie back on to the street, there are 10 shots, averaging a little over 3 seconds a shot. Most of the cuts are between a medium close-up (MCU) of Noah and a MCU of Allie, but there is also a wider 2-shot thrown in, as well. As soon as they join again, to begin their dance, the pacing of the cutting slows down. It seems that whenever Noah and Allie are physically together, the film relaxes, but whenever they are physically apart, the director and editor emphasize this with a faster pace of cutting.

Kuleshov, if you remember, back in the 1920s (see Chapter 1), created a performance out of nothing by splicing one image into the middle of a different context. In a drama such as *The Notebook*, the editor controls the performances by *not* cutting so frequently, thereby keeping our attention focused on what the actors are doing. Since these two actors are appealing and have real physical chemistry, it is quite pleasant to watch them interact. We fall a little in love with them while they fall in love with each other.

From 17:14 to 17:28, Noah and Allie make their way back into the middle of the street. At 17:28, he spins her, and we have a nice match cut into a tighter MCU 2-shot. For the next 30 seconds, we don't cut, as they dance closely together. Then, from 17:58 to 18:14, we are in a wider full shot of both of them in the street; at 18:14, we cut back to the tight 2-shot. Finally, at 18:47 – 33 seconds later – we cut into the same overhead wide shot we have seen earlier, while the older Noah, played by James Garner (1928–), begins a voiceover narration (reading from the notebook), that takes us into the next scene, into which we cut at 18:54.

Between 17:14 and 18:54 – 1 minute and 40 seconds – we cut only four times. The scene begins with no cuts – that long tracking shot – and ends with a very similar slow pace as Noah and Allie end their date very much on the way to falling love.

Whether or not you have seen this film – or seen it and liked it – you can appreciate the intelligence behind most of these editing choices. Even 3 seconds can feel like a long time on-screen, yet here we have shots that are much longer than that. All of these decisions have been taken in service of allowing the emotions to play out in front of us, which is what a drama should do for the viewer.

Now let's look at a scene from a comedy – *Four Weddings and a Funeral* – and see how that is cut.

Four Weddings and a Funeral – a comedy

Four Weddings and a Funeral is best described as a comedy, since most of the time it makes us laugh. It has a few sad moments, but these only serve to heighten the comedy. They help us to better appreciate why it is so important, in life, to enjoy the happy moments. *The Notebook*, though a drama, has funny moments. Contrast is good.

It is important in your opening scenes to indicate to your audience the style and genre of the film they are watching. *Four Weddings and a Funeral* opens with a wedding. It is not, however, a serious wedding scene. Instead, we get, right away, an indication of the hilarity ahead.

D.W. Griffith showed us the power of *parallel editing*, which is when you cut back and forth between scenes and characters. This simple technique – radical for its time – helps a filmmaker build tension, for dramatic, comedic, or suspenseful effect (or some combination of all three). Let's see how director Mike Newell and his editor, Jon Gregory, used parallel editing in the opening of *Four Weddings and a Funeral*.

The movie begins with some sentimental music playing underneath black title cards. The first actual image we see is a close-up (CU) on a white floral corsage, out from which we quickly zoom, so that the frame shows the corsage and the title of the movie, printed on a white wedding invitation card. Then, at 40 seconds into the film, we dissolve into Charles, played by Hugh Grant (1960–), asleep in bed. An alarm goes off, and he starts to move his arm towards it. At 47 seconds, we cut into a CU of the clock, as his arm comes into the frame, in a nice match cut. In this shot, he turns off the alarm, and then we pan with his arm over to his face as he rolls over, still asleep. At 54 seconds, we cut away.

We stay away from Charles until 1:47. In that interval, we are introduced to other characters – some of the people who, we will later learn, make up Charles's social circle. They, pointedly, do *not* turn the alarm off, and are all clearly getting ready for something fancy, based on the clothes we see. Then, at 1:47, we cut back to Charles, still asleep. And cut away again at 1:52.

So here we have an interesting setup. We assume, just as Kuleshov's audiences assumed when he presented his experiment, that there must be some relationship between the different scenes. When we return to Charles, asleep, we guess that it is a bad idea for him to be so.

We then cut away from Charles, again, and stay away until 2:43. During that time, we see the other characters, and some new ones, getting even more ready than before. We eventually see them gather in a car together and driving through London. Charles, however, doesn't wake up yet, because at 2:43 we return to him for about 2 1/2 seconds, still asleep. And then we cut back to his friends' car, no longer in London, driving on a highway.

At approximately 2:56, we return to Charles, who now slowly opens his eyes as the music that has played throughout this entire sequence fades down and ends. He reaches off camera for the alarm, pulls it to him (he is in a CU), and we watch as the horror of what must be a very late hour registers on his face. Still in the same shot, we hear him utter the first of what will be many profanities in this opening, at 3:12, before he leaps out of frame, and we cut to the next shot at 3:14.

What is wonderful about this opening is the economy of the editing and storytelling. It is now less than 3 minutes since we saw the first image, and yet we have a very firm sense of what the story is about, so far. And because we have cut back and forth between the sleeping Charles and other people who are *not* sleeping, we can't help but laugh when the first word out of Charles's mouth is a desperate obscenity.

Now, up until this point, even though the film has told its story very efficiently, the cutting has not felt particularly rapid. That changes here. At 3:14, we cut into a different room, where a redheaded woman is lying in bed, asleep. This is Scarlett, played by Charlotte Coleman (1968–2001), who is, we learn later, Charles's flatmate. Immediately, Charles's legs appear from camera right as he runs in. At 3:16 we cut into a CU of Scarlett as Charles shoves her alarm into her face. After a beat, she, too, curses. Then she gets up out of frame.

At 3:20, we cut to a medium shot of Charles, now with a dress shirt and pants on, struggling with suspenders. The camera tilts up to his face, then follows him down again as he bends over. The suspenders come off, and he curses again. Immediately, with the sound of the obscenity still in our ears, we cut to a 2-shot of Charles and Scarlett in a car. We stay on the 2-shot for 8 seconds, while Charles tries to start the car. It won't start. He suggests they take Scarlett's car, to which she replies that her car only goes 40 miles an hour.

NOTE

When you can still hear audio from a previous shot as you cut to a new shot, or when you hear audio from an upcoming shot before you cut to it, it is called a split edit. *If it is a case, like this one, where the audio continues into the next shot, it is also called an L cut. If it is a case where the audio starts before the shot from which it emanates, it is called a J cut. These cuts are named after these letters of the alphabet because of the way they look on an editing timeline when you overlap sound and picture one way or the other. Editors make these kinds of* split edits *because they help make cuts between shots smoother, especially when we have an abrupt scene transition like this one. Sudden transitions like this are sometimes called* smash cuts.

At 3:35, we smash cut into a new scene in which we follow what is apparently Scarlett's car, from behind, speeding (as best it can), on the highway. The engine sounds like it is working hard, revving high. We'll stay on this shot – hopefully laughing – for 10 seconds.

For comedy, these rapid smash cuts help in at least three ways. First, they make us dispense with unnecessary (and unfunny) footage. For example, do we need to see Charles and Scarlett walk from their apartment to the car? Do we need to see them walk out of his car and into hers? Secondly, they help us feel as if the film is picking up speed, generating excitement, and priming us for the jokes. And finally, they allow for very funny juxtapositions. Scarlett says, "It only goes 40 miles per hour," and before we can even imagine what that means, we see the actual car, straining. It's a funny cut.

At 3:45, we cut into a CU of Charles inside the car. He turns his head, asking, "What's the turn-off?" At 3:46, we see their POV from within the car: a road sign for the B359 highway, as they drive past the turn-off for it. At 3:47, we cut back to Charles, he asks "It's not the B359?" At 3:49, in the middle of his question, we cut to Scarlett, struggling with a map, as she says, reading, "It's the B359." Immediately, at 3:51, we cut to an exterior shot, panning from the side of the road, as their car passes us from left to right, slamming on the brakes. At 3:54 we get a tight insert of the gear shaft, with Charles's hand putting the car into reverse. Then, at 3:55, we have Charles's CU again, as he turns to face the rear. And then, at 3:57, we see his POV through the rear window: a big truck is barreling towards them as they head towards it. Not quite at 3:58, we cut to Scarlett, turning away, swearing. Then, at 3:59, we have a wide exterior shot, from the side of the road, of the car speeding in reverse and the truck swerving out of the way. At 4:00, in the middle of the truck's swerve, we cut to a tighter shot of the car as it comes to a stop at the beginning of the turn-off. At 4:01, we cut back to a shot of the gear shaft, as Charles's hand puts the car back into a forward gear, and then, at 4:03, we cut back to the wide exterior as the car now successfully drives onto the B359. The shot ends at 4:05.

In 20 seconds, we have 13 shots, which is a lot of cutting. It's an action scene played for laughs. If the director and editor do it right, then the adrenaline rush we get from watching this high-tension scene play out brings us to a state of excitement that makes our laughter even more powerful. It's true catharsis.

> Catharsis, *a word that comes from Greek, means a release of emotions, usually repressed. The need for catharsis is why we go to the movies, read books, see plays, watch sports matches. We enjoy the creation of emotions within us that allow us to let go of the tension and exhaustion created by our real lives. Art and other activities that help us experience a heightened reality lead us to catharsis. The fear, the joy, the laughter, and the screams you experience during films is good for you, and a good director helps you have a* cathartic *experience by cutting the film in a way that maximizes the emotion of the scene.*

NOTE

We watch this entire opening of *Four Weddings and a Funeral* on the edge of our seat, with a final feeling of relief that they made it. Of course, the movie goes on – and this first wedding goes on – with an increasing comedy of errors that gets funnier and funnier. If you haven't seen the film, you should. And in all the scenes where you find yourself laughing very hard, stop and look at how they are cut. Just as here, with the smash cuts to punch lines and funny parallel editing juxtapositions, you'll see that everything is precisely timed to make the jokes as funny as possible.

Now let's take a look at a thriller/suspense film – *Jaws* – and see how we can create a very different set of emotions.

Jaws – a thriller

Steven Spielberg justifiably made a name for himself with this film. He had previously directed one feature-length theatrical release film, *Sugarland Express* (1974), and a number of made-for-TV films, including *Duel* (1971), which went on to have a successful theatrical release in Europe. He had also directed a number of episodes for TV shows. He showed a lot of talent, and was making a living, but it was *Jaws* that made him a superstar director. The film made a lot of money and helped show Hollywood how to finally start recovering from the collapse of the Studio System in the 1950s and 1960s.

Jaws was so successful because it scared the pants off the audience, and people like to scream as much as they like to laugh or fall in love.

What's amazing, however, is how Spielberg and his editor, Verna Fields, were able to scare the audience without showing much blood and gore, at least by the standards of later films. They didn't even show much of the shark. True, you start to see more of the shark in the last third of the film, but you are scared half to death long before you get to that point.

Let's analyze, briefly, how the director and editor build suspense by focusing on one very short sequence in a scene early in the film. The scene goes from 13:36 to 18:12, and is where we see, in daylight, the second shark attack of the film. The 4-shot sequence we will discuss begins at 16:35.

By this point in the film, we have already met the main character, Police Chief Martin Brody, played by Roy Scheider (1932–2008). He lives on Amity Island, located somewhere in the Long Island Sound/Cape Cod Area, with his family, and he is new to his job. At the very beginning of *Jaws*, before we meet Chief Brody, we witnessed a nocturnal attack on a young woman skinny-dipping in the ocean. The next day, Brody is called to the beach, sees the woman's remains, and is told by the coroner that it was a shark attack. He decides to close Amity's beaches for public safety reasons.

The town selectmen and the mayor find out what Brody is doing and tell him, without directly threatening him with these exact words, that if he closes the beaches he will lose his job. The July 4th weekend is approaching, and Amity

Island is a summer community. It survives during the year based on its summer earnings. You can't close the beaches, in other words.

So Brody doesn't close the beaches. But he knows, deep down, that he should, and this forms the subtext of the next shark attack scene. In acting, we call this the *given circumstances* of the scene. Scheider's performance is informed by the knowledge that his character has been forced to act in a way that he knows is wrong, and our appreciation of the scene is informed by the fact that we know there is a shark out there, waiting to eat its next human meal.

The scene is masterful in its presentation of information that fuels the suspense. We see various potential shark victims: a rotund middle-aged female bather, a young boy with an inflatable raft, a dog, an old male swimmer, a playful young couple, and hordes of children. Cutting back and forth between Chief Brody and the water, moving closer to Brody's face each time, Spielberg and Fields raise our tension level along with Brody's. Will it be this person who dies? That person? Will Brody have a heart attack?

Instead of breaking down this entire scene, however, let's focus on the moment when we know, for sure, that the shark is in the water, and how the way in which the filmmakers present this information increases the suspense. One of the shark-victim moments in this scene centers on a young man in a yellow shirt playing with his dog, Pippit, in the surf. We see him throw a thick wooden stick to the dog, a Golden Lab, a number of times. Then we cut away to other people, and to Chief Brody's increasing uneasiness. The shark doesn't materialize. Chief Brody begins to relax. It's all going to be OK.

And then, at 16:35, after a few more shots of children in the water, we cut to the young man in the yellow shirt, on the beach, calling for his dog, who is not there. We stay with him for 6 seconds, then cut to a medium shot at 16:41, as he continues to call "Pippit!" We stay on this medium shot for 5 more seconds. All this time, you begin to wonder – thanks to the *given circumstances* – whether or not we really should have relaxed. And then, at 16:46, we cut to what may be the simplest shot in the entire movie, and one of the most innocuously scary shots ever. Spielberg and Fields show us a cutaway of the dog's wooden stick, floating in the water, and hold on it for 3 seconds.

Those are three very important seconds. In that time, our brains can process the implications of what this floating block of wood means. If there is a stick in water, and an owner calling for his dog, that means there is no dog. If there is no dog, and we know that there is a shark loose, there's a good chance that the shark ate the dog. And we're suddenly scared.

Just as we reach that conclusion, at 16:49, we cut into one of cinema's most famous POV shots, accompanied by the composer John William's famous "dun-dun, duh-duh, dun-dun, duh-duh" *Jaws* theme. We're terrified. We've been waiting for this, we know what kind of movie we're watching, and yet we're even more scared than we thought we would be, because of the way our adrenaline and fear have been managed. That stick of wood in the water, on top of the brilliant setup before, is what makes the POV of the shark so scary. The actual attack is horrible and sad, but it's not as scary, in a way, as the anticipation of the attack.

And that anticipation – the heart of the suspenseful thriller – is accomplished with an incredibly simple shot, which is a block of wood. This moment is a direct descendent of Griffith's insert of John Wilkes Booth's gun in *The Birth of a Nation* or of Eisenstein's insert of maggots on meat in *Battleship Potemkin* (see Chapter 2). Hopefully you can have fun following in their footsteps and those of Spielberg – and inventing your own techniques – as we cut our own dramas, comedies, and thrillers in Chapters 13, 14, and 15.

SUMMARY

The purpose of this chapter was to explain the meaning of the word genre, and give you some basic editing techniques that go with each of the three main genres: drama, comedy, and thriller. Dramas make us feel something deeply, while comedies make us laugh and thrillers make us scream. We first explored the conventions of those genres, after which we analyzed many of the other genre names that are commonly applied to films. We focused on the archetypes and paradigms that make genres recognizable to the viewer.

After discussing the basics of what makes a genre a specific genre, we analyzed scenes from three different films. We selected films that were representative of the three main genres. For a drama, we chose *The Notebook* (Nick Cassavetes, 2004); for a comedy, we chose *Four Weddings and a Funeral* (Mike Newell, 1993); and for a thriller, we chose *Jaws* (Steven Spielberg, 1975).

SUMMARY

In our discussion of *The Notebook*, we broke down the scene where the two main characters fall in love. Through a close shot-by-shot analysis, we were able to see how the director and editor controlled the emotions of the scene through editing. We then performed the same kind of breakdown on the opening of *Four Weddings and Funeral* and saw how comedy can demand a faster pace of editing than a drama. Finally, we analyzed a short moment in a pivotal scene in *Jaws* and discovered the importance of anticipation in creating thrills. The real scare comes from our own imagination, and a well-edited film like *Jaws* provides us with plenty of opportunities to imagine the worst.

Now that we are done exploring the meaning of genre and how genre conventions affect the editing process, we are ready to move on to the differences between documentary and narrative filmmaking, the subject of the next chapter. In the final three chapters of this book, you will have an opportunity to apply the genre techniques we studied here to the editing of your own drama, comedy, or thriller using the footage we provide on the DVD that accompanies this book.

REVIEW QUESTIONS: CHAPTER 3

1. Describe and discuss the three main film genres.
2. Name five of the many sub-genres of cinema. Which are your favorites?
3. What is the most important role of a drama?
4. What is the most important role of a comedy?
5. What is the most important role of a thriller?

1. Choose a film you like that is a hybrid of different genres. Discuss how the filmmakers handle transitions between comedy, drama, and/or suspense.

2. Discuss, in shot-by-shot detail, a scene from one of your favorite comedies. How do the director and editor maximize the laughs?

3. Do the same with a drama, except discuss how the serious emotional content of the film is maximized.

4. Select a thriller and give it the same treatment. How is the suspense heightened?

Further Research

As in the previous chapters, your assignment is to watch more movies. Here is a list of selected films mentioned in this chapter:

- *The Cabinet of Dr. Caligari* (Robert Wiene, 1919)
- *The Kid* (Charles Chaplin, 1921)
- *Metropolis* (Fritz Lang, 1927)
- *Napoléon* (Abel Gance, 1927)
- *Sunrise* (F.W. Murnau, 1927)
- *Duck Soup* (Leo McCarey, 1933)
- *King Kong* (Merian Cooper and Ernest Schoedsack, 1933)
- *The 39 Steps* (Alfred Hitchcock, 1935)
- *Destry Rides Again* (George Marshall, 1939)
- *The Wizard of Oz* (Victor Fleming, 1939)
- *The Grapes of Wrath* (John Ford, 1940)

- *The Lady Eve* (Preston Sturges, 1941)
- *Cat People* (Jacques Tourneur, 1942)
- *Ivan the Terrible, Part 1* (Sergei Eisenstein, 1944)
- *Stray Dog* (Akira Kurosawa, 1949)
- *The Day the Earth Stood Still* (Robert Wise, 1951)
- *The Bad and the Beautiful* (Vincente Minnelli, 1952)
- *The Hitch-Hiker* (Ida Lupino, 1953)
- *Ugetsu Monogatari* (Kenji Mizoguchi, 1953)
- *Shane* (George Stevens, 1953)
- *The Cranes Are Flying* (Mikhail Kalatozov, 1957)
- *North by Northwest* (Alfred Hitchcock, 1959)
- *Some Like It Hot* (Billy Wilder, 1959)
- *The Man Who Shot Liberty Valance* (John Ford, 1962)
- *Goldfinger* (Guy Hamilton, 1964)
- *Mary Poppins* (Robert Stevenson, 1964)
- *Andrei Rublev* (Andrei Tarkovsky, 1965–66)
- *Blow-Up* (Michelangelo Antonioni, 1966)
- *THX: 1138* (George Lucas, 1970)
- *The Last Picture Show* (Peter Bogdanovich, 1971)
- *The Conversation* (Francis Ford Coppola, 1974)
- *Jaws* (Steven Spielberg, 1975)
- *Three Days of the Condor* (Sydney Pollack, 1975)
- *Halloween* (John Carpenter, 1978)
- *La Cage aux Folles* (Edouard Molinaro, 1978)
- *The Howling* (Joe Dante, 1981)
- *Raiders of the Lost Ark* (Steven Spielberg, 1981)
- *Tender Mercies* (Bruce Beresford, 1983)

- *Blue Velvet* (David Lynch, 1986)

- *Coming to America* (John Landis, 1988)

- *Die Hard* (John McTiernan, 1988)

- *Edward Scissorhands* (Tim Burton, 1990)

- *The Russia House* (Fred Schepisi, 1990)

- *Point Break* (Kathryn Bigelow, 1991)

- *A League of Their Own* (Penny Marshall, 1992)

- *Unforgiven* (Clint Eastwood, 1992)

- *Four Weddings and a Funeral* (Mike Newell, 1993)

- *Schindler's List* (Steven Spielberg, 1993)

- *Babe* (Chris Noonan, 1995)

- *Face/Off* (John Woo, 1997)

- *Ratcatcher* (Lynne Ramsay, 1999)

- *Monsters, Inc.* (Pete Docter, David Silverman, and Lee Unkrich, 2001)

- *Signs* (M. Night Shyamalan, 2002)

- *Elf* (Jon Favreau, 2003)

- *The Notebook* (Nick Cassavetes, 2004)

- *Pan's Labyrinth* (Guillermo Del Toro, 2006)

- *Tell No One* (Guillaume Canet, 2006)

- *The Edge of Heaven* (Fatih Akin, 2007)

- *Juno* (Jason Reitman, 2007)

CHAPTER 4

DOCUMENTARY VS. NARRATIVE

OVERVIEW AND LEARNING OBJECTIVES

In this chapter, you will:

- Learn the difference between documentary and narrative films
- Explore the history of the documentary film
- Analyze documentary filmmaking techniques
- Discuss how to organize yourself for documentary post-production
- Understand the difference between various documentary genres

What is a Documentary Film?

Here are 10 noteworthy documentaries from the first decade of the 21st century:

- *Winged Migration* (Jacques Perrin, Jacques Cluzaud, and Michel Debats, 2001)

- *Lost in La Mancha* (Keith Fulton and Louis Pepe, 2002)

- *The Fog of War* (Errol Morris, 2003)

- *My Architect* (Nathaniel Kahn, 2003)

- *The Cutting Edge – The Magic of Movie Editing* (Wendy Apple, 2004)

- *Unforgivable Blackness: The Rise and Fall of Jack Johnson* (Ken Burns, 2004)

- *The Wild Parrots of Telegraph Hill* (Judy Irving, 2004)

- *Grizzly Man* (Werner Herzog, 2005)

- *Murderball* (Henry Alex Rubin and Dana Adam Shapiro, 2005)

- *Helvetica* (Gary Hustwit, 2007)

These films cover a wide range of subjects. Some are portraits of people; others are portraits of groups; one is instructional; another historical. They all, however, purport to be about actual people and/or events, using the actual people and/or events as the *actors* in the film. They are, in short, *documents* of the real, rather than fictionalized accounts of these actual people and events.

A film that uses actors is usually what we call a *narrative*, or fiction film. Narrative films, even if they are based on real events and people, are made from a script. The screenwriter, in order to structure a story in as interesting a way as possible, may take liberties with the historical record. This means that a narrative based on actual events is an interpretation of history, rather than a document of history. This does not mean that a documentary filmmaker does not manipulate the footage she gathers to make her film. On the contrary: filmmaking is all about manipulation of the images and sound. The difference is that a documentary film is supposed to tell a story that is truer than a narrative would, since it uses non-actors who tell their own story.

The movie *Milk* (Gus Van Sant, 2008) is a fictionalized account of the life and murder of the gay San Francisco activist and politician, Harvey Milk (1930–1978). It's a powerful and well-made film, but it's a narrative and works from a script. This makes it "based on a true story," rather than an actual true story. The movie *The Times of Harvey Milk* (Rob Epstein, 1984), on the other hand, is a documentary. It features footage of the real Harvey Milk, interviews with people who knew him, and voiceover narration. The director arranges the information of Harvey Milk's life in a way that makes for maximum dramatic impact on the viewer, but he does not tweak any of the facts of his life. It's like a news account of his life.

Neither kind of film is better than the other. They're just different. Just as some people like reading non-fiction books because they like learning about things that are true, or about events that actually happened, some people like to watch documentary films for the knowledge that they are watching a true story. That very fact – the truth – can heighten the effect of the film.

People who make documentaries like to manipulate facts (through editing) as much as people who make narratives. You need to be careful how much you play with the truth, however. If you are going to rearrange footage or interviews – even if they're real – in such a way that the story changes, then you might as well cast real actors, write a script, and make a narrative.

Then again, there have been some truly interesting films that have played with the boundaries between documentary and narrative. But they've usually been honest about it, so the viewer can enjoy the experience as a hybrid work of art, knowing that it's a hybrid. We'll look at some of these later in this chapter. For now, let's take a very brief tour through the history of documentary filmmaking and look at the different kinds of documentaries that have been made.

A (Brief) History of the Documentary Film

The following outlines a brief history of pioneers in film editing.

Documentary pioneers

It all started with the Lumière Brothers. That first publicly projected motion picture, the 50-second "Workers Leaving the Factory," was, in fact, a documentary film. Auguste and Louis Lumière just stood their Cinématographe in front of their own factory and filmed the workers leaving.

In the beginning, then, there was documentary. At least in France. Edison, in the United States, made staged films right away, in addition to documentaries. Both the Europeans and the Americans, however, quickly saw the value in producing early newsreels, or *Actualities*, in addition to making short fiction films. People on one side of the planet liked to see how people on the other side lived. In fact, even though they made a few short narratives (including the highly popular "The Sprinkler Sprinkled"), the Lumière Brothers didn't see much use for their invention beyond this kind of short newsreel.

If you want to learn more about documentary filmmaking, read Documentary Film: A Very Short Introduction *by Patricia Aufderheide (New York: Oxford University Press, 2007).*

Up until the rise of the feature-length film, in the 1910s, there were a fair amount of both narrative and documentary works made. It was clear early on, however, that the fiction works were more popular. World War I came and went, and so did the Russian Revolution, and we have already discussed how those two cataclysmic events affected narrative filmmaking. Now let's see what happened in the world of documentary. Let's start with an American by the name of Robert Flaherty (1884–1951).

During the first part of the 20th century, many American explorers went to both the North and South poles. There was therefore some real interest in the people of the North (no one lived in Antarctica), who they were, and what they did. There was also interest in the gold and other minerals of the Far North.

Robert Flaherty was a prospector who took a movie camera with him on one of his expeditions and ended up becoming the world's first *ethnographic* filmmaker. *Ethnography* is the study of specific peoples and cultures.

In 1922, Flaherty released what is now known as the world's first commercially successful feature-length documentary film, *Nanook of the North*, which follows the story of a group of "Eskimos" (the Inuit people) and focuses on one family, in particular, headed up by "Nanook" (not his real name).

Using real Inuit people, and filming them as they went about their real tasks, Flaherty created a portrait of one man that has become, in many ways, the template for all documentaries to come. Some historians and filmmakers, however, take issue with Flaherty for staging a lot of what we see on the screen.

Instead of just following an Inuit family as they went about their daily life, Flaherty asked his subjects to do things for the camera, following a story that he created, based on his previous experiences with other Inuit people. In many ways, the only *documentary* aspect of the film is that it uses real people as actors. At the same time, however, Flaherty was not inventing fictional facts of Inuit life. Everything that he had his subjects do he had seen done before.

This means that the first commercially successful documentary feature is a kind of hybrid work. It's both fictional and real. In some ways, it foreshadows the reality TV shows of our current era, since it has real people performing in scripted scenarios. Still, much of the world considered the film to be a document of reality, and since Flaherty made money off of it, it guaranteed that other filmmakers would follow suit. The documentary tradition was born.

Russian documentarians - beyond montage

Let's look at the Russians now. We have already met Kuleshov and Eisenstein. Now let's explore the work of Dziga Vertov (1896–1954) whose real name was Denis Kaufman. He chose the name Dziga Vertov as a young artist in the 1910s. The name sounds like a play on sounds that mean "spinning top" in Russian. He had two brothers. One of them, Boris Kaufman (1897–1980), became a highly regarded cinematographer in the United States, shooting such films as *On the Waterfront* (Elia Kazan, 1953) and *12 Angry Men* (Sidney Lumet, 1956).

Vertov was as radical in his artistic views as Kuleshov and Eisenstein, but he put his energies into making non-fiction films. Throughout the 1920s, working on newsreel films, which he called Kino-Pravda, or "Cinema Truth" (Pravda – "Truth" – was the name of the official State newspaper), Vertov made highly effective propaganda films for the Soviet Union, organizing footage of real events into montages that supported whatever agenda he had for that particular film. He argued for the future of cinema as one that eschewed narrative storylines. He liked these mash-ups of *Actualities* that became his stock in trade.

Unfortunately for Vertov, the real radicals in the government fell out of favor, and Joseph Stalin took over. Stalin thought these experimental documentaries were hard for the masses to understand, and, by the early 1930s had helped establish something called *Socialist Realism*, which encouraged filmmakers to make stories about simple folk doing simple things in simple settings: two factory workers falling in love while building a tractor, for example. Vertov made an important film called *Man with a Movie Camera* (1929), as a result.

Ironically, while this was considered a documentary, Vertov staged a fair amount of scenes in this movie and inserted shots of the cameraman running around the city. While there is no real story, there is a main character, the man with the movie camera. The film is about what film can capture in the hands of a clever artist. There are double-exposures, wild compositions, and fast moving shots, all cut together in creative ways. In some ways, this is far more what we might call an experimental film, since even documentaries usually try to have some sort of story. And yet it is a film made up primarily of real events and real people, which makes it also a documentary.

Vertov's ideas on filmmaking - whether he was always true to them or not - would resonate 30 years later as the filmmakers of the late 1950s and 1960s would start movements called *Cinéma Vérité* (which means "Cinema Truth," like Kino Pravda) in France and *Direct Cinema* in Canada and the United States. Vertov himself, however, for the rest of his own life, would be forced to make far more audience-friendly fare.

Propaganda and newsreels

In the 1930s, as totalitarian regimes rose in Europe, filmmakers pushed the propaganda angle of filmmaking, particularly in Nazi Germany. Filmmaker Leni Riefenstahl (1902–2003) became famous for two films: *Triumph of the Will* (1935) and *The Olympiad* (1938). Both are beautifully photographed and edited films made in the service of a fascist ideology. The first film is actually about a Nazi party rally, while the second is about the 1936 Olympic games in Berlin. As controversial as these films are, they are, like *The Birth of a Nation*, extremely well made. And if you watch George Lucas's original *Star Wars* (1977), since renamed as *Episode IV: A New Hope*, after watching *Triumph of the Will*, you might be surprised by some similar imagery that pops up.

So far, we have documentary as newsreel, documentary as ethnographic film, documentary as experimental art, and documentary as propaganda. Hollywood at this time was producing its own newsreels. *Time* magazine had a longer format series called *The March of Time*, spoofed in the opening of *Citizen Kane* (Orson Welles, 1941), and then, during World War II, the Warner Brothers Studio partnered with the U.S. government to produce the *Why We Fight* series. These were feature-length films that used archival footage, newsreel footage, and voiceover narration to sell the idea of war to the American public. These films also served as historical documents of the moment, and top Hollywood directors like Frank Capra were drafted to make them.

After World War II, as mentioned in Chapter 1, Italian filmmakers, their studios destroyed, took to the streets with cameras and non-actors to make gritty dramas that became known as the Italian Neo-Realist movement. These were narrative films made using documentary techniques, and they showed that compelling stories could be created with very few resources. Along with the theories of Dziga Vertov, this style would have a great influence on other filmmakers a little over 10 years later.

Until the late 1950s, however, the documentary films that most mainstream audiences would see were of the newsreel variety, whether in short format or feature-length. These films usually featured authoritative voiceover narrations that guided viewers through the film. Though these films were, indeed, documents of some kind of reality, the stories were shaped by the point of view of the narrator and by what facts were shown, or not shown.

Cinéma vérité and its cousins

By the late 1950s, just as the French New Wave filmmakers were about to launch themselves, advances in camera and sound technology suddenly allowed for the development of small, quiet, and very portable consistent frame-rate film cameras. These convenient cameras could run at a constant 24 fps rate so you could synchronize sound reliably. Even more importantly, there appeared small, synchronized sound recording devices that were easily portable. Suddenly, a small film crew of just two people could gather high quality footage – with sound – without intimidating their subjects with a lot of large equipment.

With the new kind of cameras and sound equipment available, it became much easier to think about going down to the street and capturing reality, as is, without adulteration. It certainly helped news-gathering crews. Until the invention of light, decent quality, portable video cameras, which made shooting even easier (and allowed news and documentary crews to bring only one device into the field), this dual-system technology is what was used.

The French *Cinéma Vérité* movement and its North American *Direct Cinema* counterpart both focused on the idea that the camera could just capture what was there, so that audiences would be able to see the unadulterated truth. As we have already established, the mere act of editing footage creates a reality influenced by the filmmaker's point of view, but these kinds of cameras certainly helped foster the illusion that what was presented was as real as possible.

These kinds of films generally avoided voiceover, interviews, soundtracks (other than music that might appear naturally while filming was going on), and just presented scenes as they unfolded. Since most non-filmmakers are unaware of the editing, the aesthetic of these films felt very pure, as if the viewer were a fly on the wall. A terrific early example of this is Robert Drew's 1960 film *Primary*, about the Democratic Party's primary election that year, which ended in John F. Kennedy's ascension to the top of the ticket.

In the film, Drew (1924–) used no narration, and instead just followed the various candidates as they campaigned across the country. He cut, and inter-cut scenes of the different candidates, and sometimes overlapped sound from one scene onto another scene, thereby creating a makeshift soundtrack that is nevertheless organic to the world of the movie. No music or dialogue was created specifically *for* the movie. This would have gone against the ideals of *Direct Cinema*.

Throughout the 1960s, this style of documentary filmmaking, also now known as *observational cinema*, became increasingly popular. D.A. Pennebaker (1925–) mastered this approach in his brilliant 1967 *Don't Look Back*, about Bob Dylan's 1965 concert tour of England. Using only the shots and sounds recorded while following Dylan on his trip, Pennebaker assembled a story devoid of any apparent editorial artifice.

Albert (1926–) and David (1931–1987) Maysles were two other pioneers of this style. Three noteworthy films of theirs were: *Salesman* (1968), *Gimme Shelter* (1970), and *Grey Gardens* (1975). The first is about bible salesmen on the road; the second is about the ill-fated Rolling Stones concert where the Hell's Angels, acting as bodyguards for the rockers, killed a man; and the third is about a mother and daughter, relatives of Jacqueline Kennedy Onassis, who live in a huge decrepit mansion on Long Island. This last film has since been adapted as a stage musical and as an HBO® film starring Jessica Lange (1949–) and Drew Barrymore(1975–).

Another noted filmmaker of that era was Frederick Wiseman (1930–), still very active today. His film *Titicut Follies* (1967) is about an institution for the criminally insane in Massachusetts. Being a fly on the wall in such a place is an incredible experience. It is a perfect film for the *Direct Cinema* approach.

Documentaries today

Starting in the 1970s, we began to see filmmakers adopt a documentary style that is more like what we see today. Directors started to interview their subjects, or people who knew their subjects, and include these interviews – what we now call *talking heads* – in the film. Sometimes these *talking head* interviews were nicely staged and photographed, with the person sitting comfortably in a room, with good lighting and sound. Other times, these interviews were gathered on the run, outside, and not always so beautifully shot. But the point of view of these actual participants in the drama now started to be included in the final film.

A good example of this evolution is a film by Barbara Kopple (1946–), *Harlan County, USA* (1976), about a miner's strike in Kentucky. The film felt very similar to a purely observational film in many ways, but Kopple filmed gritty interviews of the miners as well. It's a powerful movie, and the filmmakers' really committed to the project; at one point, they were caught up in a strike-breaking riot and suffered physical injuries.

Since the 1970s, video technology has improved enough so that documentaries shot on film – which are very expensive, given the amount of footage you have to gather for a good story – have gradually become more rare. Also, with the invention of cable TV in the 1980s, and the growth in channels, and news channels, in particular, there has been a blurring of the line between documentaries made for theatrical release and documentaries made for broadcast on television. There has also been a blurring of styles between newscasts and films. And with reality TV and crime shows, we are now used to seeing documentary film techniques in a variety of different contexts. Since the broadcasting of the future is unknown, we can assume that the Internet and other broadband delivery devices will affect how we make and watch movies in the years ahead.

For now, however, we will briefly discuss current documentary shooting and editing techniques.

Documentary Production Techniques

As always, we need to define our terms. While we do that, we can also discuss the reasons for which these various techniques might be used.

Observational footage

This footage is the main part of your film. As the name suggests, this is footage that comes from spending a significant amount of time with your subject. In order to capture interesting activities or events, you must film for long periods of time. This is why the invention of relatively inexpensive high-quality video cameras was such a boon to the documentary filmmaker; it allowed her to shoot without worrying too much about cost. Film is expensive to develop.

It's always a good idea to spend time with the people you are going to film, before you film them. This way you can truly start to become part of the background, and there is a better chance that you will not affect their behavior. The movie *Hoop Dreams* (Steve James, 1994), which follows two inner-city African-American teenage boys as they navigate basketball programs in exclusive white private schools, took five years to make. During that time, the young men at the center of the film became increasingly comfortable with the presence of the camera, to the point where it doesn't seem to be a factor in how they behave.

B-roll

This term comes from the days before non-linear digital editing systems. In the film world, you would have a strip of film – the a-roll – on one track of your editing table. This might have your interviews. Then, on a second track, you might have observational footage, to which you could cut when someone said something in the interview that needed supporting imagery. In the linear video-editing world, the same kind of process would happen, but with two tape decks instead.

Some would argue that the b-roll – the shots of real life and of your subjects doing things – is more important to the story than the interviews. After all, interviews, no matter how interesting, are visually static and boring, for the most part. In this school of thought, you would therefore cut your b-roll first, shaping your story that way, and then use interviews, if you must use them, to support the b-roll. But this takes time.

Others would argue, among them news programmers who make many short documentaries a day for broadcast, and who therefore do not have that much time, that the b-roll supports the interview. Whenever your subject talks about an activity or an event for which you have some available footage, you cut to it. Hence, the a-roll and b-roll model.

B-roll, in any case, is really just observational footage by another name. Regardless of what you call it, if it's interesting and serves the story, then put it in the film.

Talking heads

A talking head is an interview. It is usually framed in a medium shot or a close-up. If you have the time, you should make sure that the talking head is a well-composed and well-lit shot with good sound. If all goes well, you can even use the audio from the interview as a voiceover for parts of the film.

In a situation where you envision having multiple people talk about a similar topic, it's a good idea to shoot different talking head interviews on alternate sides of the frame. In other words, shoot Person A's interview with him on the right. Then, when you film Person B, shoot her on the left side of the frame. That way, when you cut back and forth, it's a more visually dynamic experience for the viewer.

Try to avoid a situation where you have to include the interviewer's voice in order for the subject's answer to make sense. Make sure that the interviewee answers in complete sentences. Also, shoot a long interview. It's much easier to spend more time at someone's house or office on one day than to realize you didn't get all the information you needed and have to go back. That said, if, as in *Hoop Dreams*, you are filming over months or years, there is nothing wrong with returning for multiple interviews with the same people. If you do so, try filming these different interviews with the same people on alternate sides of the frame each time. Visually, it will be more interesting.

If the only way that you can shoot an interview with someone is quickly, on the run, then that's what you do, even if you don't have time to frame a nice shot. Interesting information is always better than no information. Do try, however, to make sure the audio is decent, or it will most likely be unusable.

A great film that shoots interviews this way is *Blindsight* (Lucy Walker, 2006) about a group of Tibetan blind children climbing a peak next to Everest. The higher the crew climbs, the less oxygen there is, and some of the shots don't always look as good as others. But they're usable, and that's the most important thing.

Archival footage and stills

This just means footage, or photographs, that existed from before you started making the film. In the case of an historical documentary, this might be all you have, in terms of imagery. If you're making a biographical film, you might use home movies from the childhood of your subject. If you are making a film about the history of cinematography, as in the terrific *Visions of Light*

(Arnold Glassman, Todd McCarthy, and Stuart Samuels, 1992), the archival footage might consist largely of old movies. You should always get written permission, however, from the owners of the films, before using something like that.

Ken Burns (1953–), the creator of many an historical documentaries, was faced with an enormous visual challenge when he made his seminal 11-hour masterpiece for PBS®, *The Civil War* (1990). The events at the center of his film took place in 1865, thirty years before the invention of movies. So Burns took old photographs (photography, fortunately, was invented in the 1830s and 1840s) and animated them, creating slow zooms in and out, and gentle pans and tilts across and up and down each image. He turned them into movies, in other words, thereby making the viewer's experience more interesting. This creative solution to a significant problem was seen as innovative, and the film series was so successful, that iMovie®, Apple's beginning editing program, named their similar effect the "Ken Burns" effect.

Reenactments

Sometimes, however, you just have to spend time and money and recreate a scene for which you have no actual footage. If you're making a film about the invasion of Gaul (the ancient word for France) by the Romans, you will obviously have to recreate scenes, but even contemporary subjects sometimes require reenactments.

Errol Morris (1948–), another great documentarian, used a reenactment in his 1988 film *The Thin Blue Line*. Morris wanted to show the event that led to his subject's conviction of murder, for which there was no footage, so he filmed a reenactment in a variety of ways. In his finished movie, each time new facts come out about the case, or a different point of view is being discussed, he shows a new version of the reenactment.

Errol Morris is also responsible, in his later work, for showing how interesting talking head interviews can be made to look. In *The Fog of War* (2003), about Robert McNamara (1916–2009), the Secretary of Defense under Presidents Kennedy and Johnson, there is only one interview – with McNamara – but it was shot over a number of days, and with a variety of compositions, many of which are quite striking.

Another documentary film with an interesting reenactment is *Touching the Void* (Kevin MacDonald, 2003). This film is about a disastrous attempt, in 1985, by two British climbers to ascend a peak in Peru. The two men almost died, and one of them did something to the other one that, under normal circumstances, would have resulted in his death.

The film consists of interviews with the two climbers and a third man who helped them reach their base station, and a reenactment of the climb. That reenactment takes up half of the movie. MacDonald cuts back and forth between his real-life subjects and the actors who portray them, following their descriptions as he recreates what it must have been like.

Voiceover narration

The advantage of a narrator is that you can write a script for him or her, and thereby make sure that the information you want to deliver to the audience is actually delivered. Even better, since this script is written after the film is edited, you can tailor the voiceover to each specific moment in the film, for dramatic effect.

For historical documentaries, this can be quite effective. Ken Burns' films use voiceover as well as individual actors reading from historical documents, which creates a nice variety in the voices we hear. He does this particularly well in *Unforgivable Blackness: The Rise and Fall of Jack Johnson* (2004).

In addition to the *Why We Fight* series, other films about World War II, and the Holocaust, have used narrators to take us through the horrors of what happened. Examples of this are *Night and Fog* (Alain Resnais, 1955) and *The Sorrow and the Pity* (Marcel Ophuls, 1971). In *Night and Fog*, which takes us on a tour of the death camp Auschwitz, the narrator provides just the authoritative presence we need to help us deal with the disturbing subject matter.

Music: Diegetic vs. Non-diegetic

Diegetic sound is sound that comes from people or events or things that happen within your film. If you use sound from a talking head interview as voiceover, that is diegetic sound. If you record a live concert, as D.A. Pennebaker does in *Don't Look Back*, with Bob Dylan, that is also diegetic sound. Pennebaker frequently cuts away from shots of Dylan playing to show the post-concert departure, or the next day's trip, while keeping the music from the concert on the soundtrack. That is still diegetic sound, even if it is not diegetic to that scene. Think of this kind of sound as the *insert* of the sound design world: It exists within the scene.

NOTE

On the other hand, non-diegetic sound comes from outside the world of the movie. It has been recorded completely separately from any activities on-screen. Voiceover narration that does not come from talking heads is non-diegetic sound. So is music that you have hired a composer to write for the film, and later used on the soundtrack. Think of non-diegetic sound as the *cutaway* of sound design: It exists just outside of the scene.

Music can be a powerful tool, even in a documentary film that is supposed to show real people in real events. It is one more way, as in a narrative, that you can manipulate how the audience perceives your story.

Errol Morris really likes to use music. In both *The Fog of War* and *A Brief History of Time* (1991) – a film about the great English physicist Stephen Hawking – he uses the music of composer Philip Glass (1937–) to great effect. Glass's music lends itself well to soundtracks: The repetitive minimalist strains slowly build in intensity, affecting the viewer in subtle ways. Glass also provided the music for the strangely beautiful experimental documentary *Koyaanisqatsi: Life Out of Balance* (Godfrey Reggio, 1982).

Ken Burns uses music, as well, although he often uses it as a complement to the particular historical period he is discussing. In *Unforgivable Blackness*, for example, he uses music from the turn of the 20th century as his main soundtrack

Music can be stirring in a documentary; it can be funny; it can be sad. The effect is no different than it is in a narrative. The more you use it, however, the more you depart from the professed aesthetic of observational cinema. Keep this in mind.

Title cards and other textual explanations

Another technique that you might see used in documentaries is the title or text card. Sometimes that's the only way to introduce a sequence or concept without hiring a voiceover artist. The card can be as simple as putting up a definition of a word, or it can be a way of dividing your film into different sections. In *The Fog of War*, Errol Morris has Robert McNamara's philosophy broken down into 11 lessons, and he opens each lesson section with a card. For example: "Lesson 10: Never say never."

It's called a title card *because, in the old days of film, you would print text on a card and then film the card.*

Final consideration: To include yourself or not

Have you seen any documentaries by Michael Moore (1954–)? His films take the forms of quests, such as, "I will track down the head of General Motors," or, "I will figure out what happened at Columbine High School." And in the context of these quests, he puts himself at the center of the story. In a way, this makes sense because he gives the story a clear trajectory and one main protagonist.

Other filmmakers have put themselves in their films as well. This makes sense if, in fact, the film is about the filmmaker. Autobiographical films that have done this well are *Sherman's March* (Ross McElwee, 1986) and *Halving the Bones* (Ruth Ozeki Lounsbury, 1996), both of which play with our expectations of what an autobiography should look like.

Or there are films like the one Morgan Spurlock (1970–) made in 2004, in which the filmmaker experiments on himself. He is not so much the story – in this case, the film is about how bad fast food can be for you – as the driving vehicle of the story. His is a quest, as well, as in Michael Moore's films. The only difference is that Moore doesn't use himself as a human guinea pig.

Werner Herzog (1942–), who has made both narratives and documentaries, likes to use himself as the narrator of his films, and occasionally appears as a peripheral subject. *Grizzly Man* (2005) is a film about a very troubled but well-intentioned man, Timothy Treadwell (1957–2003), who spent many years trying to save grizzly bears in Alaska. He had no training as a wildlife biologist, but nevertheless lived among the bears (and foxes) for months at a time, filming himself. He was, in short, the subject of his own documentary. The only problem was that he was eaten by a bear before he could make the film. Instead, Herzog, who loves extreme personalities, made a film about him, which he narrated, using Treadwell's own footage. It's a disturbing portrait of a disturbing man.

It's your choice whether to include yourself in the film or not. Just make sure that if you do, it serves the story. That should be your guiding principle at all times.

Documentary Post-Production

So you've gone out and spent a year filming a documentary about a family that built a house out of duct tape. HBO has funded the project, and you have to deliver a rough cut in 2 months. Now what?

The number one way to keep yourself from losing your way in the editing process, whether you're cutting a narrative or a documentary, is to organize, organize, organize. If you're a little sloppy when working with a narrative, it will slow you down, and might make the film worse, but you'll get it done. If you're a mess with a documentary, however, beware the disaster that awaits you. When we get to the chapters on Final Cut Express, we'll learn how to organize, but for now, it's enough to just understand the importance of it.

One of the dangers that arose when high-quality video cameras began to be readily available was that filmmakers could now shoot and shoot and shoot. In many ways, this was a boon to documentary filmmaking, since there was no concern about not capturing important moments in the lives of your subjects. The problem, however, is that if you were to film for a year, and film just one hour a day, you would have 365 hours of footage. That would then take you 15 days and 5 hours just to watch all of that footage, not counting the times you might have to stop and go back because you missed something. You can see how, given this possibility, that you would want to adopt very organized editing practices. Let's discuss some of these practices.

First of all, you obviously watch the footage during the filming process, taking notes, and doing something called *logging*. This means that you write down everything important that happens in a shot, for future reference. If it's an interview, you might want to pay someone to transcribe it, if you don't have the energy to do it yourself. Then again, the more time you spend getting to know your footage, the faster the actual creative part of the editing will be. The amount of time inherent in cutting a documentary, however, does explain why it is more common to see multiple names listed as editors of these films than in narrative work.

Secondly, you must keep all of your files labeled in folders that make them relatively easy to find. Final Cut has something called a *Browser* (we'll get to that in Chapter 7), where your footage is stored, and in it you can create as many folders, called *Bins*, as you like. In these *Bins*, you can store your observational footage, archival footage, still photos, music, text cards, etc. Keep all of these kinds of material organized in a way that makes sense to you, so that you can access them quickly. Before you file something, however, make sure you have watched that bit of footage and taken notes. Never file anything away without watching it and labeling it.

Documentary Genres

In the last chapter, we discussed narrative film genres. Here is a very brief list of some different kinds of documentary genres.

Cinéma vérité

We know what this is by now. All observational documentaries, without voiceover or interviews, fit into this category. You can find examples earlier in this chapter.

Ethnographic

You might see films like this on PBS or the Discovery Channel®, but it all began with Flaherty. This is any kind of film that explores a specific culture or people, different, usually, from that of the filmmaker. In some ways, you could argue that *Harlan County USA*, a film about Kentucky miners made by a New Yorker, is an ethnographic film. Most people, however, think of something like *First Contact* (Bob Connolly and Robin Anderson, 1983), a film about a people discovered on the island of New Guinea in 1930, untouched by European civilization.

Event films

This is any kind of film that tells a story by focusing on a contest or event that lends the movie a convenient trajectory. There is a beginning (getting ready for the contest), a middle (the contest), and an end (somebody wins or loses). These films very nicely lend themselves to telling stories about interesting groups of people – a sort of ethnographic study – while seeming to be about the contest. They make it easier for the filmmaker to know what to film as well. Some films in this category are *Mad Hot Ballroom* (Marilyn Agrelo, 2005), a film about a group of middle-school kids competing in a ballroom dancing contest in New York, and *Murderball* (Henry Alex Rubin and Dana Adam Shapiro 2005), a film about quadriplegic rugby players.

Historical

We've mentioned a number of these documentaries. Depending on how far back the history goes, filmmakers have to decide how to present the material. Do they use the "Ken Burns" effect and hire actors to read historical documents? Do they use a narrator? Do they stage reenactments? If you watch the History Channel, you've seen all kinds of historical documentaries. Some historical films can also focus on the modern legacy of an historical topic or event. One such extremely well-made film is *Helvetica* (Gary Hustwit, 2007), which takes the viewer on a journey through the history of modern typography and graphic design.

Nature

The 2006 BBC® series *Planet Earth* is an amazing work that takes the viewer on a journey through the flora and fauna or our planet. At the end of every episode is a 10-minute behind-the-scenes documentary that shows how much work went in to gathering the material. In general, nature films explore the natural world. You can see many of these movies on Animal Planet®. Nature documentaries that have had theatrical releases include *Microcosmos* (Claude Nuridsany and Marie Pérennou, 1996), a film about tiny creatures we can barely see, and *Winged Migration* (Jacques Perrin, Jacques Cluzaud, and Michel Debats, 2001), a film about birds and their migration patterns. *March of the Penguins* (Luc Jacquet, 2005) was a very commercially successful nature documentary.

Polemical/Political

This is any film with a strong opinion that it wants you to share. We already mentioned Michael Moore, who makes films with strong political opinions. Other films that take on potentially controversial subjects are *The Ground Truth* (Patricia Foulkrod, 2006), a film about the failed reconstruction of Iraq, and *The Trials of Henry Kissinger* (Eugene Jarecki, 2002), a film about the alleged war crimes of our former Secretary of State.

Other documentaries

There are plenty of other genre categories out there that we could discuss, such as biographical films, *making-of* or *behind-the-scenes* films (now standard on most DVDs), and concert films. There are also experimental works that don't really document anything tangible, but that use footage of real people and events, as Dziga Vertov did. To make matters even more complicated, some films that are really narratives nevertheless employ documentary techniques, creating interesting hybrids. One example of this kind of hybrid is *American Splendor* (Shari Springer Berman and Robert Pulcini, 2003) in which the real-life characters who are played by actors in half of the film make actual appearances – as themselves – in the film, as well. Or there's *The Class (Entre les murs)* (Laurent Cantet, 2008), a fictionalized account of a French middle-school teacher's troubles, based on a book by that teacher, in which the actual teacher plays himself in the movie.

And then there are *mockumentaries*, which are really narratives pretending to be documentaries. Two of the best-known examples of this are *This Is Spinal Tap* (Rob Reiner, 1984), a film about a fake 1960s rock band (which really launched this genre), and *Best in Show* (Christopher Guest, 2000), about a fake dog show.

But it's all cinema, and it all involves careful shooting and editing, regardless of genre or style. If you think of yourself as more of one kind of director than another, keep in mind that plenty of directors, like Werner Herzog, make both documentaries and narratives. Make the movies you want to make.

SUMMARY

The purpose of this chapter was to explain the difference between documentaries and narratives, and to discuss, in brief, the history of the documentary film. In addition, we discussed the many different techniques used in making a documentary as well the importance of organization in the editing process. Finally, we ended by exploring genres within the documentary realm.

As we did in Chapter 1, we started at the beginning, revisiting the films of Auguste and Louis Lumière and Thomas Edison, and moving quickly to the first documentary feature, *Nanook of the North* (Robert Flaherty, 1922). We ended our journey in the reality TV tradition of today by way of the *Cinema Vérité* movement of the 1960s. Along the way, we learned how the invention of lightweight cameras and sound recording devices affected the development of documentary techniques.

We then spent some time learning the terminology of the medium. We studied the differences between *talking heads* and *b-roll*, *diegetic* and *non-diegetic* sound, *archival footage* and *reenactments*. We looked at examples of how these different techniques have been used in specific films. After analyzing these techniques, we emphasized the monumental importance of organization in the post-production process and touched briefly on the ways in which Final Cut makes good organization possible. We will learn more about what Final Cut can do, starting in Chapter 7.

Finally, we ended this chapter with a quick survey of the different kinds of genres within the documentary tradition. From *ethnographic* to *nature* films, from *historical* to *polemical* films, we explored examples of each style. We even discussed films that are hard to categorize because they combine elements of documentary and narrative filmmaking. Whatever the genre, however, we decided that what counts the most is a good story, regardless of technique.

Now it is time, in Chapter 5, to explore the differences between short films and features.

REVIEW QUESTIONS: CHAPTER 4

1. Define "documentary film."

2. What are some documentary genres?

3. What was the first successful documentary feature?

4. Who was Dziga Vertov?

5. What is *Cinéma Vérité*?

6. What is the difference between observational footage and b-roll?

1. How truthful do you think a documentary film should be? Is it possible to achieve "cinema truth," and should we even try?

2. Do you have a favorite director of documentary films, or just a favorite documentary film? Does the director usually have an opinion, or does the film in question have an opinion? How is that opinion delivered to the audience?

3. What do you think of *reality TV*? Do you have a favorite show? Do you think it's truthful, or can you see how reality is manipulated?

4. What do you think of the news on TV or cable? Is it objective? Should it be?

Further Research

Here is a list of documentary films to watch, some of which have already been mentioned in this chapter:

- *Nanook of the North* (Robert Flaherty, 1922)
- *Berlin: Symphony of a Great City* (Walter Ruttmann, 1927)
- *Man with a Movie Camera* (Dziga Vertov, 1929)
- *Land without Bread* (Luis Buñuel, 1933)
- *Why We Fight* film series (Frank Capra and others, 1940s)
- *Night and Fog* (Alain Resnais, 1955)
- *Primary* (Robert Drew, 1960)
- *Don't Look Back* (D.A. Pennebaker, 1967)
- *Titicut Follies* (Frederick Wiseman, 1967)
- *Salesman* (Albert and David Maysles, 1968)

- *Gimme Shelter* (Albert and David Maysles, 1970)

- *The Sorrow and the Pity* (Marcel Ophuls, 1971)

- *Grey Gardens* (Albert and David Maysles, 1975)

- *Harlan County U.S.A.* (Barbara Kopple, 1976)

- *Pumping Iron* (George Butler and Robert Fiore, 1977)

- *Koyaanisqatsi: Life Out of Balance* (Godfrey Reggio, 1982)

- *First Contact* (Bob Connolly and Robin Anderson, 1983)

- *Stop Making Sense* (Jonathan Demme, 1984)

- *Streetwise* (Martin Bell, 1984)

- *The Times of Harvey Milk* (Rob Epstein, 1984)

- *Shoah* (Claude Lanzmann, 1985)

- *Sherman's March* (Ross McElwee, 1986)

- *Who Killed Vincent Chin?* (Christine Choy, 1987)

- *Buena Vista Social Club* (Wim Wenders, 1988)

- *The Thin Blue Line* (Errol Morris, 1988)

- *The Civil War* – PBS series (Ken Burns, 1990)

- *A Brief History of Time* (Errol Morris, 1991)

- *Visions of Light* (Arnold Glassman, Todd McCarthy, and Stuart Samuels, 1992)

- *The War Room* (Chris Hegedus and D.A. Pennebaker, 1993)

- *Bauhaus: The Face of the Twentieth Century* (Frank Whitford, 1994)

- *Crumb* (Terry Zwigoff, 1994)

- *Hoop Dreams* (Steve James, 1994)

- *The Celluloid Closet* (Rob Epstein, 1995)

- *Halving the Bones* (Ruth Ozeki Lounsbury, 1996)

- *Microcosmos* (Claude Nuridsany and Marie Pérennou, 1996)

- *Fast, Cheap & Out of Control* (Errol Morris, 1997)

- *4 Little Girls* (Spike Lee, 1997)
- *Little Dieter Needs to Fly* (Werner Herzog, 1998)
- *Regret to Inform* (Barbara Sonneborn, 1998)
- *American Movie* (Chris Smith, 1999)
- *The Original Kings of Comedy* (Spike Lee, 2000)
- *Promises* (Carlos Bolado, B.Z. Goldberg, and Justine Shapiro, 2001)
- *Winged Migration* (Jacques Perrin, Jacques Cluzaud, and Michel Debats, 2001)
- *Bowling for Columbine* (Michael Moore, 2002)
- *Lost in La Mancha* (Keith Fulton and Louis Pepe, 2002)
- *The Trials of Henry Kissinger* (Eugene Jarecki, 2002)
- *The Corporation* (Mark Achbar and Jennifer Abbot, 2003)
- *The Fog of War* (Errol Morris, 2003)
- *My Architect* (Nathaniel Kahn, 2003)
- *Born into Brothels* (Zana Briski and Ross Kauffman, 2004)
- *Control Room* (Jehane Noujaim, 2004)
- *The Cutting Edge - The Magic of Movie Editing* (Wendy Apple, 2004)
- *Fahrenheit 9/11* (Michael Moore, 2004)
- *Super Size Me* (Morgan Spurlock, 2004)
- *Unforgivable Blackness: The Rise and Fall of Jack Johnson* (Ken Burns, 2004)
- *The Wild Parrots of Telegraph Hill* (Judy Irving, 2004)
- *Dave Chappelle's Block Party* (Michel Gondry, 2005)
- *Enron: The Smartest Guys in the Room* (Alex Gibney, 2005)
- *Grizzly Man* (Werner Herzog, 2005)
- *Mad Hot Ballroom* (Marilyn Agrelo, 2005)
- *March of the Penguins* (Luc Jacquet, 2005)
- *Murderball* (Henry Alex Rubin and Dana Adam Shapiro, 2005)

- *Blindsight* (Lucy Walker, 2006)

- *The Ground Truth* (Patricia Foulkrod, 2006)

- *An Inconvenient Truth* (Davis Guggenheim, 2006)

- *Planet Earth - The Complete BBC Series* (Alastair Fothergill, 2006)

- *Pete Seeger: The Power of Song* (Jim Brown, 2007)

- *Helvetica* (Gary Hustwit, 2007)

- *Harvard Beats Yale 29–29* (Kevin Rafferty, 2008)

- *Roman Polanksi: Wanted and Desired* (Marina Zenovich, 2008)

CHAPTER 5

FEATURES VS. SHORTS

OVERVIEW AND LEARNING OBJECTIVES

In this chapter, you will:

- Compare and contrast short films and features
- Explore the history of the short film
- Consider the specific needs that go into editing a short film
- Study the short film, *Nail Polish*, that we will work with in later chapters
- Discuss distribution possibilities for short films

What is a Short Film?

In some ways, the only difference between a short film and a feature is length.[1] Back in 1894, when Edison made his films using the Kinetoscope, and in 1895, when the Lumière Brothers used their Cinématographe, a short film was all there was. Short meant about 50 seconds long. But by the 1910s, if you remember from Chapter 1, films had increased in length to be *one-reelers* (10 minutes) or *two-reelers* (20 minutes), and an evening's entertainment would consist of a number of these projected in a row. Then, the *feature* was born, which was a film that was long enough, in and of itself to constitute the entire show. There might have been a short film or two before the main *feature*, but that 2-hour film was the main event.

Did the short film die after that? Well, yes and no. Some filmmakers, such as Mack Sennet (1880–1960), had invested a significant amount of time, effort, and money in producing short films. Sennet's Keystone Studios had a successful run in the 1910s with slapstick comedies (comedies with a lot of physical humor), such as his *Keystone Kops* series. If you watch the movie *Chaplin* (Richard Attenborough, 1992), Sennet is played by Dan Aykroyd (1952–) as a boisterous producer who is eventually outmaneuvered by Charlie Chapin, played by Robert Downey, Jr. (1965–). Sennet gave Chaplin his start in Hollywood by putting him in a series of very funny short films. Chaplin then transitioned seamlessly into the world of the feature film.

That is just one example. Once the feature-length film came, however, it supplanted the shorter format. That did not mean, however, that short films disappeared.

There were newsreels such as *The March of Time*, created by *Time* magazine (as we discussed in Chapter 4), which were basically short documentaries about current events. These films would play before the longer feature programs. Once Americans began to watch more and more television in the 1950s, however, this series eventually ended.

There were also short films for children, such as Walt Disney's *Silly Symphonies* or Hal Roach's *Our Gang/Little Rascals* series. These were wildly popular and could play as short programs of just one film, longer programs of many films, or as pre-feature preludes. After that time, however, the art of visual short storytelling began to move more and more into the realm of TV. After all, television news programs, dramas, and situational comedies are really just short films presented on a small screen. And today's cartoons are direct descendents of Walt Disney's early works.

Finally, today, as the influence of television may be on the wane, the networked world of the present and future promises untold possibilities for showing short films in ways undreamed of by the Lumière Brothers and their early followers. Web sites and streaming devices that allow you to play films from Netflix®, Amazon®, and Hulu® give you faster and better access to content than ever before. And since it's so easy, with almost zero distribution costs, the reasons to actually make short films are back in full force. Until recently, since there was no clear market for distribution, there was little reason for someone to spend many hours and lots of money on a work that no one would ever see. The short had become, instead, a way for many aspiring feature filmmakers to demonstrate their ability to tell a visual story. It was like a business card, in other words, to announce to the world (or a producer) that you know how to make a movie.

Over the years, film festivals and film markets, like the ones at Cannes, Sundance, or Toronto, have provided filmmakers, both new and experienced, with an opportunity to show their work. Jim Jarmusch (1953–), Spike Lee (1957–), Jane Campion (1954–), and others, now established feature film directors, began their careers by having their short films admired in festivals. Sometimes a filmmaker will make a short version of a story that they hope to then turn into a feature, as Billy Bob Thornton (1955–) did with *Some Folks Call It a Sling Blade* (George Hickenlooper, 1994). Thornton wrote the script for the film, starred in it, and when it was a critical success, adapted it into the 1996 feature film *Sling Blade*, which he directed, himself.

There are other kinds of short films, as well, which provide work, artistic fulfillment, and income to countless filmmakers: commercials, movie trailers, music videos, and promotional films for businesses, to name a few.

Is there a cut-off length, after which a film ceases to be considered a "short?" If you look at the descriptions that most film festivals list on their submission forms for shorts vs. features, 50 minutes seems to be the magic number, at least in the United States. The Cannes Film Festival, in France, considers films to be of feature-length if the film is over 60 minutes. Interestingly, Cannes does not accept films that run between 15 and 60 minutes. For them, a short film is 15 minutes or less.

You can think of a short film as you would a short story and its relationship to a novel. They belong to the same family, but they are not quite the same thing. You make different decisions concerning pacing and emphasis based on the length of the material. In a short work, most story details should count directly towards an understanding of the plot, whereas you might be slightly looser in a longer piece. Not too loose, however, as good stories are usually tightly plotted.

Still, a story should have a clear beginning, middle, and end. So how does editing a short film differ from editing a feature film? The only real difference is that you need to be even more organized when you cut a feature than you are when you cut a short, since there is more footage.

Cutting a Short

Have you seen a short film, other than a commercial or trailer? If so, you've probably seen it online, or through a cable channel such as the Independent Film Channel (IFC).

Films – long or short – exist as art because we intend them to be art. Is there, however, a different approach to creating a short work of art vs. a longer work of art? Perhaps.

Let's look at the YouTube® phenomenon. Clips that might be boring and repetitive at 3 minutes are very funny at 30 seconds. Sketch comedy skits that work for the first 2 minutes start to get boring at the fourth minute. Ideas that are interesting without much development for a short period of time, in other words, start to require more story development as time drags on.

If you are making a short film with strong dramatic intent, you are going to want to structure it just like you would a feature. Instead of taking 20 minutes or so to set up the world of your movie and establish character, you'll take 1 or 2 minutes. But the plot will flow from this setup, and reach an eventual conclusion.

Where the short film can differ from the longer format is in its choice to be plot-driven or idea-driven. As with *Saturday Night Live*® skits, as long as the film is short, if the idea being explored is interesting (and visual), viewers will keep watching. Commercials do this very well. Sometimes there is no plot, but it's highly visual and it ends before it gets boring.

Many commercials are structured around ideas like this, but there are plenty that manage to tell stories with amazingly well-developed plots for their short lengths. If you visit the CLIO Awards Web site,[2] you can watch a wide variety of work, both idea-driven and plot-driven.

The *Nail Polish* script

Let's now take a look at one specific short film, included on this book's accompanying DVD, titled *Nail Polish* (Christopher L. Reed, 2004).[3]

It's 8 minutes long, and the story focuses on what happens on a hot summer afternoon when a boy doing yard work is observed by a bored girl doing nothing. There are multiple versions of this film on the DVD, since we will later cut and recut the footage as a comedy, drama, and thriller. For now, just look at the one called, simply, *Nail Polish*.

At 8 minutes, there is plenty of time to set up the characters, the world of the movie, and the general tone of the piece for a few minutes before putting the plot into motion. Here is the script, presented in the proper script format and font (12-point Courier):

```
EXT. BACKYARD - DAY

MICHAEL, a sweet teen with man-like
aspirations, works hard in the overgrown
backyard of an upper-middle-class home.
He pulls weeds in one spot, then moves on
to the next. It's a hot summer day, and he
begins to tire.

INT. BEDROOM - CONTINUOUS

LISA, mid-teens, cute and aware of it, lies
in bed, bored. She reads but gives up. She
turns an electrical fan on and off. She
annoys her DOG, a Westie. Finally, she gets
up and looks out the window at . . .

EXT. BACKYARD - CONTINUOUS

. . . Michael, who takes off his shirt and
takes a drink from a spigot by the back door
of the house. He goes back to weeding, less
enthusiastically than before, while . . .

INT. BEDROOM - CONTINUOUS

. . . Lisa watches, her boredom gone. She
smiles to herself and appears to consider
something. She exits.
```

EXT. BACKYARD - DAY

While Michael is some distance away from the door, Lisa quietly pops out of the house and grabs his shirt.

INT. BASEMENT - DAY

Lisa turns the main house water switch to off.

INT. BEDROOM - DAY

Lisa sits back on the bed, a towel and nail polish in her hand. She scratches her dog's head and laughs a little.

EXT. BACKYARD - DAY

Michael continues weeding, though only because he must. The vigor is all gone now. He looks back at the house as Lisa looks away from her window. He stops, stretches, and looks down at his filthy hands.

He walks back to the spigot and turns it on. No water comes out. He frowns. After a beat he considers the back screen door. He gets up and looks for his shirt. After another beat, he walks tentatively towards the screen.

                    MICHAEL
          Hello?

                    (beat)
          Hello?

There is no answer. After a pause, Michael pushes open the door and goes in.

INT. HALLWAY - CONTINUOUS

Michael kicks his dirty shoes off and
proceeds, slowly, down the hall.

                    MICHAEL
          Hello?

This time Lisa's voice answers, muffled, from
down the hall in the bedroom.

                    LISA
          Yeah?

Michael goes to the bedroom door and pushes
it open.

INT. BEDROOM - CONTINUOUS

Lisa sits, leaning forward on the bed, a
towel under her feet, painting her nails.
Her dog is on the bed.

Michael blushes and says nothing.

Lisa continues painting her nails, barely
acknowledging him. Then, still without
looking at him, she breaks the silence.

                    LISA
          What's up?

                    MICHAEL
          Water's out.

                    LISA
          Oh.

                          MICHAEL
                Got any water in the
                fridge?

                          LISA
                Think so.

Lisa looks up at Michael for the first time.

                          LISA
                Hey, will you help me get
                some of this off?

She holds up her foot. Some excess nail
polish is on the big toe.

                          MICHAEL
                Huh?

Lisa holds out a box of q-tips.

                          LISA
                Please? My hands are
                tired.

Michael looks down at his own, grimy, hands,
considering. He takes a q-tip and wipes
the excess nail polish from her toe. Lisa
watches Michael closely as he does it,
considering him. Michael gets a little lost
in the moment, not noticing that he has
gotten some nail polish on his finger and
some dirt on her foot.

In the background, the front door opens and
an older MALE VOICE calls, after a beat.

```
                    MALE VOICE (O.S.)
                  Hello? Honey? Lisa?

                  Anybody home?

      Michael comes to himself and exits quickly.

      EXT. BACKYARD - DAY

      Michael weeds. He looks down at the spot of
      nail polish on his finger, thinking.

      INT. BEDROOM - DAY

      Lisa, still on her bed, looks down at the
      spot of dirt Michael left on her foot,
      thinking.

      FADE OUT
```

Whatever you think of the script, it tells a story with a clear beginning, middle, and end. There is conflict, and there is change. And although very little actually happens, plot-wise, the two characters – Michael and Lisa – connect in some way, and perhaps will now pursue another interaction in the future.

In order for this story to work, then, we need to create an atmosphere of heat and ennui (without making the film, itself, boring). In the original script, which you have just read, there is one page of description before Michael discovers that the water has been shut off. In the finished film, that opening part of the movie takes 3 minutes to unfold. This is because, in the editing process, it became clear that we needed more time for the setup. The natural rhythm and pace of the story took over. As it stands now, we cut back and forth between the two scenes of Michael and Lisa, developing each person's point of view before finally setting up their meeting.

In the fourth minute of the film, we head in a new direction. Lisa turns off the water and steals Michael's shirt to see what he'll do. And so the real story begins. Michael has to come into the house, looking for water, and he and Lisa meet. Their meeting was another section where the pacing had to be just right. This section is also a bit longer than it is in the script. We linger on their respective gazes, allowing enough time on each close-up for their emotions to register, while also cutting away from each close-up in a way that helps increase the tension we feel as we watch them.

Since *Nail Polish* is the film we will use, as Kuleshov and his cohorts used Griffith's *Intolerance*, in Chapters 13–15, we will refrain from breaking down every bit here. But you should definitely watch the entire film to familiarize yourself with the footage.

Professionally Made Shorts to Study

Let's now take a look at a group of short films from which you can learn more about pacing and rhythm. The 2006 film *Paris, je t'aime* is a feature comprised of 18 five-minute short films (all separate from each other). Each film is about love, in some way, and each takes place in Paris. In English, the title of the film means "Paris, I love you." Here are some of the stronger films in the collection:

#1. *Montmartre* (Bruno Podalydes)

#2. *Quais de Seine* (Gurinder Chadha)

#4. *Tuileries* (Joel & Ethan Coen)

#7. *Bastille* (Isabel Coixet)

#9. *Tour Eiffel* (Sylvain Chomet)

#11. *Quartier des enfants rouges* (Olivier Assayas)

#12. *Place des fêtes* (Oliver Schmitz)

#14. *Quartier de la Madeleine* (Vincenzo Natali)

#16. *Faubourg Saint-Denis* (Tom Tykwer)

#18. *14e Arrondissement* (Alexander Payne)

These ten shorts are the ones that have the best writing, editing, and acting. Let's analyze the Coen Brothers' *Tuileries*. While we won't break it down shot by shot, let's see how these feature film directors go about making a short film.

The movie starts at 20:25 (that's the time within the entire film of 18 shorts). Each film is separated from the other shorts via exterior shots of Paris, and before we enter the world of this particular movie, we are shown a shot, above ground, of the subway station in which this story takes place. The very next shot after that is inside that same subway station, Tuileries. This happens to be a stop highly frequented by tourists, since it is near major museums. After a beat, the actor Steve Buscemi (1957–) lowers his face, back of the head to us, in extreme foreground, into the shot, and the story begins. It's an engaging moment because the camera racks focus to him and then he turns his face towards us, looking highly confused. This tells us all we need to know, really, to understand the film.

KEY TERM:

A **rack focus** is when there are multiple planes of focus in a given shot, and you shift between them by rotating the focus ring on the lens. In this way you can have two subjects in a shot, and have one be out of focus while the other is in focus, and then, as one person turns his or her head, rack focus to the other person.

The best kind of filmmaking is visual. The stories are told with shots, and it is more efficient to communicate ideas with images than with dialogue. When Buscemi, who, it turns out, is a very confused American tourist, enters frame, looking helpless and lost, we don't need extraneous words to explain the situation. It's a perfect cinematic setup.

In *Nail Polish*, a drama, we needed time to create a feeling of boredom. Here, in the Coen Brothers' *Tuileries*, a comedy, we want to jump into the fun part as quickly as we can. And so they do.

Over the course of the first minute, Steve Buscemi's character looks though his bag of knick-knacks, including a Paris guide, and begins to read about how Paris is a city of love, and of lovers. Four minutes later, this expectation will have been turned on its head by the events of the story, but for now Buscemi is blissfully unaware of how Paris will treat him. He notices a young couple across the tracks, on the opposite subway platform, groping and kissing each other. He continues to read his guide.

As he does so, a young boy blows a spitball at him. Buscemi next reads a passage in his guide about how important it is to avoid eye contact in the Paris subway. And just at that moment, he looks up and makes eye contact with the lovers across the way. If a good dramatic structure is made up of three acts, then this is the transition point between the opening setup – Act I – and the conflict that the main character will face – Act II. It happens at a little less than 2 minutes into the film.

Over the course of the next 3 minutes, Buscemi's character will deal with the challenge of how these two lovers react to his "eye contact." The boyfriend challenges Buscemi, and his girlfriend gets angry with him for yelling at the poor guy. Buscemi consults his guide to understand what they are saying to him. The woman and the man escalate their argument, and when a subway stops on their side and then departs, she is gone. Only she has not gone very far, since she has merely come over to Buscemi's side of the station.

To anger her boyfriend even more, she kisses Buscemi. Earlier in the film, he had read, in his guide, a warning about "social diseases" (i.e., STDs) in Paris, and after the woman kisses him, he notices a disturbing welt (like the ones in the photos of his book) on her lip. Before Buscemi can really react to this gross detail, the kid with the spitball straws hits him again, and then the boyfriend shows up to beat him up.

The resolution of the film – Act III – has the French couple walking away (the woman was really just testing her boyfriend to see what he would do), starting at 25:25, leaving Buscemi lying on the platform, while the spitball boy blows one last missile his way. At a little over 5 minutes, we have just seen a complete story, with perfect setup, conflict, and ending, paced for comedy, with no extraneous detail in the frame. The American 19th-century writer Edgar Allan Poe (1809–1949) believed in the importance of making sure that everything in a work of short fiction serves a central idea. This is especially true in a short film.

In *Tuileries*, every shot and every visual detail ends up playing a part in this story, which subverts the idea that Paris is a city of love, and they make it work by using every minute of screen time to sell their central conceit. Even the items in Buscemi's shopping bag are important, as they include dozens of Mona Lisa postcards, which get dumped on him. Earlier in the film, we had seen Buscemi looking, with pleasure, at a picture of the Mona Lisa in his guidebook.

If you watch the other films in this collection, you will see that the ones that are most effective tend to follow this rule: make everything count. They all tend to have about the same amount of story setup – between 1 and 2 minutes – about the same amount of conflict development – about 3 minutes – and the same quick resolutions and endings – less than a minute. We go in, learn a little bit about new people, follow them through a crisis, and then we leave. The good short film doesn't spend too much doing any of this.

Distributing a Short

Distribution of shorts is both easier and more complicated than distribution of features. It's also always in flux, and it's hard to say how distribution will look even just a few years from now. For a comprehensive study of modern distribution techniques, see a book in this series by Jason Moore, *Short Film Distribution*. But one thing that you must spend some time learning to understand is *compression*.

KEY TERM:

Compression is the way you take the format in which your film was shot, or edited, and change it to fit the distribution medium you may choose. If you shoot in high-resolution high-definition video, for example, the size of your file will be far too large for playback on a Web site. It may also be too large for burning to a DVD. So you need to know how to choose a compression format that is a good compromise between visual quality and file size.

Technically, compression is not the editor's job. However, filmmakers are increasingly finding that they need to be one-person production and distribution houses. Knowing how to do as much as possible on your own can make you less dependent on others doing the work for you.

In any case, not everyone can get a contract to make a film for a collection such as *Paris, je t'aime*. Most beginning filmmakers try to shoot as inexpensively as possible and then submit their films to festivals, whether live or online. Or they post them on sites like YouTube, or on their own personal Web pages. There are plenty of other sites around, including atomfilms.com, which was one of the first markets for online film content.

If you want your film to be seen, you'll need to figure out the best venue for it. First, you'll need to make it as well as you can, of course, but then you'll need to export it using the right compression for that venue. We'll cover some of this in Chapter 10.

In this chapter, we examined some of the differences between shorts and features, while also taking a brief journey through the history of shorts from 1894 to the present. We looked at some examples of short films, from commercials to a film on the accompanying DVD to a film that is part of the feature-length *Paris, je t'aime*. We also discussed some of the issues that you might face when considering distribution options.

In some ways, the way we make shorts vs. the way we make features is not that different. The storytelling needs are the same, but in the shorter format we have to pay more attention to the rhythm of the cutting. In a feature, we have a little more time to set up the story.

We saw how short films have thrived at various times since 1894, and how we might be entering a new Golden Age of short filmmaking and distribution. The ease of new technologies and the pervasive reach of current broadband streaming sites make it far simpler to make and distribute your work. Still, easy access does not necessarily lead to quality work, and your films should still tell good stories. Making shorts can be good training for your future career, and you should use this opportunity to develop good editing habits. Always be organized. This will become especially important as you transition form shorts to features.

We also looked at the script for the short film *Nail Polish*, which we will later dissect and reconstruct in Chapters 13–15. The movie, itself, is available on the accompanying DVD, and you should watch it now so you are familiar with it. Finally, we analyzed a short film, *Tuileries*, from the feature-length collection *Paris, je t'aime*, as a further study of good editing rhythm.

1. What is a short film vs. a feature film?

2. What came first, the short or the feature?

3. What kinds of short films exist today?

4. What does Poe have to do with short films?

5. What are some distribution options for short films today?

DISCUSSION / ESSAY QUESTIONS

1. Are there different structural concerns when telling a story as a short vs. a feature? If so, what are they?

2. What are some of the best short films you have seen, whether they are commercials, music videos, or actual short film stories? How were they structured?

3. How (in what venue) do you see most of the short films that you see? Do you think this is going to change in the years ahead?

Further Research

There are many collections of short films available on DVD, and there are many Web sites where you can see shorts as well. We have mentioned YouTube many times, but there is also Hulu, Cinemaspot, Shortfilms.com, Atomfilms.com, etc. We mentioned the CLIO Awards, but you can also see commercials that have aired during recent Super Bowls by going to Superbowl-ads.com.

There is also a DVD collection called *The Director's Series*. Volume 1 presents some of the non-feature work of Spike Jonze (1969–) who directed *Being John Malkovich* (1999), *Adaptation* (2002), and *Where the Wild Things Are* (2009).Volume 3 presents the non-feature work of Michel Gondry (1963–) who directed *Eternal Sunshine of the Spotless Mind* (2004), *The Science of Sleep* (2006), and *The Green Hornet* (2011), among others. It's worth looking at both of these directors' short films to see how efficiently they tell stories.

Finally, you should really start familiarizing yourself with the movie *Nail Polish*, included on this text's DVD. We will spend some time taking it apart later, so get to know it now in its unedited form.

References

1. There are some excellent books that deal specifically with short film writing and short film production. Here are two:

    Cowgill, Linda J. *Writing Short Films: Structure and Content for Screenwriters*. New York: Watson-Guptill Publications, 2005.

    Irving, David K. and Peter W. Rea. *Producing and Directing the Short Film and Video*. New York: Focal Press, 2006.

    These authors explain the logistics of preparing for and shooting the shorter film format.

2. www.clioawards.com: Clios are given to the best commercials of a given year.

3. This film was originally supposed to be an acting exercise for the young man and the young woman, but it turned into a completed short film.

CHAPTER 6

THE NLE EDITING REVOLUTION

OVERVIEW AND LEARNING OBJECTIVES

In this chapter, you will:

- Learn the difference between linear and non-linear editing (NLE)
- Journey briefly through the history of NLE platforms
- Understand important NLE terminology
- Explore how the NLE revolution has affected editing procedures

The Very Recent Past

Not so very long ago, all movie editing was done using actual film, and all video editing was done on dual-deck video editing stations, cutting from one tape to another.

If you are at all a fan of films made before you were born, remember that they were cut without the benefit of Avid, Final Cut, or Adobe Premiere®. And yet many of them are quite good. Keep this in mind as you learn how to edit using the latest new technologies. The software and computer innovations of the past few decades are stunning, but they are merely tools to be used in the service of art.[1]

Knowing how to operate a tool is very important, but it is not enough to create meaningful works of art, or even just fun entertainment. In this book, we will learn the tools, but we will also learn the art and the craft of editing. Without the tools, your art and craft will never be expressed, but without art and craft, your tools will produce work that expresses nothing. In other words, let's learn how to edit using non-linear editing technologies, but let's do so knowing that that is only part of becoming a successful filmmaker.

Before we get into non-linear editing, let's make sure that you understand a few basic computer terms. Here is a list of some useful words, along with their synonyms and definitions.

KEY TERMS:

Application Also known as software, or a program, designed to do a specific thing on your computer, smartphone, or other digital device. In the smartphone world, this has been shortened to just *app*. Examples of applications are Microsoft Word®, Adobe Photoshop®, and Final Cut Express.

Operating System or OS. This is the main program that runs your computer. The two most common computer operating systems are Microsoft Windows® and Mac OSX®.

Platform The meaning of this word depends somewhat on the context. If one is comparing Macs to PCs, then a discussion of platform will refer to the OS. If one is discussing non-linear editing programs, then platform might refer to the difference between Avid and Final Cut Pro (which will be explained later in the chapter).

What is Linear and Non-Linear Editing?

Until the late 1980s, the editing of anything shot on actual film was primarily done by men and women who touched and handled strips of celluloid film, cutting and splicing the movie together in ways not that different from how Griffith, Kuleshov, and Eisenstein cut their own films. Today, we use the terms *cut* and *splice* rather loosely, but before the arrival of computer programs that could simulate the physical process, editors actually cut the film with a razor, or with something razor-like attached to a solid metal block known as a *film splicer*, and then *spliced* the film back together with tape or glue. It was hard physical labor. And it was *linear*.

So what does that mean? *Linear editing*, which was just called "editing" before *non-linear* systems were invented, is a way of working in which you watch and assemble your footage from beginning to end in a straightforward, chronological way.

In this system, your footage would come back from the lab on a reel, and you would have to watch the reel in order, removing the shots you thought you might want to use in your film. You would hang these shots on little pegs, hanging into a *bin* (like a laundry bin), and return to them once you had finished going through all of the developed footage. There was no way, really, to watch the shots in anything but the order in which they came to you on the reel, which was also the order in which they were filmed. You could fast forward through a shot if you decided you didn't like it, but you still had to watch each shot in turn, and you couldn't access the next shot until you had gone through the previous shot.

Finally, after all the shots were viewed, you could start the process of assembling your movie. You would pick the first shot, then splice it to the next shot, and so on until your film was done or you had, at least, a rough cut. Nothing said you had to assemble each scene or sequence in the order they appeared in the script, but within each scene or sequence you had no choice but to put your shots in the approximate order you wanted to view them.

Although there were many different kinds of physical editing systems, most resembled something like a reel-to-reel tape player, except with a viewing screen. You would load the film, just as you would inside the camera or on a projector, on rollers with sprockets, since all film is perforated on one side or both. This player, which could be an upright system, or a flatbed table, was a mechanical device with a motor, which you controlled with some kind of switch or foot pedal. When you flicked the switch, your footage would flow – linearly – through the brightly lit aperture, projecting that image onto the viewing screen. There was no way to jump from one frame at the start of a shot to a frame at the end of a shot, unless you blinked. Likewise, there was no way to jump from a shot at the start of a scene to a shot at the end of a scene. You had to watch everything in the order it appeared on the reel.

You could certainly assemble a scene from the start of the movie, put that aside on a reel, then assemble a scene from the end of the film, and then jump around in that way, but that was as *non-linear* as it got.

In the video world, editing happened in somewhat similar ways. The footage you shot was available, in the exact order in which you shot it, on the tape on which it was recorded, in whatever format that might have been. You would have to watch each shot in sequence, in order to determine what takes you might want to use in your movie (or news piece, or commercial, etc.). In some ways, this process was even more *linear* than in the film world, because you couldn't cut out the shots you wanted and hang them on a bin. You could always record them onto a new tape – perhaps some sort of "best of" collection (called *selects*), but even then, in order to watch one shot in the middle of a tape, you would have to fast forward or rewind to that shot.

The editing of films or TV pieces was done using dual-tape deck systems. Tape A would hold the original, uncut footage, and Tape B would be the fresh tape, onto which you would record the bits of the shots that you wanted to use. You would control each deck using large rotating dial knobs. One by one, you would record each shot – or part of a shot – onto the new tape, in the order you wanted, in a strictly linear fashion. Once you had recorded a sequence, there would be no easy way to insert a new shot within that sequence. You could certainly go back to a certain point in your film, and record over from that section forward, but you couldn't insert a shot and have all of the other shots move over to make room for it.

But then, starting in the 1970s, engineers began to work on what became known as *non-linear* systems. In the late 1980s, a software program that would evolve into what is now the film industry standard, Avid, was released, and film and television editors began to make the move – some quickly, some reluctantly – away from the *linear* world.

So what is *non-linear* editing? Quite simply, it is a system of editing where you can jump around from shot to shot, and within each shot, as much as you want. The usual rules of frame sequence do not apply.

Basically, what happened with the arrival of Avid and subsequent systems is that the creators of the software developed technology that allowed the original video or film image to be converted into a digital format. This digital format, comprised, as are all digital objects, of a sequence of 1s and 0s, allowed the user of the program to move through and around the footage. You could insert shots in the middle of a previously cut sequence, for example, and you could undo actions taken without undoing everything you had done.

While the speed and the cleanliness and the ability to manipulate footage in untold ways was incredibly valuable, suddenly editors were no longer forced to watch discarded shots anymore, just to get the shot they wanted. But one of the useful things about having to revisit old footage over and over again is that you sometimes see things that you hadn't noticed before. Good film editing is a balance between the old and the new.

In the next chapter, we will begin to learn the ins and outs of our non-linear editing program of choice, Final Cut Express, but right now, let's take a quick look at the issues that face all non-linear editing programs, regardless of manufacturer.

Online, Offline, and Timecode

There are three terms to know before going further: the first two are *online* and *offline*. These are important words in the world of film editing programs, since they deal with the resolution and quality of the files with which you work. The higher the resolution of the video files, the more storage space they take up on your hard drive. These days, memory is measure in terabytes, rather than gigabytes, but not so long ago it was measured in megabytes. 1000 megabytes = 1 gigabyte. 1000 gigabytes = 1 terabyte.

As hard drives get bigger, so do video files. Before *high-definition* video formats were invented, *standard-definition* video files took up 12.6 gigabytes of memory for 1 hour of footage. In the current world of many different kinds of high-definition resolutions, you can easily take up 1 minute per gigabyte, or even more. You can see how quickly a 2 terabyte hard drive might fill up if you're shooting a long project.

KEY TERM:

Online resolution means that you are editing in the same resolution in which you shot. **Offline** means that you have reduced the quality of your work files enough so that your computer can handle them. Later, when you have edited your project down to a manageable length, you can, using the offline files as a reference, bring your film back up to the original resolution in which you shot. Since it is now much shorter, your computer should be able handle the film at full resolution.

The third term we need to know is *timecode*.

KEY TERM:

Timecode is a reference number for each frame of video. Standard modern timecode has eight digits, which look like this: 00:00:00:00. The first two digits are for the hours, the second two for the minutes, the third two for the seconds, and the final two for the frames.

It is timecode – a frame-by-frame exact reference marker for your video – that has actually allowed modern non-linear editing to take place. When you shoot your video, the camera embeds this code into the frames, and then, when you transfer your video digitally – either via tape or the newer flash memory systems – this timecode remains. Every frame has a number. This is what allows you to edit in one kind of resolution – *offline* – and then upgrade to the original resolution – *online*. Every frame is marked, and no matter how much you chop up the footage in whatever program you are using, these markers do not change.

This is also what allows you to cut, in a non-linear editing (NLE) program, a movie shot on film, and then take your work and conform the film negative to the cuts you have made in the NLE program. When you convert the film negative to a digital video image, timecode is embedded into each frame of that image, matching the equivalent *edge code* numbers that exist on film. These edge code numbers are coded references for each frame of the film strip, printed on the edge of that strip. When you are all done, there is a clear trail of what video frame matches what film frame.

Finally, timecode is what lets you make cuts to your movie in one kind of NLE program, and then, if you have to, switch to a different program, keeping your work. All of these NLE programs have the capability to export an *EDL*, or *edit decision list*, which references the original timecode of your video, and all of the decisions you have made in the editing process. These days, there are even more advanced kinds of EDLs, known as *XMLs* (short for *eXtensible Markup Language* – this is a language also used in HTML, or Web-based, encoding), which allow for even more kinds of information to be exchanged between editing applications.

A Brief Journey through NLE Platforms

Let's now go back and see how this digital revolution in the editing world began. Here is an historical breakdown of NLE systems:

1971: CBS® and Memorex® get together and create the CMX600. This is long before the digital age of video, and it is really strictly an offline system, with functional capabilities limited to working in black & white. Still, it's a step toward the systems we have today.

1980s: George Lucas and others try their hand at various attempts at non-linear systems and start inventing technology that will eventually allow for digital imaging, which will be the key to the future non-linear editing systems. Lucas, whose ex-wife Marcia was a film editor, pioneered the now common timeline feature and digital bins that we see in most non-linear programs these days.

1989: Avid releases its first Media Composer program, on the Mac platform. Much of what is now standard in non-linear programs was present in this revolutionary system, including similar kinds of tools as those we will see in Final Cut Express, in the next chapter. The resolution of the video in this generation of NLE programs was low, however.

1991: Adobe, one the world's leading makers of creative video, graphics, and other imaging software, releases Premiere, a video editing program for the Mac. It is more for the home user and less expensive than Avid. It is very similar, in terms of its basic interface, to what Avid does, with a timeline, editing tools, etc.

1992–1993: A major breakthrough occurred, thanks to some engineers at Disney, allowing for more storage capability in the Avid system. Suddenly, it was possible for projects longer than short commercials to be edited on this platform, and editors worldwide started to migrate to Avid, away from both editing on film and editing on dual tape decks. For the budget or student filmmakers, without access to high-end computers with a lot of memory, Avid also developed the whole offline/online standards that are still in use, to some degree, today.

Late 1990s: Avid began to consider abandoning its original operating system of choice – the Mac – for Windows.

Also late 1990s: The DV standard for digital video was introduced, along with Firewire systems of data transfer (also known as IEEE1394, and called iLink® for PCs). With video that was already in a digital, non-analog format, this allowed for a transfer of footage from tape to computer with zero loss of quality.

1999: Apple, abandoned by Avid, and with the successful release of its new G3 computers and iMacs the year before, came out with what would become, eventually, the main competitor to Avid: Final Cut Pro. It's is less expensive than Avid and designed to take advantage of the new DV standard. It has become, since then, the software of choice for the budget and student filmmaker.

2003: Apple releases Final Cut Express. It lacks some of the more advanced features of the Pro program, but has the same basic interface, and many of the same capabilities.

2011: Apple releases Final Cut Pro X. While this new program solved many of the issues with slow effects creation that plagued other versions, it lacks many of the features of the earlier programs.

What All Digital Editing Programs Have in Common

One thing all non-linear programs have in common with each other is that, unlike in the film world where you are cutting up an actual film print, you never touch the original media files when you are editing. These digitized files exist somewhere on your hard drive and you are only manipulating virtual copies of them.

So – for filmmakers both indie and Hollywood – the tools of choice, right now, are Avid, Final Cut Pro, and Adobe Premiere. Avid is the most expensive, and Adobe Premiere is the least expensive – for now. All three applications do an excellent job of allowing you to edit your movie in a user-friendly manner. Because Avid was first, more people use it; plus, the program has stayed current with new technologies. For a long time, Avid was the best non-linear program for conforming video edits of a project shot on film back to the original negative of that film. It was designed with this exact issue in mind, and therefore handled timecode to edge code number matching seamlessly. Final Cut Pro came of age with the rise of the DV standard and Firewire, and the relative affordability of mini-DV cameras, so it focused more on issues related solely to projects shot on video. Since it was, at the time, much less expensive than Avid, it was popular with film students and low-budget filmmakers.

> *With the recent invention of the Red One™ camera, the line between film and video may eventually become blurred. The Red camera is – for now – rather revolutionary. It shoots raw (completely uncompressed) image files at incredible resolutions. It's as if you had all of the flexibility and range of exposure that you get with the best film stocks, but with the ability to bypass laboratories and transfer the data directly to your computer. It's like a digital film stock. It's very expensive, however, and outside the scope of this book.*

NOTE

Adobe Premiere has much of the same functionality as both Avid and Final Cut, but it first started out, in the 1990s, as a very simple home movie application. Today, it is capable of handling most video formats, including newer HD ones.

All three programs have a similar type of timeline, in which you lay down your video and audio tracks and make your cuts (as we'll see in the next chapter), and all three have the same kinds of tools.

Final Cut Express is the software we chose for this book because it is inexpensive and has the same exact interface as the more expensive Final Cut Pro. If you master how this application works, it is easy to move on to the next level. It can handle a variety of different video formats, and has many great tools and effects.

> *Final Cut Express and Final Cut Pro only run on Mac systems.*

NOTE

SUMMARY

In this chapter, we studied the history of NLE programs and how they have affected film editing. We discussed the revolution in editing techniques that occurred as the new technologies were adopted, and what was both gained and lost. While the tools of today seem incredibly advanced compared to the tools of the past, it is important not to lose sight of the importance of art and craft in the editing process.

We learned the difference between *linear* and *non-linear* systems and *online* and *offline* resolution. We also learned the importance of *timecode* and *EDLs*. We discovered that all non-linear editing programs share certain features, and that it is possible to communicate between the various platforms.

We reviewed the development of different – and competing – editing systems, and compared them. Depending on your needs, Avid, Final Cut Pro or Express, and Adobe Premiere are all good programs to use. In this book, however – starting in Chapter 7 – we will learn how to use Final Cut Express.

REVIEW QUESTIONS: CHAPTER 6

1. What is an NLE system?

2. What is timecode?

3. When was the first NLE system invented?

4. When did the NLE revolution really begin?

5. What are the main NLE programs available today?

1. Describe the process of editing films on film, before NLE systems were invented.

2. What are some advantages to editing under the old system?

3. Compare a film edited in the 1980s, right before NLE systems were adopted, with a film released this year. Can you detect how the NLE revolution has affected how the more modern film was cut?

Further Research

You should watch, if you haven't already, *The Cutting Edge: The Magic of Movie Editing* (Wendy Apple, 2004). This is a film that traces the history of editing methods and technologies from 1895 to the present. It features interviews with contemporary directors and editors and is a finely crafted documentary.

You might want to also visit the websites of the various applications and other technologies in common use today. Here are a few to get you started:

- Final Cut Express: http://www.apple.com/finalcutexpress/

- Final Cut Pro and Final Cut Studio: http://www.apple.com/finalcutstudio/

- Avid Media Composer: http://www.avid.com/video/

- Adobe Premiere: http://www.adobe.com/products/premiere/

- Red One Camera: http://www.red.com/

- Panasonic HD: http://www.panasonic.com/business/provideo/app_hd.asp

- Sony HD: http://pro.sony.com/bbsc/ssr/micro-xdcam/

Reference

1. A good book that teaches you how to be extremely organized in the editing process, and that also offers a brief history of video editing systems, is the following:

   Hollyn, Norman. *The Film Editing Handbook: How to Tame the Chaos of the Editing Room*, 4th Edition. Berkeley, CA: Peachpit Press, 2010.

FINAL CUT EXPRESS: BASIC INTERFACE

OVERVIEW AND LEARNING OBJECTIVES

In this chapter, you will:

- Learn the basic interface of Final Cut Express (FCE)
- Explore the editing tools you need to get started
- Use the video clips included on the DVD to master simple techniques

Opening FCE for the First Time

If you're already familiar with the basic interface of Final Cut Express,(FCE) you might want to skip ahead to the next chapter. You can always come back here if you need help. For those of you who know little to nothing about the application, let's proceed.

Let's assume that you own a copy of the latest version of Final Cut Express. As we discussed in Chapter 6, you can only use Final Cut Express on a computer running some version MAC OSX. Click on the FCE icon in your dock, or double-click on the icon in your Applications folder. You will be greeted with the welcome window, as shown in Figure 7.1.

Final Cut Express
Volume License

Licensed To:

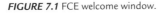

Version:
Final Cut Express 4.0.1

© 2002–2008 Apple Inc. All rights reserved. Apple, the Apple logo, and Final Cut Express are trademarks of Apple Inc., registered in the U.S. and elsewhere.
See www.apple.com/legal/trademark for more information.

FIGURE 7.1 FCE welcome window.

 All figures appear in color on the companion DVD.

After a few seconds, a second window – a pop-up menu – as shown in Figure 7.2, should appear over the first one. But if this is not the first time the program has been opened on your computer, you might not see this. This screen allows you to set the default preferences of FCE. If the default preferences have already been set, FCE will likely bring up a different window, as shown in Figure 7.3. For now, let's focus on what to do with the setup preferences.

The following figure shows the FCE External A/V window.

The settings in this menu determine the default video format that FCE will use every time you open it. They also determine the default location – called

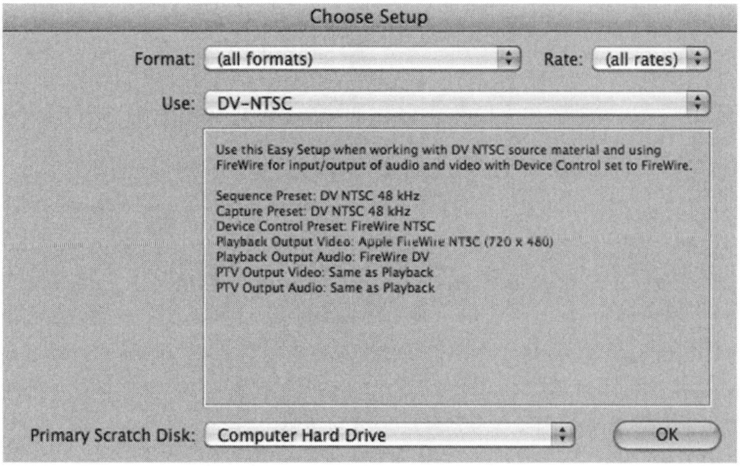

FIGURE 7.2 FCE Setup Preferences pop-up menu.

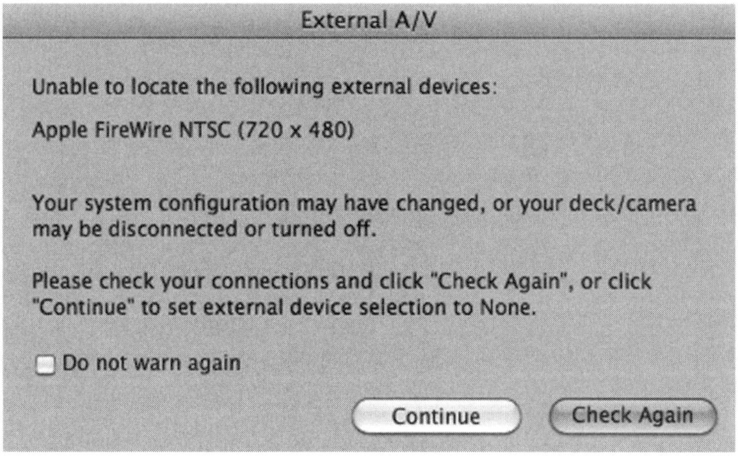

FIGURE 7.3 FCE External A/V window.

a *scratch disk* – in which you store the files created in FCE. Scratch disks are extremely important – and we will learn more about them soon – but for now you can just click *OK*.

After you click OK, you will probably see the External A/V window (Figure 7.3). This window tells us that FCE is unable to locate an "external device." Unless you have some kind of digital video camera or video player turned on and hooked up to the computer via a Firewire cable, FCE is going to look for one and not find it. Since the program, by default, assumes you might want to capture or export video, for which you would need either a camera or player, it warns you that you do not have such a device attached.

At this point, we don't need such a device, so we can safely click on *Continue* and move on.

Now, you may notice, on the left, a little box that says "do not warn again." If you click in that box before clicking on *Continue*, then you won't see this warning the next time you open FCE. You can later reset this option in one of the preferences menu, so it's your choice whether to click in the box or not. It's not a bad idea to leave it unchecked, however, since it can be useful to know that your camera or player is not connected, just in case you want to capture or export video. If you're shooting to flash-based media, rather than to tape, then this menu is useless, and you can click in the box with impunity. If you don't see this menu, it's either because you have a player or camera that is on and connected, or someone, using the program before you, chose to click in the "do not warn again" box.

If you saw the Setup Preferences pop-up menu and clicked *OK*, you automatically set your scratch disks to the default location, and the program will now open. If this is the case, you can skip the next section, going straight to Figure 7.9. However, if someone has used FCE before you, or you're on a computer at an institution – like a university or video lab – you may get a different screen. Let's look at that possibility now.

First, we have to define the term *scratch disk*.

KEY TERM:

The **scratch disk** is a folder, somewhere on your computer (hopefully designated by you) where all of the media associated with your project is stored.

If you're not the first person to use this version of FCE, then the person who used it before you might have set the scratch disks to a removable external hard drive. If that hard drive is now no longer attached to the computer, then a new window will pop up, as shown in Figure 7.4, warning of you of this fact.

There is no need to panic, however. Click on the blue button that reads *Reset Scratch Disks*. As soon as you do this, another, smaller window, as shown in Figure 7.5, pops up on top of the Missing Disks window. This dialogue box warns you that FCE cannot find the last scratch disk location. Click *OK*. The Scratch Disks window, as shown in Figure 7.6, will now pop up. This gives you the opportunity to choose your own scratch disk location. For now,

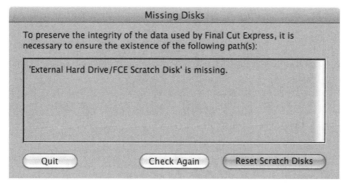

FIGURE 7.4 Missing Disks window.

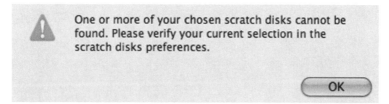

FIGURE 7.5 Missing Disk pop-up warning.

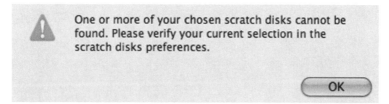

FIGURE 7.6 Scratch Disks window.

pick an easy-to-remember location, such as the default Documents folder on your computer. Let's look at how to do that.

The following figure shows the Scratch Disks window.

You will see that there are a number of buttons labeled *Set*. Click on the topmost one, to the right of the top *Video Capture*, *Audio Capture*, *Video*

Render, and *Audio Render* boxes. Another window will open, as shown in Figure 7.7. This window allows you to choose your scratch disk location. Find the Documents folder, and click *Choose.* Once you do so, you will be taken back to the Scratch Disks window.

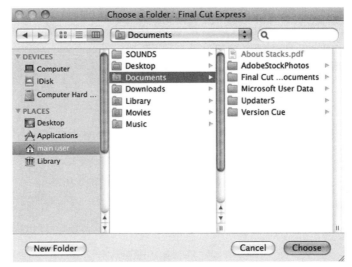

FIGURE 7.7 Choose a folder for Scratch Disks window.

Notice the three lines that read *Waveform Cache, Thumbnail Cache,* and *Autosave Vault,* located below the main box. On each of those lines, click the *Set* button. Each time, you will be brought to the same *Choose a Folder* window (Figure 7.7) we just visited. For each item, choose the same folder you chose the first time. Do not try and set a second main scratch disk by clicking on the *Set* button just below the top line that you clicked on first. You'll just confuse FCE. There are reasons to set multiple main scratch disks, but we will not discuss them now.

When you are done setting all of your scratch disks, click *OK* in the Scratch Disks window. You'll be immediately taken back to the Missing Disks window that started us on this process, but now it is blank, as shown in Figure 7.8. That's because the program no longer has a missing scratch disk, since you just set a new one. Click on the *Continue* button, and you will enter the actual FCE application, as shown in Figure 7.9.

The following figure shows the FCE interface.

Next time you open the program, you should be sent directly to this interface. If, in the interim, you delete the folder you had set as a Scratch Disk,

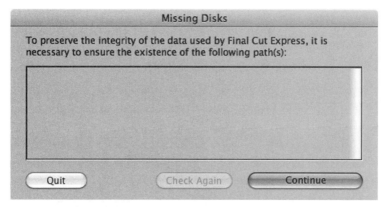

FIGURE 7.8 Return to the Missing Disk pop-up warning, but without any Missing Disks, since you set a new scratch disk.

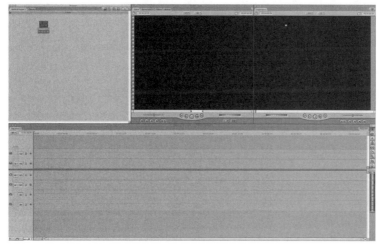

FIGURE 7.9 The FCE interface.

or eject the external hard drive to which you had set your Scratch Disk, you will have to redo all of the steps that we just went through. The application is set up in this way to warn you that folders are missing, in case you expect them to be present.

The Four Main Windows of FCE

Now that the program is open, you should see something similar to Figure 7.9. If you don't, you can press the *control* key on your keyboard and the letter *U* key at the same time to put the windows back in their default order.

If you only see two windows, as shown in Figure 7.10, the *Timeline/Sequence* window is closed. In order to get this back, all you have to do is double-click on the icon in the upper-left window, as shown. This icon represents a *Sequence*, and when you double-click on it, the *Timeline* of the *Sequence* – which is where you will do your editing – will open up. Then your application should look like Figure 7.9.

FIGURE 7.10 Double-click the icon in the upper-left window, if the other two windows of the interface are missing.

There is one other thing that might be different, as shown in Figure 7.11. This just shows the *Browser* window. The icon of the *Sequence* is much smaller than it is in Figures 7.9 and 7.10. It doesn't matter – it's still the same thing. It's just that you can change the settings of the program to show the items in the *Browser* in something called *List View* or *Icon View*. In Figures 7.9 and 7.10, we see *Icon View*, which is the default setting, whereas in Figure 7.11, we see *List View*.

The reason we have to be so specific for so many different possibilities is that we want to anticipate the different ways in which you might have to approach Final Cut Express for the first time. The program, on your computer, may never have been touched, or you might be using it after many other people have used it. If this is the case, then the default settings will probably have been changed.

Now look, again, at your *Browser* window (Figure 7.11). Does it read *Untitled Project 1* at the top? If so, that means that a new project has opened. If not, then it probably shows you the name of the last project that was being used. Instead of making changes to someone else's project, let's close the project, and create a new one. This works in the same way as it does for any other computer application.

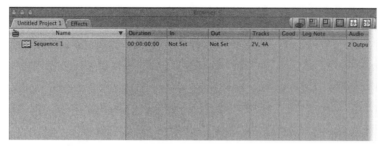

FIGURE 7.11 Browser window in List View instead of Icon View.

At the top of your screen, click on *File*, as shown in Figure 7.12. You will see a number of options. Scroll down to *Close Project* and click on that. After the project closes, go back to the same menu and scroll down to *New Project*.

File	Edit	View	Mark	Modify

New	▶
New Project	⇧⌘N
Open...	⌘O
Close Window	⌘W
Close Tab	⌃W
Close Project	
Save Project	⌘S
Save Project As...	⇧⌘S
Save All	⌥⌘S
Revert Project	
Restore Project...	
Import	▶
Export	▶
Capture Project...	⌃C
Capture...	⌘8
Log and Transfer...	⇧⌘8
Reconnect Media...	
Print to Video...	⌃M

FIGURE 7.12 File dropdown menu to close project and open a new one.

Let's now take a look back at the four main windows that make up the basic interface of FCE (refer back to Figure 7.9). Here is a description of each one, including its location on the screen, under the default settings.

If you hover your mouse over most icons, controls, or other items in FCE, a little yellow note will pop up and describe its function.

Browser

This is where you organize your project. It is located in the upper-left corner of the application interface. As you learn more about how FCE works, you will use the Browser to create folders in which to store various kinds of media, and to keep track of all of your footage. The Browser is equivalent to the Finder of your computer's operating system and is a very important tool to help you stay organized.

If we look back at Figure 7.10 or Figure 7.11, we see just a single item in the Browser. This item, as we noted, is an icon for the *Sequence*, which we will learn more about in a moment. If you hold down the *control* key and click anywhere in the Browser (or simply right-click if you have a mouse with that option) – except on the icon itself – you will see a new menu pop-up, as shown in Figure 7.13. The default setting when you open FCE is *View as Medium Icons*. Choose whichever option you prefer. In this text, however,

FIGURE 7.13 Browser pop-up menu.

we will be working with the setting *View as List*, because that option allows for more items to be viewed in the Browser at once.

Notice the two tabs (like the tabs on a manila folder) at the top of the Browser window. One reads *Untitled Project 1*, because we haven't saved this project yet, and one reads *Effects*. If you click on that second tab, you will see a number of new folders, as shown in Figure 7.14. There are several useful features here, but let's focus on the basic interface of the program.

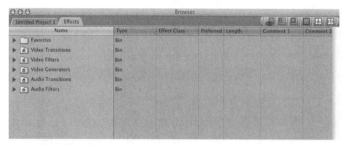

FIGURE 7.14 Effects tab of Browser.

If the second tab is missing, go to the one dropdown menu at the top of the screen labeled *Window*, which is the next to last one on the upper right, and click on it. As shown in Figure 7.15, there are a number of FCE windows listed. Near the bottom you will see *Effects*, without a check mark next to it. Click to the left of it. A check mark appears, and the *Effects* tab pops back into place. It will appear before the *Untitled Project 1* tab, however, rather than after it, but this doesn't matter.

Window	Help	
Minimize		⌘M
Send Behind		
Arrange		▶
✓ Tool Palette		
✓ Viewer		⌘1
✓ Canvas		⌘2
✓ Timeline		⌘3
✓ Audio Meters		⌥4
✓ Browser		⌘4
Effects		⌘5
Browser		
Timeline: Sequence 1 in Untitled Project 1		
Canvas: Sequence 1 in Untitled Project 1		
Viewer: Slug		

FIGURE 7.15 Window dropdown menu with *Effects* un-checked.

Viewer

This is the window, located just to the right of the Browser, where you can view or play any video or audio clip or image file you double-click from within FCE. Think of this window, as shown in Figure 7.16, as the equivalent of the window that opens in QuickTime® when you double-click any video file *outside* of FCE. Later, we will see how we can modify files from within this window by setting in and out points and modifying any filters we might add to the clip. The reason this window, under the default settings, reads *Viewer: Slug* at the top is because *slug* is the generic term for blank, black filler. Since there is no media in this project yet, all we see is this empty clip.

FIGURE 7.16 Viewer window.

At the top of the window, there are four tabs: *Video, Stereo (a1a2), Filters,* and *Motion*. Click on each tab to see what it contains. You might want to click on them each right now, just to see what they display. Once we have an actual clip, we'll go over each tab in more detail.

Underneath these four tabs, but still at the top, are two small white windows with room for timecode (which we discussed in Chapter 6). The one on the left tells you the length of the media that you double-clicked. The one on the right lets you know the position, in terms of the timecode of the clip, of the cursor at the bottom. If you grab that cursor and scroll along the bottom, you will see the numbers in the window to the right change. Nothing will change in the window to the left.

In between these two windows are two buttons with various menu options. The one that is a little to the left of center, with 97% displayed, lets you change the viewing size of the clip in the window, without affecting the actual size of the clip. The button just to the right of center has four options in its menu, which we will discuss later.

There are also a number of buttons at the bottom of this window; some might look familiar (like the standard play button icon), but others may not. There are two other controls as well: the shuttle slider and the jog wheel. We'll explore these when we import media.

Canvas

This is the window that displays whatever is in your *Timeline*. If you close it, the *Timeline* closes as well and if you close the *Timeline*, this window closes. There are controls and buttons at the top and bottom of the screen, as you can see in Figure 7.17. Some of these look just like the ones in the Viewer window. At the top of the Canvas, you see the title *Canvas: Sequence 1 in Untitled Project 1*. As you can imagine, when you work on a project of some length, knowing which *Sequence* is displayed in the Canvas can be important.

You also see a blue band running vertically at the right side of the frame. This band is present when you are at the end of an editing sequence. It lets you know you are at the final frame of your movie. Since there is nothing currently in the Timeline, the blue band is automatically present. Once you have some media in the Timeline, you can scroll from start to finish, and the blue band will only appear when you are at the end.

FIGURE 7.17 Canvas window.

Timeline

This is a representation of your *Sequence* and is also where you cut your movie. There is a ton of information in this window, as seen in Figure 7.18 . Much of it will make sense, as with the other windows, once we add actual media.

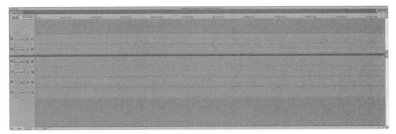

FIGURE 7.18 Timeline window.

For now, look at the dividing line that runs horizontally through the Timeline. Above the line is where your video clips will reside; below is for audio. If you look to the left, you can see the *V1*, *A1*, and *A2* indicators. If you have a clip with both video and audio, then it will be split into respective components, the one above, the other below. Most audio is recorded in two stereo channels, so for every one track of video, there are two audio tracks.

Notice how, along the entire upper length of the Timeline, there are a series of 8-digit timecode numbers (increasing by 4 seconds each time). These let you orient yourself in the Sequence. We will soon learn how to change the intervals by which the timecode changes (i.e., the viewing size of the Timeline), which would change what these numbers read.

At the upper right of the Timeline, there are two buttons, currently highlighted, as shown in Figure 7.19. The left one, which looks like an infinity symbol, controls *Linking* (the joining of video to audio) and the other one, which looks like a star, controls *Snapping*. If you click on them, they become black, which means they are turned off. Click on them again and they become green again. The *Linking* button, if you turn it off, allows you to separate your video and audio tracks together. The *Snapping* button, if it is turned on, allows you to have the cursor *snap* to edit points. Both of these controls will prove extremely useful, as you will see.

On the bottom left are two other important controls, as seen in Figure 7.20. One looks like a mountain with a valley next to it. This is the *Toggle Clip Overlays* button, which allows you to manage audio levels, as well as the opacity of your video. You can use this feature to create quick fades, up and down. The control to the right of this is the *Toggle Timeline Track Height* button. Click on the different options inside the box and notice that your tracks change size. Choose the track height you like best. You can change it at any time.

Above these buttons, to the left of each track, are buttons that have either a tiny icon of a film strip on them (for video) or an icon of a speaker with a curved line next to it (for audio), as shown in Figure 7.21. These buttons are green when they are activated and black when deactivated. When turned off, they make the track invisible or inaudible. It's a good way, when you're editing, to quickly see what something might look or sound like without a particular piece of audio or video, without having to delete all the work you have done.

A little to the right of these buttons, aligned with each track, are small icons

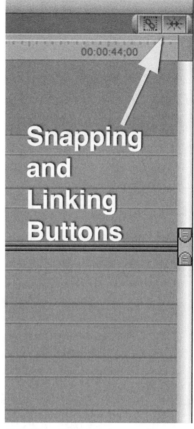

FIGURE 7.19 *Linking* and *Snapping* buttons at upper right of the Timeline.

FIGURE 7.20 *Toggle Clip Overlays* and *Toggle Timeline Track Height* buttons in bottom left of Timeline.

FIGURE 7.21 Track Visibility buttons.

that look like padlocks, which you can see in Figure 7.22. Right now they are open and unlocked. If you lock a track, you will not be able to make changes to it. The program places black diagonal bars over the tracks, as shown in Figure 7.23, so you know they're locked.

The following figure shows locked tracks on the Timeline.

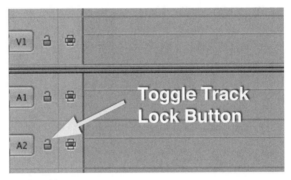

FIGURE 7.22 *Toggle Track Lock* button.

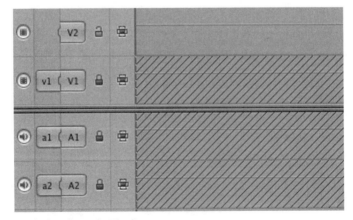

FIGURE 7.23 Locked tracks on the Timeline.

There are many more controls on the Timeline, but that's enough for now. Let's move on to the Tool Palette and Audio Meter.

The *Tool Palette* and *Audio Meter* are the two small vertical rectangular windows to the right of the Timeline (refer back to Figure 7.9). Both are important. In the default configuration of the program, the *Tool Palette* sits on top of the *Audio Meter*.

Tool Palette

As shown in Figure 7.24, the Tool Palette has nine separate icons embedded in it. If you hover over each of them, FCE tells you what the icon does. If you click on the icon, that tool is activated. If you click and hold on a particular tool, then you are usually given multiple variants of that tool to choose from. For example, the bottom tool, in the shape of a pen, allows you to create markers (more on these later). Right now, by default, the top tool is highlighted. This tool – the *Selection Tool* – lets you click on and select clips. We will look more closely at the rest of these tools in Chapter 8.

FIGURE 7.24
Tool Palette.

Audio Meter

This window, as shown in Figure 7.25, would show the levels of a clip's audio if we had one playing. This is a very useful window, since we don't always edit our films in the most optimum sound conditions. You might think your sound is loud enough because the computer's speakers are turned up all the way, only to find out that the sound ends up being too quiet in certain passages. That's where the Audio Meter comes in. If you make sure that the dialogue hovers around the –12db (decibel) level, your sound should be good. Sound design is more complicated than that, but knowing this is a good place to start.

FIGURE 7.25
Audio Meter.

If you can't see either the Tool Palette or the Audio Meter, then one of two things might be the cause. As noted with the Effects tab of the Browser, the windows might be turned off. Go up to the Window dropdown menu (Figure 7.15) again and select the Tool Palette and

Audio Meter, and they will reappear. Another possibility is that, even though you have opened FCE, and are looking at the program, you might have clicked away from it. Click on any of the windows of FCE, and you will be back in the program, and the Tool Palette and Audio Meter will reappear.

Finding and Arranging Windows

Click on any of the four main windows, so that it is selected. Notice that when a window is selected the gray bar at the very top of that window becomes a much lighter shade of gray. Click on a different window, and the window you were just in now has a much darker gray bar up top.

Click and hold in that top bar, and you can drag the window anywhere. Try it now. Choose a different window, and look at the bottom-right corner, as shown in Figure 7.26, which has little diagonal ridges. Click and drag on the corner, and the window will expand or contract, depending on the direction in which you move. You can't expand or contract the Tool Palette or the Audio Meter, but you can move them.

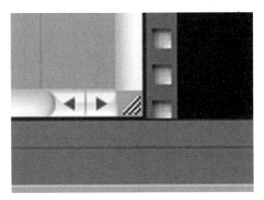

FIGURE 7.26 Corner of the FCE window.

After you have re-arranged the windows, you're probably going to want to know a quick fix to put them back into the default arrangement. You could try to reset each window, one at a time, but there is an easier way. Go back to the Window dropdown menu and scroll down to *Arrange*, as shown in Figure 7.27. Choose *Standard* and the windows will be arranged by default.

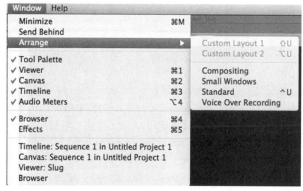

FIGURE 7.27 Arrange windows in the standard configuration.

Keyboard Shortcuts

There is no one right way to do things in FCE. You will be the best judge of the techniques that work best for you. But most professional editors use keyboard shortcuts because they allow you to work more quickly. Fortunately, FCE makes that easy, because, to the right of most of the commands listed in the menus is the keyboard shortcut. And, whenever you hover over a button or a tool, you are usually given, in addition to information about what that tool does, the keyboard shortcut. For example, if you hover know over the top tool on the Tool Palette, the yellow pop-up window reads *Selection Tool – a*. Scroll down to the tool that looks like a razor blade and hover over that. The pop-window reads *Razor Blade Tool – b*. Now, press the A key and B key in quick succession, and see how each tool is highlighted.

In order to understand the keyboard shortcuts, you have to know how Apple represents, graphically, the non-letter keys on your keyboard. As shown in Figure 7.28, there are four keys on a Mac: *shift, control, option*, and *command* (this key is sometimes referred to as the *Apple* key, since it used to have an symbol on it). Once you know these symbols, it is easy to understand the shortcuts.

4 MAIN APPLE KEYBOARD SYMBOLS

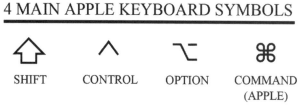

FIGURE 7.28 Apple keyboard symbols.

Importing Media

If you haven't already saved your project, FCE has probably prompted you to save. About every 30 minutes, FCE will show an Autosave message, as shown in Figure 7.29. Click *OK*. You will then be prompted to give your project a name, when the next menu pops up, as shown in Figure 7.30. Go ahead and change the name of the project from *Untitled Project 1* to something more useful by typing in a new name. Ideally, you would organize your entire project by having a single folder on an external hard drive, where you would set your scratch disks, and then save your project with a relevant name. For now, it doesn't matter that much. For more on how to name or re-name your projects, see the beginning of Chapter 8.

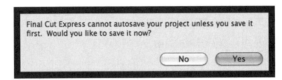

FIGURE 7.29 Initial Autosave prompt.

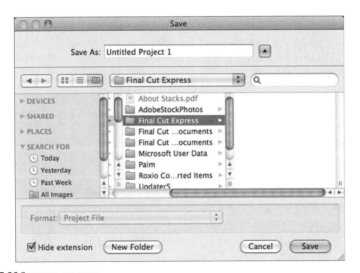

FIGURE 7.30 Save pop-up menu.

Now let's get started with some actual media. You will find a variety of video clips on the book's companion DVD. Go to the folder labeled *Video_01*. These are video files from the short movie we discussed in Chapter 5, *Nail Polish*. Drag that folder from the DVD to your computer, and make sure a copy is placed on your desktop.

Once the media is copied, go back to FCE. As shown in Figure 7.31, go to the File dropdown menu and scroll down to *Import*. You can choose either *Import Files* or *Import Folder*. If you choose *Import Files*, you'll have to highlight all of the files in the folder to import them all at once. If you choose *Import Folder*, then all you have to do is select the folder, and the program does the rest.

Once you're done, the files should now appear in your Browser. If you used the *Import Folder* option, then the clips are inside a folder labeled *Video_01*, as shown in Figure 7.32. If you used the *Import Files* command, your Browser will look as it does in Figure 7.33. If you use the first option, then FCE automatically creates the folder – called a *bin* – with the files. In Chapter 8, you will learn how to create bins on your own to help you stay organized. If you want to see what is in the bin, just click on the little triangle to the left of it, and it will display the files within it, as shown in Figure 7.34.

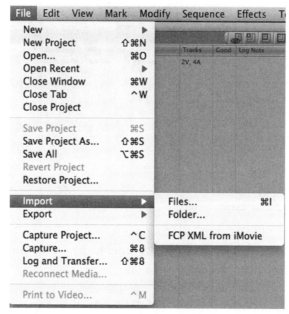

FIGURE 7.31 File dropdown menu with *Import* option highlighted.

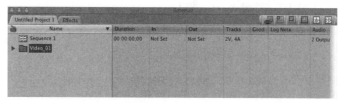

FIGURE 7.32 Browser after you chose *Import Folder*.

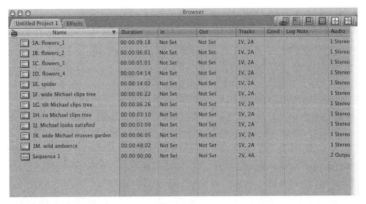

FIGURE 7.33 Browser after you chose *Import Files*.

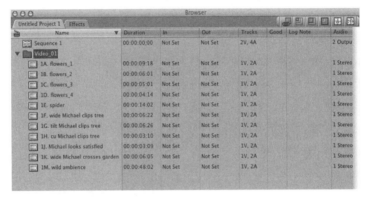

FIGURE 7.34 The bin, opened in the Browser.

Using Media

These are all of the clips used in the opening of the film *Nail Polish*. If you haven't done so already, you should first watch the actual film. You can find it on the DVD in the folder labeled *Completed Films*.

Starting slow and easy with basic tools

Look carefully at the Browser. Notice how there are columns to the right of the clips, as shown in Figure 7.35. The first one is *Duration*. This tells you the length of the clip. This column's value will change if you do anything to the clip to make it shorter, as we will do shortly. The next two columns read *In* and *Out*. We will tweak the clips by changing the values here, too. The next column is labeled *Tracks*, which tells you how many video and audio tracks are in your clips and sequences. Notice how the sequence has two video and four audio tracks, while the clips all have one video and two audio tracks.

Duration	In	Out	Tracks
00:00:00;00	Not Set	Not Set	2V, 4A
00:00:09:18	Not Set	Not Set	1V, 2A
00:00:06:01	Not Set	Not Set	1V, 2A

FIGURE 7.35 The columns in the Browser. Choose the clip labeled *1M. Wild Ambience*.

KEY TERM:

In the filmmaking world, the word **wild** refers to sound that you record that is not synchronized to any particular picture. You record it to be used later in your sound design.

This clip was filmed for its background noise, but also has a video component. It is always a good idea to make sure you capture sounds on location to help with your post-production work.

This clip is the longest, which means we will have few more options in a moment. Double-click on the clip. We now have an image in the Viewer, as shown in Figure 7.36.

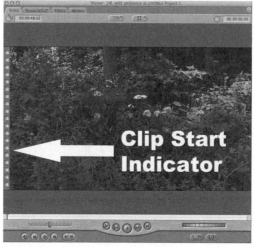

FIGURE 7.36 Clip *1M. Wild Ambience*, double-clicked in the Viewer.

Notice that on the left side of the screen there is a line up and down the side of the frame that looks like a film strip with perforations. This means that you are at the start of the clip. At the bottom left of the Viewer is a yellow cursor icon – the *playhead* – as you can see in Figure 7.37.

Click and drag it all the way to the right. Now your screen should have that same column of film perforations, but on the right side, as shown in Figure 7.38. Drag the playhead back and forth. Look at the timecode display windows at the top of the Viewer. See how the value on the right changes as you drag. That window indicates the position of the cursor.

FIGURE 7.37 The Viewer's yellow playhead icon.

FIGURE 7.38 Clip *1M. Wild Ambience*, with the playhead dragged to the right.

All of these clips are in what is called a 16:9 aspect ratio, like your widescreen TV at home. If you are working in the default format with which FCE starts, you will see gray bars above and below the clip in the Viewer. This is because the program starts up in a 4:3 aspect ratio, which is square. When we drag clips down to the Timeline, we automatically change the program's video settings, and the gray bars go away.

Changing the length of clips

Now we are going to change the length of the clip by applying *In* and *Out* points. At the bottom of the Viewer, there is a block of buttons, as shown in Figure 7.39, called *Transport Controls*. The two right-most buttons, as shown in Figure 7.40, are the controls for setting your *In* and *Out* points. Go ahead and hover over each one. You will see that the yellow pop-up window reads *Mark In – i* and *Mark Out – o*.

FIGURE 7.39 The Viewer's Transport Controls.

The following figure shows the Mark *In* and Mark *Out* icons.

Scroll anywhere in the clip. Now press the *I* key. You should see a new division appear on your Viewer window scroll bar, with an area of darker gray to the left, as shown in Figure 7.41. In addition, the top timeline display values have changed: the one on the left shows the new length of the clip, while the one on the right shows the location of the *In* point. The information to the left of the *In* point is still there, and you can scroll through it, but if you were to drag this clip down to the Timeline, it would only play from the *In* point forwards.

FIGURE 7.40
Mark *In* and
Mark *Out* icons.

FIGURE 7.41 The clip in the Viewer with an *In* point.

Scroll past the *In* point in the Viewer – or just click anywhere in the scroll area – and stop on a new spot. Now press the *O* key. You have just created an *Out* point, as shown in Figure 7.42. Again, the timecode values, above, have

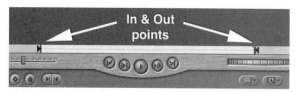

FIGURE 7.42 The Clip in the Viewer with both an *In* point and an *Out* point.

changed. Look back at the Browser. As shown in Figure 7.43, the duration of the clip has changed, and there are now timecode values for both the *In* and the *Out* points.

The following figure show how the timecode values have changed.

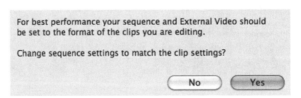

FIGURE 7.43 The Clip in the Browser with a new duration and new *In* and *Out* point timecode values.

Bring clips into the Timeline

Let's now take it to the next level and drag a clip down to the Timeline. Let's use *1D. flowers_4*. Click on it once (twice and you will open it up in the Viewer), then hold and drag it down to the Timeline. Drop it in the V1 track. Before you see the clip appear in the Timeline, however, you will probably see a new pop-up window, as shown in Figure 7.44. This window warns you that the clip's video settings do not match the Sequence settings. If you kept the default FCE settings, the Sequence is set for a 4:3 aspect ratio, while the clip is in a 16:9 ratio. All you have to do is click *Yes*, and the program will adjust the Sequence settings. The next time you drag a clip down during these exercises, you will not see this pop-up warning.

> For best performance your sequence and External Video should be set to the format of the clips you are editing.
>
> Change sequence settings to match the clip settings?
>
> No   Yes

FIGURE 7.44 Clip and sequence format difference pop-up warning.

After you click *Yes*, you should see your clip in the Timeline, as shown in Figure 7.45. If you look at this configuration, you will see that the first clip we worked with – *1M. Wild Ambience* – is still up in the Viewer, while the new clip – *1D. flowers_4* – sits in the Timeline, in Tracks V1, A1, and A2. Because the Canvas shows what is in the Timeline, the image we see there is different than the image in the Viewer. By default, when you drag a clip to the Timeline, the playhead appears at the end of that clip, so the Canvas shows us the final frame of the new shot.

FIGURE 7.45 If you have successfully dragged the new shot to the Timeline, the windows should look something like this.

Notice how we still see the gray bars above and below the clips in both the Viewer and the Canvas. Despite the change in the aspect ratio of the Sequence, the window arrangement is still set to a 4:3 project. If you remember, we looked at the Window dropdown menu (Figure 7.27) to learn how to reset the configuration back to the standard setting. There was a keyboard shortcut associated with that command: *control* key + *U* key. Press those two keys at the same time, and you will see how FCE now arranges the windows, as shown in Figure 7.46. The gray bars are gone. The application has adjusted the display settings to match the new aspect ratio.

FIGURE 7.46 After you reset the windows to the standard arrangement, the gray bars above and below the clips will be gone.

How the Timeline and Viewer Interact

From the Timeline, double-click the clip we just dragged there. It should now show up in the Viewer Window, as shown in Figure 7.47. Any time you

CHAPTER 7 ▓ FINAL CUT EXPRESS: BASIC INTERFACE ▓▓▓ **157**

FIGURE 7.47 After you double-click the clip in the Timeline, both the Viewer and the Canvas show the same image.

double-click a piece of media, it appears in the Viewer, but the location from which you double-click the media makes a difference.

Look at the bottom of the Viewer, in the scroll bar. The light gray line there now has texture, as if mildly perforated, as shown in Figure 7.48. Go back up to the Browser and double-click the same clip – *1D. flowers_4*. Now look at the Viewer. The scroll bar area is free of texture, as we can see in Figure 7.49. This is a very important distinction. Later, when working with effects and other filters, you will want to know whether you are working on a clip from your Timeline or from the Browser. At the top of the Viewer, there is always a line of text that tells you what clip you are viewing and its location. If you know that the scroll bar can also tell you the location of the clip, you can tell at an even quicker glance if you need to double-click the clip from a different location.

FIGURE 7.48 If the Viewer's scroll bar is perforated, you have double-clicked the clip from the Timeline.

FIGURE 7.49 If the Viewer's scroll bar is smooth, you have double-clicked the clip from the Browser.

Double-click the new clip – *1D. flowers_4* – from the Timeline. Now set an *In* and *Out* point, as we did with the previous clip. Because we are working with a clip that resides in your Sequence, you should see the way that clip looks in the Timeline change as you set your *In* and *Out* points, as shown in Figure 7.50. It is shorter.

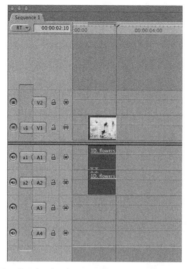

FIGURE 7.50 The clip in the Timeline looks shorter after you set *In* and *Out* points in the Viewer.

Now go to the Browser, and instead of double-clicking, just click and drag a clip from there to the Viewer. It's the same as if you had double-clicked on the clip: the clip appears in the Viewer. In the future, you can use whatever method works best for you. On this new clip, set an *In* and *Out* point, and then click and drag the clip down from the Viewer to the Timeline. This new clip now appears on the Timeline, shorter than its original length.

If you ever want to simply delete something from the Timeline, all you have to do is click on it – provided the Selection Tool is highlighted in the Tool Palette – and press the delete *key.*

Basic Editing Tool and Techniques

It is time to experiment a little. Take all of the clips that are in the Browser and place them in the Timeline, whether by dragging or double-clicking them into the Viewer, setting *In* and *Out* points, or just dragging them directly into the Timeline. If you want to play any one clip, or the jumble of clips that you have thrown into your Sequence, press the *spacebar*. Just make sure that you first click the Window in which you wish to play the clip, so that that Window is highlighted.

Notice how each video and audio track has a thin dividing line about a third of the way down from the top. Grab a piece of video from the Browser and drag it down to the Timeline, but don't let go. An icon of an arrow appears once you drag the clip into the Timeline. Notice what happens when you hover around the dividing line; it changes from an arrow pointing sideways to an arrow pointing down. If you let go of the clip while your cursor is in the top third of the destination track, FCE will make what is called an *Insert* edit, which moves everything over to the right from the point where you drop the clip. If you let go of the clip while your cursor is in the bottom two thirds of the destination track, FCE makes an *Overwrite* edit, which just places the clip down on top of whatever is there, writing over it. Both are useful edits.

Note that you do not have to drop clips into the same tracks. You can drop some clips into V1 (and A1 and A2) and some into V2 (and A3 and A4). You could even create a new track by hovering with the clip above V2 and then letting go. The application will then create a V3 (and A5 and A6) track and so on. While you can play and hear multiple tracks of layered audio at a time, you will only be able to see one video track at a time. You can always change the opacity of a video clip using the *Toggle Clip Overlays* command (Figure 7.20) we discussed earlier. If you do that, then you will be able to see another video clip underneath the one whose opacity you have changed.

While editing, it is often useful to checkerboard your scenes, as shown in Figure 7.51. *As you become more advanced, and learn more tools, you will be able to see why this is sometimes useful, depending on the scene you are cutting. All you would need to do now, if you hadn't dragged your clips into this pattern already, would be to click and drag them, in the Timeline, to the track above. The audio will always follow the video on to the corresponding new audio tracks, unless Linking (Figure 7.19) has been turned off.*

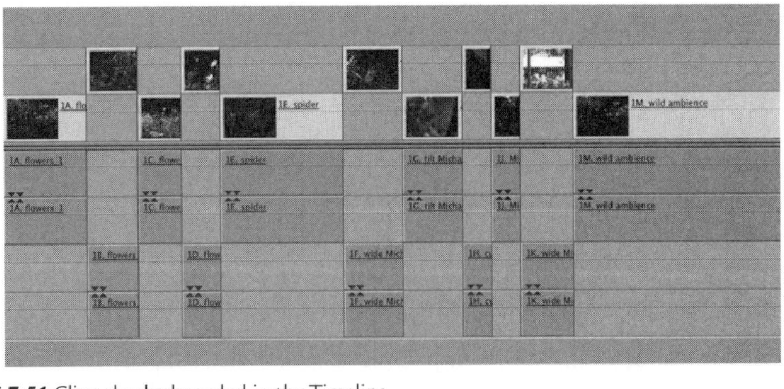

FIGURE 7.51 Clips checkerboarded in the Timeline.

Let's try *Linking/Unlinking* and *Snapping*. Figure 7.19 shows where these buttons are located. Try deleting parts of a clip (audio or video) by turning *Linking* on and off. Highlight the part of the clip you don't want – make sure the top, *Selection*, tool is on in the Tool Palette – and press the *delete* key. You can also turn *Linking* on and off by pressing the *shift* key and *L* key.

Snapping is also very useful. If it's on, then the cursor and clips in the Timeline will always *snap* to the closest edit point. An edit point is the end of one clip and the start of another. It's also wherever the playhead has stopped. If you find a good spot to which you want to drag a clip, leave the playhead in that spot and drag the clip to it. If *Snapping* is on, then the clip will *snap* to that spot. If *Snapping* is off, it can be very hard to pinpoint the exact spot that marks the end of the last clip, without leaving a tiny bit of a gap between the two clips. This gap will look like blank frames when you play the Sequence. The keyboard shortcut for *Snapping* is the *N* key.

The Viewer, Canvas, and Timeline Windows all have the same kind of playhead. If you want to move the playhead's position, you can either drag it through the scrollbar, or just click on a new point in the scrollbar, and the playhead will automatically move to that point. Note that if *Snapping* is on, and you have clips in the Timeline, then you will not be able to scroll smoothly, as the cursor will jump forward as it *snaps* to each edit point.

If you turn *Linking* off you may accidentally separate your video and audio clips, moving them out of synchronization (or *sync*) with each other, and they will remain out of sync once you turn *Linking* back on. They may still be *linked*, but the picture and sound will no longer match up. If this happens, turn *Snapping* on and keep *Linking* off for a moment, move the audio and video so that they snap back together at the end points, and then turn *Linking* back on.

If you have trouble seeing all of your clips in the Timeline at once, it is because your Timeline is set to intervals that are too small to offer a wider view. There is an easy way to zoom in and out. Start by making sure you are clicked in the Timeline, then press the *command* key and the *minus* key (that's "–") to zoom out, or the *command* key and the *plus* key (that's "+"), to zoom in. In the next chapter, we will explore at least one other way to do the same thing. Once you are done experimenting, you will probably have a lot of questions. Don't worry, as we will start answering them in the very next chapter. Before we end this chapter, here are a few final words of encouragement.

Don't be afraid to experiment. There is nothing you can do to your media, from within FCE, that will affect the original media on your hard drive. You can cut up, lighten, darken, delete, speed up, or do many other things, but the source media remains unchanged. Even within FCE, if you drag a piece of media down to the Timeline and add filters, or cut it up, or anything else, and then change your mind, you can always delete that piece of media from the Timeline and drag it down again, fresh, from the Browser. If you make changes within the Browser, however, you will have to undo them, as they are a little more permanent than changes made in the Timeline. But "permanent" is a relative concept here, since you can always re-import the media from your hard drive if you can't figure out how to reset it.

Also remember that you can always undo your actions up to 32 times. As in most Apple-based programs, there is an *Undo* command. If you go up to the *Edit* dropdown menu at the top of the program, the very first line is *Undo*, as shown in Figure 7.52. The keyboard shortcut is the same as it is in most other applications: *command* and the Z key.

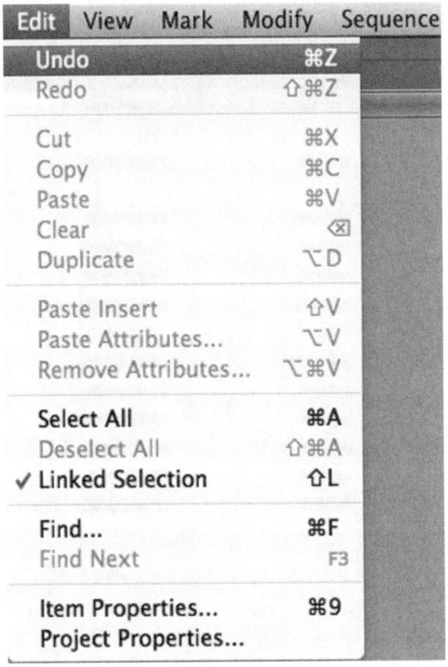

FIGURE 7.52 Edit dropdown menu with *Undo* highlighted.

The default setting for the program is for only 10 levels of undo, but you can change this setting. Go up to the top of the screen, to the *FCE* dropdown menu, and scroll down to *User Preferences*, as shown in Figure 7.53. Click on that option, and a new menu will pop up, as shown in Figure 7.54. To the right of the *Levels of Undo*, at the top, you can see that the number *10*.

Final Cut Express File Edit

About Final Cut Express

User Preferences... ⌥Q
System Settings... ⇧Q

Easy Setup... ^Q

Provide Feedback

Services ▶

Hide Final Cut Express ⌘H
Hide Others ⌥⌘H
Show All

Quit Final Cut Express ⌘Q

FIGURE 7.53 Go to the Final Cut Express Menu and select User Preferences.

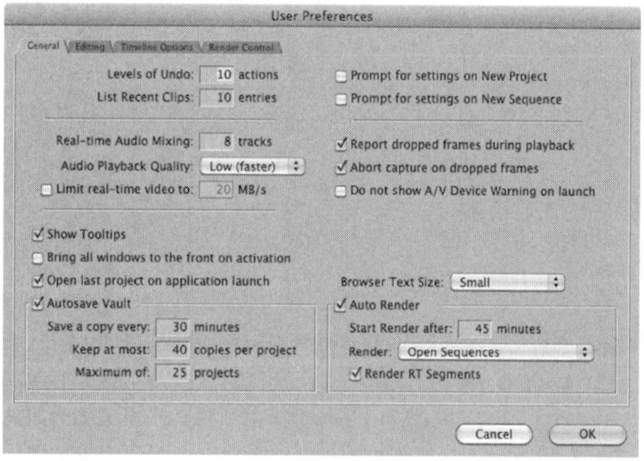

User Preferences

General Editing Timeline Options Render Control

Levels of Undo: 10 actions ☐ Prompt for settings on New Project
List Recent Clips: 10 entries ☐ Prompt for settings on New Sequence

Real-time Audio Mixing: 8 tracks ☑ Report dropped frames during playback
Audio Playback Quality: Low (faster) ☑ Abort capture on dropped frames
☐ Limit real-time video to: 20 MB/s ☐ Do not show A/V Device Warning on launch

☑ Show Tooltips
☐ Bring all windows to the front on activation
☑ Open last project on application launch   Browser Text Size: Small
☑ Autosave Vault   ☑ Auto Render
   Save a copy every: 30 minutes   Start Render after: 45 minutes
   Keep at most: 40 copies per project   Render: Open Sequences
   Maximum of: 25 projects   ☑ Render RT Segments

Cancel   OK

FIGURE 7.54 User Preferences menu.

Click in that box and change the number to 32, as shown in Figure 7.55. While you are in this menu, change one other thing. Towards the bottom, there is a line, under *Autosave Vault*, that reads *Save a copy every,* as seen in Figure 7.56. The default setting for this is 30 minutes. Change it to 5 minutes. This way, if the program crashes (which is very rare these days), you only lose, at the most, 4 minutes and 59 seconds of work. Click *OK*, and we are done with this chapter.

The following figure shows how you can change the levels of Undo.

Figure 7.56 shows how to change the Autosave settings.

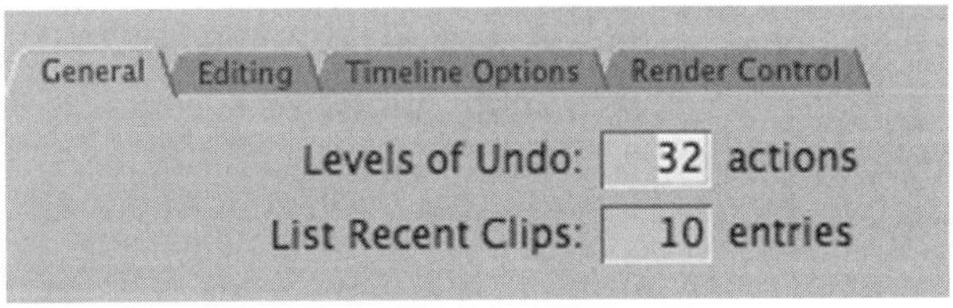

FIGURE 7.55 Levels of Undo changed to 32.

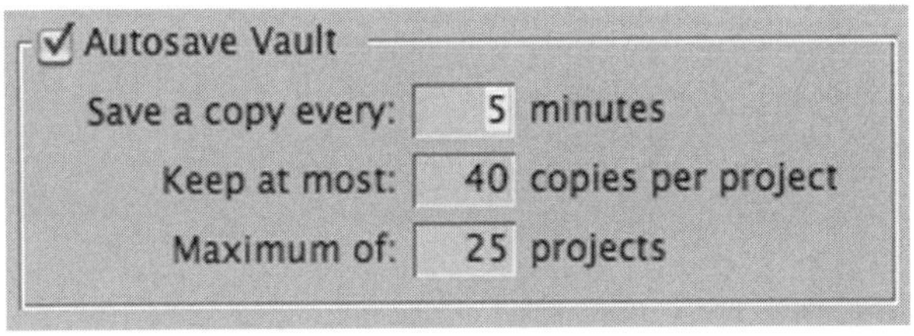

FIGURE 7.56 Autosave set to every 5 minutes.

SUMMARY

In this chapter, we covered the basic interface of FCE and some of its tools. We began with the four main windows – the Browser, the Viewer, the Canvas, and the Timeline. We then moved on to the Tool Palette and Audio Meter. We also learned how to change – and reset – the arrangement of the windows on the screen.

We then imported video from the companion DVD. Once we had the video in the program, we began learning simple tools to manipulate the clips. We set *In* and *Out* points and practiced clicking and dragging video to the Timeline. Along the way, we learned how to recognize keyboard shortcut keys.

While experimenting with video, we discussed the usefulness of the *Linking* and *Snapping* buttons and also discovered how to change some of the default settings of the program, such as aspect ratio. We learned that there is nothing fear in the editing process in FCE, because you can always undo you actions up to 32 times. Plus, the source media is never altered, no matter what you do to it in FCE.

In this chapter we created a foundation on which we can now build as we move on to more advanced techniques.

1. What is a *scratch disk*?

2. What are the four main windows in FCE?

3. What is a keyboard shortcut key?

4. What are *In* and *Out* points for?

5. What happens to the original source media that we manipulate in FCE?

DISCUSSION / ESSAY QUESTIONS

1. Describe what each of the four main windows in FCE is used for.

2. Based on what you've learned so far, what kinds of problems do you think a disorganized editor might face?

3. If you have used other NLE programs, how is FCE different?

Further Research

If you haven't done so already, watch *Nail Polish*. After doing so, take the tools we have discussed so far and try to recreate the opening of the film with the clips we imported in this chapter. Don't worry about titles and credits, and don't worry about sound issues. Just cut for picture.

You know how to shorten clips using *In* and *Out* points, and you know how to drag your media to the Timeline and within the Timeline, so you can make an attempt to put the clips in the same order as they appear in the movie.

You can always undo your actions, and you can always delete everything and start over. The goal here is for you to lose your fear of the basic interface before we start doing more complicated things. So be brave, experiment, and make mistakes.

CHAPTER 8

BEYOND THE BASICS: UNDERSTANDING THE TOOLS OF FINAL CUT EXPRESS

OVERVIEW AND LEARNING OBJECTIVES

In this chapter, you will:

- Work with clips in the Timeline
- Begin to explore the Tool Palette
- Create a match on action
- Manipulate audio levels and video opacity using keyframes
- Learn how to use the built-in fades and dissolves
- Render the effects you have created

Editing, Part I – Cutting a Clip in the Timeline

If you didn't already do it, let's now save the project we started in Chapter 7 with a name other than *Untitled Project 1*. Go up to the *File* dropdown menu up top and scroll down to *Save Project As*, as shown in Figure 8.1. Click on that option, and another menu will pop up, as we see in Figure 8.2. Whenever you use the *Save Project As* feature, the default name that is given to use is always the current name of the project, followed by the word *copy*. Notice that if you have never used this menu before, it is somewhat compressed, in terms of the location options it offers. Click on the blue triangle box to the right of the *Untitled Project 1 copy* line, and the menu will magically expand, as you can see in Figure 8.3. This menu expansion is a feature throughout MAC OSX, and not unique to FCE. Now choose a name, and a location, that works for you. As shown in Figure 8.4, we have renamed this project *Nail Polish Files*.

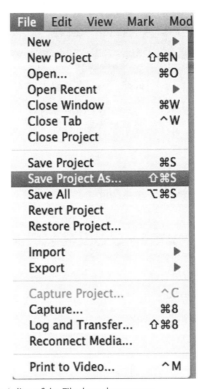

FIGURE 8.1 The *Save Project As* line of the File drop-down menu.

All figures appear in color on the companion DVD.

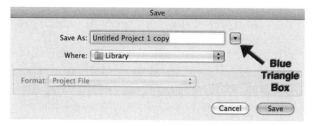

FIGURE 8.2 The FCE *Save Project* menu. Click on the blue triangle box, as marked, to expand the menu.

FIGURE 8.3 The *Save Project* menu, expanded.

FIGURE 8.4 Renaming our project as *Nail Polish Files*.

It's a good idea, as you save a project for the first time, to also create a folder, either on an external hard drive or on your computer's internal hard drive, into which you will save this project. This folder can also be the location of your scratch disks. Never forget the importance of scratch disks.

When we left our project last, we had cut together the first scene of *Nail Polish*, checkerboarding our footage, as shown in Figure 8.5. In this chapter we will take the basic skills we learned in the last chapter and add some new techniques. If you did not do the exercises in Chapter 7, but are an experienced user of FCE, try and recreate something with the footage from the *Video_01* folder on this book's DVD that looks similar to what you see in Figure 8.5. If you did the exercises, but your project doesn't look exactly like what you see here, don't worry. As long as you have some footage in the Timeline and in the Browser, you will be able to follow along.

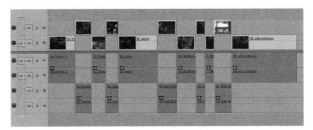

FIGURE 8.5 Scene 1 from *Nail Polish*, as completed in Chapter 7, with the footage checkerboarded.

Beginning with the first shot

Starting from the Timeline, then, let's double-click the first shot, *1A. flowers_1*. This shot will now appear in the Viewer window. If the playhead is in a different spot than at the head of the shot we just clicked, as shown in Figure 8.6, you will see a different image in the Canvas window. Remember that this window always shows us the exact spot where the playhead lies in the Timeline.

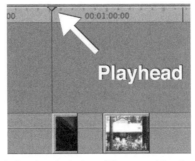

FIGURE 8.6 The Timeline's playhead might be in a different position from that of the clip you double-clicked.

We can set in and out points, as we did in Chapter 7, from within the Viewer window, which would make the length of the clip in the Timeline change. Let's do something different now, however. Go over to the Tool Palette, on the right, and select the *Razor Blade* tool, as shown in Figure 8.7. It's one of the icons that actually looks like what it is, which in this case is a razor blade. Don't forget to hover, for a moment, above this icon, so that FCE can remind you of the keyboard shortcut (which is the *B* key).

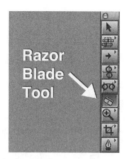

FIGURE 8.7 The *Razor Blade* tool on the Tool Palette.

Using the Razor Blade tool

Once you have selected the Razor Blade tool, drag the cursor over to the Timeline. You'll notice that, if and when you position the cursor over a shot in the Timeline, and the Razor Blade tool is selected, the cursor turns into a razor blade, rather than a pointer. If you notice that the cursor *snaps* to the points between shots as you are dragging the cursor across the various shots, remember what that means: *Snapping* is on (as we discussed in Chapter 7). You can turn it on and off by clicking the *N* key.

Find a spot on a clip where you might want to make a cut. Are you zoomed out too far on the Timeline? Are you having trouble seeing the clips? Remember that, as discussed in Chapter 7, you can easily zoom in and out. There's a tool for that on the Tool Palette as well, but rather than switch away from the Razor Blade tool, let's just use the *command* key and the *plus* key (that's "+"), or the *command* key and the *minus* key (that's "–"). If you do the former, then you zoom in on the timeline, as shown in Figure 8.8, and if you do the latter, then you zoom out on, as shown in Figure 8.9.

FIGURE 8.8 Zoomed in on your Timeline.

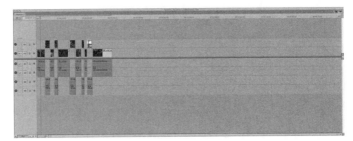

FIGURE 8.9 Zoomed out on your Timeline.

Find a spot, hover over it, and click with your mouse button, and your one clip will be cut into two clips, as shown in Figure 8.10. Once this is done, you can switch back to the top tool on the Tool Palette – the *Selection Tool* – and select either half of the clip that used to be a single clip, as shown in Figure 8.11. The darkly shaded half is the one selected. You could click on that half and drag it anywhere you want in the Timeline. You could also bring it up in the Viewer. Let's do that now by double-clicking on the second half.

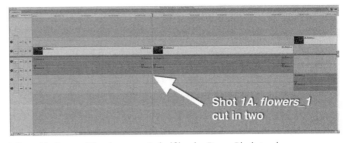

Shot 1A. flowers_1
cut in two

FIGURE 8.10 Shot *1A. flowers_1* has been cut in half by the Razor Blade tool.

The next figure shows the second half of the clip selected using the Selection Tool.

FIGURE 8.11 Using the Selection Tool, we select the second half of the clip.

The second half of the clip now appears in the Viewer, as shown in Figure 8.12, but with the first half still showing as part of the clip, only not highlighted. Notice again, as we saw in Chapter 7, the dotted lines at the bottom of the Viewer, which indicate that we double-clicked from the Timeline and not from the Browser. Approximately halfway through the clip is an *In* point. To the left of the *In* point is the footage that is in the first half of the clip. It's as if we had done what we did in Chapter 7, and simply set an *In* point directly in the Viewer window, rather than by chopping the clip in two with the Razor Blade. FCE offers multiple ways to do the same thing, as you can see.

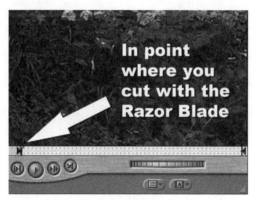

FIGURE 8.12 After you double-click the split shot *1A. flowers_1*, it appears in the Viewer as if you had set an *In* point directly in that window.

Deleting with the Selection Tool

Now delete the first half of the clip, in the Timeline. With the *Selection Tool* highlighted in the Tool Palette, click on it, then press the *delete* key on your keyboard. As we can see in Figure 8.13, it is gone. But back up in the Viewer, the second half of the clip is still there, since it's still in your Timeline. To undo this last action, press the *command key* and the Z key. The half of the clip that you just deleted should reappear.

FIGURE 8.13 After you highlight the first half of the clip and press the *delete* key, it disappears.

How the Browser and Timeline interact

Look up at your Browser window. When last we looked up there, the bin in which the video clips reside was open, as shown in Figure 8.14. Let's close it by clicking to the left of the bin icon, on the little triangle pointing down. The bin closes, as shown in Figure 8.15.

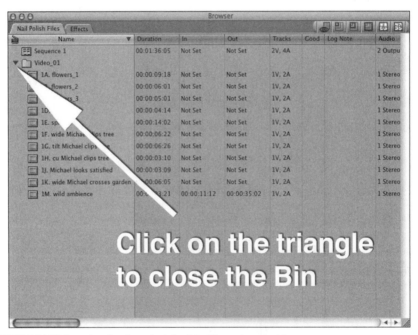

FIGURE 8.14 Click on the triangle to the left of the bin to close the bin.

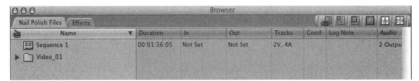

FIGURE 8.15 After you click on the triangle to the left of the bin, it closes.

Let's click once on the first half of the clip and drag it up to the Browser. Drop it there. Do the same thing with the second half of the clip. Notice how both clips stay in the Timeline, but now also appear in the Browser – with the same name, *1A. flowers_1* – above the bin, as shown in Figure 8.16. Dragging a clip to the Browser from the Timeline does not remove it from the Timeline. All that happens is that you make an exact copy of it. If you have made changes to the clip, in the Timeline (like cutting it in two), those changes will be copied as well.

FIGURE 8.16 Both halves of shot *1A.flowers_1* appear above the bin in the Browser after you drag them from the Timeline.

Renaming a clip in the Browser

It's awkward to have two shots with the same name, however, so let's rename each half. Lightly click on the text part of the clip in the Browser; do not click on the icon. If you do it right, the text will highlight, as shown in Figure 8.17. After the text has been highlighted, click the text again and the text bar will turn into a text box that you can edit, as you can see in Figure 8.18.

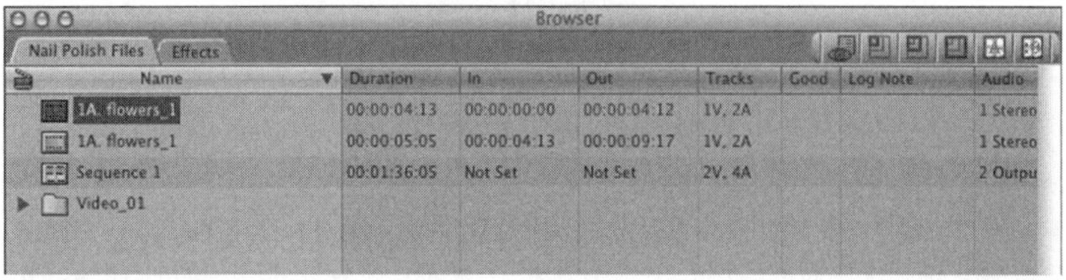

FIGURE 8.17 The text of the top clip highlighted in the Browser.

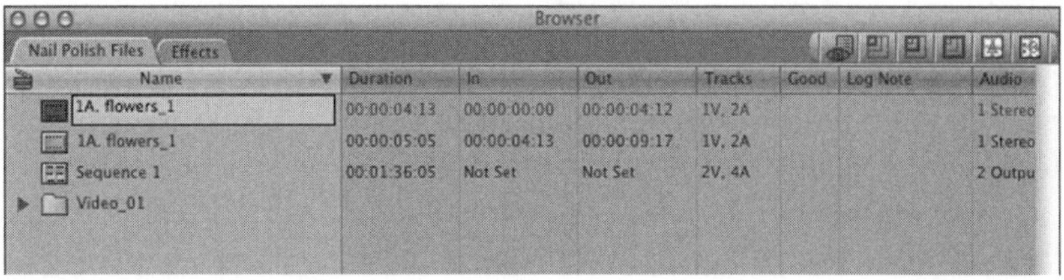

FIGURE 8.18 After you click gently on the text of a clip, it becomes an editable text box.

Go ahead and type *First Half*, as shown in Figure 8.19. Now hit Enter. The text is edited, and the name of that clip has changed. You will notice, however, that the name of the clip below it has changed as well, as shown in Figure 8.20. If you look down at the Timeline now, you will see that both halves of that original clip now also bear the name *First Half*, as shown in Figure 8.21. That's not what we intended, so let's figure out what happened.

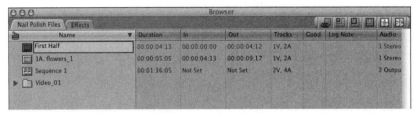

FIGURE 8.19 Type *First Half* into the highlighted text box.

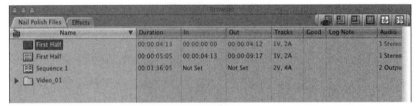

FIGURE 8.20 After you hit Enter, both clips' names change to *First Half*.

FIGURE 8.21 The names of both clips change in the Timeline as well.

This has happened because the icons in the Browser each still represent the footage associated with that original clip. We have not created new clips – just copies of the original clip. These are both really the same clip, even if they represent different halves of the clip.

Later, when we create *subclips*, you will discover a way to take bits of an original clip and rename them separately. For now, it is enough to understand the relationship that clips and their icons have to each other in both the Browser and the Timeline, as we have just demonstrated. And, using the method we just used, you can also rename your bin and your sequence icons by clicking on their text descriptions.

Undoing our actions to start again

We have just learned how to make a basic cut. Using that skill, we could take the footage in the Timeline, chop it up, and rearrange it fairly easily. Before we do anymore cutting, however, let's clean up our Timeline and undo the renaming of the clips we just did. To undo, remember that you simply press the *command* key and the Z key.

In the Timeline, highlight the first half of the clip. Since we were previously working in the Browser, click once in the Timeline to reactivate that window. Press the A key to make sure the Selection Tool is active. Then click once on the first half of the clip, as shown in Figure 8.22. Press the *delete* key, and it disappears, as shown in Figure 8.23.

FIGURE 8.22 Highlight the first half of the clip *1A. flowers_1* in the Timeline.

FIGURE 8.23 Delete the first half of the clip *1A. flowers_1* in the Timeline.

Now go to the left side of the remaining half of the clip and grab the left edge by clicking once with your mouse. Without letting go, drag the edge all the way left and back to the start of the Timeline. The Timeline should look just as it did before we cut the clip in half (see Figure 8.8). How did this happen? Even though we deleted half of the original clip, the information is still there, but invisible. So we can drag the clip back to its original size, if we want, and if there is enough empty space in the Timeline to accommodate the full clip.

Be careful, however, when you try to do that. If you click on the entire clip, rather than on the edge, and then drag left, the entire clip will move. You will not extend the clip back to its original length, but just shift the clip over, as shown in Figure 8.24.

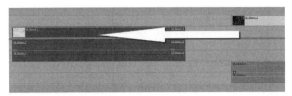

FIGURE 8.24 Shot 1A. *flowers_1*, shifted to the left.

 Now let's start working with the opening of *Nail Polish* again. As a departure point, we'll use the project we completed in Chapter 7.

Editing, Part II – Adding More Tools to Our Repertoire

If you've been working in a Timeline window that is zoomed in so that you can't see all of the clips, you will now need to zoom out a bit.

Zooming out on the Timeline

The easiest way to do this is, again, by pressing the *command* key and the *minus* key.

NOTE
If you do not know how to import video footage into FCE, or if you have forgotten, review Chapter 7.

Changing the speed of a clip

We have labeled the shots on the DVD in the same order in which they appear in the movie. You will notice, however, if you compare the very first shot as it appears in the finished movie and the very first shot as it appears in your clips, that the movie version is longer. This is because that first shot was slowed down to allow that moment to last longer. So, the first thing we have to learn how to do is to change the speed of a clip.

Highlight the shot – *1A. flowers_1* – which should still be in the Timeline. Now go up to the *Modify* dropdown menu and select *Speed*, as shown in Figure 8.25. Notice that the keyboard shortcut for this option is the *command* key and the *J* key. The *Speed* pop-up menu appears, as shown in Figure 8.26.

FIGURE 8.25 Modify dropdown menu with *Speed* selected.

The following figure shows the clip *Speed* menu.

FIGURE 8.26 Clip *Speed* menu.

There are two ways to change the speed of a clip using this menu. First of all, we could simply type in a different number in the speed category. A higher number would speed the clip up; a lower number would slow the clip down. This is easy enough. What we're going to do, however, is change the length of the clip.

If you watch the opening of *Nail Polish*, you'll notice that the length of the opening, from the first frame of black to the last frame of the first shot, is 15 seconds and 19 frames. There are 2 seconds of black *slug* (blank film) at the start and end of the movie, so we can subtract those 2 seconds from the length of the opening. To make things easier for us, let's just say we need 14 seconds for this first clip. In the small window in the menu next to the word *Duration*, which indicates a length of 9 seconds and 18 frames, let's type in 14 seconds and zero frames, as shown in Figure 8.27. When we do that, the speed of the clip automatically changes to 68.57 percent. We have, in effect, slowed the clip down by making it longer. Before you click on the *OK* button, notice the little checkbox labeled *Reverse*. Don't check it now, but remember it for later. This is how you can make a clip play backward.

FIGURE 8.27 The Speed menu with a new clip duration.

Click on the *OK* button. The clip on the Timeline grows longer and shoves all of the clips over and to the right. There is also a green line that appears above the clip, at the top of the Timeline, along with a new speed percentage indicator in the middle of the clip, both of which are shown in Figure 8.28. We will discuss effects in Chapter 9, but you should know what this colored line indicates.

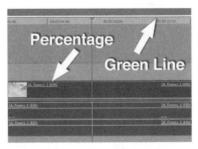

FIGURE 8.28 Shot *1A. flowers_1* after we changed the speed, with a green to-be-rendered indicator above it and a new speed percentage indicator in the middle of it.

How FCE creates effects

Whenever you do something to a clip that requires the program to change the way the clip looks, or sounds, or the speed at which it plays, FCE has to *render* the effect. This means that it has to create a new piece of video, to be stored in the scratch disks, to play the new effect you want (*render* here is synonymous with "create"). After you *render* an effect, the two files – the original video and the new overlaid effect – exist as separate files in the scratch disk folder. If you ever accidentally delete the render file, you'll have to recreate it, or rerender it. Once you export your finished movie at the end of the editing process, that rendered piece of new video becomes part of the film, and no longer exists separately.

In the early days of FCE (before there were Pro and Express versions), almost every effect you created, no matter how simple, had to be rendered before you could see what it looked like. That has changed. Now there are effects that you can see in real time, and others that can only be seen once you render them. A minor speed change like the one we just did is available in real-time viewing. You would want to render it before exporting the film, but for now, you don't need to. If the line were red, however, then we would need to render it to see it. We will discuss this issue in greater depth in the next chapter.

Now click on the upper-left corner of the Timeline, above the start of the first clip, and the playhead moves to that position, as shown in Figure 8.29. Press the *spacebar* key on your keyboard, and the clip will start playing. At 68.57 percent, the objects floating through the frame look a little slow, as if in a dream, which works for the opening garden scene. There are some problems with the sound (we hear a microphone bump, for instance), but we'll fix those issues later.

FIGURE 8.29 When you click at the top-left corner of the Timeline, the playhead moves to the beginning of the sequence.

Removing and replacing audio

Let the Timeline continue playing through to the next clip. At the transition point between the two shots, where the sound from the one collides with the sound from the other, you'll hear a loud "blip." We'll have to fix that, too. Keep the Timeline playing until the section of *1E. spider* where you hear the voice of the director talking to the actor. Now press the *spacebar* key and the playhead stops.

We will need to replace all of the sound up to the part just after the director's voice. Let's do that now, using our new Razor Blade tool. First, let's mark the spot where the voice stops. It's simple to do. Every keyboard has arrow keys somewhere on it, usually in the lower-right corner. You can either drag the playhead back through the clip, or you can use the right arrow key to scrub backwards. By default, *audio scrubbing*, which lets you hear sound as you move through a clip, is turned on. If you don't hear anything as you scroll backwards, stop and click on the *View* dropdown menu. At the bottom of that menu is *Audio Scrubbing*, as shown in Figure 8.30. If it is unchecked, then highlight it and let go. Note that the keyboard shortcut is the *shift* key plus the *S* key.

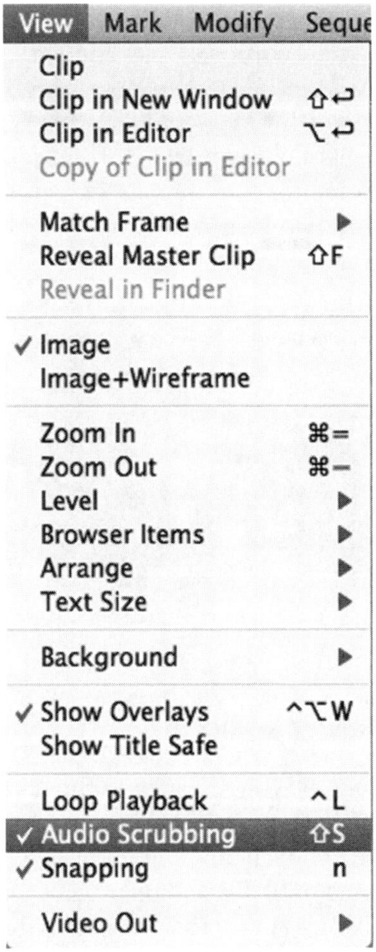

View	Mark	Modify	Seque

Clip
Clip in New Window ⇧↵
Clip in Editor ⌥↵
Copy of Clip in Editor

Match Frame ▶
Reveal Master Clip ⇧F
Reveal in Finder

✓ **Image**
Image+Wireframe

Zoom In ⌘=
Zoom Out ⌘−
Level ▶
Browser Items ▶
Arrange ▶
Text Size ▶

Background ▶

✓ **Show Overlays** ^⌥W
Show Title Safe

Loop Playback ^L
✓ **Audio Scrubbing** ⇧S
✓ **Snapping** n

Video Out ▶

FIGURE 8.30 The View dropdown menu, with *Audio Scrubbing* highlighted.

Scrub back until you hear the tail end of the director's voice. Then go forward, just past it, until you hear no more voices. Make sure that the clip is highlighted and press the *M* key. This places a *marker* at the spot at which

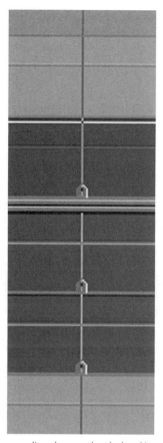

FIGURE 8.31 A marker appears in your clip, wherever the playhead is stopped, when you press the *M* key.

the playhead is stopped, as shown in Figure 8.31. This *marker* lets us know the point at which the good audio, without voices, begins.

Alternately, you could set a marker in a different way. Double-click the audio portion of the clip, so that the clip appears up above, in the Viewer. Since you've double-clicked the audio, the audio tab in the Viewer will be the one highlighted. Using either the playhead or the arrow keys, scroll past the audio of the voices. Then press either the *M* key or the ` key (both are valid shortcuts), and the marker will appear where the playhead sits, as shown in Figure 8.32. One advantage of doing things this second way is that you can actually *see* the audio waveforms and thereby know that you are close to the spot you want. You can turn on these audio waveforms in the Timeline. We'll learn about this in Chapter 9.

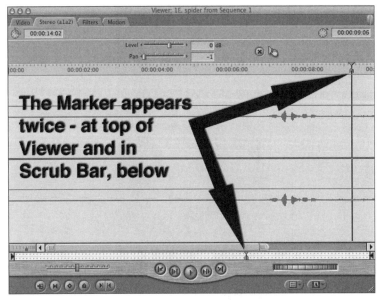

FIGURE 8.32 You can also set a marker in the Viewer, and it will appear at both the top and bottom of the window.

If you ever forget the keyboard shortcut for markers, or if you want to remove markers, there is a *Mark* dropdown menu up top. Scroll down to *Markers*, as shown in Figure 8.33, to set a marker this way.

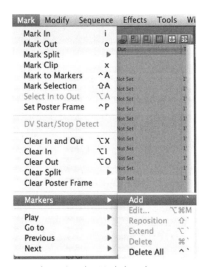

FIGURE 8.33 You can also set a marker using the *Mark* dropdown menu.

Now that we have the spot clearly marked, we'll have to *unlink* the video and audio tracks. Go the green infinity-like symbol all the way on the upper right of the Timeline, which we discussed in Chapter 7: green is on; black is off. Turn *linking* off now.

Next, we are going to remove the audio up to the point just after the director's voice, including the audio from the clips without any voice at all. We will then replace all of this audio with a separate *ambience* – background sound – clip to get rid of the "blips" between shots in the garden. This way all of the shots will play smoothly one after the other, with no difference in sound. We are keeping the audio in shot *1E. spiders*, after the director's voice, because the actor enters the frame, and we need to hear the sound of his steps and rustling in synchronization with the picture.

So, highlight the four tracks of audio before shot *1E. spiders*. Since linking is now off, if you highlight just the audio tracks, the video will remain unselected, as shown in Figure 8.34. There are two easy ways to select multiple tracks at once. The first way is to place your cursor to the left, under the first audio track, then click once with your trackpad or mouse, hold, and drag up and to your right until all four separate audio tracks are selected. The other way would be to click on the first audio track, then hold down the *command* key as you click, one by one, on all of the tracks you wish to highlight.

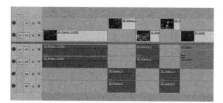

FIGURE 8.34 With linking off, you are able to select just audio, or just video.

Once all four sets of audio are highlighted, press the *delete* key. They should all disappear, as shown in Figure 8.35. Now we will work with the audio in the fifth clip, *1E. spiders*. Before we proceed, make sure that *snapping* (right next to linking) is on. This way the Razor Blade tool will *snap* to the marker.

FIGURE 8.35 By highlighting just the audio and pressing the *delete* key, we have successfully removed the audio from the Timeline.

Next, switch to the Razor Blade tool and cut the fifth audio track at the point where we placed our marker, as shown in Figure 8.36. Now highlight the part of that audio track to the left of the cut we just made, as shown in Figure 8.37. Once that is done, delete it, as shown in Figure 8.38.

FIGURE 8.36 With snapping on, we successfully cut the clip at the exact spot where we placed our marker.

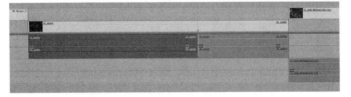

FIGURE 8.37 We then highlight the first part of the audio in that same clip.

FIGURE 8.38 Finally, we delete the first part of that audio.

Now that we have successfully removed audio, we are going to have to replace it with something else. That's where the *ambience* we discussed comes in. The final shot in the *Video_01* bin is labeled *1M. wild ambience*. When this particular shot was recorded, the intent was to use it as background sound, without the image that it came with.

KEY TERM:

Wild sound, in film and video production, refers to sound that has been recorded without regards to synchronization with the image.

If shot *1M. wild ambience* is not already in your Timeline, drag it down there now, placing it at the end of the sequence, after the other clips. Then go ahead and delete the video track. Repeat the action we just completed with the previous clips, but delete the video component this time. Highlight the video and press delete. Now the Timeline should have a clip with audio only at the end of it, as shown in Figure 8.39.

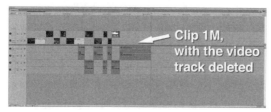

FIGURE 8.39 If you have successfully deleted the video track of *1M. wild ambience*, your Timeline should show that clip at the end, without video.

Unfortunately, the ambient sound in that clip is not long enough to fill the blank spots that we created by deleting the other audio, but we can make it work.

Grab the wild ambience and drag it to the start of the Timeline. However, as you do so, drag it below the tracks labeled A3 and A4, so that we create two new tracks (you can create as many new tracks as you like in this way), as shown in Figure 8.40. Now, with the clip still highlighted, press the *command* key and the *C* key. This is the universal keyboard shortcut for copy, in all Mac-based applications. You can also go up to the *Edit* dropdown menu and scroll down to the *Copy* line, as shown in Figure 8.41.

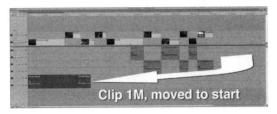

FIGURE 8.40 Clip *1M. wild ambience*, moved to the start of the Timeline.

The following figure shows the *Edit* dropdown menu where you can select *Copy* and *Paste*.

Edit	View	Mark	Modify	S(
Undo			⌘Z	
Redo			⇧⌘Z	
Cut			⌘X	
Copy			⌘C	
Paste			⌘V	
Clear			⌫	
Duplicate			⌥D	
Paste Insert			⇧V	
Paste Attributes...			⌥V	
Remove Attributes...			⌥⌘V	
Select All			⌘A	
Deselect All			⇧⌘A	
Linked Selection			⇧L	
Find...			⌘F	
Find Next			F3	
Item Properties...			⌘9	
Project Properties...				

FIGURE 8.41 The *Edit* dropdown menu, from which you can select *Copy* and *Paste*.

Once the clip is copied, paste it as many times as you need to fill the Timeline to the end of the clips. The keyboard shortcut for this is the *command* key and the *V* key. You can also select Paste from the same Edit dropdown menu we just used. Wherever the playhead is located is where the first paste will take place. If you want to have the first copy appear at the end of the ambience, make sure the playhead is positioned at the end of that clip. After the first paste, the playhead will automatically position itself at the end of that new clip. When you are all done, your Timeline should have three copies of *1M. wild ambience*, as shown in Figure 8.42.

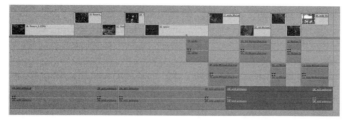

FIGURE 8.12 Three copies of clip *1M. wild ambience* are sufficient to fill the Timeline.

Go ahead and watch the movie now, with this new sound. You'll find that the ambience clip is long enough (23 seconds and 21 frames) that you don't really hear that it is repeating itself. You'll also notice that in shot *1G. tilt Michael clips tree*, you can hear the director talking again. Let's fix that quickly before proceeding further.

Listen carefully to the audio in *1G*. Do we actually need any of the sound? In *1E*, we needed the sound of the actor's arrival – tramping through the brush – at the end, since we see him walk through the frame. Here, however, the ambience from *1M* might be enough. While it is true that we can see the actor's hand in motion, it is not until the next shot that there is an action requiring synchronized sound. So let's just delete the entire sound of *1G*. Highlight that track and press the delete key. When you are done, the only sound below that shot will be one of the copies of *1M*, as shown in Figure 8.43.

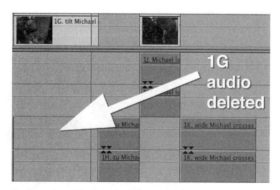

FIGURE 8.43 The audio from shot *1G. tilt Michael clips tree*, deleted.

Now that we have practiced some basic editing techniques working directly in the Timeline, let's try something a little more complicated. Let's make a *match on action*.

Editing, Part III – Matching Action

If you remember correctly, a *match on action* is a cut where an action from one shot is completed in the shot that follows. Let's look at the transition point between shots *1G* and *1H*. *cu Michael clips tree*. If you place the playhead at the start of *1G*, and let it play through the end of *1H*, you'll notice that there's a lot of wasted screen time. In *1G*, we see the clippers, in an extreme close-up, as they disappear behind the leaves. In *1H*, it takes a second or so before they come into frame. Let's cut away that dead time.

Finding the first edit point

Watch shot *1G* until you see the clippers disappear behind the leaves. Take the Razor Blade tool and make a cut at that spot, as shown in Figure 8.44. The frame on which you are paused should show primarily out-of-focus leaves, as seen in the Canvas window in Figure 8.45. Remember that the Canvas will always show you the frame at which the playhead is currently positioned. Next, highlight the part of the clip after the cut you have made, and delete it. After that, highlight the clips to the right of the resulting gap, as shown in Figure 8.46. Then, drag them to the left until the gap is closed, as shown in Figure 8.47. If *snapping* is turned off, you will have a hard time being precise as you drag the clips, so make sure it is turned on. There are other ways to close gaps like this, but this method will do, for now.

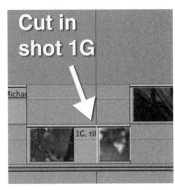

FIGURE 8.44 Cut shot *1G* after the clippers disappear from frame.

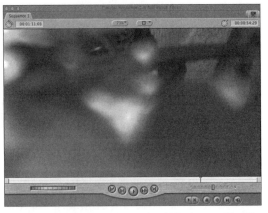

FIGURE 8.45 The frame in *1G* should look something like this image, as seen in the Canvas.

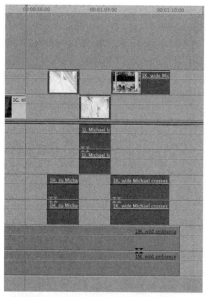

FIGURE 8.46 After you delete the second part of the clip, highlight the remaining clips to the right of the gap.

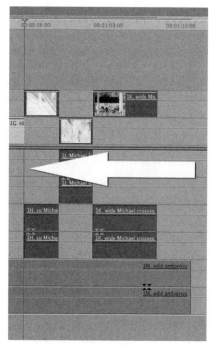

FIGURE 8.47 Drag these clips to the left, closing the gap.

Finding the second edit point

Now we will have to examine shot *1H*. Watch this shot until the clippers close on the stem and cut through it. Using the arrow keys on your keyboard, scroll back until just before the clippers cut. Using the Razor Blade tool, cut the shot at that point, and then delete the section of the shot to the left of the cut you just made.

At some point, you may accidentally hit the caps *lock key as you edit. If that happens, you will see, in both the Viewer and the Canvas, a warning screen, as shown in Figure 8.48. Don't panic; just hit* caps *lock again, and the problem will go away.*

The Caps Lock key is on; rendering is disabled.

FIGURE 8.48 If you accidentally hit the *caps lock* key at any point, you will see this warning screen appear in the Viewer and Canvas.

Making the edit points match

As before, with shot *1G*, we will now highlight the clips, including the remaining portion of shot *1H*, to the right of the gap, and drag them left to close that gap. There should be no more open spaces in your Timeline, as we can see in Figure 8.49. However, a portion of the third copy of the ambient audio is now longer than the picture. Using the Razor Blade and the *delete* key, cut away the part that sticks out, as shown in Figure 8.50.

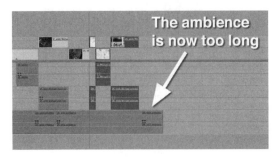

The ambience is now too long

FIGURE 8.49 After the cuts we have made, the ambience is now longer than the picture.

FIGURE 8.50 We cut off the end of the ambience to match the length of our sequence.

Once you are done with this exercise, you may want to turn linking *back on, so that you won't accidentally separate your picture and sound.*

!
TIP

Now watch the sequence. We have made, from shot *1G* to shot *1H*, a rough kind of *match cut*. We can see the clippers grasp a stem and then, in the next shot, we see the clippers cut the stem. The action should flow smoothly from one shot to the next.

There is still a little problem left. If you turn up the volume on your computer high enough, you will notice major differences in the quality of the sound between the various tracks of audio in the scene we just cut. The next thing we're going to do is fix that issue to help make the audio transitions a little smoother. We'll need a few more tools to do this.

Editing, Part IV – Clip Overlays and Keyframes

Take a look at the bottom left of the Timeline and find the *Toggle Clip Overlays* button (discussed in Chapter 7), which looks like a mountain followed by a valley, as shown in Figure 8.51. If the button is a light grey, then it is off; if it is a darker grey, as shown in Figure 8.52, then it is on. Click the button on, and you will see horizontal lines appear in each clip on the Timeline: red for audio, as shown in Figure 8.53, and black for video. What these lines allow you to do is to raise or lower audio levels and raise or lower the opacity of a video clip.

FIGURE 8.51 The *Toggle Clip Overlays* button, turned off.

FIGURE 8.52 The *Toggle Clip Overlays* button, turned on.

| 1F. wide Michael clips tree | 1F. wide Michael clips tree |
| 1F. wide Michael clips tree | 1F. wide Michael clips tree |

FIGURE 8.53 Audio overlays visible in clip *1F. wide Michael clips tree.*

Video overlays

For video overlays, if you were to place one video clip on top of another one and lower the opacity of the clip above, you would get a ghostly double-exposure effect. At 100% opacity, we see only the clip on top. At 50%, we see that top clip at half intensity and the clip underneath at half intensity. If there is no video clip underneath, then all we're doing is making that one clip less and less intense, until it disappears entirely. We will work with this kind of effect in future chapters.

Audio overlays

We're going to need another tool, however, in order to modify audio levels with a certain amount of precision. If, with the Selection Tool selected, you bring your cursor to the red line in any piece of audio, you can raise or lower the audio levels of that clip by clicking and dragging the red line up or down. If the line is below the middle point of the clip, as shown in Figure 8.54, then the audio level is lower than its original setting. That can be very important if you have recorded sound at too high a level and that level is too high throughout the track. But that's not what we want to do right now. We want to be able to do more than just raise or lower the level of the entire track. We're going to make some fades up and fades down using something called the *Pen Tool*.

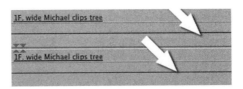

FIGURE 8.54 The audio level in clip *1F. wide Michael clips tree* has been lowered from its original setting.

The Pen Tool and keyframes

You can find the *Pen Tool* on the toolbar to the right of the Timeline. It looks like an old-fashioned fountain pen head, as shown in Figure 8.55. The keyboard shortcut for this tool is the *P* key. Once you have selected this tool, whether by clicking on it or pressing the *P* key, your cursor in the Timeline will look just like the tool in the Toolbar.

FIGURE 8.55 The *Pen Tool* in the toolbar.

With the Pen Tool activated, go to the first audio clip, at the start of the Timeline. About a second after the start, click on the red clip overlay line. A red diamond-shaped dot, called a *keyframe*, should appear, as shown in Figure 8.56. Now, go to the very start of the clip, click to create a keyframe there, and drag that keyframe down, pulling the line of the audio clip overlay down with it, as shown in Figure 8.57. The line should now have a curved arc to it, moving up from the start of the clip. You have created a fade up.

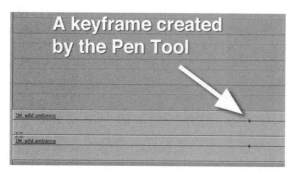

FIGURE 8.56 A *keyframe*, as created by the Pen Tool, in the audio track of your clip.

The following figure shows another keyframe pulled down to create a fade up.

FIGURE 8.57 Another keyframe set in the same audio track, at the start, pulled down to create a fade up.

Do the same with the video track above the audio. But first drag your playhead to the spot where the second dot (the end of the curve) is located on the audio track. If snapping is on, the playhead will automatically click to this point. Now repeat what we just did for the audio, but do it on the video track. Remember that the video clip overlay line is black; instead of a default position in the middle, it resides at the top of the clip. The result will not be a curved line, but a straight diagonal, as shown in Figure 8.58. You have made a video fade up to match the audio fade up.

FIGURE 8.58 Using the Pen Tool, we have set two keyframes in the video clip to create a fade up there as well.

Play the movie from the beginning, and you will see how it looks and sounds. The picture fades up from black, and the sound fades up from silence. Now undo what we just did, until all of the keyframe marks and fades disappear, and also turn off the toggle clip overlays button. We're going to create fades in a different way.

Editing, Part V – Fades and Dissolves

Final Cut Express has a number of built-in effects that you can use. Doing what we just did takes time, but we did it so you could develop some initial familiarity with the Pen Tool and with keyframes. Both functions are very useful to know, and we will work with them more in Chapter 9.

Let's go up to the Browser, and click on the Effects tab, shown in Figure 8.59. First, open the bin marked *Video Transitions*, as shown in Figure 8.60. Remember that to open a bin, you click on the little triangle to the left of it. Within the *Video Transitions* bin, open the bin marked *Dissolve*, as shown in Figure 8.61. Right now we are interested in the *Cross Dissolve* and the *Fade In Fade Out Dissolve*. All transitions are applied in the same way, so once we learn how to use one, it's easy to use the others. The *Cross Dissolve* is used to create dissolves between shots. These are overlaps between shots, where one shot slowly – or quickly – turns into the next shot. The *Fade In Fade Out Dissolve* is for fading up from, or down to, black.

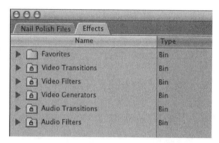

FIGURE 8.59 The *Effects* tab in the Browser.

The following figure shows the Video Transitions bin.

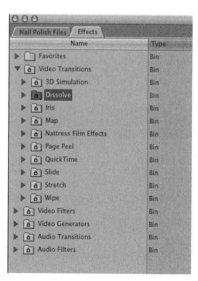

FIGURE 8.60 The *Video Transitions* bin under the Effects tab.

The following figure shows the two keyframes we set using the Pen Tool.

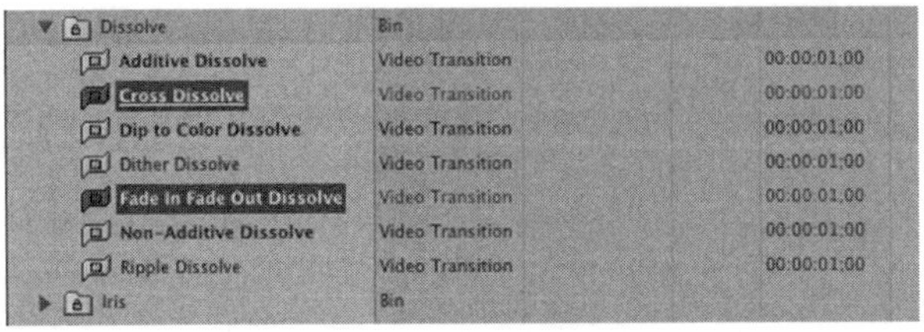

	Dissolve	Bin	
	Additive Dissolve	Video Transition	00:00:01;00
	Cross Dissolve	Video Transition	00:00:01;00
	Dip to Color Dissolve	Video Transition	00:00:01;00
	Dither Dissolve	Video Transition	00:00:01;00
	Fade In Fade Out Dissolve	Video Transition	00:00:01;00
	Non-Additive Dissolve	Video Transition	00:00:01;00
	Ripple Dissolve	Video Transition	00:00:01;00
	Iris	Bin	

FIGURE 8.61 Using the Pen Tool, we have set two keyframes in the video clip to create a fade up there as well.

Click on the *Fade In Fade Out Dissolve* effect and drag it down to the Timeline, to the very start of the first clip. Drop it on top of the clip. If you try and place it anywhere but at the head or tail of the shot, FCE won't let you. When you are done, the effect should sit snugly on top of the start of the clip, as shown in Figure 8.62.

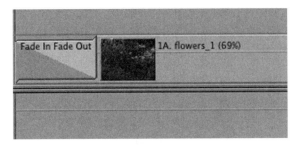

FIGURE 8.62 The *Fade In Fade Out Dissolve* effect on top of the head of the video clip.

Now let's add an audio fade to match the video fade. Back under the Effects tab, go ahead and close the *Video Transitions* bin, then open up the *Audio Transitions* bin, as shown in Figure 8.63. You'll notice that there are two of them: *Cross Fade (0db)* and *Cross Fade (+3db)*. The former creates a slight dip in the audio levels between the two shots, while the latter boosts the level at the transition, to avoid that dip. Depending on what kind of transition you are trying to create, you may or may not want a slight dip. At the head of a clip, it doesn't matter, so let's take the *Cross Fade (0db)* transition for now. Do as you did with the video fade – click and drag it down and drop it at the head of the audio clip, as shown in Figure 8.64.

FIGURE 8.63 The *Audio Transitions* bin under the Effects tab.

The following figure shows the audio effect on top of the head of the audio clip.

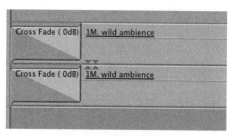

FIGURE 8.64 The *Cross Fade (0db)* audio effect on top of the head of the audio clip, to match the fade on the video clip.

db *stands for* decibels, *the unit of measurement for sound intensity.*

NOTE

Notice how both fades are the same length. That's because the default length of these transitions is 1 second. You can lengthen or shorten the transition by grabbing the edge of it and dragging left or right. Here, we cannot drag left, as the left side is the start of the Timeline, but we could drag right. Try it. You can make the fades as long or as short as want.

Let's now apply fades and dissolves throughout the sequence, where appropriate. Try adding them at the head and tail of each audio clip, and between audio clips that intersect, like the ambience tracks. The only really appropriate place to add another video fade would be at the very end of the last shot. When you are done, you should have a scene where the first shot fades up from black and the last shot fades down to black, and where those abrupt audio blips we mentioned earlier have disappeared, as shown in Figure 8.65.

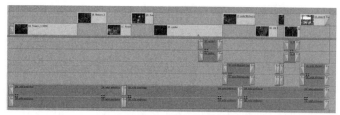

FIGURE 8.65 A version of what your sequence should look like after you have applied fades and dissolves throughout.

If you have edited films before, all this might seem pretty basic. You need to walk yourself through these steps, however, in order to understand the application well enough to do more advanced editing.

Editing, Part VI – Rendering Effects

Because of the video fades at the beginning and end of the sequence, and also because of the speed adjustment we made to that first clip, we have to render a few items. Go up to the *Sequence* dropdown menu and scroll down to the first *Render All* menu item, as shown in Figure 8.66. In that submenu, notice that not all types of rendering are checked, as shown in Figure 8.67, and we have some green-colored items in the Timeline, which won't be rendered unless the green line is checked here. You could either just check the items that match that color, or check all of them, as shown in Figure 8.68, to be safe. Unfortunately, after you check each item, the menu closes, and you have to reopen it to check the next one, but the program will remember your most recent render settings and you will only have to set them once.

FIGURE 8.66 The *Render All* item under the *Sequence* dropdown menu.

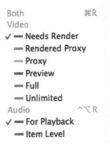

FIGURE 8.67 Not all render lines are checked when you first access the *Render All* menu item.

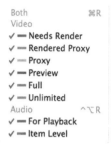

FIGURE 8.68 Once you check the render lines, FCE will keep them checked until you change them again.

When you are done checking render lines, you can then select the top *Both* line in that same submenu, or you can press the *command* key and the *R* key. As soon as you do that, FCE will render your effects, and the colored lines in your sequence will become an almost indistinct blue, as shown in Figure 8.69. For what we needed, the program only had to render video files – the audio fades and dissolves were simple adjustments that FCE could handle without creating any new audio render files.

FIGURE 8.69 When effects are rendered, the line above the effect in the Timeline turns blue.

Now watch the sequence again. What do you think? You have just cut a scene together by working with Timeline tools, rather than with the Viewer, and done some basic effects work and sound design.

In the next chapter, we will explore more tools and effects in greater detail. Don't delete this project, however, since the first thing we are going to do in Chapter 9 is make titles for it.

SUMMARY

In this chapter, you moved beyond the basic interface of FCE and cut a sequence together using some of the tools available in the Tool Palette, including the *Razor Blade* tool. Continuing to use the *Nail Polish* clips, we worked primarily in the Timeline this time, rather than in the Viewer.

As we re-cut the first scene of *Nail Polish*, we practiced a *match cut*, one of the foundational techniques of continuity editing. This proved to be an excellent way to solidify our understanding of how the *Razor Blade* tool works. We also discovered how easy it is to click and move clips around in the Timeline, or to extend and shorten them by clicking and dragging their end points.

We also learned some basic effects, such as speed control. We explored how to manage audio levels and video opacity using keyframes. We discovered that we could create fades up and down with these keyframes by using clip overlays and the *Pen* tool.

From the *Pen* tool, we moved on to the built-in fades and dissolves that come with FCE. We learned how to apply these effects to our clips, and then we learned how to render them. We are now ready to learn some more advanced effects and editing techniques in the next chapter.

REVIEW QUESTIONS: CHAPTER 8

1. What does *rendering* mean?

2. What do clip overlays allow you to do?

3. What are the tools on the Tool Palette that you have used so far?

4. How can you create audio and video fades and dissolves?

5. What is a *keyframe*?

1. So far, we have learned two ways to shorten clips – using the Viewer and *In* and *Out* points and using the *Razor Blade* tool in the Timeline. Which do you prefer, and why?

2. When is it wise to leave snapping off, and when is it wise to leave it on?

3. What are some potential pitfalls to leaving the clip overlays turned on when you don't need them?

4. What are some potential pitfalls to leaving the linking function turned off?

Further Research

Delete the wild ambience clips that we copied and pasted into the Timeline. Drag a fresh wild ambience down to the timeline, delete the video portion of it, and try figuring out how to slow it down enough so that it fills the entirety of the scene, so that we don't need to have three separate clips. If you succeed in doing that, watch the scene again with this new ambience. Don't forget to apply dissolves at the head and the tail of the clip. Does the audio sound strange to you, or does it work? Can you hear the fact that is slowed down? Try it!

CHAPTER 9

EFFECTS AND ADVANCED EDITING TECHNIQUES

OVERVIEW AND LEARNING OBJECTIVES

In this chapter, you will:

- Review the dropdown menus in FCE
- Learn how to customize the Browser and Timeline windows
- Discover alternate ways to perform insert and overwrite edits
- Explore the full range of filters and tools available in FCE for media manipulation
- Work with wireframes and keyframes
- Create basic text titles

Dropdown Menus – A Quick Overview

As with most computer applications, FCE comes with a variety of dropdown menus to help you easily find the commands you need. Most of these commands come with keyboard shortcuts, and you should familiarize yourself with what each dropdown menu has to offer, so that you know where to look when you need a specific tool.

Let's take a moment to briefly look at each menu. You should also explore each menu's full functionality on your own.

At times, some of the dropdown menu options will appear in a light grey text, rather than in black bold. This means that that particular function is unavailable at that time. This might be because:

1. *You were not clicked in the right window of the program before you selected this menu.*

2. *You have not performed an action that is a prerequisite to the unhighlighted action (e.g., before you can paste, you have to first copy).*

3. *You have not highlighted any particular piece of media (by clicking it once), so that the menu has nothing on which to perform the action.*

FCE dropdown menu

Among other things, this menu allows you to set your scratch disks (through the *System Settings* – see Chapter 7) and preferences, such as how many levels of undo you want (through the *User Preferences* – see Chapter 7). You can also use *Easy Setup* to set the video format of your project. We will learn more about video formats in the next chapter. The FCE dropdown menu is shown in Figure 9.1.

FIGURE 9.1 The *FCE* dropdown menu.

 All figures appear in color on the companion DVD.

File dropdown menu

This menu allows you to create new bins, new sequences, and even new projects. You can save a copy of your existing project with a different name (using *Save Project As ...*). You can also save your current project using this menu. You can also restore a project from the *Autosave Vault* (which is automatically created inside your scratch disks). Although we will cover video capturing – whether from tape or from flash memory – in the next chapter, note that this is the menu through which you set up the capture of your footage. Finally, beyond capturing video from your camera, you can also *Import* footage or files that are already on your computer or hard drive, and *Export* your finished movie. The File dropdown menu is shown in Figure 9.2.

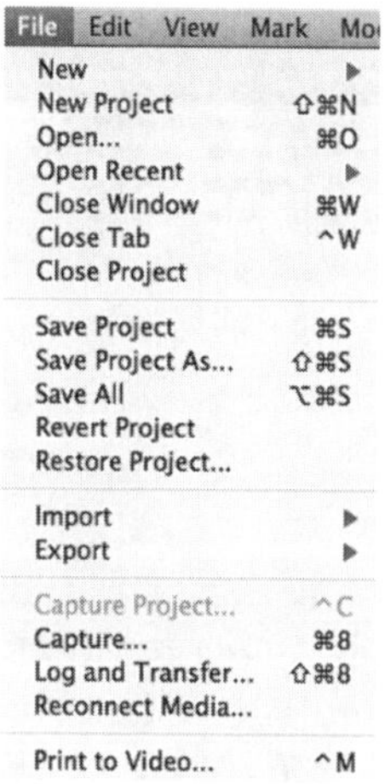

FIGURE 9.2 The *File* dropdown menu.

Many people forget to save as often as they should. If the program or the computer crashes, and you haven't saved, you could lose your work. The Restore Project *function is useful, but it's a good idea to train yourself to press the* command *key and the S key, which is the keyboard shortcut for* Save Project. *If you do it often enough, you'll even forget that you're doing it, and be thankful – if the program does crash – to discover that you saved just a few seconds before.*

Edit dropdown menu

This menu allows you to perform the *Undo* and/or *Redo* function. You can also cut, copy, paste, etc., any and all media in your project. You can also *Link* and/or *Unlink* your audio and video in the Timeline. This is the same as clicking the green infinity symbol on the upper right of the Timeline itself (see Chapters 7 and 8). The Edit dropdown menu is shown in Figure 9.3.

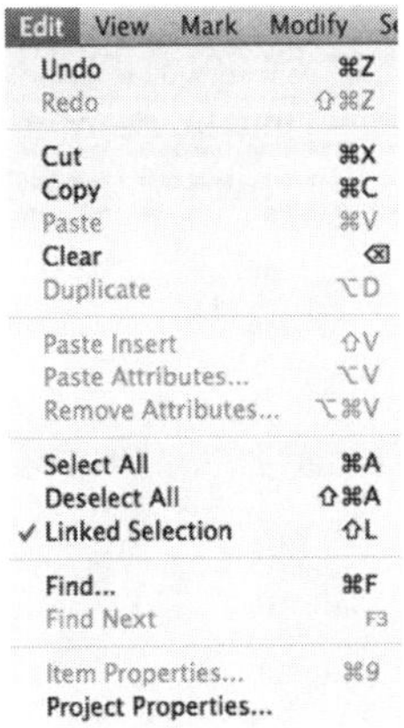

FIGURE 9.3 The *Edit* dropdown menu.

View dropdown menu

This menu allows you to do many things that you can also do from within the Browser, Viewer, Canvas, and Timeline windows. We will learn how to use many of these tools in this and later chapters. Final Cut Express provides multiple ways to do the same thing, so you can find the way that works best for you for each tool. In this menu, you can also choose *Loop Playback*, which means that a given clip or sequence will play start to finish, and then start again at the beginning once done. You can likewise turn *Audio Scrubbing* on and off here. This allows you to hear (or not hear) the audio of a given clip or sequence as you drag the playhead through it. The View dropdown menu is shown in Figure 9.4.

Mark dropdown menu

As we learned in the last chapter, setting *Markers* can be very useful. So can setting *In* and *Out* points. This menu gives you other ways to perform

FIGURE 9.4 The *View* dropdown menu.

these same actions. If you have a large, unbroken piece of video, comprised of many different shots, captured from a tape, the *DV Start/Stop Detect* function in this menu will allow you to break up that long bit of video. The program will automatically detect the breaks and separate the video into its separate shots. The Mark dropdown menu is shown in Figure 9.5.

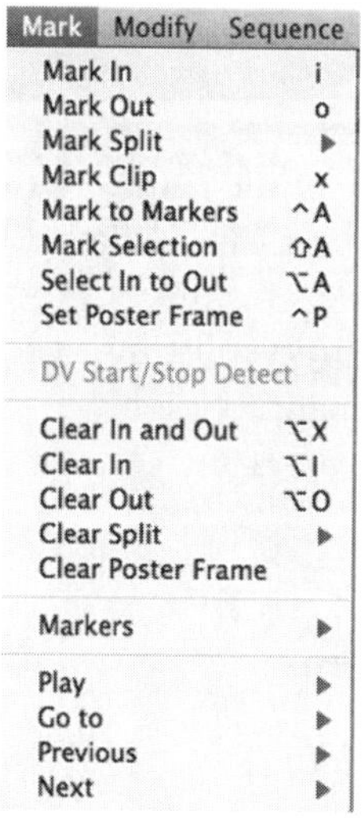

FIGURE 9.5 The *Mark* dropdown menu.

Modify dropdown menu

This menu has several important options. You can create a *subclip* from a longer clip (more on this later in the chapter). You can also make an *independent clip* from a *Master clip*. This means that you can copy video clips from the Browser and then tell FCE to treat them as brand new clips, rather than copies. You can then change the names of the clips. If you remember, in Chapter 8 we couldn't change the name of a part of a clip, or a copy of a clip, without all versions of the clip adopting that new name. All clips captured or imported into the Browser are considered, by default, *Master clips*. If you highlight a clip in the Browser before clicking on this menu, the line *Make Independent Clip* will change to *Duplicate as New Master Clip*. Go ahead and try it.

FIGURE 9.6 The *Modify* dropdown menu.

You can also *Link* or *Unlink* audio and video clips through this menu. If you *Unlink* them this way, then the audio and video tracks will always be separate, even when that green infinity symbol is clicked on the Timeline. Other things you can do include splitting two tracks of audio into a *Stereo Pair*, changing the speed of a clip (which we did in Chapter 8), and making a *Freeze Frame* – or still image – from a clip of video. The Modify dropdown menu is shown in Figure 9.6.

Sequence dropdown menu

This menu allows you to tweak the settings of a sequence as well as render any effects you have created (we covered what *rendering* means in Chapter 8). We will discuss the *Lift* and *Ripple Delete* functions later in this chapter. This Sequence dropdown menu is shown in Figure 9.7.

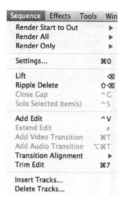

FIGURE 9.7 The *Sequence* dropdown menu.

Effects dropdown menu

This menu offers you the same functions that you find under the *Effects* tab of the Browser. We will discuss that tab shortly. Again, in FCE you are offered multiple ways to do the same thing. The Effects dropdown menu is shown in Figure 9.8.

FIGURE 9.8 The *Effects* dropdown menu.

Tools dropdown menu

This menu allows you to use the *Voiceover* tool when you want to record audio directly into the Timeline (provided you have a microphone built in or attached to the computer). This can be useful for ADR (Automated Dialog Replacement) or voiceover narration. You can also use the *Button List* function to add more menu buttons (in addition to the *Snapping* and *Linking* buttons) to the top-right corner of the Timeline and other windows. We will discuss how to add buttons later in this chapter. The Tools dropdown menu is shown in Figure 9.9.

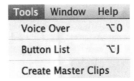

FIGURE 9.9 The *Tools* dropdown menu.

Window dropdown menu

This menu is used to change the arrangement of the various windows – the Browser, the Viewer, etc. – in FCE. You can either manually move and resize the windows, or you can change the configuration using some of the defaults under the *Arrange* function. If a window has a check mark next to it in this menu, then it is visible. At the bottom of this menu, you have a list of what files are currently open in each window. This Window dropdown menu is shown in Figure 9.10.

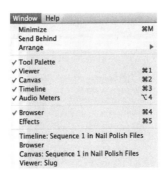

FIGURE 9.10 The *Window* dropdown menu.

Help dropdown menu

This is the usual Help menu that you find in all applications in the Mac OSX. The best part of this menu is that you can open up the *FCE User Manual* just by clicking on the top link. Use this link to search the manual for answers. The Help dropdown menu is shown in Figure 9.11.

Now that we've covered the 11 dropdown menus in FCE we will start to learn some more advanced ways of interacting with the program's interface. Let's look at the Browser first.

FIGURE 9.11 The *Help* dropdown menu.

Customizing Your Browser

There are several ways to customize the Browser and change its configuration. We have been working with our clips in *List View*. This option, as shown in Figure 9.12, allows you to see your clips as tiny icons with the text description almost the same size as the icon. This layout offers you the ability to see many clips at once, but some people prefer to see larger icons instead.

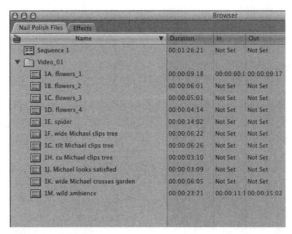

FIGURE 9.12 The Browser in *List View*.

To change your Browser viewing options, press the *control* key and click with your mouse (hereafter referred to as *control-click*) anywhere in the Browser (but not on an actual video clip). If you have a mouse with multiple buttons, you could also *right-click* instead. After you do so, a pop-up menu will appear, as shown in Figure 9.13, which allows you to perform a number of actions, including switching to different icon views. Scroll down to *View as Large Icons* and select that option.

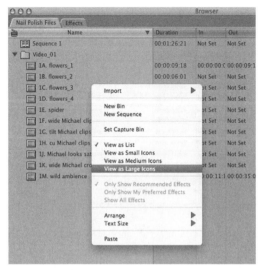

FIGURE 9.13 *The Icon pop-up menu* in the Browser.

Now you can see the largest of the icon views, as shown in Figure 9.14. Notice that the bin (Video_01) that was open in the previous view is now closed. Go ahead and double-click on it, and the bin will open as a new window, as shown in Figure 9.15, with each clip represented as a large icon of the shot. One of the advantages of this view option is that the clip icons are thumbnail images of the content of each shot.

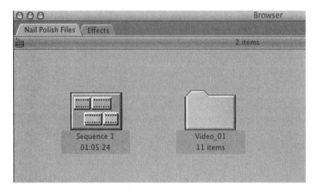

FIGURE 9.14 The Browser with *View as Large Icons* selected.

The following figure shows the open bin with the large icons.

There are three small buttons in the upper left of the open bin window. When you want to close the bin, you'll have to click on the first of the three

FIGURE 9.15 The open Video_01 bin with *View as Large Icons* selected.

buttons. Pressing the *control* key and the W key will also close the window. Make sure you don't press the *command* key, instead, or you will close the Project. The middle button minimizes the window, storing it in the Mac OSX dock, and the right-most button resizes the window to fit the vertical length of your computer's monitor. Go ahead and try those buttons now. You've got nothing to lose. When you are done, close the bin.

You can also change the size of the text description of each clip. If you like the text in the Browser to look really big, you can do that. That same pop-up menu we just used to change the icon size allows you to change the text size as well (so does the *View* dropdown menu). This time, scroll down to *Text Size* and choose *small*, *medium*, or *large*. The large text, together with the large icon, makes it easy to see the details of a clip, sequence, or bin, as shown in Figure 9.16. However, those options also create a very crowded Browser. In this book, we will use the *List View* and the *Small* text options.

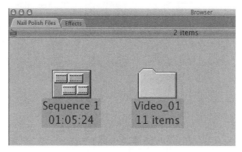

FIGURE 9.16 The large text option and the large icon option, combined.

In the upper-right corner of the Browser there are some preconfigured buttons, as shown in Figure 9.17. Hover over them to see what options they offer. You will discover that these buttons give you another way to do the same types of things we have just done, such as changing the icon and text sizes. Soon, we will learn how to customize these kinds of button groupings in all of the windows.

FIGURE 9.17 The button tool options in the Browser.

Insert vs. Overwrite Edits

In the last chapter, we spent some time putting together a sequence of shots by dragging clips directly to the Timeline from the Browser. Now we will look at different ways of doing the same thing.

Before we start, let's remind ourselves of what our sequence looked like at the end of Chapter 8. We cut the first scene of the movie *Nail Polish*, as shown in Figure 9.18. Open your own comparable sequence now, and make sure that the playhead is at the beginning.

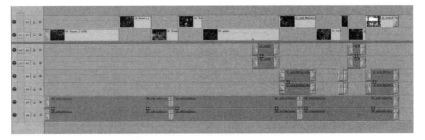

FIGURE 9.18 Scene 1 of *Nail Polish*, in the sequence we cut in Chapter 8.

Look at the left side of the *Sequence* window. To the left of each track are *Video* and *Audio Source & Destination* buttons, as shown in Figure 9.19. These buttons are labeled as *v1*, *a1*, and *a2* (note the lowercase letters), while the tracks themselves are labeled as *V1*, *A1*, and *A2* (note the upper-case letters). Also notice how these buttons are positioned.

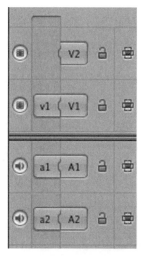

FIGURE 9.19 The left side of the sequence, where the *Video* and *Audio Source & Destination* buttons reside.

If you click on any of the buttons, it detaches itself from the track, as shown in Figure 9.20. If you drag them up or down, you can then attach them to different tracks. What these buttons do is tell FCE what the default destination tracks are when you drag items down to the Timeline, or when you use the tools we are about to use. For now, let's keep them where they are.

Now that we understand the concept of destination tracks, let's choose a clip from the *Video_01* bin in our Browser. Let's use *1J. Michael looks satisfied*, as we have done in Figure 9.21. Click on it and drag it over to the Canvas window.

FIGURE 9.20 Two *Video* and *Audio Source & Destination* buttons detached from their tracks.

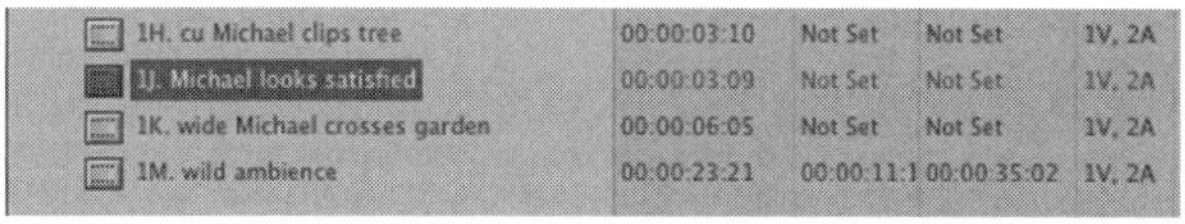

1H. cu Michael clips tree 00:00:03:10 Not Set Not Set 1V, 2A
1J. Michael looks satisfied 00:00:03:09 Not Set Not Set 1V, 2A
1K. wide Michael crosses garden 00:00:06:05 Not Set Not Set 1V, 2A
1M. wild ambience 00:00:23:21 00:00:11:1 00:00:35:02 1V, 2A

FIGURE 9.21 The clip *1J. Michael looks satisfied*, highlighted, and ready to be dragged to the Canvas.

Insert edits

When you drag the clip over to the Canvas, you will see a group of seven multi-colored buttons pop up. Drag the clip onto the *Insert* button, as shown in Figure 9.22, and release. Now look down at the Timeline. The *Insert* function has placed the clip where the playhead was and shoved every other clip over to the right, as shown in Figure 9.23. If the playhead had been in

Sequence 1
00:01:05:23
00:00:00:00
Insert
1J. Michael looks satisfied
with Transition
Overwrite

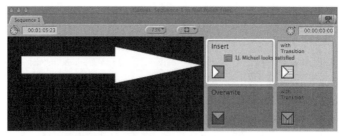

FIGURE 9.22 The *Insert/Overwrite Menu* in the Canvas.

V2
v1 V1
1A. flowers_1 (69%)
a1 A1
1J. Michael loo
a2 A2
A3
A4
A5
A6
1M. wild ambience
1M. wild ambience

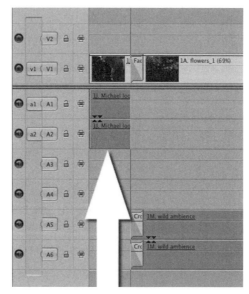

FIGURE 9.23 The clip *1J. Michael looks satisfied*, inserted at the head of the Timeline.

the middle of a clip, FCE would have broken that clip in two and inserted this clip in the middle. That's what *Insert* does. It's the same as dragging a clip down to the Timeline and dropping the clip when the cursor is in the top third of the track (and looks like an arrow pointing right) rather than an arrow pointing down (which you remember from Chapter 7).

The following figure shows our clip inserted at the head of the Timeline.

Undo (*command* key + Z key) what we just did. Now take the same clip we just used and drag it to the *Insert with Transition* button, as shown in Figure 9.24. Again, look down at the Timeline to see what it looks like. It's the same as before, but with a dissolve at the head of the shot, as shown in Figure 9.25. As we did after the last action, undo this action.

The following figure shows our clip inserted with a dissolve at its head.

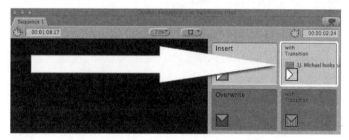

FIGURE 9.24 The *Insert with Transition* option is now highlighted in the Canvas.

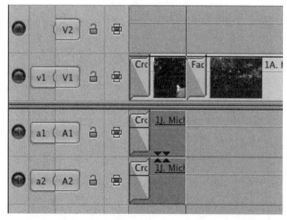

FIGURE 9.25 The clip *1J. Michael looks satisfied* has been inserted with a dissolve at its head.

Overwrite edits

Now drag the same clip to the Canvas, but drop it on the *Overwrite* button, as shown in Figure 9.26. If you look down at the Timeline, you'll notice that something new has happened. Instead of shoving all of the clips over, FCE has placed this clip on top of the clip that was there, as shown in Figure 9.27. This is the same as if you had dragged a clip down from the Browser to the Timeline, but dropped it in the sequence while hovering in the bottom two-thirds of the track, with the arrow icon pointing down (again, see Chapter 7). Don't forget to undo before you move to the next action.

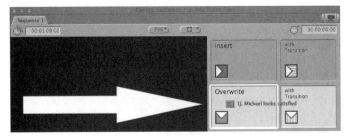

FIGURE 9.26 The *Overwrite* option is now highlighted in the Canvas.

The following figure shows that our *1J. Michael looks satisfied* clip has overwritten the clip that was at the head of the Timeline.

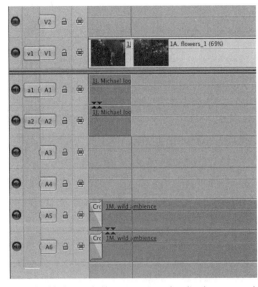

FIGURE 9.27 The clip *1J. Michael looks satisfied* has *overwritten* the clip that was at the head of the Timeline.

We will skip the *Overwrite with Transition* button, as you can try it on your own. It does what we just did, but with a dissolve at the head of the clip. Instead, we'll move on to a different tool, *Replace*.

Replace edits

The *Replace* button allows you to replace a clip in your Timeline with another clip, matching the length of the clip already in the Timeline, and keeping any effects or transitions that may be on that original clip. This is actually an extremely convenient tool if, for example, you have been shooting multiple angles of the same activity (as you so often should), or if you want to replace a medium shot with a close-up, or some such similar action. In that case, you want the shot with which you are replacing your current shot to have the same properties, including length, effects, and transitions. It's just a different angle or shot size.

In order for this tool to work, however, the shot you drag down to the Timeline has to be at least as long as the shot you are replacing. You cannot replace a 10-second shot with a 2-second shot, in other words (at least not while using *this* tool). To further complicate matters, FCE will consider the length of the replacement shot from the point where the playhead, within that shot, last stopped.

Let's say you have a 5-second shot in your sequence and you wish to replace it with a different angle. So you find a shot in the Browser and double-click it so you can watch it in the Viewer and make sure it offers you what you want. If it's a 15-second shot, then it will work. However, you watch it to the 11-second mark and leave the playhead there. When you then try to drag the shot to the *Replace* button, you'll see an error message telling you that there is *Insufficient Content for Edit*. That's because FCE, at that point, considers the shot only 4 seconds long. Move the playhead back, and it will accept the edit.

To perform the action as it should be performed, let's choose a different clip than the one we were using before. Let's use *1E. spider*, as shown in Figure 9.28. Double-click it and, in the Viewer, make sure the playhead is at the head of the shot, just to be safe. Now let's place the playhead, in the Timeline, at the start of the final shot of the sequence, which is, in this case, *1K. wide Michael crosses garden*, as shown in Figure 9.29. We are going to have to remove the audio transition, shown in Figure 9.30, that we placed (in Chapter 8) at the head of this shot, because this tool doesn't like to perform its function with such a transition at the head. To delete the fade, just click on the transition and press delete. It disappears, as shown in Figure 9.31.

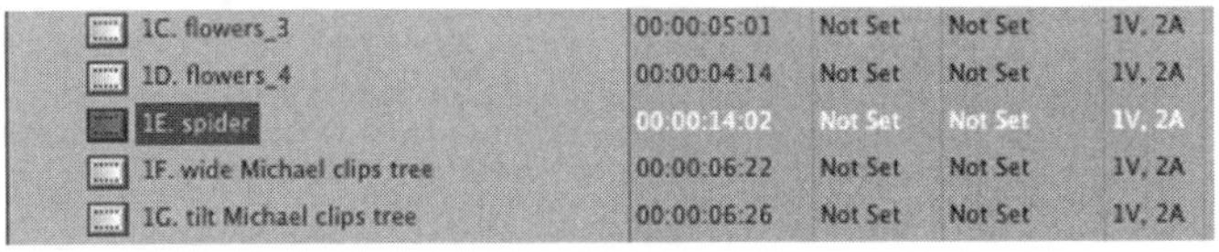

▦	1C. flowers_3	00:00:05:01	Not Set	Not Set	1V, 2A
▦	1D. flowers_4	00:00:04:14	Not Set	Not Set	1V, 2A
▦	1E. spider	00:00:14:02	Not Set	Not Set	1V, 2A
▦	1F. wide Michael clips tree	00:00:06:22	Not Set	Not Set	1V, 2A
▦	1G. tilt Michael clips tree	00:00:06:26	Not Set	Not Set	1V, 2A

FIGURE 9.28 Select shot *1E. spider*.

FIGURE 9.29 Place the playhead at the head of the final shot in the sequence.

The following two figures show how to remove the audio fade at the head of the shot *1K. wide Michael crosses garden*.

FIGURE 9.30 We have to remove the audio fade at the head of *1K. wide Michael crosses garden*.

Notice how the clip we are about to replace is on the second video track (*V2*) and third and fourth audio tracks (*A3* & *A4*). That means that we will first have to move the *Video* and *Audio Source & Destination* buttons from their

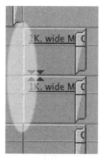

FIGURE 9.31 We can remove the audio fade at the head of *1K. wide Michael crosses garden* by selecting the fade and pressing delete.

default positions. Let's do that now. Click on the *v1* button to separate it from the *V1* track, and then drag it to the *V2* track. Do the same thing with the *a1* and *a2* buttons and drag them to the *A3* and *A4* tracks. When you are done, you will have successfully repositioned the buttons, as shown in Figure 9.32, thereby designated new tracks as the default destinations.

Now, grab the *1E. spider* shot and drag it to the *Replace* button, as shown in Figure 9.33. Look down at the Timeline. The final shot has been replaced with the new clip, as shown in Figure 9.34. What we just did doesn't make sense, artistically, but it helped us learn how to use a new tool. Let's undo however many times it takes us to get back to the way the Timeline looked before we started this last exercise. When you undo, however, it doesn't reset the *Source* & *Destination* buttons. They will remain in the last position to which you dragged them. In this case that's acceptable because our next exercise involves the same final clip, on tracks *V2*, *A3*, and *A4*.

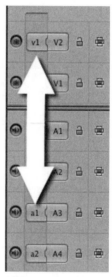

FIGURE 9.32 After you have moved the *Video* and *Audio Source* & *Destination* buttons, they should appear next to tracks *V2*, *A3*, and *A4*.

FIGURE 9.33 Drag shot *1E. spider* to the *Replace* button in the Canvas.

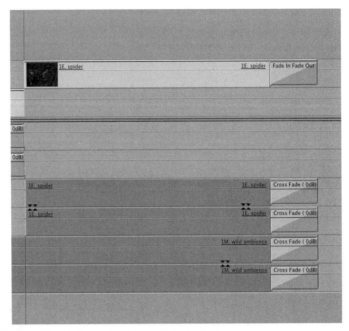

FIGURE 9.34 Shot *1E. spider* has *replaced* shot *1K. wide Michael crosses garden.*

Notice that when we had the playhead at the head of the Timeline the Canvas window appeared black, as shown in Figures 9.22, 9.24, and 9.26. When we placed the playhead later in the sequence, the Canvas showed a frame from a particular shot, as shown in Figure 9.33. That's because the Canvas always shows you the exact frame on which the playhead is stopped in the Timeline.

Fit to fill edits

Now we will use the *Fit to Fill* button. It allows you to drag a clip, of any length, to replace a clip – or many clips – of any length, in the Timeline. This process is also referred to as *three-point editing*. You'll need at least one *In* and one *Out* point, either on the clip you are moving or the sequence you are moving it to, and then either another *In* or another *Out* point, on either the clip or the sequence.

To begin, let's focus once more on that last clip in our sequence, *1K. wide Michael crosses garden*. In the Timeline, set an *In* and *Out* point at either end of the clip. You do this the same way you would set an *In* and *Out* point in the Viewer. Place the playhead at the head of the clip and press the *I* key. Then place the playhead at the end of the clip and press the *O* key. The result will highlight whatever is inside the *In* and *Out* points, as shown in Figure 9.35.

Let's use the same *1E. spider* clip as before. When using this tool, it doesn't matter where the playhead is located. As far as *three-point editing* is concerned, if you do not set either an *In* or an *Out* point in this clip, then, by default, FCE will consider the beginning of the clip as the *In* point. But you could also set an *In* (or an *Out*) point that would shorten this clip, before you drag it.

Now drag the clip to the *Fit to Fill* button, as shown in Figure 9.36. Once dropped, the clip should replace the clip that was inside the *In* and *Out* points in the Timeline, which have now disappeared, as shown in Figure 9.37. Interestingly, since the *1E. spider* clip was longer than the clip it was replacing, it has been sped up, in order to *fit to fill* (hence the name of this tool). It is now running at 226% of its original speed. Play it. The sound has a much higher pitch now, and the spider runs much faster. If the shot had been shorter, then it would have been stretched to *fit to fill* and would have played at a rate of less than 100%. The difference between *Replace* and *Fit to Fill*, then, is that, in the latter case, all of the new clip is placed in the sequence, even if it has to be compressed or stretched to do so. Before moving on, don't forget to undo enough times to return to the same starting point as before.

FIGURE 9.35 Shot *1K. wide Michael crosses garden* with an *In* and an *Out* point in the Timeline.

Superimpositions

There is one more tool in this collection. Make sure the playhead is at the start of the last clip in the Timeline, and then drag the same *1E. spider* clip to the final button, *Superimpose*, as shown in Figure 9.38. This time the clip has been placed in the video and audio tracks (*V3*, *A5*, and *A6*) just above the clip that was there at the playhead, as shown in Figure 9.39. Final Cut Express automatically had to create a new set of video and audio tracks. The new video track (*V3*) houses the video component of our new clip. On the audio side, FCE actually moved the existing audio, from *1M. wild ambience*,

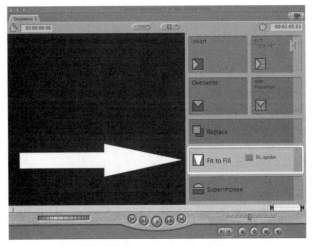

FIGURE 9.36 Drag shot *1E. spider* to the *Fit to Fill* button in the Canvas.

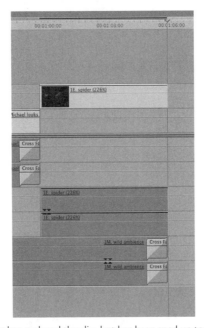

FIGURE 9.37 Shot *1E. spider* has replaced the clip, but has been sped up to do so.

below, onto a set of new audio tracks (*A7* and *A8*), and placed the companion audio to *1E. spider* on tracks *A5* and *A6*. Why? Because FCE, by default, likes to keep linked audio and video paired in this way: *V1* goes with *A1* and *A2*; *V2* goes with *A3* and *A4*; *V3* goes with *A5* and *A6*; and so on.

FIGURE 9.38 Drag shot *1E. spider* to the *Superimpose* button in the Canvas.

FIGURE 9.39 Shot *1E. spider* has been placed on top of *1K. wide Michael crosses garden*, and new tracks have been created to make this possible.

What is this tool used for? If one video clip sits on top of another, we will only see the top clip, after all. But once you have a clip placed over another, then you can adjust the opacity, using the *Clip Overlays*, which we discussed in Chapters 7 and 8. In this way, you can create simple double-exposures and other effects. You could also more easily cut back and forth between two shots if one is above the other using the *Razor Blade* tool to cut away parts of the shot on top.

Don't forget to undo everything we just did. Now that we have examined the many ways to place footage into the Timeline using the Canvas let's take a closer look at the rest of the tools in the *Tool Palette*. (An overview of the Tool Palette and its tools was given in Chapter 8, but we will go into more detail here.)

The Tool Palette, in Detail

Even though we explored some of these tools before, we will now go through each one in the order it appears on the Tool Palette, from top to bottom. We will discuss each tool, how it would appear to you if you hovered over it, and how it would appear to you if you clicked and held on the tool itself. We will also indicate the keyboard shortcut for each tool next to the name of that tool.

Selection tool (*A* key)

As the name implies, this is the tool you use to select items and to click and drag, etc. Its keyboard shortcut is easy to remember: the *A* key (no *command* key needed). As with many tools that allow you to select items in other computer applications, if you hold down the *shift* key, you can select a range of clips from the first area where you clicked to the last area where you click. If you hold down the *command* key, you can select multiple items, regardless of whether they follow in order. The Selection tool is shown in Figure 9.40.

FIGURE 9.40 The *Selection* tool in the Tool Palette.

Edit selection tool (*G* key)

This tool is actually a series of three tools that also includes the *Group Selection tool* (*G* key + *G* key) and the *Range Selection tool* (*G* key + *G* key + *G* key). If you scroll from the first tool to the second or third tool, the little yellow pop-up window tells you the name of each tool. All of these tools, in different ways, allow you to select part or all of a clip. The *Edit Selection* tool allows you to select one edit point per track, as shown in Figure 9.42. If you click and drag across clips with this tool selected, you will see the edit points between clips highlighted. You can then adjust the edit points in the *Trim Edit* window, which we will discuss later in this chapter. The Edit Selection tool is shown in Figure 9.41.

FIGURE 9.41 The *Edit Selection* tool in the Tool Palette.

The following figure shows how you can use the Edit Selection tool to select an edit point.

FIGURE 9.42 Using the *Edit Selection* tool, you can select an edit point.

Like the Selection tool, the *Group Selection* tool allows multiple clips to be selected. Unlike with the Selection tool, however, you can't move any clips with this tool selected (although you can delete them once they are highlighted). Some people prefer to use this tool to select clips, as there is no way to accidentally move a clip with this tool.

The *Range Selection* tool allows you to select just part of a clip, or clips, on a track. You can then delete or move just the section that is selected.

Select track forward tool (*T* key)

This series of five tools includes four others: the *Select track Backward* tool (*T* key + *T* key); the *Select track* tool (*T* key + *T* key + *T* key); the *Select All tracks Forward* tool (*T* key + *T* key + *T* key + *T* key); and the *Select All tracks Backward* tool (*T* key + *T* key + *T* key + *T* key + *T* key). These are great tools, as they allow you to very quickly select all items on a particular track (and any audio or video items associated with those clips on other tracks). The first two tools select items on the track on which you click either forward or backward from your click point. The *Select Track* tool lets you select all items on a particular track, no matter where you click. The final two tool options let you select all items in the sequence, either forward or backward from your click point. The Select Track Forward tool is shown in Figure 9.43.

FIGURE 9.43 The *Select Track Forward* tool in the Tool Palette.

Whenever you select a number of clips simultaneously, you can always deselect just one item by going back to the main *Selection* tool, holding down the *command* key, and clicking on the one item that you wish to deselect.

Roll and Ripple tools (*R* key)

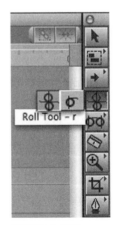

There are two tools available in this grouping; the *Roll* tool (*R* key) and the *Ripple* tool (*R* key + *R* key). Both of these tools can be very useful for fine-tuning edit points. The *Roll* tool (shown in Figure 9.44) converts the Canvas window – as you click and drag across an edit point – into a display for two mini-windows; one for each shot on either side of the edit point, as shown in Figure 9.45. As you drag back and forth over the edit point, each shot extends or shortens as you move, and you can very quickly find a better spot for a potential match cut this way. The *Ripple* tool works in a similar way, except that, depending on which side of the edit point you click and drag, you only affect one clip, rather than both simultaneously.

FIGURE 9.44 The *Roll* tool in the Tool Palette.

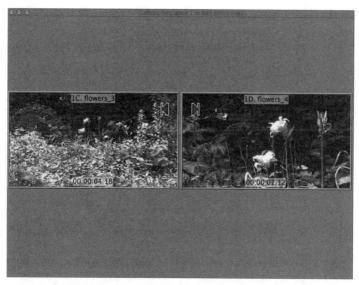

FIGURE 9.45 The *Roll* tool's edit point, as displayed in the Canvas.

If you do not have *handles* of extra footage, beyond what is in the Timeline, then you will only be able to shorten a clip.

KEY TERM:

A **handle** is extra footage that exists within the shot, but is invisible in the Timeline because you have either cut it away, or shortened the master clip using *In* and *Out* points before dragging it to the Timeline.

If you have two clips side by side, and neither of them have such *handles*, or only one of them does, this will complicate the effectiveness of these tools. Finally, if you checkerboarded your footage, as we did when we created this sequence in Chapter 7, then there is no shot side by side with another shot; the shots need to be on the same track in order for you to be able to use *Roll* or *Ripple* between them. If they are not, then you will just be *rolling* or *rippling* between one shot and empty space.

Slip and slide tools (*S* key)

There are two tools available in this grouping: the *Slip* tool (*S* key) and the *Slide* tool (*S* key + *S* key). As with the *Roll* and *Ripple* tools, these two tools let you trim and adjust edit points. The *Slip* tool allows you to keep the clip on which you have clicked at its original length, and in the same position between other clips, but with different parts of the clip displayed. Let's say you have a 10-second clip, which has been trimmed to 2 seconds, and is positioned between two other clips (of whatever length). If you click on that clip with the *Slip* tool and slide back and forth, it will remain at 2 seconds of length, but a different part of the original clip will be displayed. This tool can also be useful when trying to fine-tune match cuts. While you're dragging over the clip, the two-part window in the Canvas appears again, as it did for the *Roll* tool, allowing you to see your work in progress. The Slip tool is shown in Figure 9.46.

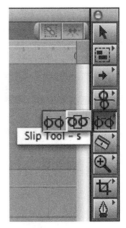

FIGURE 9.46 The *Slip* tool in the Tool Palette.

The *Slide* tool allows you to tweak the clips on either side of the clip on which you have clicked. As you drag back and forth, each clip, on either side, is shortened or lengthened. Again, the two-part window displays your work in the Canvas.

For all of these adjustment tools, however, you should be aware that transitions, of any kind, can get in the way of allowing the clips to lengthen or shorten. Sometimes you might have to remove the transitions before using with these tools. And as with the *Roll* and *Ripple* tools, you will need *handles* of actual footage beyond each edit point. If every clip is being used in its entirety, in the Timeline, then there will be no extra, unshown footage with which to *roll*, *ripple*, *slide*, or *slip*.

Razor blade (*B* key)

We have already used this tool extensively, but we have not used its companion tool, the *Razor Blade All* tool. The keyboard shortcut for this second tool is the *B* key + the *B* key. It is a very useful tool, and it works in the same way as the standard *Razor Blade* tool, except that it cuts all items, up and down, on all tracks, at the point at which you click. The Razor Blade tool is shown in Figure 9.47.

FIGURE 9.47 The *Razor Blade* tool in the Tool Palette.

Zoom and hand tools

This series of four tools includes three others, and for the first time the different tools under one heading do not share the same shortcut key. These tools are the *Zoom In* tool (Z key); the *Zoom Out* tool (Z key + Z key); the *Hand* tool (H key); and the *Scrub* tool (*control* key + II key, or H key + H key).

FIGURE 9.48 The *Zoom In* tool in the Tool Palette.

In Chapters 7 and 8, we used the *command* key and the *plus* key or *minus* key to zoom in or out. Now you have a new tool to do the same thing. The advantage of using the *Zoom* tools is that you can focus the point of the zoom more precisely. With our previous method, the focus of the zoom is wherever the playhead is positioned. With the *Zoom In* tool, wherever you click is the place to which you zoom, and with the *Zoom Out* tool, the same is true, but in reverse. The Zoom In tool is shown in Figure 9.48.

The *Hand* tool does not let you actually do anything to the footage. Instead, it lets you grab the Timeline and scroll right or left. The *Scrub* tool lets you see, in the little preview window that appears on each clip in the Timeline, a quick view into the action within that clip. As you drag right or left over the clip, you can see what footage resides inside.

Crop and distort tools (*C* key and *D* key)

There are two tools under this heading; the *Crop* tool (*C* key) and the *Distort* tool (*D* key, or *C* key + *C* key). Both of these tools are used to change the size or dimensions of a clip by cropping the edges or distorting it in some way. In order to be able to use this tool, you first have to turn on the *wireframe*, which we will discuss later. Then you click once on a clip, in the Timeline, to highlight it, and then make sure the playhead is over it, so you can see it in the Canvas. You would then be able to crop the edges or distort the image by dragging the edges that appear in the wireframe. Once we go over the wireframe, you can try these tools out. You will also be to crop and distort your clips by using the *Motion* tab in the Viewer, which we will also discuss later in this chapter. The Crop tool is shown in Figure 9.49.

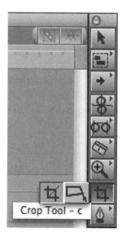

FIGURE 9.49 The *Crop* tool in the Tool Palette.

Pen and Smooth Point tools (*P* key)

There are three tools under this heading: the *Pen* tool (*P* key); the *Delete Point* tool (*P* key + *P* key); and the *Smooth Point* tool (*P* key + *P* key + *P* key). We've already discussed, and used, the *Pen* tool in Chapter 8. The *Delete Pen* tool option let's you click on a spot where you marked a pen marker and remove it. The *Smooth Point* tool allows you to adjust the way the *Pen* tool's effect works. Using *Pen* tools is really just another way of applying and using *keyframes*, which we will learn about before the end of this chapter. By using the *Smooth Point* tool, you can adjust the way the *keyframes* are applied, referred to as their *interpolation*. The Pen tool is shown in Figure 9.50.

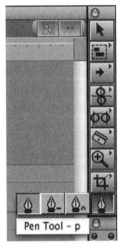

FIGURE 9.50 The *Pen* tool in the Tool Palette.

Trim Edit Window

Now it's time to explore the *Trim Edit* window. This is a convenient window arrangement that looks and behaves somewhat like the two-part window that pops up when you use the *Roll, Ripple, Slip,* and *Slide* tools. The difference is that the Trim Edit window appears on top of the Viewer and the Canvas, and is as large as those two windows, combined, while the *Roll* tool window fits inside of the Canvas. Like those other tools, however, the Trim Edit window exists to provide you with some easy ways to tweak your edit points.

Before proceeding, we will need to drag a clip from track *V2* down to *V1*, since we checkerboarded before, and this tool won't work unless the clips with which you want to work are on the same track. Make sure the *Selection* tool is chosen, and then go ahead and grab shot *1F. wide Michael clips tree*, as shown in Figure 9.51, and drag it down from track V2 to V1, as shown in Figure 9.52.

Next, you will need to select the edit point between the two shots, which you can do in two ways. You can either use the regular Selection tool and double-click on the spot where the two shots touch, or you can use the *Edit Selection* tool and click (once) on the exact same spot. Whichever method you use, you should end up highlighting the edit point, as shown in Figure 9.53. As soon as you do that, the Trim Edit window appears, above, where the Viewer and Canvas windows used to be, as shown in Figure 9.54. The top-left side

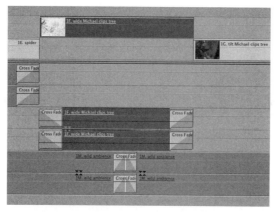

FIGURE 9.51 Select *1F. wide Michael clips tree* on track V2.

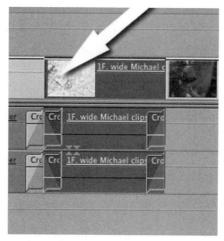

FIGURE 9.52 Drag the shot down to track V1.

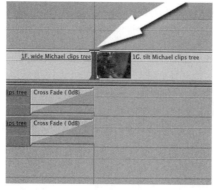

FIGURE 9.53 After you double-click it with the Selection tool, or click it once with the Edit Selection tool, the edit point between the two shots is highlighted.

FIGURE 9.54 The *Trim Edit* window.

of the two-part window is labeled *Outgoing Clip* (which is shot *1F*), and the upper-right side of the window is labeled *Incoming Clip* (which is shot *1G*).

The following figure shows the Trim Edit window.

In the bottom center are the window's playback controls, as shown in Figure 9.55, which let you play through the edit (the center button), go to the edit points before and after the one you clicked on (the two outer buttons), play through both shots in their entirety (just to the left of center), and stop playing (just to the right center). Again, if you hover over any of these buttons, FCE gives you a yellow pop-up menu that tells you what each button does.

FIGURE 9.55 The *Trim Edit* window's edit point playback controls.

Notice, on the right side of the Outgoing Clip window, and on the left side of the *Incoming Clip* window, the frame edges that look like filmstrips. These edges let you know when you are stopped at the original edit point. You can move through the clip in each window, as well, where the controls match the controls you are used to from the Viewer and the Canvas.

Also at the bottom of each window are buttons marked "*–5*," "*–1*," "*+1*," or "*+5*," which let you shift the edit point in either direction by 1 or 5 frames at a time. Finally, there are buttons that let you manually set new *In* and *Out* points on either side. No matter how you tweak the edit point between your shots, however, the overall length of the two clips put together remains the same. Depending on how much extra room – the *handles* – you had in each shot, you can only shift the edit point so far in either direction. Eventually, you will run out of media, and see a *media limit* message.

This Trim Edit tool can really help you create the perfect match-on-action cuts. To exit this window, just click away from the edit point in the Timeline.

General Window Controls

Both the Viewer and the Canvas have the exact same controls at the bottom of the window, called *Transport Controls*, as shown in Figure 9.56. In the middle of each window, we see very similar controls to what we just saw in the Trim Edit window. Hover over each button to see what it does, and then try clicking on it. Remember to pay attention to the keyboard shortcut for each button. The spacebar is the universal keyboard command for play, no matter the window. To the left and right of these general controls is the *Shuttle Control*, as shown in Figure 9.57, and the *Jog Control*, as shown in Figure 9.58. Go ahead and drag the center button left and right in the *Shuttle Control*, and drag the wheel left and right in the *Jog Control*. Each tool allows you to move through the clip in a different way.

FIGURE 9.56 The *Transport Controls* of the Viewer and Canvas.

FIGURE 9.57 The Shuttle Control.

FIGURE 9.58 The Jog Control.

You might also like to know that there are three keyboard shortcuts for shuttling through a clip, as well. They are the *J* key, the *K* key, and the *L* key: *J* moves backwards; *L* moves forward (as does the space bar); and *K* stops (as does the spacebar, when the clip has been moving). Try all three keys at once, and see what happens.

Audio Meter

To the right of the Timeline, underneath the Tool Palette, is the Audio Meter (Figure 9.59), which shows you the decibel level of an audio clip at the point where the playhead passes over it (Figure 9.60). In general, for sound that is the main sound we are meant to hear, such as dialogue, the rule of thumb is to keep it in the –6db to –12db range. If your dialogue is considerably below these levels, you should raise it using the Clip Overlays, which we used in Chapter 8.

FIGURE 9.59 The *Audio Meter* with no sound levels.

FIGURE 9.60 The *Audio Meter* with sound levels just below –18db.

Customizing the Timeline

Now it's time to look at the different ways to customize the Timeline.

Adding buttons

Let's start by adding buttons to the upper-right corner of the Timeline. Conveniently, this lesson is also applicable if you wish to add buttons to the Browser, Viewer, and/or Canvas as well. By default, the Timeline comes with two buttons that control *Linking* and *Snapping* – which we used in Chapters 7 and 8 – as shown in Figure 9.61.

FIGURE 9.61 The *Linking* and *Snapping* buttons on the upper right of the Timeline.

To add more buttons, go to the *Tools* dropdown menu and select the *Button List*, as shown in Figure 9.62. When you do this, the *Button List* pop-up menu appears, as shown in Figure 9.63. This menu has many options, listed here by category. Open the *Sequence Menu* category, as shown in Figure 9.64, by clicking on the little dark triangle to the left of the category header. All you have to do next is grab and drag the button of your choice

FIGURE 9.62 The *Tools* dropdown menu with the *Button List* selected.

FIGURE 9.63 The *Button List*.

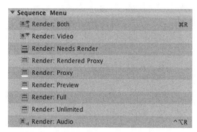

FIGURE 9.64 The *Sequence Menu* category of the *Button List*.

over to the button bar on the Timeline. Drop it there, and you will now have a new button where before there were only two, as shown in Figure 9.65. You can add as many buttons as will fit, and can click and drag to choose the arrangement of buttons you prefer. To delete a button, all you have to do is grab it and pull it away from the button bar and let go, and it will disappear. You can add and delete buttons to the upper-right corner of the Browser, Viewer, and Canvas in exactly the same way.

FIGURE 9.65 You can click and drag a button from the *Button List* to the button area of the Timeline to add a new button.

Changing the size of the tracks

You can also change the size of tracks in the Timeline to show more or less detail. Go down to the bottom left of the Timeline and click on the *Toggle Timeline Track Height* control, as shown in Figure 9.66. Each track size is represented by a larger or smaller column on which you click to set a new size. To cycle – or *toggle* – through all four sizes, you can just hit the *shift* key + the *T key* over and over. Try it. When you find the size that works for you, stop. Be aware, however, that the greater the track height that you choose, the fewer tracks you will see on your screen, unless you have a very large monitor. You can always change heights many times during an edit session, to suit your needs at various times in the editing process.

FIGURE 9.66 The *Toggle Timeline Track Height* control.

Adding and deleting tracks

We already know that it is possible to add more tracks to the Timeline simply by dragging clips to spots above and below existing tracks, but there is also another way to do it.

Go up to the *Sequence* dropdown menu and scroll down to *Insert Tracks*, as shown in Figure 9.67. If neither *Insert Tracks* nor *Delete Tracks* are highlighted, as shown in Figure 9.68, the Timeline window was not selected when

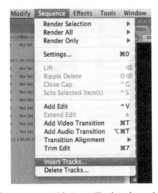

FIGURE 9.67 The *Sequence* dropdown menu with *Insert Tracks* selected.

you jumped up to the dropdown menu. Go back down to the Timeline window, click once inside it, and then go back to the Sequence dropdown menu. Now both the Insert Tracks and Delete Tracks options will be highlighted.

FIGURE 9.68 The *Sequence* dropdown menu with *Insert Tracks* unavailable for selection, because the Timeline is not selected.

How can you recognize if a given window is selected or not? If the top bar of the window is a dark *grey, as shown in Figure 9.69, then that window is* not *selected. If the top bar is a* light *grey, however, as shown in Figure 9.70, then that window is* selected.

FIGURE 9.69 An *unselected* window has a dark grey top bar.

FIGURE 9.70 A *selected* window has a light grey top bar.

Select *Insert Tracks*, and a new pop-up menu will appear, as shown in Figure 9.71. Type in the number of extra tracks you wish to add, click *OK*, and the tracks will be instantly added to the Timeline. It's up to you whether you want to create new tracks this way, or simply by dragging media to the Timeline and placing it above or below existing tracks.

FIGURE 9.71 The *Insert Tracks* pop-up menu.

The *Delete Tracks* pop-up menu lets you conveniently remove tracks that have no media on them. Since there is no other way to perform this function, you will probably find yourself using this menu more than you will the Insert Tracks option. When you pull up the menu, you have to choose whether or not you want to delete *Video Tracks* or *Audio Tracks*, as shown in Figure 9.72. Once you click on one or both of those options, you can choose either *All Empty Tracks* or *All Empty Tracks at End of Sequence*, as shown in Figure 9.73. The difference between these two functions is that the former will remove every track that is completely empty, while the latter will only remove empty tracks that are above or below the last track on which there is media. In other words, if you have been keeping some empty audio or video tracks inside other full tracks – just in case you wanted to add media there – the second option will keep those tracks in your sequence, while the first option will delete them.

FIGURE 9.72 The *Delete Tracks* pop-up menu.

FIGURE 9.73 The *Delete Tracks* pop-up menu, with *All Empty Tracks* selected for both video and audio.

Audio Waveforms

We will review the different tabs available to you in the Viewer shortly, and one of them – the Audio tab – allows you to do some of the same things with sound as the *Audio Waveforms*. You can tell FCE to show you a graph of the sound in your audio clip, so that you can see, in a rough way, what sound is happening where. Go to the *Sequence* dropdown menu and scroll down to *Settings*, as shown in Figure 9.74. The *Sequence Settings* pop-up menu will appear, as shown in Figure 9.75. Underneath *Track Display*, you can see a box that you can check to the left of *Show Audio Waveforms*. Check that box, and then click *OK*.

FIGURE 9.74 The *Sequence* dropdown menu with *Settings* selected.

FIGURE 9.75 The *Sequence Settings* pop-up menu.

Now you will see a loose visual representation of the audio in each track, as shown in Figure 9.76. These clips from the beginning of *Nail Polish* do not have much sound in them, so the graph. With more sound, the graph would reflect greater variance. And if you change your track size to the largest possible option, you will see more variance as well.

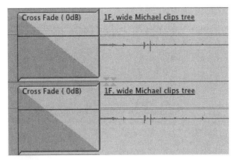

FIGURE 9.76 The audio from shot *1F. wide Michael clips tree*, with the *Audio Waveforms* turned on.

There is a slight downside to using the *Audio Waveforms*, however. With sound that requires a lot of visual graphing, FCE can stutter every time you zoom in or out on the Timeline, since it takes a split second to render the drawing of the graph. If you have a powerful computer, this may not be an issue. If it is an issue, you may find that it is easier to double-click the clip, then go into the Audio tab in the Viewer and work with the sound in that window.

Shifting by frame numbers

This is a highly useful tool for moving clips quickly, especially if you need to move those clips very precisely. In the Timeline, select shot *1E. spider*, then hit the *plus* key (without the *command* key). If you do not have a stand-alone numeric keypad, with the *plus* key on its own keypad, you will need to hit the *shift* key as you press the *plus* key; otherwise, FCE will read the key as an *equals sign*. Once you press the *plus* key, a small pop-up box – an entry field – appears, into which you will can type a number, as shown in Figure 9.77. That number is the amount of frames you would like the highlighted clip to slide forward. Here, we have typed 30, which is about a second in *Standard Definition NTSC Video* (we will discuss video formats in Chapter 10). If we then hit return, we will see that the clip has moved forwards by 30 frames. If two clips are touching on the same track, then FCE will give you a *Clip Collision* error message, since there is no empty space into which the clip could move.

FIGURE 9.77 The pop-up entry field that appears in the Timeline when you press either *plus* or *minus*.

You have to be careful, however, because if *Linking* is off, you might accidentally move your audio and video out of synchronization. If that happens, you will see red numbers appear inside both the audio and video clips, as shown in Figure 9.78. Here, they are indicating that we are a second behind on the audio side. You can rectify this by repeating the process in reverse, using the *minus* key (you don't have to use the *shift* key) instead of the *plus* key, and entering *30* again.

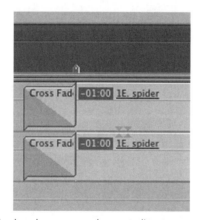

FIGURE 9.78 The red warning box that appears when your clips are out synchronization.

Closing the gap between clips

Often, whether because you have deleted a clip, or because you have simply left a space between clips as you worked on different parts of a sequence, you will have a gap between shots that needs to be closed. You could, with *Snapping* on, just drag the clip, or group of clips, back to the previous clip, thereby closing the gap. But if there are many clips, then you would have to select them all and drag them back, and you may not want to do that. Here is another, simpler way to do it.

To demonstrate, let's place a shot after the end of our sequence, so that there is a gap. We can use *1D. flowers_4*, but it doesn't matter, as any shot will do. Place the playhead anywhere in the gap, as shown in Figure 9.79. Now press the *control* key plus the *G* key. This closes the gap, as shown in Figure 9.80. As easy that seems, however, note that, in order for this tool to work, there must be a complete gap between clips. There can be no other clip in any track within the gap. If there is, FCE won't see a gap, and the tool won't work. If you forget this keyboard command, you can find the tool in the *sequence* dropdown menu.

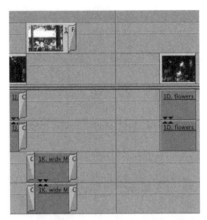

FIGURE 9.79 We have placed shot *1D. flowers_4* after the end of our sequence, to create a gap.

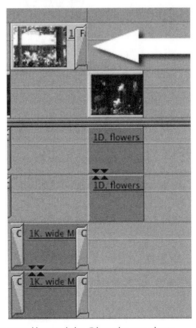

FIGURE 9.80 After we press the *control* key and the *G* key, the gap closes.

Lift vs. Ripple delete

There is yet another method to close gaps or, rather, to avoid them entirely. FCE makes a distinction between what it calls a *Lift Delete* and a *Ripple Delete*. A *Lift Delete*, which you perform by selecting a clip and pressing the *delete* key, removes whatever has been highlighted, without touching or affecting anything on either side. It's how a proper building demolition is supposed to work: the structures on both sides remain untouched. A *Ripple Delete*, on the other hand, which you perform by selecting a clip and pressing the *shift* key and the *delete* key, moves all of the clips to the right of the newly deleted clip over to the left, thereby closing the gap before it appears. Sometimes the *Ripple Delete* won't work if there is something blocking the rest of the clips from moving over, at which point you will be shown a *Clip Collision* error message.

We know how a *Lift Delete* works, so let's just try a *Ripple Delete*. Let's highlight shot *1J. Michael looks satisfied*, as shown in Figure 9.81. Now press the *shift* key and the *delete* key, and then look at the Timeline. As shown in Figure 9.82, the shot has been deleted, and there is no gap. Notice how the audio on tracks *A5* and *A6* hasn't moved. That's because there is no room on those two tracks for any clip to move to the left. Again, make sure you undo this action before we proceed.

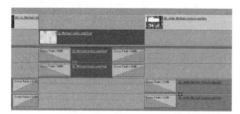

FIGURE 9.81 Select shot *1J. Michael looks satisfied.*

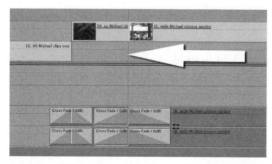

FIGURE 9.82 You can press the *shift* key and the *delete* key to delete the shot and close the gap.

In case you forget the keyboard shortcut for this function, you can also perform a *Ripple Delete* by going to *Sequence* dropdown menu and scrolling down to the *Ripple Delete* line, as shown in Figure 9.83. If you are using a standard Apple desktop keyboard, then you have even another option to perform a *Ripple Delete*. To the right of the standard QWERTY keys, look under the F13 button, and you will see a secondary *delete* key, as shown in Figure 9.84. If you press this key, instead of the regular *delete* key, then it will make a *Ripple Delete* automatically. As mentioned, there are always multiple ways to do the same thing in FCE.

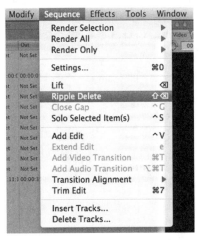

FIGURE 9.83 The *Ripple Delete* option in the *Sequence* dropdown menu.

Video and audio source and destination controls

We have already discussed these controls earlier in this chapter, but there is one more feature you should know about. In addition to being able to move the *v1* and *a1/a2* indicators to any track – which then designates that track as the default destination track – you can also simply detach them, as shown Figure 9.85. What this does is tell FCE that no audio, or video,.. should be inserted or overwritten on any track. If you want to bring a clip down, but only for its audio content, then you would detach the *v1* button and then drag the clip to the Timeline.

FIGURE 9.84 The secondary delete key on a Mac keyboard.

Muting and locking tracks

You can also *mute* and/or *lock* tracks in a sequence. *Muting* effectively turns a track off, so that the video is invisible or the audio inaudible. *Locking* safeguards the contents of a track, preventing any changes of any kind being made. To *lock*, you click on the open padlock icon immediately to the left of each track. Once clicked, it becomes a closed padlock, and a series of diagonal lines appear on the track, indicating that it is locked. To mute, you click on the left-most green buttons on each track, which look like audio or video symbols, depending on the track. Once the track is muted, it becomes shaded. You can mute and lock tracks at the same time, as shown in Figure 9.86.

FIGURE 9.85 The *Video and Audio Source and Destination Controls*, separated from the video and audio tracks.

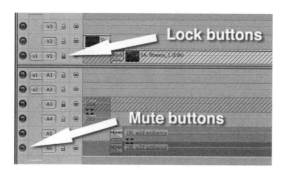

FIGURE 9.86 Here, tracks *V1* and *A3* are locked, and track *A6* is muted.

Sometimes, when you mute a track, you might see a *Warning* pop-up screen, as shown in Figure 9.87. This warning means that if there are any effects that have been rendered on a given track, then muting a track undoes the render, and if you don't undo, you will have to re-render. This is certainly not a major problem, unless, of course, the initial render took a long time.

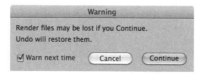

FIGURE 9.87 The *Warning* pop-up screen that appears when you mute a track that has rendered effects.

Clip collisions and other problems

At various times, you may find yourself frustrated as you try and apply a tool, only to see a *Clip Collision* or *Media Limit* error message. Don't get frustrated. Final Cut Express is an intelligent program, but it is only a computer application. It has its set of rules and protocols. Always double-check to see if there is an actual gap through all the tracks (if you are trying to close a gap); and always check to make sure that you have actual *handles* of extra, unused footage to either side of an edit point if you are trying to *ripple*, *roll*, *slide*, or *slip*.

You should also always be careful when you are dragging clips within the Timeline. If you are not careful, you can, fairly easily, accidentally drag one clip over another, or over part of another clip (particularly if *Snapping* is turned off). Pay close attention, however, and you will avoid this problem. The same goes for your video and audio clip synchronization, particularly if you have turned off the *Linking* button. Watch for those red out-of-synchronization number indicators, and you'll be fine.

Effects Tab

Now it's time to start exploring the *Effects* tab. Here, you have access to all of the special filters, transitions, and generators that FCE has to offer. In the last chapter, we used some of the built-in transitions. Let's find out what else is there.

Remember, the *Effects* tab is located in the Browser, next to the *Project* tab, as shown in Figure 9.88. If, for some reason, the *Effects* tab is missing, you can bring it back by going up to the *Window* dropdown menu and scrolling down to the *Effects* line, as shown in Figure 9.89. Just click on that line, and you will bring the *Effects* tab back.

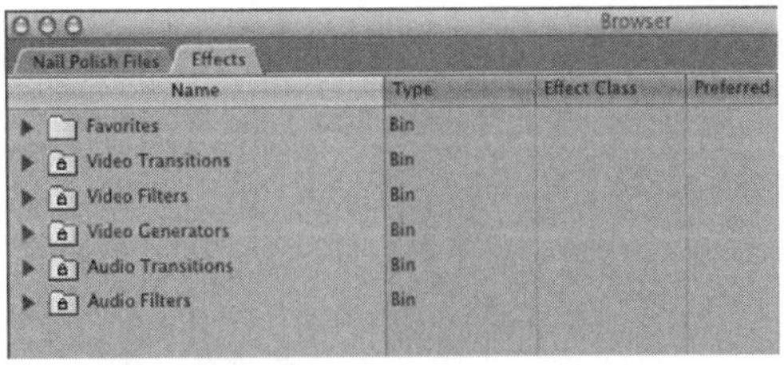

FIGURE 9.88 The *Effects* tab of the Browser.

There are six bins under the *Effects* tab, and within each bin are other bins. We will now look within each bin, in turn, to briefly explore the contents. In order to open a bin, you can either click on the triangle to the left of it, making it open within the current Browser, as shown in Figure 9.90, or you can double-click it. If you do the latter, then a new window will open, showing the

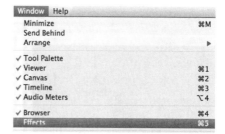

FIGURE 9.89 The *Effects* line of the *Window* dropdown menu.

content of that bin, as shown in Figure 9.91 To close that window, just press the *control* key and the *W* key. If you press the *command* key, instead, you will close the project.

FIGURE 9.90 You can open a bin by clicking on the triangle to the left of it.

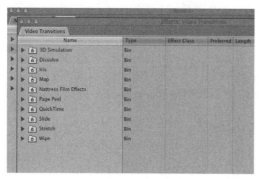

FIGURE 9.91 You can also open a bin by double-clicking on the bin, itself, thereby by making it open in a new window.

Favorites

Open the *Favorites* bin. Most likely, it will be empty, but as you find effects, transitions, and generators that you like, you can drag them into this bin for quick future reference. They won't disappear from their original location, but will be duplicated here, so that you don't have to search for them again. Also, if you tweak an effect's parameters before dragging it to this bin, or after double-clicking it from this bin, then those changes will be recorded in that version of the effect. This makes this a very convenient bin.

Video transitions

We visited this bin in Chapter 8, so it should be familiar to you. You should experiment with as many of these transitions as possible to see which ones you like. All you have to do is drag the transition down to the head or tail of a clip, or to the edit point between clips, and let go. By default, every transition is 1 second long. If you want to make it longer or shorter, just grab the end of it and drag one way or the other, as shown in Figure 9.92. Final Cut Express will show the length of the change you are making in that little yellow pop-up field.

FIGURE 9.92 It is easy to change the length of a transition just by dragging its edge to the left or right.

NOTE *Some computers may have different transitions and effects than the ones you see in this book's illustrations. That is because other users may have installed extra third-party plug-ins. Don't worry. You will have plenty of options to work with, even with the default settings.*

The only way for you to effectively learn how the different transitions work is to experiment. As you look around, notice how some transitions are listed in bold print, while others are not, as shown in Figure 9.93. The same will be true in the effects. The transitions and effects in bold do not require as much computer processing power to be viewed, so you do not have to render them to see how they look (we discussed rendering in Chapter 8, if you remember). The transitions and effects *not* in bold will show up on the Timeline with the red to-be-rendered line above them, and will only be playable if you render them first. If you ever try to apply a transition and an *Insufficient Content for Edit* warning pops up, this is because you do not have the *handles* necessary for the transition to work.

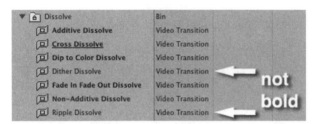

FIGURE 9.93 The transitions in bold do *not* require rendering to be viewed, while the others do.

Video Filters

Open up the *Video Filters* bin now, as shown in Figure 9.94. There are many choices here as well. All you need to do is drag an effect down to a clip on the Timeline, and then render it (if it's in regular non-bold font), or just view it (if it's in bold). What are these effects, exactly? Video filters let you apply simple visual effects, such as a blur, or let you change the color of the shot. Some even let you distort the image with various funhouse mirror adjustments. There are plenty more as well. In the chapters ahead, when we start cutting more footage, we will use some of these filters, but not all. You should therefore feel free to experiment as you go along. Again, it's the way to really learn what they look like.

Sometimes, as in this case, you cannot see all of the filter options in the space of the Browser window. But you can always resize the window by clicking on the bottom-right corner and dragging until all items are visible, as shown in Figure 9.95. If you want to tweak an effect, once it is on your clip, then you need to double-click that clip in the Timeline and go to the *Filters* tab in the Viewer, which we will explore shortly.

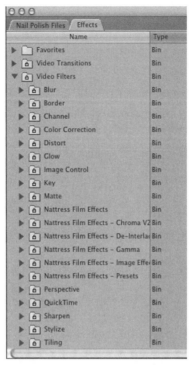

FIGURE 9.94 The *Video Filters* bin has many bins within it, with many different effects.

FIGURE 9.95 The *Video Filters* bin, after you have resized it, shows all of its contents now.

Video Generators

Open the *Video Generator* bin next, as shown in Figure 9.96, to see what it offers. You can find color bars, black slug (blank video), interesting shapes and images, and title generators (which we will explore at the end of this chapter). Try dragging any of these down to the Timeline to see what the generators look like. Just be aware that these are not effects, but actual pieces of video that will overwrite another piece of video if you drop them on top of it. The generators have the same bold/non-bold scheme as the transitions and effects. If you want to change how they look, then double-click them once you have dragged them to the Timeline and go to the *Controls* tab in the Viewer. We will explore this tab before the end of the chapter, when we work on titles.

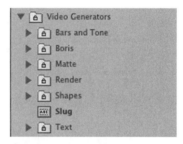

FIGURE 9.96 The *Video Generators* bin.

Audio Transitions

Next, open the *Audio Transitions* bin, as shown in Figure 9.97. We used these transitions in Chapter 8, so they should look familiar. There are only two of them, and you drag and drop them the way you would drag and drop video transitions (except that you apply them to audio only).

9.97 The *Audio Transitions* bin.

Audio Filters

Finally, open up the *Audio Filters* bin, as shown in Figure 9.98. Final Cut Express offers two different bins of filters within this bin: one labeled *Apple*, as shown in Figure 9.99, and the other labeled *FCE*, as shown in Figure 9.100. The former are audio filters that come as part of your Mac OS, and the latter are bundled with the FCE application. These function just like video filters, except that they only apply to the audio side of things. Drag any down to any clip, double-click that clip, and then play with the effect settings in the *Filters* tab.

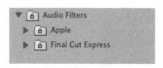

FIGURE 9.98 The *Audio Filters* bin.

FIGURE 9.99 The *Apple* bin within the *Audio Filters* bin.

FIGURE 9.100 The *FCE* bin within the *Audio Filters* bin.

Now that we are done looking at all of the bins in the *Effects* tab, you should know that there are two other ways to access some of these tools. First, you can scroll through the options in the *Effects* dropdown menu, as shown in Figure 9.101, and find all of the transitions and filters. Put your playhead at the edit point between two shots, in the Timeline, and then select the transition you wish to apply. If you want to find the generators, you can use the *Generator* pop-up menu in the bottom right of the Viewer, as shown in Figure 9.102. Select the generator you want, and it will appear in the Viewer, ready to use.

Viewer Tabs

Now let's discuss the tabs in the Viewer. To begin, let's double-click a shot from the Timeline, *1F. Michael clips tree*. Let's go through each tab in the Viewer, one by one.

FIGURE 9.101 You can also access the filters and transitions in the *Effects* dropdown menu.

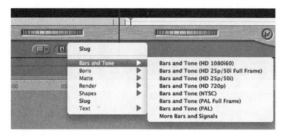

FIGURE 9.102 The *Generator* pop-up menu in the Viewer.

Video tab

The default tab is the *Video* tab, as shown in Figure 9.103. This is a very familiar tab, since it is the one we have been working in primarily. This is where you can see what your video looks like.

FIGURE 9.103 The *Video* tab of the Viewer.

Audio tab

Now click on the next tab – the *Audio* tab – as shown in Figure 9.104. This is also a familiar tab. In many ways, it's easier to work with audio here, rather than directly in the Timeline, with *Audio Waveforms* enabled, as we discussed earlier. You can easily adjust the level of the audio track and whether the channels are panned left, right, or centered using the controls at the top of the window. You can see the *Level* and *Pan Bars* just above the center part of the audio graph.

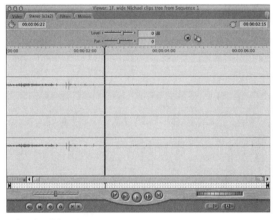

FIGURE 9.104 The *Audio* tab of the Viewer.

Filters tab

Next, go ahead and click on the *Filters* tab. It should be empty, as shown in Figure 9.105. Let's go ahead and drag both a video and an audio filter to the clip that we double-clicked from the Timeline, shot *1F. Michael clips tree*. You can either drag the filters directly into the Viewer, or you can drag them onto the clip itself. Either way, the result will be the same. For now, we'll use a video filter from the *Blur* bin called *Prism* and an audio filter from the *Apple bin* called *AUPitch*, as shown in Figure 9.106. As you can see, we have a number of control options for each filter.

Within the *Prism* video filter, you can change the amount of the blur, the angle of the blur, and how the effect is applied (called the *mix*). In order to see how this filter affects the shot, place the playhead in the Timeline directly over the clip, so you can see the effect in the Canvas. As you adjust the controls, you will see how much leeway you have in determining the look of the shot using this particular effect.

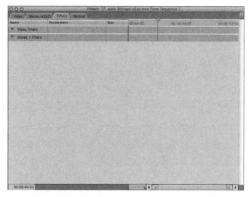

FIGURE 9.105 The *Filters* tab of the Viewer, empty.

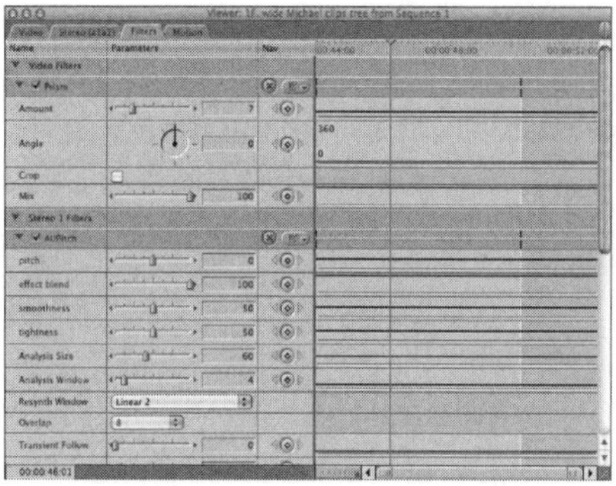

FIGURE 9.106 The *Filters* tab of the Viewer, with the *Prism* video filter and the *AUPitch* audio filter.

On the *AUPitch* audio filter, you have several settings you can adjust. This filter also lets you change the pitch of the audio. If you raise the pitch control above zero, the sounds plays in a higher register; if you dip below zero, it is lower. The other controls help you control the amount of the effect applied to the clip, the smoothness of the audio (which can sound tinny as you adjust the filter), etc.

From these two examples, you should have a basic understanding of how all filters in FCE can be adjusted. It's fairly simple. You click and drag sliders and/or change numbers manually. If you ever want to reset the values of the filter to their default settings, just click on the red *X* on the right side of the filter, as shown in Figure 9.107. If you want to keep the effect on the clip, just in case you might want it later, but want to disable it while you decide, you can uncheck the blue box on the left side, as shown in Figure 9.108. If you wish to delete the effect entirely, just click in the grey area around the filter's name, so that it is highlighted, and press the *delete* key.

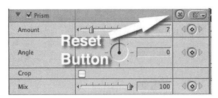

FIGURE 9.107 The *Reset Button* for filter values.

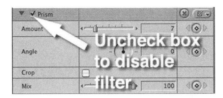

FIGURE 9.108 Uncheck this box to disable the filter.

Before you delete these filters, however, take a look at the Timeline. You should see two different colors, one on top of the other, as shown in Figure 9.109. These are the to-be-rendered indicators, also known as *Render Bars*. The top color (green) is for the video filter, and the bottom color (red) is for the audio filter. This means that the video filter can be watched in real time, without rendering, but the audio filter requires rendering just to be able to play. Different filters require different amounts of processing power, as we mentioned earlier, so your computer may handle these filters differently.

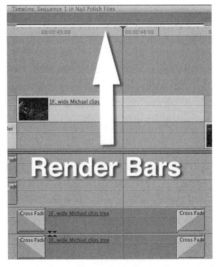

FIGURE 9.109 After you have applied your filters, check the *Render Bars* in the Timeline.

Motion tab

Now let's take a look at the final tab in the Viewer, the *Motion* tab, as shown in Figure 9.110. When we work with generators, at the end of this chapter, we will discover one more tab – the *Controls* tab – but that tab does not exist for regular media. Here, you can tweak the way a shot looks without using filters. You can change the scale of the shot (the default is 100%), which makes you zoom in or out on the image. You can rotate the shot. You can move the shot right or left using the center button. You can crop the edges. You can change the opacity. You can distort the aspect ratio. You can even tell it, using the anchor points, to rotate on an axis other than the actual center of the shot. Combined with *keyframing*, which we will learn about soon, this tab offers many possibilities.

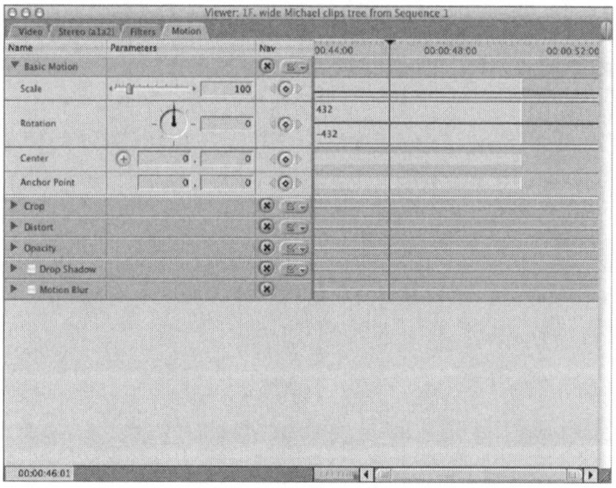

FIGURE 9.110 The *Motion* tab in the Viewer.

No matter what you do, you can always click on the same red *X* that we saw in the *Filters* tab to reset the shot to the default settings. If you do change things, you will need to render the new piece of video, just as you would with an actual filter.

Viewer and Canvas Controls

Now let's look at a few of the controls (some of which we are already familiar) that exist in both the Viewer and Canvas windows.

Transport Controls

The *Transport Controls*, as shown in Figure 9.111, are the series of five buttons at the bottom of both the Viewer and Canvas, which let you control the Playback of your clip or sequence. The most commonly used is the middle, or *Play*, button. The keyboard shortcut for this is the *spacebar* key. Hover each of the other buttons to see what they do.

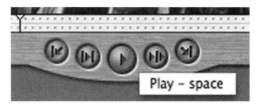

FIGURE 9.111 The *Transport Controls* in the Viewer.

Playhead Controls

To the left and right of the *Transport Controls* are the *Playhead Controls*, as shown in Figure 9.112. The *Shuttle Control* is on the left and the *Jog Control* is on the right. They provide you with more precise ways to move through a clip than just dragging the playhead through the scrubber bar. To be even more precise, you can use the arrow keys on your keyboard to move forward and backward, one frame at a time.

FIGURE 9.112 The *Playhead Controls* in the Viewer.

Marking Controls

To the left, under the *Shuttle Control* in the Viewer, is a set of controls that lets you set *In* and *Out* points, *Markers* and *Keyframes*, as shown in Figure 9.113. We already know how to set *Markers* and *In* and *Out* points manually. This gives us an additional way to do it.

FIGURE 9.113 The *Marking Controls* in the Viewer.

The first button on the left of the *Marking Controls* in the Viewer is called the *Show Match Frame* button (hover over it to see), and it either moves the playhead in the Viewer to match the position of the playhead in the Timeline, or the other way around, so that you are looking at the same frame in both windows, if that is what you need to do.

Zoom pop-up menu

At the top of both the Viewer and the Canvas are two buttons that reveal pop-up menus when clicked. The first is the *Zoom* pop-up menu, as shown in Figure 9.114. Using this menu, you can change the viewing size of the clip in the window. This does not create an actual zoom effect on the shot, but just zooms in or out for you to see more detail. You can also zoom in or out within the window using the *command* key plus the *plus* or *minus* key (as discussed earlier). When you want to reset to the default, choose *Fit to Window*, rather than *100%*, since every computer screen is different in size, and *100%* will be either too big or too small for the clip, depending on the format.

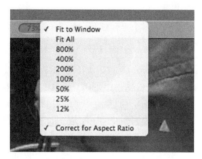

FIGURE 9.114 The *Zoom* pop-up menu in the Viewer.

View pop-up menu

The *View* pop-up menu is the other button at the top of both the Viewer and Canvas, as shown in Figure 9.115. You can make the window display a *wireframe* on top of the image (which we will discuss shortly), and you can have the window show the *Title Safe* area (which we will discuss when creating titles in at the end of the chapter). Click on the *Image + Wireframe* line, and you will see a white *X* spread across the window, as shown in Figure 9.116. Don't leave the *wireframe* on, however, when you don't need it, because it will keep you from being able to click and drag clips from the Viewer or Canvas to another window.

FIGURE 9.115 The *View* pop-up menu in the Viewer.

FIGURE 9.116 *Image + Wireframe* in the Viewer.

Recent clips pop-up menu

This is a pop-up menu that exists solely in the Viewer. Just under the *Jog Control* are two buttons. The right one is the *Generator* pop-up menu, which we discussed earlier. The left menu is the *Recent Clips* pop-up menu, as shown in Figure 9.117, and is for displaying all of the clips that you have recently dragged here from the Browser (not from the Timeline), so you can quickly shuffle between different shots. If you have been working on a shot, and then think you have lost your work because you double-clicked on a new shot, which appears in the Viewer in place of the old shot, just go to this button, and the clip you were originally working on will be there.

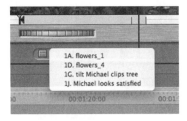

FIGURE 9.117 The *Recent Clips* pop-up menu in the Viewer.

And now, it is time to discuss keyframes.

Keyframes

Using *keyframes* – which we can also call *keyframing* – can be both compli-cated and simple. If you understand the basic principles behind *keyframes* here, you will be able to go on and do more advanced work in applications such as Adobe After Effects® or Motion®.

Let's start by going back to the *Motion* tab. If you have double-clicked on other media since we placed shot *1F. wide Michael clips tree* in the Viewer, take the time now to double-click on *1F*, from the Timeline, again. In the *Motion* tab, notice that underneath the red *X* on which you would click to reset all values to their defaults there are a series of black diamonds, to the right of each property of *Basic Motion* (*Scale, Rotation, Center, Anchor Point*), as shown in Figure 9.118. These diamonds are actually buttons with which you can set a *keyframe*.

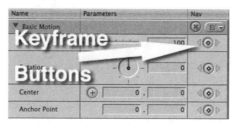

FIGURE 9.118 The *keyframe* buttons in *Motion* tab.

What, then, is a *keyframe*? Simply put, a *keyframe* is a marker, before which or after which you set in motion some kind of change or animation. In Chapter 8, when you created fades up for the first video and audio clips, we used the Pen tool to place a dot at the beginning of the clip and another dot about a second later. These "dots" were actually *keyframes*. That is actually what the Pen tool creates when you click with it on a Clip Overlay. You can even set *keyframes* in the *Motion* tab using the Pen tool instead of using the *keyframe* buttons. It would have the same result.

Place the playhead somewhere in the middle of the window, and click on the black diamond next to the *Scale* parameter. When you do this, the diamond turns green, as does the line extending to the right, and a green dot (a *key-frame*) appears where the playhead was stopped, as shown in Figure 9.119. Now move the playhead to a later spot on the line. Note that the lighter portion of the line in the *Motion* tab represents the visible part of the clip. Add another *keyframe* by clicking on the diamond again, as shown in

Figure 9.120. Now drag the second *keyframe* as far up as it will go, as shown in Figure 9.121. In so doing, you have just created an artificial zoom, and have successfully *keyframed* your first animation. The number in the box to the right of the *Scale* slider should read *1000* at the second *keyframe*, which means you have zoomed in 10 times. Go ahead and watch it in the Timeline (it doesn't need to be rendered to be shown). It looks bad, because of massive pixelation, but it works.

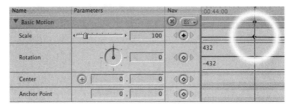

FIGURE 9.119 Set your first *keyframe* along the *Scale* parameter line in the *Motion* tab.

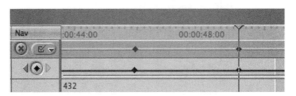

FIGURE 9.120 Set a second *keyframe* a little further along the line.

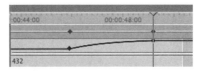

FIGURE 9.121 To create the animation, pull the second *keyframe* up to the top of the line, thereby creating a zoom.

What you should take away from this simple exercise is that all animations require two *keyframes*, and you can set two different values and have the parameters of whatever effect you are adjusting shift from one point to the next. Now, if you drag a video filter to this clip and open the *Filters* tab, you will notice that each effect has the exact same kind of overlay line extending to the right of each parameter. You will also see the same *keyframe* marker diamonds, which means you can make the filter change during the shot. Practice with either more filters and/or more of the effects available in the *Motion* tab. Just make sure you undo your work.

Copying and Pasting Clip Attributes

It's important to know how to make changes to one particular clip and then apply these changes to all the similar clips in a scene. Let's say you shot your movie beautifully, except for one interior scene, where all of the shots are improperly color-balanced. You spend an hour using some of the color correction filters, which you'll find under *Color Correction* and *Image Control* in the *Video Filters* bin, and then you worry that you're going to have to do the same thing over and over again for each clip. Don't worry – in FCE, there are several things you can do in this type of situation.

This series has a book (Digital Filmmaking *by Pete Shaner*) *on how to properly use a video camera, and you should consult it for information on how to both expose and balance the color of an image. Video (and film) reacts differently to light that comes from the sun vs. light that comes from a traditional tungsten light bulb vs. that from a fluorescent bulb. If you shoot your footage incorrectly, your image could end up looking blue, or orange, or green. Fortunately, programs like FCE offer you the means to correct the image … up to a point.***

NOTE

First, you can highlight all of the clips in the Timeline that do not have the filter on them, go to the *Filter* tab of the clip that *does* have the filter, and simply click and drag that filter to all of the other clips simultaneously.

Let's imagine, however, that you made several changes to your clip. Perhaps there was a microphone that was visible in all shots, so you had to crop the image slightly, and the audio was too low, so you had to raise the audio levels, etc. Now you have some things that won't drag so easily from shot to shot. What can you do? All you need is to first highlight, in the Timeline, the clip that has everything corrected. Then press the *command* key and the *C* key, or go to the *Edit* dropdown menu and highlight *Copy*. Once that is done, you should select all of the clips in the Timeline that have not been corrected. Then go back up to the *Edit* dropdown menu and scroll down to *Paste Attributes*, as shown in Figure 9.122. The keyboard shortcut for this is the *control* key + the V key.

FIGURE 9.122 Choose *Paste Attributes* from the *Edit* dropdown menu when you want to easily copy and paste filters and other corrections from one shot to another.

The *Paste Attributes Menu* will then pop up, as shown in Figure 9.123. Whatever had been changed in the clip that you copied will appear in *full strength black* (as opposed to the *Speed* attribute here) and ready for you to check. Whatever attributes are available for pasting - those attributes that you changed in the source clip that you copied - will appear in this menu with their text description in black, rather than a faded gray color. The check boxes to the left of these available attributes will allow you to place a check mark within them, if you click on the box. You don't have to paste all of the attributes;

FIGURE 9.123 The *Paste Attributes* pop-up menu.

you can choose only what you need. If you were to check *Content*, however, that would replace all of the clips with the actual video and/or audio in the original clip, which might be what you want to do. When you have the boxes you want, click *OK*, and the attributes will be paste on to the new clip or clips.

Subclipping

In Chapter 8, we discovered that if you duplicate clips, they will all be linked as duplicates. If you try to rename one, the names of all of the duplicates will change, too. At the start of this chapter we discussed how to make *independent clips* from the *Master clips*, when we looked at the *Modify* dropdown menu.

Using that same dropdown menu, we can also create *subclips*, which behave as *independent clips* once created, and can be renamed. *Subclips* are very useful when you have a very long shot from which you want to isolate some shorter moments. You can make FCE treat that shorter moment as its own *independent clip*, without the extra parts of the shot that don't belong in that moment. Creating a *subclip* does not in any way affect the original clip. It simply creates a new, shorter clip inside FCE.

Let double-click on shot *1M. wild ambience*, from the Browser. In the Viewer, set your *In* and *Out* points, choosing just part of the shot, as shown in Figure 9.124. Next, go to the *Modify* dropdown menu and select *Make Subclip*, as shown in Figure 9.125, or press the *command* key + the *U key*. As soon as you do so, a new clip – the *subclip* – appears in the Browser, as shown in Figure 9.126. You can rename it or choose not to. If you don't rename it, it will have, by default, the name of the original clip with the word *subclip* tacked on. Notice how the new clip has jagged, rather than smooth, edges. This lets you know that it's a *subclip*, which can be important if you are later trying to figure out where this clip came from.

FIGURE 9.124 Shot *1M. wild ambience*, with *In* and *Out* points marked, ready for *subclipping*.

FIGURE 9.125 *Make Subclip* selected in the *Modify* dropdown menu.

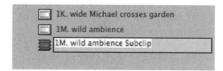

FIGURE 9.126 The new *subclip* as it appears in the Browser, ready for renaming.

Title Creation

Let's end this chapter with some basic title creation. We are going to practice, briefly, with the two main options available within FCE. In Chapter 11, we will work with *LiveType*, an additional piece of software that comes bundled with FCE and offers you far greater title creation possibilities.

Open the *Video Generators* bin, and you will see two other bins therein, among others, which offer title generation: *Boris* and *Text*, as shown in Figure 9.127. *Boris* used to be a third-party text generator plug-in that you had to install separately (although it came on the FCE installation disc). However, a few years ago it started coming pre-installed. The quality of the title cards that you can make with *Boris* is slightly better than what you can do with the plain *Text* generators, although most people find the *Text* generators adequate (and easier to use).

FIGURE 9.127 The *Boris* and *Text* bins inside the *Video Generators* bin are where we will find the title generating tools.

Let's start with *Text*. Within the *Text* bin are a variety of options. The straightforward title card is the one labeled *Text*. Drag that *Text* icon down to the Timeline, as shown in Figure 9.128, and drop it over the first clip, in track *V2*. If you drop it on top of the first clip, in track *V1*, it will actually delete part of that clip. It is not a filter, but a generator, and FCE treats it as a new piece of media.

FIGURE 9.128 Drag the *Text* generator down to the beginning of the Timeline, above the first shot.

Make sure the playhead in the Timeline is placed over the middle of those two clips, and you will see, in the Canvas, the first shot of the movie with the words *Sample Text* in the center, as shown in Figure 9.129. The reason why the *Text* clip doesn't block out the entire shot below it is because all text generators come with a built-in layer of transparency (called an *alpha channel*). The text portion is built over a buffer of empty space. If you place the title over nothing, the background will appear black; if you place it over another shot, that shot will be visible beneath the text. If you've ever used Adobe Photoshop, you might be familiar with layers and transparency.

FIGURE 9.129 This is what the *Text* generator looks like over the first shot, as shown in the Canvas.

Now, double-click, in the Timeline, the *Text* clip, to open it in the Viewer, as shown in Figure 9.130. Notice the new tab mentioned earlier in the chapter. This is the *Controls* tab that appears for all video generators. Click on that tab now, and you will see a menu specific to the generator with which you are working. You will see a menu to change the default text, as shown in Figure 9.131. Next, click in the Text window and change the text, by selecting it, deleting it, and typing the words *Nail Polish*. Then choose a new font, like Arial Black, and increase the font size from *36* to *48*. All of these changes are reflected in the text box, as shown in Figure 9.132. Take a quick look at the Canvas now to see what the new text looks like on top of the shot.

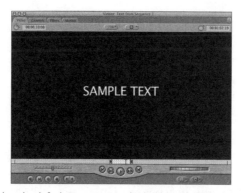

FIGURE 9.130 This is what the default *Text* generator looks like in the Viewer.

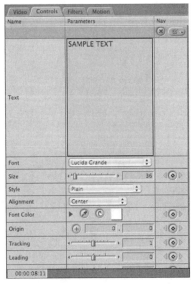

FIGURE 9.131 Click on the *Controls* tab to change the way the text looks.

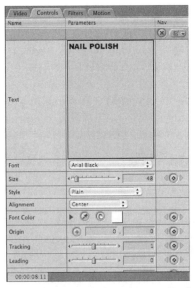

FIGURE 9.132 After you make changes to the text, these changes are reflected in the text box.

Have you ever seen white text over an image and noticed how difficult it is to read? Let's fix it. Click now on the *Motion* tab, and go down to the *Drop Shadow* line, and click open that parameter, as shown in Figure 9.133. Make sure you check the box next to *Drop Shadow*, or the effect won't be visible. You can leave the default settings as is, or you can tweak them. If you increase the *Opacity* to *100*, the shadow behind the text becomes solid black. It's up to you.

FIGURE 9.133 You can apply a *Drop Shadow* to your text in the *Motion* tab.

Now let's take a step back and check out our work, as shown in Figure 9.134. Notice how the *Text* clip now requires rendering, with the *Render Bar* in red. If you looked before we applied the *Drop Shadow*, that line was green. Certain actions require more processing power, and adding that extra effect is too much for the computer to play without rendering first.

FIGURE 9.134 Adding the *Drop Shadow* to your text turns the *Render Bar* red.

Let's do one more thing with this title card, using the *wireframe*, which we access through the *View* pop-up menu (refer back to Figure 9.115). We worked in the Viewer before, but let's turn it on in the Canvas this time. Let's also turn on the *Title Safe* area, using the same *View* pop-up menu. Then make sure that you have highlighted the *Text* clip in the Timeline by selecting it and place the playhead over it, so we can watch our work in progress. Lastly, go up to the *Zoom* pop-up menu (refer back to Figure 9.112), and reduce the screen size to 50%. When you are done, your Canvas will show shot *1A. flowers_1*, with the *Nail Polish* title and the *Wireframe* and *Title Safe* lines laid over it, in an image that does not quite fill the window, as shown in Figure 9.135.

FIGURE 9.135 The Canvas with the *Wireframe* and *Title Safe* lines activated and the viewing sixe reduced to *50%*.

Now grab the center point of the *wireframe* and drag downward. Note that if you have failed to properly select the *Text* clip in the Timeline, the *wireframe* will not appear. Stop when the text is just above the innermost *Title Safe* line, as shown in Figure 9.136. The *Title Safe* line ensures that, no matter what the dimensions of the TV or projector on which this might be screened, anything within these lines will be visible. The safest line is the innermost one, although most TVs can handle the outer one. Using the *wireframe* in this way, you could also move your title up, sideways, or anyway you want. It's your choice. This is just one of the many ways in which the *wireframe* can be useful.

FIGURE 9.136 Grab the center of the *wireframe* and move the title to just above the *Title Safe* line.

Look back on the Timeline. If you want to shorten or lengthen the title, all you have to do is grab the edge of the *Text* clip and pull to the right to lengthen, as shown in Figure 9.137, or to the left to shorten. This is the same way we learned to lengthen or shorten transitions.

FIGURE 9.137 Drag the edge of the *Text* to the right to lengthen it.

There are other kinds of title generators within the *Text* bin. Try them out.

Finally, let's look at one of the *Boris* text generators. Grab the one labeled *Title 3D*, drag it to the Timeline, and then double-click it. Go ahead and click on the *Control* tab. With *Boris*, however, we can't just change the text inside the *Control* tab. We also have to click where it says *Click for Options*, as shown in Figure 9.138. Once we do that, the *Boris Title 3D* pop-up window appears, and we can type in all the text we want, as shown in Figure 9.139. Once you are done typing, click *OK*, and the new text will appear on the Timeline.

FIGURE 9.138 The *Click for Options* box in *Boris* will lead you to the *Boris Title 3D* pop-up window.

FIGURE 9.139 This is where you can enter the text in a variety of different styles.

Note that in Boris, if you want to change the font or the text size or the text color, you have to highlight the text you have typed first; otherwise, the change will not occur. The advantage is that you can apply changes to individual letters or words or lines. The FCE *Text* generator does *not* give you that flexibility. You can also add outlines and drop shadows from within Boris, rather than having to rely on the *Motion* tab. Go ahead and practice. When you're done – don't forget to render! In Chapter 11, we will explore the additional title capabilities that *LiveType* offers us.

Let's move on to Chapter 10 now, where we will discuss video and audio formats and how to capture, import, and export our footage.

SUMMARY

In this chapter, we continued our exploration of the tools of FCE and discussed specific menus and customizing options. We also learned different ways to perform tasks we covered in Chapters 7 and 8, including creating transitions and making Insert and Overwrite edits. Through a series of simple exercises, we built on that foundation and further explored FCE so that we can start editing more complex sequences.

We began with the dropdown menus, learning what tools can be found in each, and then moved on to a discussion on how to customize the Browser, and by extension the other windows. Next, we tackled many of the tools in the Tool Palette and explored how to use the Insert/Overwrite menu in the Canvas. We also learned the keyboard shortcut for each tool. From the Tool Palette, we moved to the Trim Edit window, which has an interface similar to that of the Roll, Ripple, Slip, and Slide tools. All of these tools can be used to make precise changes to your edit points.

We then continued our close analysis of the Timeline, Viewer, and Canvas windows, paying close attention to the Effects Tab in the Browser, and the tabs in the Viewer related to effects and motion. As we learned the full range of possibilities offered by the audio and video filters we also reviewed the various buttons and controls found in both the Viewer and Canvas. This exploration led us to a study of keyframes and wireframes. Keyframes are an essential component for all animation and effects generation. An equally important tool that we discovered is the capability of FCE to copy and paste attributes of one clip on to another clip. Any filters and other effects work done on one piece of media can easily be applied to other clips with a few clicks of the mouse, or a few keystrokes.

We ended the chapter with a discussion on Subclipping and Titles. Subclipping allows you to easily divide long shots into smaller units, and then rename each unit separately. Titles, we discovered, are created with two separate generators within the program, Boris and Text. While our discussion here was brief, in Chapter 11, we will explore LiveType, a software application devoted to title generation, which comes with FCE.

We are now ready to learn how to capture and export footage, which we will do next, in Chapter 10.

1. How do keyframes make animation possible?

2. What does the Trim Edit window allow you to do?

3. What are the differences between the Roll, Ripple, Slip, and Slide tools?

4. How do you apply filters?

5. How can you make titles?

DISCUSSION / ESSAY QUESTIONS

1. Discuss the relative advantages to the various edit point tools. Do you think some are more useful than others and, if so, why?

2. Which method would you prefer to use to add clips to the Timeline: Using the Insert/Overwrite buttons in the Canvas, or just dragging clips down directly to the Timeline? Why?

3. Which tools, if any, in the Tool Palette, seem unnecessary at this point? If they all seem useful, explain why.

4. Is there something missing from the program that you wish were included? What?

Further Research

- Explore the various buttons in the Button List, dragging the ones you find useful to whatever window makes the most sense.

- Apply one filter from each category to a clip to familiarize yourself with the filters.

- Apply keyframes to the filters you like best, creating simple animations, and then render them and see how they look or sound.

- Create a full range of title cards for this *Nail Polish* scene with which we have worked in this chapter.

CHAPTER 10

ALL ABOUT FORMATS: CAPTURING, IMPORTING, AND EXPORTING

OVERVIEW AND LEARNING OBJECTIVES

In this chapter, you will:

- Learn about the many different kinds of audio and video formats
- Discover the right formats in which to import and edit your film
- Explore how to capture footage from both tape and flash memory cards
- Review how to import files that are already digitized and on your computer
- Understand the basic ways to export your finished movie

Introduction

Tape is on its way out. It's still here, but it won't be for too much longer. Flash memory – in all of its many manifestations on Panasonic® P2 cards, SD cards, compact flash cards, etc. – appears to be the way of the future. Some cameras shoot directly to attached or embedded hard drives; others shoot to DVD discs. Blu-Ray disc cameras may be just around the corner, or something else new and vastly different. Who knows? As soon as you invest in one kind of format, a new one arrives that makes it obsolete.

But there are periods of overlap, and we are in one now. Cameras like the Panasonic HVX200 can shoot to both MiniDV tape *and* to flash memory cards. The former only records to "old school" standard definition, while the new cards can shoot in 1080p HD.

Since you may still be shooting in MiniDV or HDV – both of which use tape – rather than in HD or AVCHD (we'll explore all of these terms shortly), we will touch on capturing footage both from tape and from non-tape sources. First, however, let's discuss audio and video formats.

Formats

Audio and video formats can be confusing to many people, so we will try to keep our explanations as simple as possible. Our goal is to allow you to know enough to be able work with formats in FCE, not to make you an expert.

If you want more information on formats, a useful resource is the book Real World Video Compression *by Andy Beach. It explains codecs, compression, file extensions, etc., in great depth, yet keeps it simple.[1]*

What do we mean by the word *format*? In brief, *format* means the quality, resolution, compression, and medium in which your video is shot. In the world of actual film, there are different kinds of film *gauges* that are used – that is, the size of the film negative – such as 8 mm, 16 mm, 35 mm, or 70 mm. Depending on the size of the filmstrip, the quality of the image will be different. A larger negative results in higher quality. Higher quality allows you to blow up the image more. This is why old home movies, shot in 8 mm, can look so grainy when projected on a screen from too far away, while 35 mm (the format of most feature films shot on film) looks sharp and clear.

The video world has similar format differences, only more of them. Formats that take up more storage space (on a tape, on a card, on a hard drive) per minute are like the 35 to 70 mm film gauges and can be blown up and projected on a screen from a faraway projection booth quite well. You might choose, however, not to use such large formats when posting a video to the Web, since the streaming or download speed would be excruciatingly slow.

Using the Browser to Read Format Information

Let's now look at some basic considerations for video formats that we will, as video editors, encounter. First, let's open our *Video_01* bin in the Browser, so we can see, once more, the clips therein, as shown in Figure 10.1. Then let's extend the size of the Browser window by grabbing the lower right-hand corner and pulling to the right, so that we can see more of the columns in the Browser, itself, as shown in Figure 10.2. You could also drag the blue slider button on the bottom of the Browser window, but this way we get a fuller view of all of the columns at once.

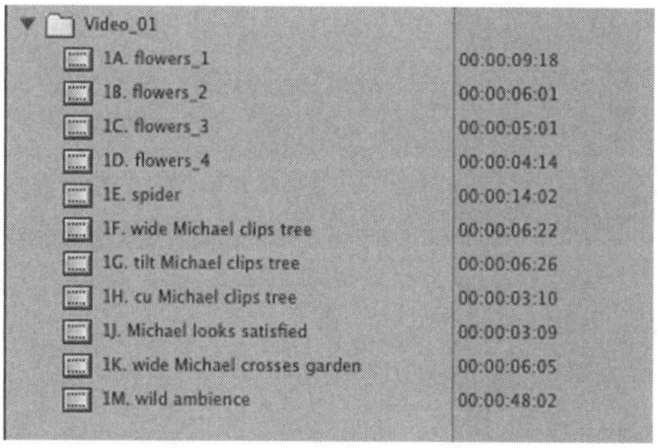

▼ 🗀 Video_01	
🎞 1A. flowers_1	00:00:09:18
🎞 1B. flowers_2	00:00:06:01
🎞 1C. flowers_3	00:00:05:01
🎞 1D. flowers_4	00:00:04:14
🎞 1E. spider	00:00:14:02
🎞 1F. wide Michael clips tree	00:00:06:22
🎞 1G. tilt Michael clips tree	00:00:06:26
🎞 1H. cu Michael clips tree	00:00:03:10
🎞 1J. Michael looks satisfied	00:00:03:09
🎞 1K. wide Michael crosses garden	00:00:06:05
🎞 1M. wild ambience	00:00:48:02

FIGURE 10.1 The *Video_01* bin open in the Browser.

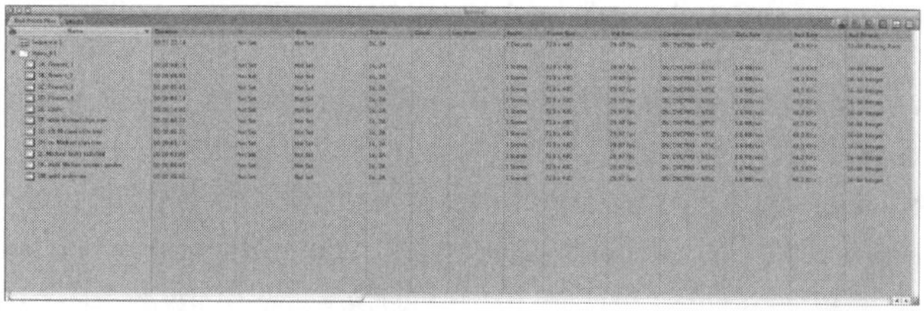

FIGURE 10.2 The Browser, extended to the right.

Audio	Frame Size	Vid Rate	Compressor	Data Rate	Aud Rate	Aud Format
2 Outputs	720 x 480	29.97 fps	DV/DVCPRO – NTSC		48.0 KHz	32-bit Floating Point
1 Stereo	720 x 480	29.97 fps	DV/DVCPRO – NTSC	3.6 MB/sec	48.0 KHz	16-bit Integer
1 Stereo	720 x 480	29.97 fps	DV/DVCPRO – NTSC	3.6 MB/sec	48.0 KHz	16-bit Integer
1 Stereo	720 x 480	29.97 fps	DV/DVCPRO – NTSC	3.6 MB/sec	48.0 KHz	16-bit Integer
1 Stereo	720 x 480	29.97 fps	DV/DVCPRO – NTSC	3.6 MB/sec	48.0 KHz	16-bit Integer
1 Stereo	720 x 480	29.97 fps	DV/DVCPRO – NTSC	3.6 MB/sec	48.0 KHz	16-bit Integer
1 Stereo	720 x 480	29.97 fps	DV/DVCPRO – NTSC	3.6 MB/sec	48.0 KHz	16-bit Integer
1 Stereo	720 x 480	29.97 fps	DV/DVCPRO – NTSC	3.6 MB/sec	48.0 KHz	16-bit Integer
1 Stereo	720 x 480	29.97 fps	DV/DVCPRO – NTSC	3.6 MB/sec	48.0 KHz	16-bit Integer
1 Stereo	720 x 480	29.97 fps	DV/DVCPRO – NTSC	3.6 MB/sec	48.0 KHz	16-bit Integer
1 Stereo	720 x 480	29.97 fps	DV/DVCPRO – NTSC	3.6 MB/sec	48.0 KHz	16-bit Integer

FIGURE 10.3 Look closely at each column, as we analyze what these categories mean.

 ON DVD   All figures appear in color on the companion DVD.

If you were to continue enlarging the window, there would be many more columns to see (if your screen is big enough), but this is enough for now. Let's see what these columns have to tell us, by taking a closer look, as shown in Figure 10.3. We'll analyze each column, from left to right.

Audio column

You probably understand the difference between *Mono* and *Stereo*. The former means that the sound plays through only one channel – or outlet – of any kind (such as a speaker), while the latter splits the sound into two channels. It is possible to capture your clips so that your audio channels are not linked, creating separate mono files, or linked in stereo. We'll look at those options later.

Frame size column

Frame size refers to the actual physical dimensions of your frame. *Frame size* refers to the actual physical dimensions of your frame. Until 1953, all feature films were shot in a relatively square-shaped format, with a 4:3 aspect ratio. This means that the horizontal length was 1.33 times the size of the vertical height. After World War II, Americans started buying televisions in increasing numbers, and Hollywood became concerned that fewer and fewer people would leave their homes to watch movies. Widescreen film was developed to draw people back to the theatres to see something they could not see on television (more and more films were shot in color, too). The first official widescreen film – shot in CinemaScope, as that film's technology was called – was *The Robe* (1953), directed by Henry Koster, about the life of Jesus Christ. The aspect ratio for that film was 2.20:1, which is considerably wider than modern-day widescreen TVs. In an interesting historical twist, today's televisions are now made in a widescreen format, to compete with the movie-going experience.

Aspect ratio is just one way of discussing *frame size*. In the video world, we more properly discuss dimensions in terms of the number of lines of resolution that are scanned by the device recording or projecting the image (like a camera or a TV), which is where terms such as 720p, 1080i, etc., come from. Those numbers measure the amount of vertical lines, in pixels, that make up the image you see. The "p" and the "i" stand for *progressive* and *interlaced*, which we'll touch upon in just a moment, when we get to *Vid Rate*. *Standard-definition* video – which is what we had before *high definition* – has 480 lines of vertical resolution. High definition begins at 720 and currently goes as high as 1080.

The vertical lines of resolution are always the second number listed under *Frame Size*. In FCE when you see the dimensions of our clips shown as 720 × 480, the first number represents the horizontal lines of resolution. This is confusing because you may mistake this for a high-definition clip, since we are now used to seeing 720 listed on most televisions and cameras. However, a high-definition clip with 720 lines of vertical resolution has *frame size* dimensions of 960 × 720 or 1080 × 720.

In FCE, standard-definition video is listed with a 720 × 480 frame size, whether or not it is in 4:3 or 16:9 (which is the standard widescreen aspect ratio). You may notice that 720 divided by 480 equals 1.5, and not 1.33, even though 4 divided by 3 equals 1.33. Technically, the *frame size* should be listed as 640 × 480 then. The reason we see this discrepancy has to do with the difference between square pixels and non-square pixels and how computers handle video vs. how cameras handle video. Such a subject is not the focus of this book, however. Just know that, in most cases, you can expect your standard-definition footage to be shown as having a 720 × 480 *frame size*.

You may also wonder why, in the case of standard-definition *widescreen* footage, the dimensions under *Frame Size* are no different than they are for the 4:3 footage. This is because the program reads the pixel resolution as the same for both aspect ratios. For widescreen, however, there is something called an *anamorphic squeeze* applied, which forces the square dimensions of the standard definition image down to the more rectangular widescreen (16:9) aspect.

You can see how this works if you scroll through the Browser window, using the blue scrubber bar at the bottom, beyond the point to which we have currently opened it. Eventually you will come to a column marked *Anamorphic*, as shown in Figure 10.4. There should be check marks next to all of the clips in the *Video_01* bin, since *Nail Polish* was shot in 16:9 standard-definition video. Double-click on the shot *1K. wide Michael crosses garden*, so that it appears in the Viewer, and then drag the playhead to the middle of the shot,

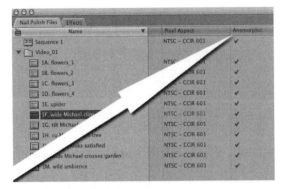

FIGURE 10.4 The *Anamorphic* column in the Browser.

FIGURE 10.5 Uncheck the *Anamorphic* column next to shot *1K. wide Michael crosses garden*.

FIGURE 10.6 Now, shot *1K. wide Michael crosses garden*, without its anamorphic squeeze, is vertically squeezed, making Michael look strange.

so we can see the actor playing Michael clearly in the frame. Now, click in the *Anamorphic* column, next to that same clip, so that the check mark goes away, as shown in Figure 10.5. You will now see that the image has been re-squeezed back into a 4:3 aspect ratio, as shown in Figure 10.6. It looks strange, as a result. The *Digital Filmmaking* book in this series will explain more about aspect ratios and how anamorphic squeezes work. Check the *Anamorphic* column again when you are done viewing the image.

The following two figures show how the shot *1K. wide Michael crosses garden* changes when you remove the check from the *Anamorphic* column.

In the world of high-definition video, all images are shot in a very rectangular aspect ratio, so there is no need for this squeeze. Widescreen is built into the new format. You will see, when you import such footage in the future, that the *Anamorphic* check mark is not there, even though the image is an at least a 16:9 aspect ratio.

Vid rate column

This column refers to the frame rate of your clips. If you remember, from Chapter 1, the traditional frame rate for the medium of film is 24 fps (frames per second).

When the North American television system, known as *NTSC* (National Television System Committee) was created, in the 1940s, the frame rate chosen was 30 fps. This number came about because of our system of electrical current works *Alternating Current,* or AC. It cycles at 60 hz, and the frame rate formula the early television engineers used halved that number. The first television systems were in black & white, and when color television was invented, the previous system didn't quite work, and they had to improvise a fix, which resulted in a frame rate of 29.97 fps, which is a slightly cumbersome number. The *PAL* (Phase Alternate Line) television system developed in Europe was based on a different electrical system, running at 50 hz. That is why PAL runs at 25 fps, which has usually been an easier system to match to 24 fps when transferring film to video.

Now we are in a world where we can shoot video in all kinds of frame rates, and the differences between NTSC, PAL, and film are merging as high definition (HD) takes over. And the types of frame rates we are seeing are 23.98, rather than 24, or 59.94, rather than 60. Both of these awkward numbers have to do, again, with the original decision to shift the NTSC frame rate from 30 to 29.97 when color arrived.

Then there is the additional factor of *progressive* vs. *interlaced* frames: that "p" and "i" you see after frame rates when you shop for players, TVs, and cameras. This has to do with *scanning*, or how a particular device reads the video signal. If a format is *progressive*, this means that your device shows you all of each of frame. If it is *interlaced*, then your frames are divided into two fields, and the scanner alternates between showing the odd fields and the even fields with each scan. The *progressive* scan rate results in a higher quality video image, without the jagged lines you may remember from the days of VHS.

And while that's the limit of how much we will explore this issue in this book, you should remember the following, at least: pay attention to your frame rates, and make sure your sequence frame rate matches your clip frame rates. We will learn how to do this later in this chapter.

Compressor column

Most video cameras capture footage in a format that has some kind of compression. This means that all of the information that makes up your images, such as color, exposure, etc. – a large amount of information – has to be contained in a digital storage unit that is, ultimately, too small to display the information as your eye sees it. In addition, you may have limited space in which to store really high quality files. So, the *compression* – or *codec* – reduces the file size to make it more manageable. This reduction in size, however, comes with a similar reduction in quality. The task of the video editor frequently involves balancing this size vs. quality equation.

If you ever go back and watch 1980s television, you'll see that, compared to what you're used to seeing today (or even to 1990s television), the video doesn't look so great. But if you watch 1980s films, or even 1950s or 1960s films, shot on film (or 1980s TV shot on film), you'll see that they look pretty good (as long as the transfer to video has been done well). That's because film has always been able to reproduce the real world with far greater resolution than video (until now, since HD improves every year). Also, the chemistry of film hasn't changed nearly as much as the technology of video over the last 40 to 50 years, so we're used to seeing film images that look very similar to those of the recent past.

But in video, the compression just keeps on getting better. What is particularly impressive is how much quality can be compressed into file sizes that aren't necessarily that large. Whichever *codec* you shoot in, you should make sure you understand it, so that you can arrange the settings of FCE appropriately. Later in this chapter we will learn how to do that. If you refer back to Figure 10.3, you will see that the *codec* of these *Nail Polish* files is *DV/DVCPRO – NTSC* compression. Always make sure, as with frame rates, that your sequence and clips are set to the same codec.

Data rate column

Later, when we capture some AVCHD footage, you will see how the *data rate* for that particular format is much larger than the *Data Rate* for these files. The *data rate* has to do with how much information is encoded into the file, per second. The larger the number, the greater the size of the video file. DV and HDV have a very similar size (as we will see), because HDV is really a hybrid format of quasi-HD resolution applied to a MiniDV tape.

Aud rate column

This number has to do with how many times your recorded audio is *sampled* (which is what *scanning* is for video), per second. The higher the number, the higher the quality of the audio. In general, all digital video these days is recorded with a sample rate of 48.0 KHz (some older cameras sample at 44.1 KHz).

Aud format column

The digital world is structured in binary numbers – or *bits* – and the value you see in this column references something called *bit depth*. As with the other numbers, discussed above, the higher the *bit depth*, the higher the quality of the audio. The standard for digital audio cameras, at present, is 16-bit. The *32-bit Floating Point* you see for the sequence, at the top of Figure 10.3, is the quality needed – twice that of the clips, themselves – to be able to apply transitions and effects to audio samples, without losing quality.

After rearranging or resizing the windows, as we have just done, you will probably want to reorganize everything to match the default configuration. You may remember, from Chapter 7, how to do that quickly and easily. If you forgot, here is a reminder: all you have to do is to press the control *key and the* U *key.Or you can go up to the* Window *dropdown menu and select* Arrange, *and then* Standard, *as shown in Figure 10.7*

Notice that there are other options available for window arrangements as well. Try them out. If you find an arrangement that you like and want FCE to remember it (until you quit the program), hold the option *key down as you access the* Window *menu. When you select the* Arrange *submenu, you will now see that, instead of* Custom Layout 1 *at the top, it reads* Set Custom Layout 1, *as shown in Figure 10.8. Highlight that line. The next time you select this menu,* Custom Layout 1 *will appear in bold, rather than light grey. Anytime you select that option (until you quit FCE), the windows will return to whatever arrangement they were in when you set this layout.*

NOTE

Video Formats

Now that we understand some basic format terminology, let's look at how we can set up our project for different codecs. There is an option, under the FCE dropdown menu – the fourth line down – labeled *Easy Setup*, as shown

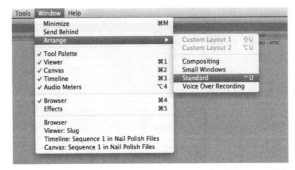

FIGURE 10.7 To reset the windows to their standard configuration, type *control* key + *U* key or select *Arrange* and *Standard* from the *Window* dropdown menu.

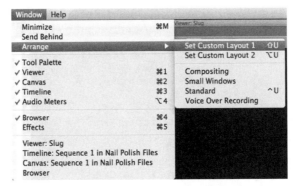

FIGURE 10.8 If you hold the *option* key down as you open the *Window* dropdown menu, you can set a *Custom Layout*.

in Figure 10.9. When you select that option, the *Easy Setup* menu pops up, as shown in Figure 10.10, and you can then choose the correct format for your project. Go to the top pop-up menu – labeled *Format* – and click on it to see your options, as shown in Figure 10.11.

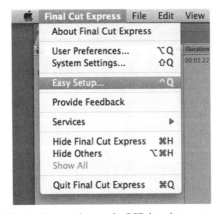

FIGURE 10.9 How to find the *Easy Setup* option on the FCE dropdown menu.

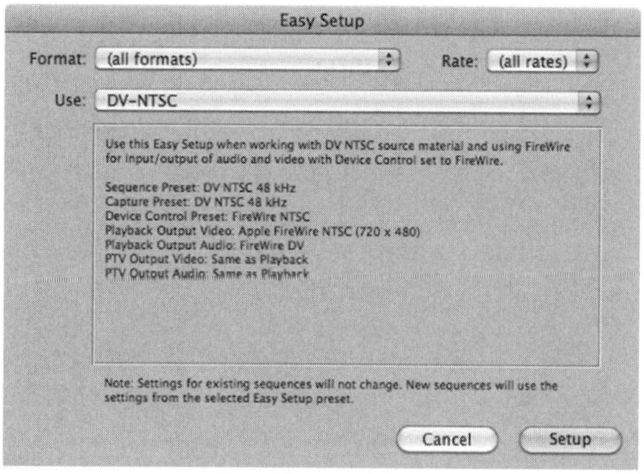

![Easy Setup menu showing Format (all formats), Rate (all rates), Use DV-NTSC with description text](image)

FIGURE 10.10 The *Easy Setup* menu.

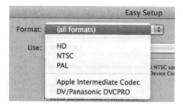

FIGURE 10.11 The Format pop-up menu in the *Easy Setup* menu.

Easy setup options

Depending on what you select under *Format*, the program then determines what you will see under the *Use* pop-up menu. For example, if this were an SPCA website, and you were choosing an animal to adopt, then if you selected *Dogs* here, you would not be given any *Cat* choices under *Adopt*. If you keep the format selection as *(all formats)* then all choices remain open, but you may then have many to sort through. You can decide what choices are appropriate for your level of experience and expertise.

We have been editing *Nail Polish* in *NTSC*, so you could choose that option here. If you choose it, then we will not see any *HD* or *PAL* options later. But you can always go back into this menu and reset your choice, so don't be afraid to do whatever you want to do.

DV vs. HDV vs. AVCHD

It is in this menu that we start to see some of the key differences between FCE and Final Cut Pro. Final Cut Express has limited format choices, and even though one of the options here is *HD*, it's really for *HDV* or *AVCHD*, both of which are hybrid formats that give you some of the resolution and quality of true HD, but not the complete package.

HDV is a format with the kinds of vertical lines of resolution you see in HD, but highly compressed onto a standard MiniDV tape. The tiny size of the magnetic strip limits what this format can actually do. That said, it looks much better than standard-definition formats, and if you have such a camera, what you shoot probably looks pretty good.

AVCHD is, likewise, a highly compressed video format – also with good lines of resolution – which is recorded onto hard drives attached to the camera or onto SD or other flash memory cards. While it is also better than standard definition, the image quality is still not quite what real HD can be.

Both HDV and AVCHD are less expensive formats that include the initials H and D, thereby allowing camcorder manufacturers to legitimately market their products as HD, but they are not professional-grade HD. One advantage, in addition to the cost, is that the files take up less storage space. And to the average eye, the video, if well exposed and focused, looks good. More important than the actual format you use is having a lens that allows for variance in depth of field, and manual focus.

Final Cut Pro allows you to capture in all of the current high-end HD codecs, and one day you may want to upgrade to it. The interface is very similar to FCE.

Choosing a frame rate

The next pop-up menu in the *Easy Setup* menu, to the right of *Format*, offers you frame rate choices, as shown in Figure 10.12. As with the first menu, whatever you choose from the *Rate* pop-up menu will alter the next set of choices, under *Use*. If you previously selected *NTSC*, under *Format*, then the 25.00 fps you see here would not appear. In fact, you would be unable to select this pop-up menu, since you would have only one frame rate available to you within the NTSC world, and that would be 29.97. Try it and see. In this way, you can see how your previous choice affects your ability to make subsequent choices.

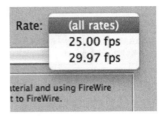

FIGURE 10.12 The *Rate* pop-up menu in the *Easy Setup* menu.

How your previous easy setup choices affect your remaining easy setup choices

Next, we have the *Use* pop-up menu, as shown in Figure 10.13. Depending on your previous choices, you may see many formats. Unless you have a very old camera or video tape deck, you should just choose *DV-NTSC* or *DV-NTSC Anamorphic*, if you are working in standard definition, or the PAL equivalents if you are shooting with a PAL camera. Final Cut Express has to include several other settings for a variety of cameras and decks. As we mentioned before, the bottom line is that you should be well aware of the format in which your camera has been recording *before* you get to this point, rather than trying to figure it out now.

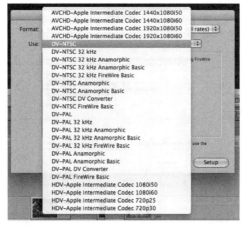

FIGURE 10.13 The *Use* pop-up menu in the *Easy Setup* menu.

Apple Intermediate Codec

We should mention one final note about how FCE (vs. Final Cut Pro) handles HD footage. Look at the full text, in the *Use* pop-up menu, when you select either *HDV* or *AVCHD*, as shown in Figures 10.14 and 10.15. There is an extra phrase there: *Apple Intermediate Codec*. This has to do with the fact that FCE is a less advanced program than Final Cut Pro. The application applies

FIGURE 10.14 *HDV-Apple Intermediate Codec* in the *Use* pop-up menu.

FIGURE 10.15 *AVCHD-Apple Intermediate Codec* in the *Use* pop-up menu.

a kind of translator to the codec in your original footage, which the more advanced Final Cut Pro does not. It will look the same, however, especially on your computer monitor, to 99.99% of people, so don't worry.

The whole purpose of the *Easy Setup* menu is to tell FCE what to expect when you import or capture footage. The settings that you have chosen will now be the settings applied to all new sequences you create. The sequences already in existence will remain in whatever format they were, as you can see in the little message posted at the bottom of this menu, as shown in Figure 10.16. Also, if you are going to hook up an HDV camera or deck to your computer, from which to capture video footage, FCE needs to know to look for *that* kind of camera, rather than for a standard DV camera.

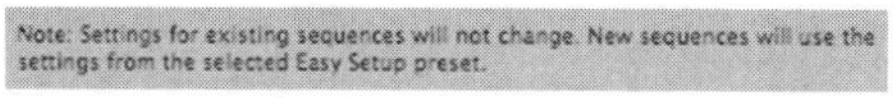

Note: Settings for existing sequences will not change. New sequences will use the settings from the selected Easy Setup preset.

FIGURE 10.16 At the bottom of the *Easy Setup* menu is a message that tells you that the changes you have made will *not* be applied retroactively to existing sequences.

Other ways to check the format of footage

Let's now leave FCE for a brief moment, and visit our scratch disks on our computer or external hard drive. You can conveniently hide most open programs in the Mac OSX, so that you can see other areas of your computer screen more easily. In FCE, go up to the FCE dropdown menu and select *Hide FCE*, as shown in Figure 10.17. After you do so, the application will vanish from view, and you will see, if you have no other programs open, the computer desktop underneath. The keyboard shortcut for this option is the *command* key + the *H* key. Later, if you wish to return to the program, just press the *command* key + the *tab* key, and a special menu – the *Application Switcher* – will pop up on your computer screen that allows you to cycle through all of the open programs, as shown in Figure 10.18. Each time you press the *tab* key, while holding down the *command key*, you will advance to

FIGURE 10.17 *Hide FCE* selected in the *FCE* dropdown menu.

FIGURE 10.18 The *Application Switcher*, accessed by pressing *command + tab*.

the next program in this menu. When you let go of the two keys as you are highlighting a particular program, that program will reappear.

Now that we have hidden FCE, go to your scratch disks, or wherever you stored the *Video_01* files with which we have been working. From within your OSX *Finder*, highlight this folder, as shown in Figure 10.19. Then, highlight the first shot in that folder, which should be *1A. flowers_1*, as shown in Figure 10.20. If your *Finder* is in *Column View*, as in these illustrations, you can see that an additional column has now opened up. Within that column is some of the same formatting information we saw in our FCE Browser earlier. Let's click on the *More info…* button (the keyboard shortcut is the *command* key + *I* key). This brings up a new pop-up window, as shown in Figure 10.21, and in this window we see even more format information, including the codec for this clip.

Now you know how to check your clip information independently of any software application. Using the *Get Info* (*command* key + *I* key) function on any file, anywhere, will always show you all you need to know for that file.

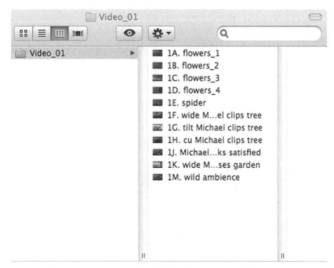

FIGURE 10.19 From within your OSX *Finder*, highlight the *Video_01* folder.

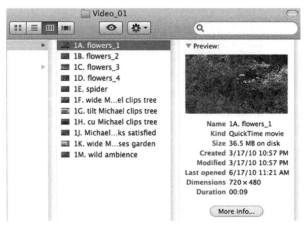

FIGURE 10.20 Highlight the first shot in the *Video_01* folder, *1A. flowers_1*, and look at the information that appears in the next column.

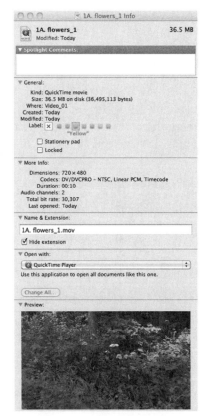

FIGURE 10.21 Look at the *Info* pop-up menu for shot *1A. flowers_1*.

QuickTime

Under the information specifications we just explored, our video file was listed as a *QuickTime* movie. QuickTime is a media player developed by Apple, which was originally only able to play video or audio files on Apple computers. As it has done with iTunes®, however, Apple has created versions of QuickTime that work on Windows systems as well.

But QuickTime is more than just a media player. It is primarily a digital audio and video encoder, which creates container files, known as *wrappers*. Think of it as a picture frame to hold your movie. Any file encoded within QuickTime (which is the default way to export files from FCE) is given the file extension *.mov*. QuickTime is not, however, a codec – files with the *.mov* extension can have a variety of different codecs. And QuickTime can read files with many different extensions, such as *.mp4* (for video) or *.mp3* (for audio). When we discuss how to export your finished film as a self-contained movie, we will revisit what QuickTime can do.

Depending on which version of OSX you are using, your default QuickTime application will either be *QuickTime Player 7*, as shown in Figure 10.22, or the newer *QuickTime Player*, as shown in Figure 10.23. There are subtle differences between how the two programs operate, but, for our purposes, they do the same thing.

David Pogue, technology correspondent for The New York Times, *has an aptdescription of the difference between the two QuickTime apps in his OSX manual.*[2]

FIGURE 10.22 The older, pre-OSX Snow Leopard *QuickTime Player 7.*

FIGURE 10.23 The newer OSX Snow Leopard version of *QuickTime Player*.

File extensions

Sometimes file extensions like *.doc* (for Microsoft Word™) or *.mp3* (the most common audio encoding) have a direct correlation to the codec of the file. Sometimes, as in the *.mov* extension, they only tell you the *wrapper*, or container file, system. It is a good idea to spend some time understanding the file extensions and codecs with which you will be working with on a given project.

We should look at one more file extension, before we get into the next section on audio formats, since it is for audio files: *.aif* (or *.aiff*). In the world of encoding, there are two different kinds of encoding: *lossy* and *lossless* compression. *MP3* and *AAC* files – two of the most common audio standards in today's world – use *lossy* compression, which is a lower quality (but smaller in size) than the *lossless* compression of *AIFF* files. AIFF stands for *Audio Interchange File Format*, and is the compression used in most professional audio encoding. When you buy a professionally formatted CD, the individual audio tracks on that CD have been encoded using AIFF compression. When you burn an audio CD (rather than an MP3 CD) in iTunes, the tracks are likewise encoded in the AIFF format. When you import music into FCE, make sure it is in AIFF.

Let's look at what music files look like when we open a CD on our computer desktop. We'll choose a movie soundtrack, such as Wong Kar-Wai's *In the Mood for Love*, as shown in Figure 10.24. Working in our OSX Finder, in *List View*, we can easily see that all of the files are in the AIFF format. Now look at what the files could possibly look like after they have been imported into iTunes from the CD, as shown in Figure 10.25. Here, they are all listed as *MPEG-4 Audio Files*, which is the description for the *AAC* (or *Advanced Audio Coding*) format that Apple developed in the late 1990s as an improvement over MP3 files. These files are much smaller than AIFF files, if you

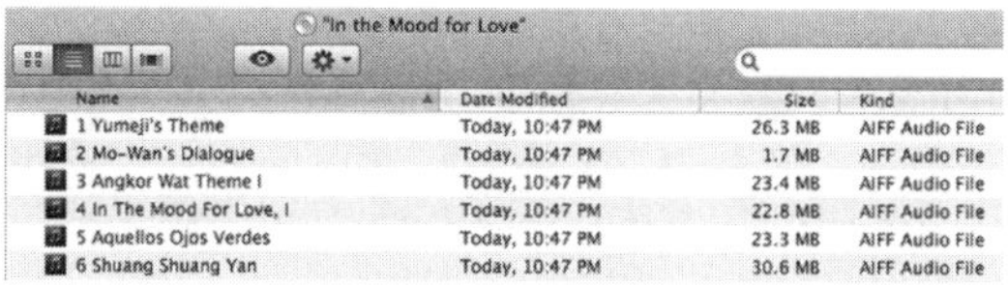

FIGURE 10.24 Audio files on a preformatted CD are automatically encoded as *AIFF* files.

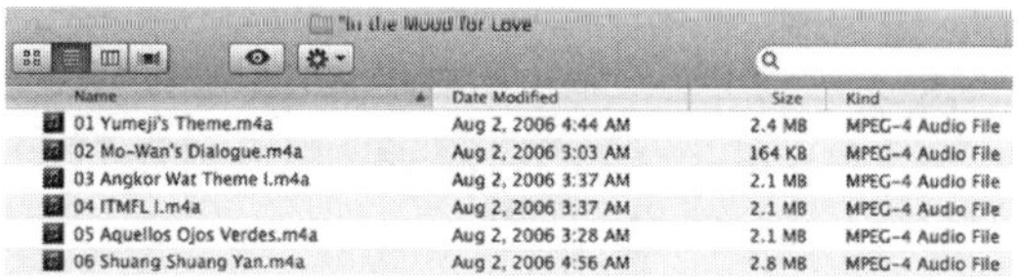

FIGURE 10.25 The default audio format of iTunes is the *AAC* file, with a *.m4a* file extension, listed as an *MPEG-4 Audio File*.

look at the *Size* column, which is good for storing most of them on your hard drive. For playing on your iPod, AAC, or MP3 quality is adequate. Not true for professional audio work. Use AIFF files. *WAV* (or *Waveform Audio File Format*) files, which are usually uncompressed, work well, too.

Audio Formats

Of course, you can import files in any kind of audio format you want, and FCE will most likely play it (it won't play *AAC* files, however). It may give you the red *must render* line at the top of the Timeline, but once you render the file, it will play. Still, if that original file is not an AIFF file, and was compressed in a *lossy*, rather than *lossless* way, the up-conversion to a *lossless* format (which is what FCE will do), sometimes results in audio blips and crackles that make the audio sound as if it is being played on an old vinyl record.

If you must use music to which you do not own the rights – and if you do, then you can never legally screen it anywhere – then the best way to get that music is to drag it directly from the CD to your computer or hard drive, let it copy from the CD, and then import it into FCE. This way it will remain encoded as an AIFF file.

Using iTunes to convert your audio formats

Instead of a CD, however, you probably buy your music online, through the iTunes store or a similar such retailer. If you do, then that music arrives as an AAC or MP3 file, most likely. The iTunes application offers you a fairly simple way to convert that music file to another format. This is how it works. Go ahead and open your iTunes application, which comes free on your Mac.

Go up to the *iTunes* dropdown menu and scroll down to *Preferences*, as shown in Figure 10.26. The *Preferences* menu will then appear, as shown in Figure 10.27, and you will see an *Import Settings* button. Click on it. The *Import Settings* menu, which appears next, as shown in Figure 10.28, offers you the option to change the compression that iTunes uses when importing new music files. Select *AIFF Encoder*. Then, in the *Settings* pop-up menu below that line, select *Custom…*, as shown in Figure 10.29. When the *AIFF Encoder* menu next appears, switch all of the options to the highest quality settings, as shown in Figure 10.30. Click *OK* on that menu and all of the other menus until you are back to the main iTunes window. Now, go to the *Advanced* dropdown menu up top, after first selecting the file(s) that you wish to convert to AIFF, and you will see that there is an option to *Create AIFF Version*, as shown in Figure 10.31. Select that option, and your file(s)

FIGURE 10.26 In iTunes, go up to the *iTunes* drop-down menu and scroll down to *Preferences*.

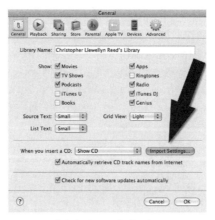

FIGURE 10.27 In the *Preferences* menu click the *Import Settings* button.

FIGURE 10.28 Select the *AIFF Encoder* in the *Import Settings* menu.

FIGURE 10.29 Then select *Custom...* in the *Settings* pop-up menu.

FIGURE 10.30 In the *AIFF Encoder* menu, choose the highest quality for all settings.

FIGURE 10.31 To convert your non-AIFF files to this format, now that you have changed the *Import Settings*, use the *Advanced* drop-down menu.

will begin to convert. The converted file(s) will be stored in whatever you have previously set as your main iTunes music folder. You can then import it into FCE just as you would a video file.

Capturing DV Footage

Although standard-definition video (DV) is on its way out, it's still here, and still a part of FCE, so we will cover how to capture this kind of footage to your computer. *Capturing* is the process by which your recorded video is transferred from the medium of tape to the medium of your computer's hard drive. Since this involves turning the information into a purely digital format and removing it from the residual analog holdover of an actual tape, we also call this process *digitizing*. While it's true that DV means *digital video*, which means that the signal is already digital, the device on which this signal is stored (i.e., the tape) is not. Once you capture the video to your computer, however, it becomes all digital 1s and 0s.

Start with your tape

So, first, we'll need a MiniDV tape – the standard consumer tape format – with some pre-recorded footage on it. The examples used in the pages ahead are taken from the original tapes of *Nail Polish*. You can use whatever tape you have. If you don't have any MiniDV footage, you can either skip this section, or just read it for future reference.

Take your tape and load it into a MiniDV video *deck* (another word for player or VCR) or camera, and make sure the deck is hooked up to your computer via a *Firewire* cable. We discussed this cable interface in Chapter 6. These days, there are two different kinds of Firewire connections: *400* and *800*. The cable connector that fits into your MiniDV camera will be smaller than either a Firewire 400 or 800 connector. It's called a *4-pin* Firewire connector. The Firewire 400 end is called a *6-pin* connector, and Firewire 800 is called a *9-pin* connector. The *pins* refer to the contact points of that end of the cable.

If you're using a Mac made before September 2008, then it has at least one Firewire 400 cable port. Post-August 2008, Apple started phasing out Firewire 400, and is now no longer using it on its computers. However, there are plenty of cable adaptors that will help you go from the 4-pin connection on your camera or deck to the 6-pin or 9-pin connections on your computer. Search online or visit your local computer store to find the right cable or adaptor. Once your deck or camera is hooked up to the computer, turn it on.

Go back to the *Easy Setup* menu, under the *FCE* dropdown menu, so we can make sure our project is set to the right format. For *Nail Polish*, that proper format would be *DV-NTSC Anamorphic*, as shown in Figure 10.32. Once you choose a particular format, the program does everything else for you. Take a look at the text in the middle of the menu. The *Sequence* and *Capture* presets are the same now, and the *Device Control* preset (this means the deck or camera) now reads *Firewire NTSC*. We are ready to capture.

FIGURE 10.32 Set the *Easy Setup* menu to *DV-NTSC Anamorphic*.

Opening the Capture menu

Now go up to the *File* dropdown menu and select *Capture...*, as shown in Figure 10.33, or press the *command* key and the *8* key. Even if you have properly followed the instructions on how to connect your camera/deck to the computer and turned it on, you will likely be confronted with an error message, as shown in Figure 10.34, letting you know that FCE cannot find a video deck or camera.

It's an easy fix, however. When you first open FCE, without a deck or camera attached, a warning screen pops up, as shown in Figure 10.35. Once you click *Continue* in that screen, you tell FCE to act as if you don't need a camera/deck. Even if you subsequently attach one to the computer and turn it on, FCE will ignore the device until you tell it to recognize it.

FIGURE 10.33 Select *Capture...* from the *File* drop-down menu.

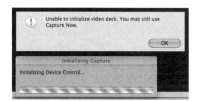

FIGURE 10.34 After you select *Capture...*, you will likely see this error message.

Click *OK* in the error message screen that reads *Unable to Initialize Video Deck*. The *Capture* menu pops up next, unusable for the moment, with text at the bottom that reads *No Communication*, as shown in Figure 10.36. We need to do something else to tell FCE to recognize our deck. So let's close this menu, either by clicking on the topmost left button, or using the *command* key and the *W* key.

FIGURE 10.35 The *External A/V* warning screen that appears when you open FCE without a deck or camera attached.

You could quit the program and restart, and since the deck or camera is on and attached now, you won't see the warning screen that tells you there is no deck again. Or, you could do something just as simple, and go up to the *View* dropdown menu, scroll down to *Video Out* and choose *Refresh Video Devices*, as shown in Figure 10.37. As long as your deck or camera is on and

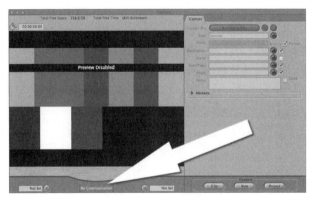

FIGURE 10.36 The *Capture* menu, open but unusable for capturing, since it cannot communicate with your camera or deck.

FIGURE 10.37 Choose *Video Out* and *Refresh Video Devices* from the View dropdown menu to force FCE to recognize your deck or camera.

attached, then after you have clicked on that line, FCE will now recognize your device. Scroll back down to *Video Out*, and now you should see some new information there, including the text *Apple Firewire NTSC (720 × 480)*, with a checkmark to the left of it, as shown in Figure 10.38. If you're working with a PAL device, then the other line will be checked. Your deck or camera is now recognized, and you can proceed with capturing.

Go back to the *File* menu, scroll down to *Capture*, and you will now be taken directly to the *Capture* menu, without the error message, and with the words *VTR OK* at the bottom, as shown in Figure 10.39. *VTR* means *Video Tape Recorder*. Don't worry about the line in the middle of the color bars that reads *Preview Disabled*. That line will be there until you first play your tape, and anytime you click away from the *Capture* screen.

FIGURE 10.38 Now, under *Video Out*, you will see information on the attached and recognized video device.

FIGURE 10.39 Back in the *Capture* menu, the *VTR* is now recognized, and we can proceed with capturing.

Let's look at the buttons above the words *VTR OK*. They should look just like the *Transport Controls* at the bottom of both the Viewer and Canvas windows. They control the playback of the tape in either your deck or camera, since once it is linked to the computer via Firewire, FCE can communicate directly with it. If you forget what the buttons do, remember that you can always just hover over each one to have FCE tell you its function.

Finding the shot you want

Find a shot on the tape, using the *Transport Controls* to fast-forward or rewind, that has some other footage you wish to capture, as shown in Figure 10.40. If you drag the *Shuttle Control*, which we discussed in Chapter 9, instead, then you can see the video on the tape as you scroll

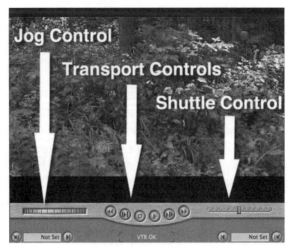

FIGURE 10.40 Use the controls you find most convenient to locate the shot you want to capture.

through it at high speed. The *Jog Control* will also let you preview your footage but will move you more slowly through the tape. If you just press the *fast-forward* button, then you will go more quickly through the tape, but you will not be able to see anything as you do so.

Stop the tape just before the point at which you wish to capture. The *Preview Disabled* and color bars are gone, and we can see the image of the stopped frame. On the right side of the *Capture* window is a data entry area, under the *Capture* tab, as shown in Figure 10.41. All information typed here will be encoded with the footage when it is captured and

FIGURE 10.41 The data entry fields under the *Capture* tab that allow you to name your shot before capture.

can be extremely helpful down the line, as we will soon see. You should always label the *Reel* – usually with the name of your movie and the tape's number, in sequence – and the *Description* of the shot. You could choose to enter the *Scene, Angle,* and *Notes* information, as well, but the more useful line is the *Shot/Take* field, as it will automatically number your shots for you, in order. Whatever you type in these fields will show up in the *Name* line (which you cannot type in). This name will be the name of the clip once captured, both in FCE and in your scratch disk folder. So choose a name for your clips that makes sense. You can always change the name, or subclip a longer clip into smaller clips, later (as we learned in Chapter 9).

Capturing the Clip

At the bottom of this tab, there are three buttons, as shown in Figure 10.42, under the heading *Capture*, labeled *Clip*, *Now*, and *Project*. The easiest function to use is *Capture Now*. To use it, start playing your tape, and then click on *Now*. A big black screen will pop up in front of all of the other windows in FCE, as shown in Figure 10.43. This screen will display the video as it captures, but in the meantime this is FCE's way of letting you know that things are starting up. At the bottom of the screen, you can read the text *Waiting for Timecode*. This means there is a slight lag in communication between the deck and the computer. This, by the way, is why you should begin playing the tape a few seconds before the actual frames that you need.

FIGURE 10.42 At the bottom of the *Capture* tab are the three buttons that allow you to capture footage from your tape.

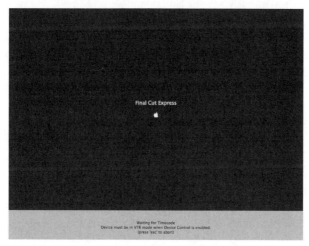

FIGURE 10.43 The black screen that appears before full communication has been established between the computer and your deck or camera.

After a few seconds the communication link is firmly established, and FCE starts digitizing video from the tape, as shown in Figure 10.44. You will not hear the sound of your clip during capture through the computer, but you can hear it through the deck or camera, if an audio output is enabled. Now that the capturing process has begun, FCE will continue capturing until either the tape runs out of footage or you press the *esc* key, per the information at the bottom of the *Capture Screen*, as shown in Figure 10.45. In the

FIGURE 10.44 The *Capture Screen* plays your footage in front of the other windows (but without sound).

System Settings menu (which we explored in Chapter 7), you can limit how much video will be captured using the *Capture Now* button. If you don't want clips that are too long, you can tell the program to only capture clips up to 30 minutes or more, or less.

Capturing Clip – NOW CAPTURING (press 'esc' to stop)

FIGURE 10.45 The text at the bottom of the *Capture Screen* tells you what to do when you want to stop capturing.

When you are ready to stop capturing, press the *esc* key. In your Browser, a new clip has appeared, labeled with the text your entered in the *Capture* tab, as shown in Figure 10.46. Let's quickly make a bin in which to put this new footage, to stay as organized as possible. Go to the *Edit* dropdown menu, or just press the *command* key and the *B* key. When the new bin appears, give it a name that makes sense, as shown in Figure 10.47.

FIGURE 10.46 After you press the *esc* key, your new clip appears in the Browser.

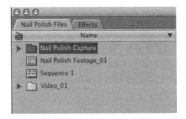

FIGURE 10.47 Make a new bin into which you can drag this clip.

Setting your Capture Bin

If you want to be really organized, you can have the clips you captured automatically show up in this bin, rather than having to drag them there. This is easy to set up. Press the *control* key as you click on the bin we just created (or right-click your mouse), and a pop-menu appears. Choose *Set Capture Bin*, as shown in Figure 10.48. Now the bin has a little icon of a FCE slate to the left of it, as shown in Figure 10.49, which means that it is the designated *Capture Bin*, and will remain so until we set a new *Capture Bin*, or quit the program. All subsequently captured clips will automatically be placed here.

FIGURE 10.48 Right-click or control-click on a bin to see a pop-up menu that lets you set this bin as the *Capture Bin.*

Let's capture a new clip, using the same *Capture Now* method, and see how this *Capture Bin* works. Back in our *Capture* tab, we don't have to do anything, because FCE has automatically increased the number of the next clip by one, and registered the new *Capture Bin*, as shown in Figure 10.50. If you hover over the two buttons to the right of the top *Capture Bin* label, you will

FIGURE 10.49 The *Capture Bin* is designated by a red icon of a film slate.

see an alternate way to create and set a new *Capture Bin*. Remember that FCE always offers more than one way to do things.

Start playing your tape, and hit the *Now* button again. When you arrive at the end of the shot, click the *esc* key. Now, this new shot has appeared, in the Browser, directly in our new bin, as shown in Figure 10.51.

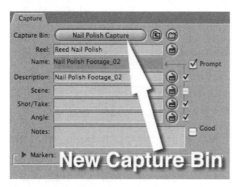

FIGURE 10.50 The *Capture* tab reflects the changes in the clip name and the new *Capture Bin*.

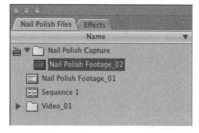

FIGURE 10.51 The new shot appears in the *Capture Bin*.

Capturing with in and out points

Now we're going to capture a shot in a slightly different way, using *In* and *Out* points. Underneath the *Transport Controls*, to the left and right of the VTR OK text, are two small white windows, as shown in Figure 10.52. The buttons on the inside side of each window should look familiar, since they are there for setting *In* and *Out* points, like the same buttons in the Viewer and Canvas windows. Find the starting point of a new shot you want to capture and click on the *In* button (or simply press the *I* key). Then play through the shot, find the end point, and click on the *Out* button (or simply press the *O* key). You are now ready to use the *Capture Clip* function.

FIGURE 10.52 The *In* and *Out* buttons of the *Capture* menu.

All you have to do, once you have set *In* and *Out* points, is to click on the *Clip* button on the bottom of the *Capture* tab, to the left of the *Now* button we previously used. This time, you don't have to start playing the deck or camera first. After you click on the *Clip* button, the *Log Clip* menu appears, as shown in Figure 10.53. You can choose not to change anything, or you can add a note, perhaps describing what is in the shot. You can also check *Mark Good*, which places a checkmark in a column (which we did not explore) in your Browser, labeled *Good*. When you are done, click *OK*.

After you click *OK*, the same black screen appears that we saw when we used the *Capture Now* function. After a few seconds, the tape deck starts to roll forward from just before the *In* point you marked. As soon as that first frame is hit, the capture screen appears, as it did before. Once the *Out* point is passed, the screen disappears, ending the capture process, and that new clip appears in the Browser, in the *Capture Bin*, as shown in Figure 10.54.

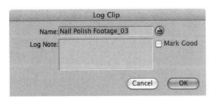

FIGURE 10.53 The *Log Clip* menu appears after your click on the *Capture Clip* button.

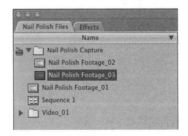

FIGURE 10.54 After you use the *Capture Clip* function, the new clip appears in our Capture *Bin*.

Capture Now vs. Capture Clip

Which is better: *Capture Now* or *Capture Clip*? *Capture Now* definitely takes less time to set up: you just find the spot on the tape where you want to start capturing, start playing, press the *Now* button, and then press *esc* when you're done. But if you want to be more precise, and capture only the exact set of frames that you want, then *Capture Clip* allows you to do that. In Final Cut Pro, you can actually go through an entire tape, *logging* (which means setting *In* and *Out* points and assigning clip names) every single shot you want, then capturing them all at once. In FCE, you can't do that, but if you just want to capture a single shot, then using *Capture Clip* is useful. Use the method that works best for you.

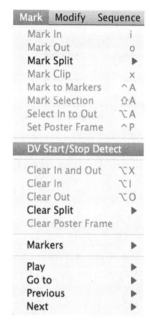

FIGURE 10.55 The *DV Start/ Stop Detect* function can be found in *Mark* dropdown menu.

If you do use *Capture Now*, then there is a way to capture a very long clip and then easily break it up. Most DV video cameras have a system that sets an internal marker every time you start and stop recording, allowing you to use the *DV Start/ Stop Detect* function available under the *Mark* dropdown menu, as shown in Figure 10.55. After you capture a long chunk of video, with many separate clips within, you can use this option, and it will add markers at every point where you stopped recording. This helps makes subsequent subclipping much easier. If, after highlighting the captured clip in your Browser, you click on this option and it informs you that there are no breaks detected (even if there should be), then that simply means that the camera on which you shot does *not* apply these start/stop markers. However, you can still, fairly easily, subclip without this function.

Setting Capture Markers

There is one more aspect of the *Capture* menu that we have yet to examine, and that is the bottom half of the *Capture* tab, where there is an expandable *Markers* submenu. Click on the triangle to open up the menu, as shown in Figure 10.56, and you will see an option to set and name a *Marker* position before you capture your clip. If there is a particularly good performance moment that you see as you preview the tape, mark it here. Or, if it turns

FIGURE 10.56 The *Markers* menu at the bottom of the *Capture* tab.

out that your camera does not allow for the *DV Start/Stop Detect* function to work, you could mark the beginnings and ends of all shots here. All of these *Markers* would then show up after capture, making it easier to subclip.

Using Capture Project

There is one more capture function to explore: *Capture Project*. But let's first prepare ourselves by discussing what is, for now, a hypothetical situation. Let's say we opened up FCE, and saw that the *Nail Polish* footage had gone *offline*. In Chapter 6, we discussed *online* vs. *offline* resolution, but this is different. Sometimes FCE cannot find the actual media, on your hard drive, that the clip data references. Perhaps your external hard drive has been disconnected, or someone has deleted your clips. If this were the case, then as long as your FCE project, itself, were intact, you would still be able to find or recapture the original media, without having to do all of the work over. If the media were missing, then your Browser would look the same, but the clips would have red lines running through them, as shown in Figure 10.57. If you then double-clicked any of these clips, the Viewer would show you a *Media Offline* message, as shown in Figure 10.58.

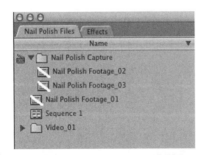

FIGURE 10.57 If your clips go *offline*, they still show up in your Browser, but have red lines running diagonally through them.

FIGURE 10.58 If you double-click one of these *offline* clips, you see a *Media Offline* message in the Viewer.

If your media has gone offline – for whatever reason – then the first thing you should do is to scroll down, within the *File* dropdown menu, and select *Reconnect Media*, as shown in Figure 10.59. This function allows FCE to search your computer and any attached hard drives for the media to which these clips were originally connected. Whichever clips you highlight before clicking on this menu is the number of clips FCE will look for; you can also highlight a bin that is filled with clips.

FIGURE 10.59 To *Reconnect Media*, select that function in the *File* dropdown menu.

After you click on *Reconnect Media*, the *Reconnect Files* menu appears, as shown in Figure 10.60. In the top window, we can see the file(s) for which FCE is now going to search. Click on the *Locate* button in the middle of the screen, and a *Reconnect* browser pops up, as shown in Figure 10.61. Navigate through this screen, which acts like any other Finder in Mac OSX, and locate the folder where you think the file(s) should be. If the file exists somewhere on your computer or attached external hard drive, FCE should be able to find it. Once the file is located, click *Choose*, and the program will reconnect this file to the clip in your FCE Browser, removing the red line and *Media Offline* message.

FIGURE 10.60 The *Reconnect Files* menu.

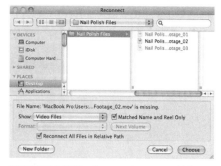

FIGURE 10.61 The *Reconnect* browser, which acts just like any other Mac OSX Finder, allows you to locate missing media.

In this hypothetical situation, however, let's assume that the files have disappeared. Perhaps you deleted them by mistake; perhaps the hard drive failed. If that has happened, but you still have the original FCE project, as well as the original tapes with the original media, then you can recapture your shots easily. This is where the final *Capture* function – *Capture Project* – comes in. You can access this option by clicking on the *Project* button in the

Capture menu. You can also scroll down to the *Capture Project...* line in the *File* dropdown menu, as shown in Figure 10.62, after having first selected the shot(s) you want to recapture.

Once you make that selection – from either menu – the *Capture Project* menu appears, as shown in Figure 10.63. Look closely at this menu. Notice that you can choose to add *handles*, extra bits of footage on either side of the original media you had captured. We discussed *handles* in Chapter 9, when we explored transitions, and the benefits of having extra footage are the same here. Perhaps you want a few more frames to play with, just in case. Whatever your decision, click *OK*. If everything is done correctly, you will *not* see an error message such as the one shown in Figure 10.64, which warns you about *Non-Drop Frame media* vs. *Drop Frame media*.

In the world of NTSC video, where 29.97 fps is sometimes rounded up to 30 fps, some cameras offer *Drop Frame* vs. *Non-Drop Frame* timecode

File	Edit	View	Mark	Mo
New				▶
New Project				⇧⌘N
Open...				⌘O
Open Recent				▶
Close Window				⌘W
Close Tab				⌃W
Close Project				
Save Project				⌘S
Save Project As...				⇧⌘S
Save All				⌥⌘S
Revert Project				
Restore Project...				
Import				▶
Export				▶
Capture Project...				⌃C
Capture...				⌘8
Log and Transfer...				⇧⌘8
Reconnect Media...				
Print to Video...				⌃M

FIGURE 10.62 You can access the *Capture Project...* function through the *File* dropdown menu, as well as through the *Capture* menu.

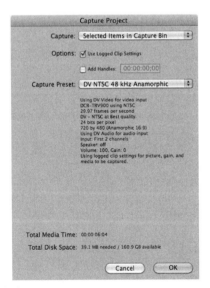

FIGURE 10.63 The *Capture Project* menu.

options. Most cameras should shoot *Non-Drop Frame* Timecode, which is more accurate, but if your capture device – if its different than the camera with which you shot – is set to *Drop Frame*, you could, over the course of a long clip, have synchronization issues.

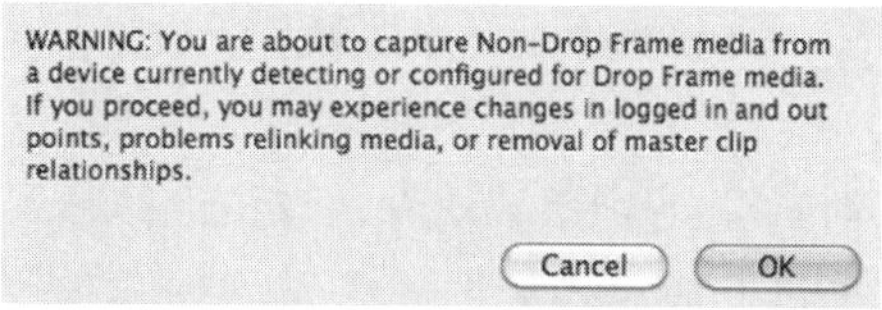

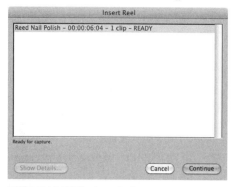

FIGURE 10.64 A possible error message you may see about *Non-Drop Frame media* vs. *Drop Frame media*, as you set out to capture footage.

It's best to go into the settings of that camera or deck and change it to *Non-Drop Frame* timecode to match the media.

Once you get past this problem or, even better, fail to have this problem, the *Insert Reel* menu pops up, as shown in Figure 10.65. This menu let's you know which *Reel* – or tape – you need to insert into the deck or camera. If you remember, we had the option of naming the *Reel* in the *Capture* tab of the *Capture* menu. It's in situations like this where your organization really pays off. Final Cut Express treats every different *Reel* label as a different tape. If your movie existed over six tapes, and

FIGURE 10.65 The *Insert Reel* menu.

each one had a different *Reel* name and/or number, you could just sit back and insert each tape as FCE finished re-capturing from the previous one.

The only obstacles preventing this process from working would be if you had timecode breaks on your actual tapes, but then this is a problem you would have encountered while capturing the media the first time, and so you would hopefully have designed a new *Reel* designation in which FCE would consider different parts of the tape as separate tapes. *Digital Filmmaking* by Pete Shaner in this book series deals with shooting without timecode breaks, so make sure you understand this process.

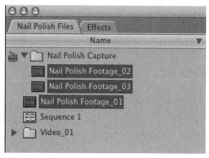

Once you have recaptured the missing media (or reconnected files that had been misplaced), the red lines disappear from the clips, as shown in Figure 10.66.

FIGURE 10.66 Once your media is recaptured/reconnected, the red offline lines go away.

Now that we're done exploring the DV capture options, let's move on to HDV.

Capturing HDV Footage

HDV – short for *high-definition video* – is a format designed to record high-definition lines of resolution on a MiniDV tape. The capture process for HDV, at least in FCE, is much simpler than the capture process for DV, because there are fewer options from which to choose. Let's start by resetting the format of our project to match our new needs. If you do not have any HDV footage, you can, as with the DV section, skip ahead, or read along and learn this process.

Go back to the *FCE* dropdown menu and the *Easy Setup* menu therein. Choose the HDV setting that matches the format of your tape, as shown in Figure 10.67. Hook up your camera/deck via Firewire, turn it on, and then

FIGURE 10.67 Choose the HDV format that matches your footage in the *Easy Setup* menu.

either repeat the same *Refresh Video Devices* process that we performed for DV, or quit and restart the program. Then type the *command* key and the 8 key, or go to the *File* dropdown menu and select *Capture*. This time, something slightly different happens.

Instead of the *Capture* window, we see something similar to what happened, in DV, when we used the *Capture Clip* function. A small pop-up window appears – the *HDV Capture* menu – giving us the option to name the clip we are about to

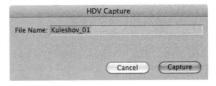

FIGURE 10.68 The *HDV Capture* menu.

capture, as shown in Figure 10.68. Choose a name that makes sense to you that can also apply, logically, to all of the footage on your tape (we'll see why in a moment). In this chapter, the illustrations of HDV footage we see are taken from the *Kuleshov Effect* clips we will use in Chapter 12. Once you have named your footage appropriately, click on the *Capture* button.

The black preview screen pops up, as before. Again, the text at the bottom of the screen tells us that the program is cueing the tape, and then, a few seconds later, the video of the actual shot pops up, as shown in Figure 10.69.

FIGURE 10.69 An HDV clip as it captures, taken from the *Kuleshov Effect* footage we will use in Chapter 12.

The HDV capture process does not let you, through FCE, fast forward or rewind the deck or camera to the exact spot where you wish to begin capturing. You have to do that using the controls on the deck or camera itself. This is a big difference from the DV capture process. On the other hand, you can leave the tape running, and every time there is a new shot, the HDV capture process automatically breaks up the shots, eliminating the need for future subclipping.

NOTE

You may have noticed that the shot in Figure 10.69 is underexposed. This was done on purpose to allow us to practice a few brightening techniques as we edit the clips in Chapter 12.

At the bottom right-corner of the *Capture* screen, you will see a text message that can be different every time you capture. If we look more closely at what it says during the capture of the first *Kuleshov* clip, as shown in Figure 10.70, we read the following: *Capture is 2% behind the camera.* Because HDV is such a hybrid format, with a lot of high resolution tightly compressed onto a MiniDV tape, the system can sometimes have trouble dealing with a smooth flow of information in the digitizing process. When this happens, there is a slight lag, and the image you see on your computer screen is slightly behind what is actually being captured at that moment. This doesn't really matter. Sometimes you see this, and sometimes you see a different

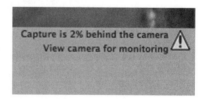

FIGURE 10.70 You might see a message like this while capturing HDV footage shows the preview screen behind the live capture.

FIGURE 10.71 Another message you might see showing preview and capture in perfect synchronization.

message, as shown in Figure 10.71: *Capture is Real-Time*. This latter message means that what you see on the screen is what is actually being captured at that moment. Regardless of which message you see, it does not affect the capture.

You can – and should – create a *Capture Bin* when working with HDV footage, just as we did with DV footage. Let's assume we did just that, and that we have now allowed FCE to capture a number of clips from our HDV tape. All on its own, the application has separated each shot, wherever there was a start/stop point on the tape, and now all of our shots sit in our bin, as shown in Figure 10.72. HDV capturing is simple, as you can see.

FIGURE 10.72 Our Browser, after we successfully captured six HDV clips into our *Capture Bin*.

As we look at our Browser before moving on to the next exercise, we may see the *Nail Polish Footage_01* shot, from the last section, still sitting outside of the bin we created after capturing it. Let's now move it inside that bin, as shown in Figure 10.73, so that we are consistent in our clip organization. And now, let's move on to AVCHD capture – or transfer, as it's called.

FIGURE 10.73 Our Browser, after we moved the *Nail Polish Footage_01* shot into the same bin, with its related clips.

Transferring AVCHD Footage

AVCHD – short for *Advanced Video Coding High Definition* – is a consumer-quality flash-memory based HD format. When you capture any kind of video footage that has been recorded to some kind of memory storage – a hard drive, an SD card, a flash card – rather than to tape, the process of bringing that footage into FCE is called *transferring*, rather than capturing. This is because the footage is already digitized – there is no old-school analog tape interface – and you are simply copying, or *transferring*, the video into the application. However, you can't just copy the files to your computer – from the hard drive or memory card – and then import them, as we imported the footage in Chapter 7. It's a little more complicated than that.

This is because, in order to maximize storage space on the cards or hard drives, the footage is encoded in a particular way to that storage device. Final Cut Express then has to decode the footage before it can become video clips that are viewable on the computer. You can, of course, copy the entire contents of your camera's SD card to your own computer's hard drive, and then log and transfer from those files, as if they were the original card. You can't, however, view the video directly from the files.

The Log and Transfer menu

To start, make sure you have some AVCHD footage on a camera or card reader that is hooked up to your computer. If you do not have any footage, then you can, as before, read along, or skip ahead. In the world of *transferring*, you can, depending on the camera, use either a USB cable or a Firewire, or both. Once you have your footage ready, go back to the *Easy Setup* menu we have already used twice before, for DV and HDV, and set the format of the application to match the format of your footage. Then, go to the *File* dropdown menu and scroll down to *Log and Transfer*, as shown in Figure 10.74, or press the *shift* key, the *command* key, and the *8* key.

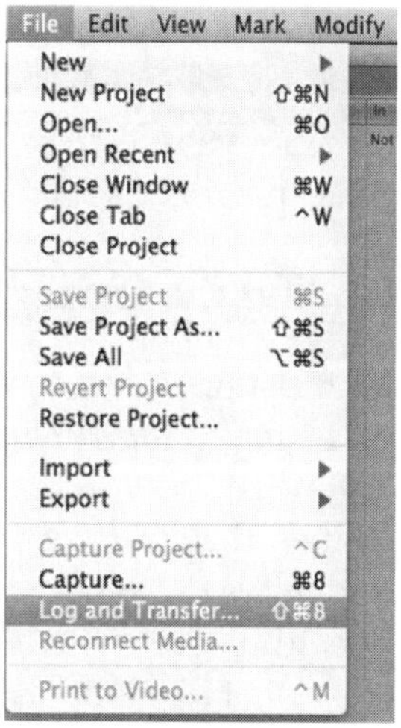

FIGURE 10.74 Select *Log and Transfer* from the *File* dropdown menu.

The *Log and Transfer* menu will then pop up, as shown in Figure 10.75. In the case of DV and HDV capture, the *Capture* menu does not appear without a warning if there is not a deck or camera attached. That is not the case for AVCHD footage, since you could, if you wanted, transfer files that had already been copied to your computer, as we just mentioned.

There are four separate sections in this screen, and as we will see, shortly, we can resize some of them to suit our needs or preferences. The upper-left quadrant is where the clips-to-be-transferred will appear. The bottom left is

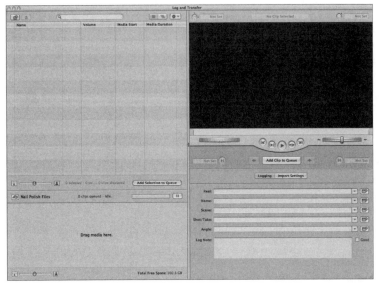

FIGURE 10.75 The *Log and Transfer* menu.

the space to which you will drag these clips. The upper right is where you can watch a selected clip before transferring, and the bottom right is where you can name the clip, the reel, etc., just as in the DV *Capture* tab.

Finding the footage to transfer

In the upper left of the upper-left quadrant is a small *Add Folder* button, as shown in Figure 10.76. This lets you tell FCE where the footage that you wish to transfer is located. If, at this point, you have connected your camera or card reader to the computer, then it is highly likely that the upper-left quadrant of the *Log and Transfer* menu is already filled with clips awaiting transfer. Your SD card (or compact flash card, or camera hard drive) is therefore visible on your computer desktop, as shown in Figure 10.77 (often labeled as *NO NAME*). If, however, you are trying to transfer clips from files that you copied to your computer, you will need to click on the *Add Folder* button, and then select the copied files from the Finder window that appears, as shown in Figure 10.78.

FIGURE 10.76 The *Add Folder* button of the *Log and Transfer* menu.

FIGURE 10.77 An SD card as it will most likely appear on your computer's desktop.

However you do it, the clips will eventually appear in the *Log and Transfer* menu, in the upper-left quadrant, known as the *Browse Area*, as shown in Figure 10.79. Whichever clip is highlighted in the *Browse Area* will appear in the *Preview Area* in the upper-right quadrant. In the lower-right quadrant – the *Logging Area* – the *Reel* (here, the folder from which

FIGURE 10.78 After you click on the *Add Folder* button, you then need to search for any copied files through the Finder that appears.

these files have been imported – if they were from the actual SD card, it would read *NO NAME*) and the *Name* appear, as shown in Figure 10.80. You can change these to suit your own organizational needs.

FIGURE 10.79 The *Log and Transfer* menu, filled with clips in the *Browse Area*, waiting to be transferred.

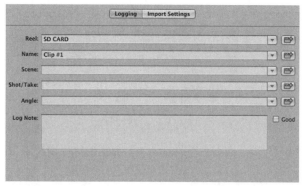

FIGURE 10.80 The *Logging Area*, with the *Reel* named after the folder from which the files were imported, and the *Name* as the default FCE clip name.

Import Settings

Notice how there are two buttons at the top of the *Logging Area*: *Logging* and *Import Settings*. Click on *Import Settings*, and that menu will appear, as shown in Figure 10.81. The only options here, in FCE, are to uncheck (or check if it's already unchecked) either *Video* or *Audio*. Doing one or the other allows you to transfer only the video or audio portions of your shot. If you want to apply these *Import Settings* to multiple shots at once, you just highlight all the shots you need, go into this section, uncheck or check the box you want, and then click on the *Apply to Selection* button on the bottom.

FIGURE 10.81 The *Import Settings* menu.

Remember that to highlight multiple clips – or any items – in any of the FCE windows, you need to either hold down the shift *key as you click, if you want to highlight items in sequence, or hold down the* command *key, if you want to highlight items out of sequence.*

Resizing the menu windows

As we noted earlier before, it is possible to resize the different quadrants or halves within the *Log and Transfer* menu. All you have to do is grab the thin gray bar that separates the windows, and drag it until the window you want to make larger has taken over the entire screen. For example, you can make the right half of the screen fill the menu, as shown in Figure 10.82, or you can make the left half fill the menu, as shown in Figure 10.83. By dragging the separation bar back to its original position, you can set things back to the way they were.

FIGURE 10.82 You can resize the *Log and Transfer* menu this way.

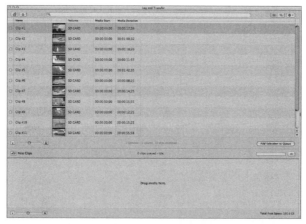

FIGURE 10.83 You can also resize the *Log and Transfer* menu this way.

Transferring footage

Let's practice transferring now. Make a new bin in the Browser, and set it as the *Capture Bin*. Then, change the *Reel* and *Name* fields in the *Logging Area*, if you want, and highlight the clips you want to transfer. Next, drag the shots down to the bottom-left quadrant – known as the *Queue* – which, conveniently, has the words *Drag Media Here* across its center, and let go, as shown in Figure 10.84. You could also have highlighted the clips

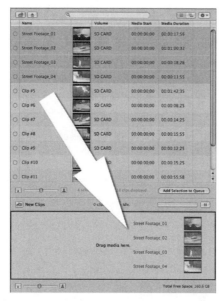

FIGURE 10.84 Drag the clips you want down to the *Queue*, and they will start transferring.

and then clicked on the *Add Selection to Queue* button at the bottom of the clip window.

Regardless of how you do it, the clips will now transfer. You can watch their progress in the *Queue*, as shown in Figure 10.85. When the process is complete, the transferred clips have, in the *Browse Area*, blue dots to the left of each one (they were clear before), as shown in Figure 10.86. Also, they now appear in the Browser, in the *Capture Bin* you created, with the names you gave them in the *Logging Area*, as shown in Figure 10.87.

FIGURE 10.85 You can watch the transfer progress of the clips in the *Queue*.

FIGURE 10.86 Once the clips are transferred, they have blue dots, instead of clear dots, to the left of them in the *Browse Area*.

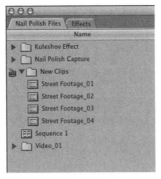

FIGURE 10.87 Once the clips are transferred, they also appear in your Browser, in the *Capture Bin* you previously set.

Flash vs. tape

One of the convenient things about transferring files from flash memory, as compared to capturing from tape, is that the transfer rate is usually much faster than in real time. When you capture, the rate for tape is a straight up

1:1 ratio. 25 minutes of taped footage takes 25 minutes to transfer. With AVCHD footage, the speed of the transfer depends on the type of camera you use, whether or not it connects via USB or Firewire, and the type of compression with which you shot (1080 vs. 720). But it will still be faster – even if only slightly so – than a 1:1 ratio.

Working with AVCHD files is easier and faster, but there are certain precautions to keep in mind as well. With tape, there is always a master copy of your footage to go back to, if your computer crashes, unless you rerecord over the tape. But once you transfer your files from your SD card, you will most likely immediately reformat that card, thereby destroying the master copy. If your computer then crashes, you're in trouble. So it is important that you make back-up copies of your work (or of the SD files), and place them somewhere safe, on a different computer or hard drive.

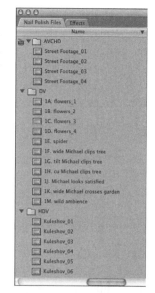

FIGURE 10.88 Now is a good time to reorganize your Browser so that your bins and clips are clearly labeled.

Let's quickly reorganize our Browser with just three bins: one for each format, as shown in Figure 10.88. If you want to rename any of the clips you have captured or transferred, go ahead and do so. This is good practice for helping you develop the essential media management skills that an editor needs. You may wonder how clips in different formats can co-exist in the same project. Don't worry. We will experiment, in Chapter 12, with what happens when you drag footage in one kind of format to a sequence that is set to a different format. For now, we are done with capturing and transferring. Let's review how to import files, and then end with a discussion of how to export files.

Importing Files Directly from Your Computer

In Chapter 7, we imported files from the movie *Nail Polish*, and explored both the *Import File* and *Import Folder* options. Remember that there is no keyboard shortcut for *Import Folder*. The shortcut for *Import File*, however, is the *command* key plus the *I* key.

Let's import an audio file, just to practice. Use the *Import File* options, either from the *File* dropdown menu or by using the keyboard shortcut, and then find an audio file – preferably in AIFF format – on your computer, as shown in Figure 10.89. If you have no AIFF files, refer back to the section, earlier in this chapter, where we discussed how to convert files in iTunes. Click on *Choose*, and the audio file now appears in your Browser, as shown in Figure 10.90. It has a different icon than the video footage, which helps you quickly tell them apart.

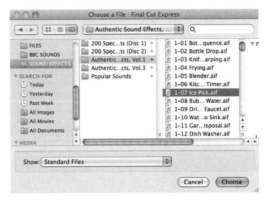

FIGURE 10.89 Import an audio file from your computer, preferably in AIFF format.

Next, let's import a folder, just to compare. Choose a folder with some type of image files, such as jpegs, as shown in Figure 10.91. Click *Choose* – this time with the entire folder selected (*Import Folder* only lets you select a folder, not individual files). Now the entire folder appears, as a bin, in your Browser, and you can open it up to see the images within, as shown in Figure 10.92, and their icons, which are different from both the video and audio icons.

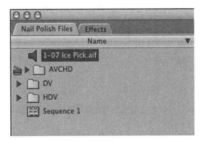

FIGURE 10.90 After you import the file, it appears in your Browser, with a different icon than the video footage.

Both audio and image files will appear in your Viewer if you double-click on them, just as video files do. The audio, as we saw in Chapter 9, shows you its waveforms – the graph of its sound waves – as shown in Figure 10.93, and the photo pops up as a video clip, as shown in Figure 10.94. The default length of this video clip is 10 seconds, but you can change this in the *User Preferences* menu. Notice how the dimensions of the photo do not match the Viewer screen. That's because the photo's

FIGURE 10.91 Import an entire folder, this time with image files.

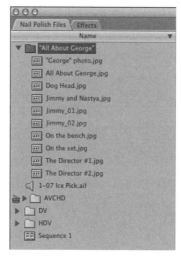

FIGURE 10.92 After you import the folder, it appears in your Browser, and the image files have different icons than the video or audio files.

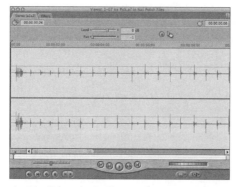

FIGURE 10.93 When you double-click an audio file, you can see its waveforms in the Viewer.

FIGURE 10.94 When you double-click an image file, it also appears in the Viewer, as a 10-second video clip.

aspect ratio does not, in this case, match the aspect ration of our chosen video format. There is nothing you can do about that, except to change the size of the photo, if you want it to fill the screen. We explored how to do that, in Chapter 9, when we discussed the *Motion* tab of the Viewer.

We should note one more thing about importing audio. A mistake that beginning editors often make is to insert a CD into their computer and then import a music track directly from the CD. Then, when they eject the CD, the audio file is shown as being offline. That's because it is offline, since the device from which it was imported is gone. What you need to do first is to drag the file from the CD to your computer or hard drive, let it copy off of the CD, and *then* import it into FCE.

Let's now discuss how to export files.

Exporting to Tape

There are two basic ways to export your finished movie: to tape and as a self-contained digital file. The former is becoming increasingly rare, while the latter is becoming the norm. If you have a self-contained file, you can use it to burn a DVD or Blu-Ray disc, or compress it for YouTube, Facebook®, Vimeo®, your own personal website, etc. In today's world, that is far more useful. Nevertheless, let's first discuss the tape method.

Before you export your movie, no matter the method of export, you always want to make sure that you have rendered all of the effects, transitions, etc. Look to see if you have any colored lines at the top of the *Timeline* window (Figure 10.112) and, if so, go up to the *Sequence* menu and choose one of the *Render* options. Once everything is rendered, you are ready to export.

Make sure you have clicked in the *Timeline* window, so that it is selected. Then, go up to the *File* drop-down menu and select the *Print to Video* option, as shown in Figure 10.95. The *Print to Video* menu that then appears, as shown in Figure 10.96, presents you with many options. You can add elements before and after your film, such as frames of *Black* (which is blank space), a *Slate*, *Color Bars*, a *Countdown*, etc. In the world of professional broadcast video, there are certain requirements for the submission of work,

FIGURE 10.95 Select the *Print to Video* option in the *File* dropdown menu.

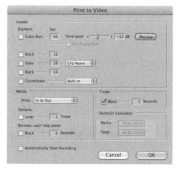

FIGURE 10.96 Choose the options you want to have added before and after your movie in the *Print to Video* menu.

and this menu lets you meet those requirements. For now, let's just leave the default 5 seconds of *Black* at the end, then click *OK*.

As soon as we do this, the computer screen is filled with a giant veil of black, on top of which a small pop-up screen appears, as shown in Figure 10.97. The text in this screen is fairly self-explanatory, as it basically tells you to start your video recorder and then to click *OK*. Hopefully, your camera or deck is attached and recognized by the program, with a fresh tape inside. Press record on that device, and then click *OK*. The movie starts playing, as shown in Figure 10.98, and, hopefully, recording to your deck or camera. When the film is done, the full FCE screen will reappear, and you can stop your device from recording.

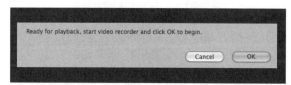

FIGURE 10.97 The pop-up screen that appears when you start the *Print to Video* is fairly self-explanatory.

FIGURE 10.98 After you click *OK*, your movie starts to export and is hopefully recorded by the device you attached.

If you had decided to add color bars, or any other item in need of generation, you would have first seen the same kind of pop-up window you see when you render effects, as shown in Figure 10.99. You would then see, before your actual movie, color bars, as shown in Figure 10.100, a slate of some sort, as shown in Figure 10.101 (this is the default text), and/or a countdown, as shown in Figure 10.102. Otherwise, the process would flow in the exact same way.

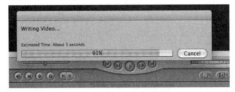

FIGURE 10.99 If you choose to include extras in the *Print to Video* process, the application first has to create them.

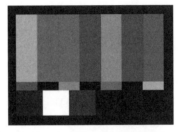

FIGURE 10.100 This is what the color bars look like, if you select them.

FIGURE 10.101 This is the default slate – the title of your sequence – if you select it.

FIGURE 10.102 This is what the countdown looks like, if you select it.

There is a slightly different way to export to tape, which is simpler, as long as you don't want or need any of the special export options. If your camera or deck is attached and recognized by FCE, you can simply place the playhead at the start of the Timeline, press play, and the signal will be received by your device. If that device is recording, then the movie will print to tape, just as if you had used the *Print to Video* menu. Nothing will look different in FCE; the playhead will move calmly through the Timeline. But if you use this method, you may want to make sure your movie doesn't just start up from the first image. If so, you can put small handles of black at the head and tail of the sequence.

In order to do this, you can either go to the *Video Generators* bin, under the *Effects* tab, or you can click on the *Generator* pop-up menu on the bottom right of your Viewer. If you use the latter option, scroll down and choose *Slug* (which is black, blank video), as shown in Figure 10.103. Now your Viewer is filled with black, as shown in Figure 10.104. The default length for *Slug*, unless you change it in the *User Preferences*, is 10 seconds.

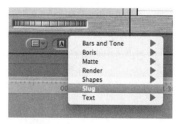

FIGURE 10.103 Choose *Slug* from the Viewer's *Generator* pop-up menu.

That's too long for our handles, so in the upper-left *Clip Duration* field of the Viewer, you can change the length to 2 seconds, as shown in Figure 10.105. We can then drag it down to the Timeline, first at the head of the movie, as shown in Figure 10.106, and then at the tail, so that the film has 2 seconds

FIGURE 10.104 *Slug* is black, blank media.

FIGURE 10.105 You can change the length of an item in the Viewer by typing in a new value in the upper-left *Clip Duration* field.

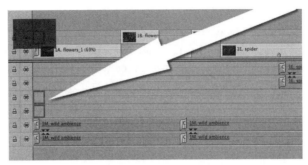

FIGURE 10.106 Drag the *Slug* down to the head of your movie, so that the film starts after a brief moment of blank media.

of nothing before it starts and after it ends. Now we can use the second tape exporting method without our film just beginning and ending abruptly. After which we can leave the world of tape behind, and look at how to export your film as a self-contained digital file.

Exporting as a Self-Contained Digital Movie File

Just under the *Import* line in the *File* dropdown menu is the *Export* option. Scroll down there now, as shown in Figure 10.107. You will see that there are three options: *QuickTime Movie*, *Using QuickTime Conversion*, and *For LiveType*. We'll talk about *LiveType* in Chapter 11, so let's focus on the first two options.

FIGURE 10.107 Scroll down to the *Export* option in the *File* dropdown menu.

The easiest option to use is the first setting, *QuickTime Movie*. What this option does is export your movie using the same format settings as the sequence in which it has been edited. If your sequence is in NTSC Anamorphic, then that is the format in which your project will be exported. If it's a 1080i HDV sequence, it will be exported as such. It's that simple. Let's try it.

Click in the Timeline, and then select *Export As QuickTime Movie*. As soon as you do so, the *Save* menu pops up, as shown in Figure 10.108. Choose the location where you would like to save the movie, and give it an appropriate name. Notice the options at the bottom of the window, in the *Include* pop-up menu. You can export both Audio and Video, Video only, or Audio only. The *Markers* pop-up menu allows you to include chapter makers for a program like iDVD®. Finally, and perhaps most importantly, is the *Make Movie Self-Contained* box. If you uncheck this, then what you are exporting is a reference file only – like an alias – that requires all of the original media you used to create the movie. You could not copy this to a different computer, or upload this to YouTube, and expect it to play. You could, however, use it to make a DVD through iDVD, if you continued to work off of the same computer or hard drive, where all of the media still exists.

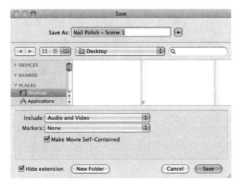

FIGURE 10.108 The *Save* menu for the *Export As QuickTime Movie* option.

We want to make sure that we know how to make a file that exists independently of the original media, and we do that by keeping the *Make Movie Self-Contained* box checked. Always look for that check mark, if you want your movie to exist as its own separate entity. As for the other check box in the bottom left – *Hide Extension* – all this will do, if checked, is hide the *.mov* file extension, which does not affect the performance of the movie. When you are all set, click *Save*, and the export begins, as shown in Figure 10.109. When it is all done, you will have a file on your desktop (or wherever you saved it) that is a self-contained movie, as shown in Figure 10.110.

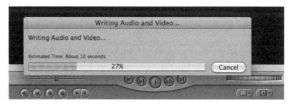

FIGURE 10.109 After you click on *Save*, the export begins.

FIGURE 10.110 When the export is done, your movie exists as a self-contained file.

Now let's go to the *QuickTime Conversion* option. When you select that option, a very similar *Save* menu appears, as shown in Figure 10.111. There are, however, some differences, if you look at the bottom of the screen. There are two pop-up menus, plus an *Options* button, that allow us to make some more detailed format choices. The *Format* pop-up menu, as shown in Figure 10.112, lets us choose a variety of ways to export files as either audio, video, or even still images. The *Use* pop-up menu, as shown in Figure 10.113, lets us choose some presets (in this case, various forms of compression for the Web) that are the relevant options for whatever format you have chosen in the *Format* pop-up menu. Let's stick to the *QuickTime Movie* format, and go into the *Options* button to see how we can change the default settings.

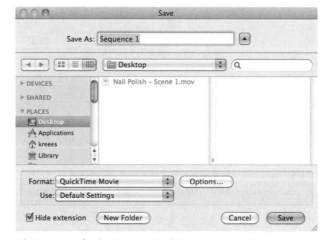

FIGURE 10.111 The *Save* menu for the *Export As QuickTime Conversion* option.

3G
AIFF
FLC
iPod
Apple TV
iPhone
✓ QuickTime Movie
AU
AVI
Wave
DV Stream
Still Image
Image Sequence
iPhone (Cellular)
MPEG-4

FIGURE 10.112 The *Format* pop-up menu.

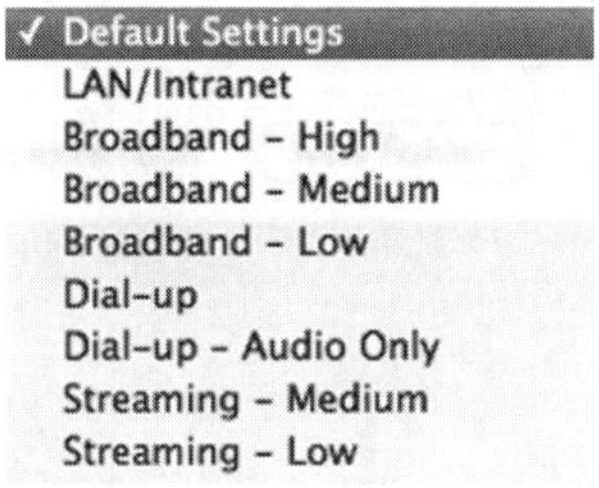

✓ Default Settings
LAN/Intranet
Broadband – High
Broadband – Medium
Broadband – Low
Dial-up
Dial-up – Audio Only
Streaming – Medium
Streaming – Low

FIGURE 10.113 The *Use* pop-up menu.

When we click on *Options*, the *Movie Settings* menu appears, as shown in Figure 10.114. There are three areas where we can tweak the settings: *Video, Sound*, and *Prepare for Internet Streaming*. Let's click on the *Settings* button within the *Video* area. That pulls up yet another pop-up screen – the *Standard Video Compression Settings* menu – as shown in Figure 10.115. Look up at the *Compression Type* pop-up menu. It's currently set to H.264, which is a type of compression typically used for Web streaming and/or downloading, as well as for some DVD's. If you were to click on this menu now, as shown in Figure 10.116, then you would see many more options than you need at this point.

FIGURE 10.114 The *Movie Settings* menu.

If you want to use this menu, then figure out what your project format is. For *Nail Polish* we know that it was shot in DV/DVCPRO – NTSC. If we can find that compression, we can ignore the other choices.

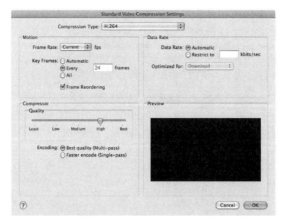

FIGURE 10.115 The *Standard Video Compression Settings* menu.

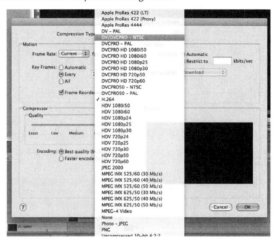

FIGURE 10.116 The *Compression Type* pop-up menu.

Once you find your format, select it, and go to the Motion area of the *Standard Video Compression Settings* menu and click on the *Frame Rate* pop-up menu to change the *Frame Rate* to match that of the sequence, as shown in Figure 10.117, which is 29.97 fps. Then, in the *Compressor* area, choose the *Quality* and the *Aspect Ratio* you want (which for *Nail Polish* would be 16:9), as well as the *Scan Mode* (*Interlaced* or *Progressive*), as shown in Figure 10.118. Once you are done, click *OK*, and we are brought back to the *Movie Settings* menu.

FIGURE 10.117 The *Frame Rate* pop-up menu.

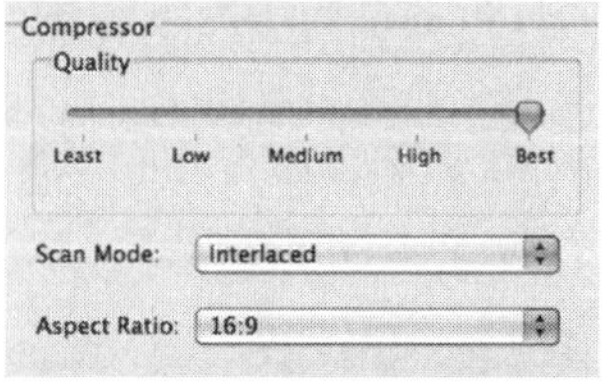

FIGURE 10.118 Choose the *Quality*, *Aspect Ratio*, and *Scan Mode* in the Compressor area.

Next, click on the *Settings* button in the *Sound* area of the *Movie Settings* menu, which brings us to the *Sound Settings* menu, as shown in Figure 10.119. Leave everything as is, for DV NTSC, except for the *Render Settings*, which you could change, if you wanted, to *Best* (most people won't be able to hear the difference). These settings already match the audio standards for professional audio, as we discussed earlier in this chapter. Click *OK*.

FIGURE 10.119 The *Sound Settings* menu.

Back in the *Movie Settings* menu, uncheck the *Prepare for Internet Streaming* box, as shown in Figure 10.120, since we are not, at present, exporting for the Web. And then click *OK* to leave the *Movie Settings* menu. Note that we used this menu as a springboard to two other menus, which allowed us to tweak both audio and video settings.

FIGURE 10.120 Uncheck *Prepare for Internet Streaming*.

We are now ready so export this sequence as a self-contained movie using the *Export As QuickTime Conversion* option. Back in the *Save* menu, give the file a name that makes sense, and then click *Save*. Movie files take a little longer to export using *QuickTime Conversion* than using *Quick-Time Movie*, since you're asking FCE to think a little more. Eventually it will finish, however, and then you will see two self-contained QuickTime movie files on your desktop, or wherever you saved them, as shown in Figure 10.121. One of them has a visible file extension, while the other one does not. For our purposes, it doesn't matter.

FIGURE 10.121 Both self-contained files – exported in two different ways – look the same, even though the file extension for one of them is hidden.

In order to view these files on the desktop, hide FCE, which we discussed how to do earlier in this chapter. Highlight both clips at once, and press the *command* key plus the *I* key (*Get Info*, if you remember). Two almost identical information windows, one for each movie, pop up, as shown in

Figure 10.122. In the middle of these windows is a box you can check if you want to unhide the file extension, as shown in Figure 10.123.

Look in the top half of both windows, under *More Info*. Notice how the dimensions, codecs, etc., are virtually the same, as shown in Figure 10.124. On the right, for the one done through the *QuickTime Movie* option, the order of the codecs is listed differently, and there is an additional *Timecode* codec, which is not important; it is just some extra code from the sequence. For all practical purposes, these are identical files.

FIGURE 10.122 After you select *Get Info* for both movie files, their information windows open up.

FIGURE 10.123 If you want to unhide the missing file extension, uncheck the *Hide extension* box in the middle of the window.

FIGURE 10.124 Look under *More Info*, and you will see how these two files are more or less identical.

There is one important difference, however. The file we exported using *QuickTime Conversion* is automatically set to be opened by QuickTime Player, while the file we exported using *QuickTime Movie*, is, by default, set to open with FCE, as shown in Figure 10.125. This can be frustrating if you want to watch your movie file and double-click on it, only to have FCE open, rather than QuickTime. You can change this, however. Click on the *Open with* pop-up menu, as shown in Figure 10.126. Choose the application that you would rather have open that file; in this case, either QuickTime Player or QuickTime Player 7. Once you select one of the QuickTime players, then both files really are, more or less, the same.

FIGURE 10.125 If we compare the *Open with* pop-up menus for our two files, we may see a difference.

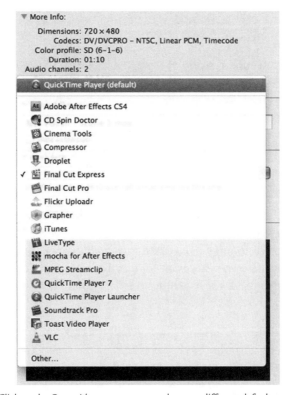

FIGURE 10.126 Click on the *Open with* pop-up menu to choose a different default application for the file.

That's it for exporting. In the next chapter we will tackle LiveType, so you can learn how to make some better titles than you can do in FCE alone.

In this chapter, we covered the current state of formats and compression, on both tape and flash memory storage units. While recognizing that the world of tape is on its way out, we nevertheless explored how to work within that world, since there are still many people and equipment that shoot to tape.

We began our exploration of formats by searching within FCE, to see how the application informs us of our current format and compression. As a result, we discovered the different types of compressions – or *codecs* – for a range of files, both audio and video. We learned how to recognize *file extensions*, and applied this knowledge to an understanding of how a few other Mac-based applications – such as QuickTime and iTunes – work. In the latter case, we even practiced converting audio files from their original compression to the AIFF codec.

We then began a systematic study of how to *capture* footage from tape. There are two tape-based formats that are compatible with FCE – *DV* and *HDV* – and we practiced with each one, in turn, paying close attention to how the capture processes for both formats intersect and diverge. As we captured, we continued to reinforce standard editing procedures and organization, such as naming files and storing them inside of clearly marked bins.

We then moved on to *AVCHD* footage, which is *transferred* to the computer, rather than captured. This is the one flash-based format currently compatible with FCE. We discovered how comparatively easy it is to work with this kind of footage vs. working with tape. We also discussed the need to have a master copy of your tape stored somewhere safe. This is one of the main reasons we continue to stress good editing practices. Back up your work frequently.

Next, we reviewed how to import files already digitized on your computer, such as music and photos. Final Cut Express treats them just as it does any other media: if the file is in a format that is readable to the application, then FCE will be able to import. By default, all still images

SUMMARY

are given a 10-second length, although you can change this in the *User Preferences*.

Finally, we explored the two ways in which you can export your finished films. You can *print to tape*, which requires you to have a deck or camera that you can attach to the computer, or you can export the file as a self-contained digital movie. Increasingly, filmmakers use the latter method, but there is still enough work being done using the former method that we needed to learn it.

Within the options to export as a self-contained movie, we looked at the differences between using the *QuickTime Movie* method and the *Quick-Time Conversion* method. Neither is better than the other, although the first way is easier; the second way gives a many more choices, and is better for the advanced user.

We are now ready to tackle LiveType, the software that Apple bundles with FCE. We will practice title creation, complete with moving fonts and special effects.

REVIEW QUESTIONS: CHAPTER 10

1. What is meant by *format* in the video world?

2. What are the different kinds of tapes from which you can capture in FCE?

3. What are the different kinds of HD footage that FCE understands?

4. What are some different ways to export your movie?

5. How do you import music and photos into your project? What is *AIFF*?

1. What are the pros and cons of exporting using the QuickTime Movie option vs. the QuickTime Conversion option?

2. Describe the differences between the three capture methods – from DV, from HDV, and from AVCHD.

3. Why is it important to understand the different video formats?

4. Describe, now that you know more, some of the potentially serious pitfalls that might occur if you do not organize your media well in the Browser.

Further Research

- Go back through this chapter and repeat the exercises, but with your own footage. If you don't have certain kinds of cameras, try and find people who do.

- Try exporting the movie in your sequence, through QuickTime Conversion, in a variety of different compressions. Compare the differences, in terms of file size and quality.

- Try exporting, through QuickTime Conversion, both still frames and audio files, to see how it works.

- Convert a music file that is *not* in AIFF format *to* AIFF format, then import both versions into FCE, and compare the difference.

References

1. Beach, Andy. *Real World Video Compression*. Berkeley, CA: Peachpit Press, 2008.

2. Pogue, David. *Mac OS X Snow Leopard: The Missing Manual*. Sebastopol, CA: O'Reilly Media, 2009.

CHAPTER 11

LIVETYPE: ADVANCED TITLING

OVERVIEW AND LEARNING OBJECTIVES

In this chapter, you will:

- Learn the basic interface of LiveType, a software application that comes bundled with FCE
- Explore how to make static titles and animated titles
- Understand the different ways to export your titles to FCE
- Practice with many of the tools and elements within LiveType

Why Make Titles?

Filmmaking is about editing, and about storytelling. Don't let today's special effects make you think differently. Successful movies still succeed primarily through their ability to move the audience, and they do that by having a good story to tell and by telling it well. It's about putting one shot next to another, and creating meaning. The lessons of Kuleshov and others still apply (as we will see in Chapter 12).

Why, then, should we care about making interesting graphics and titles? Well, credit sequences and titles can help set the mood of the film, along with music. As long as what follows is a strong story with good performances (and good editing), then the graphics that lead us in and/or take us out can only enhance the work. They shouldn't overwhelm it, and they shouldn't be better than the actual movie. In *Watchmen* (Zack Snyder, 2009), for example, the opening title sequence, designed primarily by Neil Huxley, is exciting, but the rest of the film is less interesting, and it is made more disappointing by the high expectations set in the beginning. In Zack Snyder's 2004 remake of George Romero's *Dawn of the Dead*, however, the opening title sequence, designed by Kyle Cooper, is equally brilliant, and sets the tone for a film that lives up to its title sequence.

In the last 10 years or so, television shows have given us some well-done credit sequence designs, such as those in *Six Feet Under*, *Deadwood*, *Dexter*, *Weeds*, and *Mad Men*. But credits and titles don't need to be fancy. For years, Woody Allen has used the same simple white-text-over-black title cards, accompanied by old jazz music. The simplicity of the design helps the viewer relax and know that what is coming is going to rely on the writing and acting, rather than on a major display of special effects.

Titles don't have to exist independently from the story either. You can have them appear over the opening action as well. Watch some of the openings of some of your favorite movies and pay attention to how those directors and title designers work, then figure out what you'd like to try in your own film.

LiveType, the software application we will learn in this chapter, is not After Effects, the Adobe-made software with which many of the more modern title sequences have been designed. But it is a significant step up from the possibilities that FCE, alone, can offer. So let's take a look at what it offers.

LiveType Basic Interface

Let's start by looking at the various windows within the application. Find LiveType in your *Applications* folder, or on your dock, and double-click on it. There's always the chance that you (or whoever installed FCE for you), disabled the install of LiveType, so if you can't find the program, go back to your install disk and select a LiveType only install.

After you open LiveType, you'll see the usual kind of pop-up window that always announces the opening of a piece of software, as shown in Figure 11.1. You should then see a software configuration window that shows three smaller windows sitting on top of a fourth, longer, window, as shown in Figure 11.2. If this isn't what your window arrangement looks like, don't panic. It just means that someone before you has simply decided to move things around. As in FCE, there are many dropdown menus at the top of your screen. Go up to the *Window* dropdown menu and select *Apply Default Layout*, as shown in Figure 11.3. The keyboard shortcut for this command is the *control* key plus the *U* key, as it is in FCE. Now you should see the default window setup. Let's look at each window to see what it does.

FIGURE 11.1 The LiveType opening pop-up window.

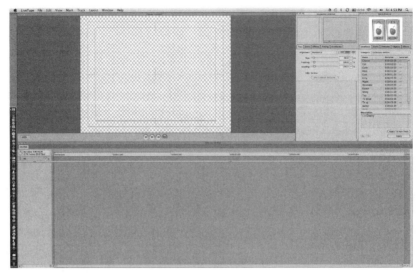

FIGURE 11.2 LiveType's default window configuration.

Layout	Window	Help
	Minimize	⌘M
	Zoom	
	Apply Default Layout	⌃U
	Inspector	⌘1
	Canvas	⌘2
	Timeline	⌘3
	Media Browser	⌘4
	Bring All to Front	
	Canvas: Untitled	
	✓ Inspector: Untitled	
	Timeline: Untitled	

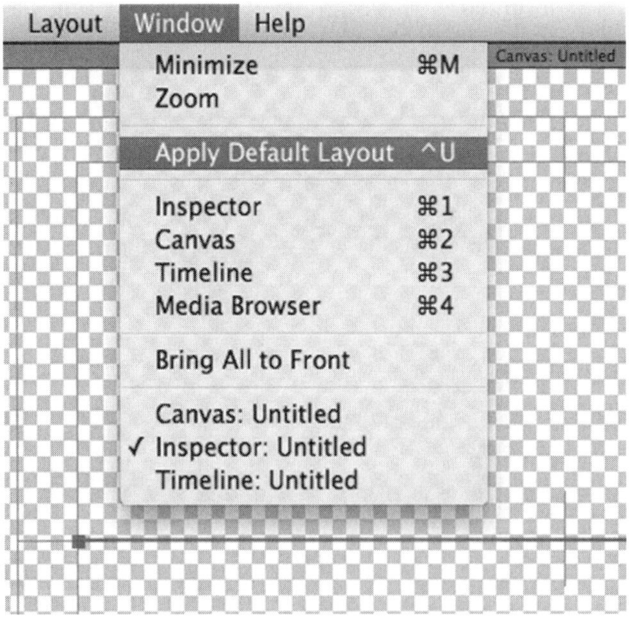

FIGURE 11.3 To set the default window configuration in LiveType, scroll down to *Apply Default Layout* in the *Window* dropdown menu.

 All figures appear in color on the companion DVD.

Canvas window

This is the window, in the upper left, where we can see what the actual credit or graphic that we create looks like. Unlike in FCE, there is only one viewing window. What we see in this window depends on which other window we happen to have clicked in first, and where the playhead may be in that window. The *Canvas* window is shown in Figure 11.4.

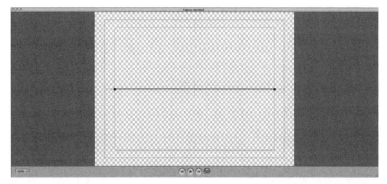

FIGURE 11.4 LiveType's *Canvas* window.

Inspector window

This is the upper middle window. Here, you make adjustments to your text, effects, and graphics. Since what you create in this program can be very simple or very complicated, you may or may not use all of the controls available in this window (especially at first). At the very top of the window are two small preview panes, which show you what specific fonts and effects look like before you apply them. The *Inspector* window is shown in Figure 11.5.

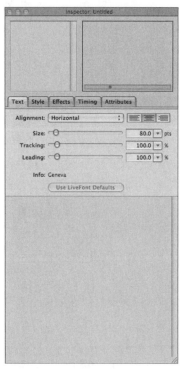

FIGURE 11.5 LiveType's *Inspector* window, with the *Text* tab open.

There are five tabs underneath the preview panes. They are, in order from left to right:

Text Tab

This is where you type the actual text, and make other adjustments, such as changing the text size. This is always the default tab that is open when you start LiveType.

Style Tab

Here, you can add or remove certain styles to the text, such as a drop shadow, outlines, glowing edges, etc. If you add an actual effect to your graphic you can change how that effect looks and acts by altering the settings under this tab. This tab is shown in Figure 11.6.

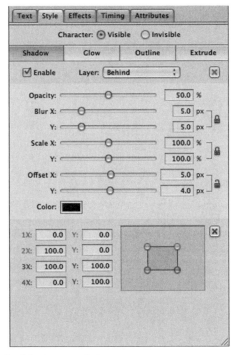

FIGURE 11.6 The *Style* tab of the *Inspector* window.

Effects Tab

If you add any effects to your title, they will be listed here. Once we create our first title, we can further explore this tab, although it is mostly used to see which effects you have applied to your title. There is not much tweaking you can do here, other than turn the effect on or off. You make the real adjustments in the *Style* tab, *Timing* tab, or *Attributes* tab. The *Effects* tab is shown in Figure 11.7.

Timing Tab

Now *this* is one of the tabs where you can tweak the settings of a particular effect. We will need an actual effect to see what we can do here, but you can tell by looking at the controls that you can switch the direction of the effect (if it's a motion effect), or its duration, and make many other changes. This tab is shown in Figure 11.8.

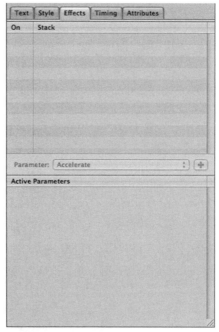

FIGURE 11.7 The *Effects* tab of the *Inspector* window.

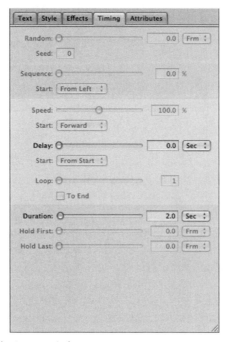

FIGURE 11.8 The *Timing* tab of the *Inspector* window.

Attributes Tab

This is another area where you can change the settings of your actual text and effects. You can change the brightness, color, and saturation, among other things. The *Attributes* tab is shown in Figure 11.9.

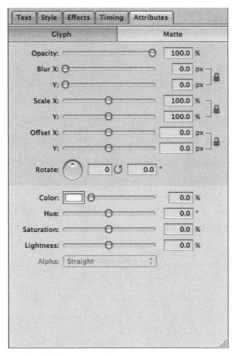

FIGURE 11.9 The *Attributes* tab of the *Inspector* window.

Sometimes the order of your actions matter. If, for example, you apply an effect to a line of text, that effect may alter the font size and color of the font, independent of any adjustments you may make in the Style tab or Attributes tab. If you have a starting font size or color that you want to use, it may become complicated to set those attributes once the effect has been added. Similarly, if you change the font size or color after an effect is applied, it may alter the way an effect behaves in unintended ways. You should therefore make sure that your text looks exactly as you want it to before you add an effect, or at least be aware of these potential issues.

Media Browser

The *Media Browser* – the window at the top right – is where you can choose the various fonts, effects, and backgrounds for your titles. Let's look at each tab in this window. As you click on an individual line, to see what a particular font, effect, or background looks like, that item will appear in the preview pane at the top of the Media Browser. It is shown in Figure 11.10.

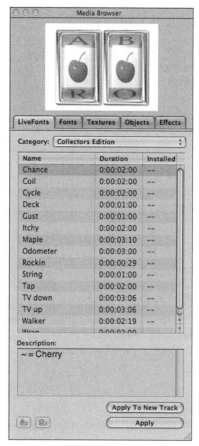

FIGURE 11.10 The *Media Browser*, with the *LiveFonts* tab open.

LiveFonts Tab

All of the fonts available under this tab are fonts that incorporate some kind of motion. If you choose your fonts wisely, even the strangest of the motion effects here can work. Just be reasonable and base your choices on the needs of your project. Click on the different fonts here to see what each one looks like.

You can change the *Category* of the LiveFonts, as shown in Figure 11.11, and you will be given more choices. Notice that at the bottom of the tab, there are two buttons: *Apply To New Track* and *Apply*, as shown in Figure 11.12. We'll look at what each button does later. But if you don't click on one of them your chosen font will not be applied to the text you type.

FIGURE 11.11 The *LiveFonts Category* pop-up menu.

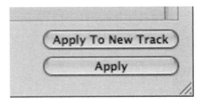

FIGURE 11.12 The two *Apply* buttons at the bottom of the *LiveFonts* tab.

Fonts Tab

Every font that is available on your computer's system should appear here. If you find the LiveFont choices have too much motion, then you can keep it simple and choose a static font here. Later, if you still want some form of motion, you can apply an effect to one of these regular fonts. The same two *Apply* buttons that appeared at the bottom of the last tab appear here as well. This tab is shown in Figure 11.13.

Textures Tab

Here, you can choose a background for your title, as shown in Figure 11.14, if you do not want your text to appear over black. You can also create your title without a background at all – just a transparent layer of nothing. We call this an *alpha channel*. If you create your title with an *alpha channel* built in, you can import it into FCE and drag it on

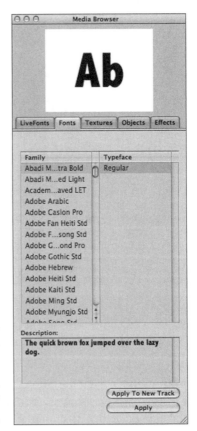

FIGURE 11.13 The *Fonts* tab of the *Media Browser*.

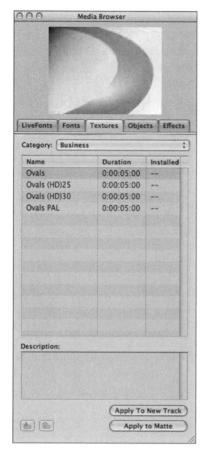

FIGURE 11.14 The *Textures* tab of the *Media Browser*.

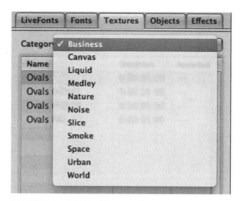

FIGURE 11.15 The *Textures Category* pop-up menu.

top of a video clip without blocking out that video, which is how title cards generated within FCE behave as well. If you want a pre-generated background, however, then scroll through the choices available to you in this tab. As in the *LiveFonts* tab, there is more than one category, as shown in Figure 11.15. At the bottom of the window are, again, two *Apply* buttons, but one of them is now labeled *Apply to Matte*. What this does is apply the texture to the actual text, rather than to the background. We will experiment with this later.

Objects Tab

At first glance, this tab (shown in Figure 11.16) looks very similar to the last one. *Objects*, however, do not fill the entire screen, the way textures do. Instead, they can be used to create *lower thirds* title bars, which are those descriptive titles or headlines you see in documentary films or on CNN®, Fox News®, or MSNBC® for the names of interviewees. There are multiple categories here, too, as shown in Figure 11.17. Again, we see two *Apply* buttons at the bottom of the window.

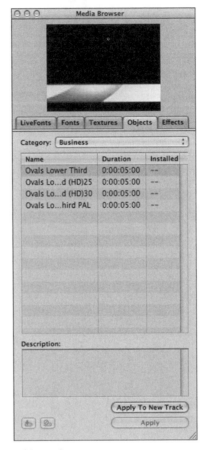

FIGURE 11.16 The *Objects* tab of the *Media Browser*.

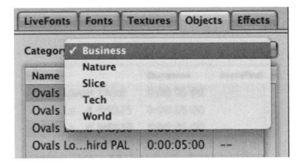

FIGURE 11.17 The *Objects Category* pop-up menu.

As you look through the textures and objects, you might consider exporting some of these to FCE, without any accompanying text. They could be used as moving backgrounds or shapes to complement the video generators that already exist within FCE.

FIGURE 11.18 The *Effects* tab of the *Media Browser*.

FIGURE 11.19 The *Effects Category* pop-up menu.

Effects Tab

As expected, here is where we find effects that we can apply directly to fonts, LiveFonts or regular ones, as shown in Figure 11.18. There are multiple categories here, too, as shown in Figure 11.19. There is only one *Apply* button at the bottom of this tab, however. Clicking on that button applies the effect to whichever font you have already chosen. If you have yet to choose a font, then the effect will be moved into the Inspector's *Effects* tab and will be applied to whatever font you choose afterwards. We will soon see how this works.

Timeline window

This window, as shown in Figure 11.20, fills the entire bottom of the screen, and should look very familiar. The LiveType Timeline has a lot in common with the Timeline in FCE. You can drag and drop stuff, and make changes in the Timeline itself, or by highlighting items in the Timeline and then changing them in the *Inspector* window. The only real difference is that double-clicking on an item does nothing, since there is no *Viewer* window, as there is in FCE. Here, you just click once to highlight.

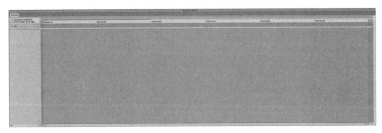

FIGURE 11.20 LiveType's Timeline.

The red line at the top of the Timeline window is, as it is in FCE, an indicator that your media needs to be rendered. Since, in effect, everything in LiveType is your *new* creation, everything needs to be rendered. Even though there is nothing in the Timeline yet, drag the playhead through the section of the Timeline where the red bar exists, or press the *spacebar* key to start the playhead playing. You will notice that the red bar turns green, as shown in Figure 11.21. The green bar indicates that you can now play your LiveType creation in real time. When we actually make something, we will see the difference between how the title plays the first time through, as the red bar becomes to green, and how it plays subsequently, once the initial rendering is done. Anytime you then make any further changes to any part of the title, the green bar will again become red. In LiveType, one of the ways to export a completed project is also called *rendering*, since you are creating new material, rather than editing pre-existing video files.

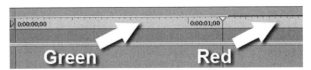

FIGURE 11.21 When you set the playhead to begin playing in the Timeline, the red to-be-rendered line turns from red to green.

Let's now look at the dropdown menus, as we did for FCE. We will touch briefly on what each one can do, and then you can experiment further on your own.

LiveType dropdown menu

In the upper left is the *LiveType* menu, as shown in Figure 11.22, which doesn't actually have much functionality, as far as our needs go. This is not the place where we can tweak the settings of the program, as we can in the equivalent FCE menu. That's in another menu, which we will discuss shortly, but we can still use the *Hide LiveType* function from here.

FIGURE 11.22 The *LiveType* dropdown menu.

File dropdown menu

Here, you can create a new project, open up a current project, save, etc. You can also *Place* files, which in LiveType means importing. And you can export your LiveType movie for other programs by either choosing *Export* or *Render*. The *File* dropdown menu is shown in Figure 11.23.

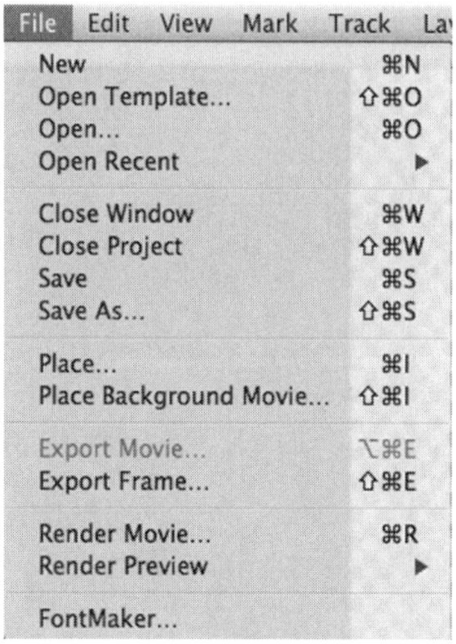

FIGURE 11.23 The File dropdown menu.

Edit dropdown menu

Just as in FCE, this menu allows you to do the usual cutting and pasting, etc. This dropdown menu is shown in Figure 11.24.

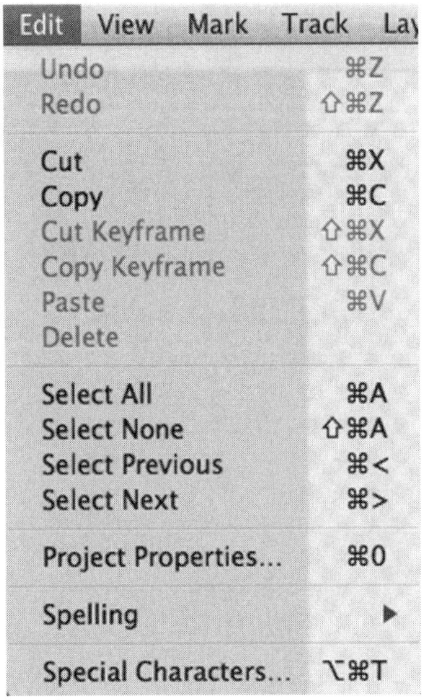

Edit	View	Mark	Track	Lay
Undo			⌘Z	
Redo			⇧⌘Z	
Cut			⌘X	
Copy			⌘C	
Cut Keyframe			⇧⌘X	
Copy Keyframe			⇧⌘C	
Paste			⌘V	
Delete				
Select All			⌘A	
Select None			⇧⌘A	
Select Previous			⌘<	
Select Next			⌘>	
Project Properties...			⌘0	
Spelling			▶	
Special Characters...			⌥⌘T	

FIGURE 11.24 The *Edit* dropdown menu.

View dropdown menu

This menu, as shown in Figure 11.25, lets you zoom in and out of a given window. You can see the keyboard shortcuts for each tool, including *Rulers* and the *Grid*. Try turning them on and off. You'll see that they can be useful devices for helping you place items or text evenly in your title card or sequence.

View	Mark	Track
Zoom In		⌘=
Zoom Out		⌘-
Zoom To Fit		⇧Z
Rulers		⇧⌘R
Grid		⌘G
Clear Guides		
✓ Title Safe		
Selected Only		

FIGURE 11.25 The *View* dropdown menu.

Mark dropdown menu

Similar to the menu in FCE, this menu lets you apply *In* and *Out* points. It also offers you another manner in which to play a particular selection. It is shown in Figure 11.26.

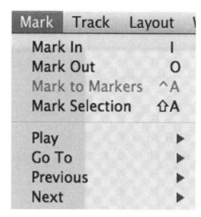

FIGURE 11.26 The *Mark* dropdown menu.

Track dropdown menu

As noted, the Timeline in LiveType is very similar to the Timeline in FCE. *This* menu lets you add or delete tracks on the Timeline, and lets you add or delete effects and keyframes. Keyframes, as we saw in FCE, are the heart of all motion effects, and since LiveType is filled with motion graphics, keyframes play a part here, too. If you keep your titles simple, you probably won't use them much. But if you use all of what LiveType has to offer, then you'll definitely be working with them in some way. We won't work with them in this chapter, but you can try working with them using your knowledge from previous chapters. The *Track* dropdown menu is shown in Figure 11.27.

FIGURE 11.27 The *Track* dropdown menu.

Layout dropdown menu

This menu, as shown in Figure 11.28, lets you move tracks in the Timeline (like moving layers in Photoshop). If you have multiple tracks, you can move them above and below each other easily this way, using the *Bring* and *Send* functions.

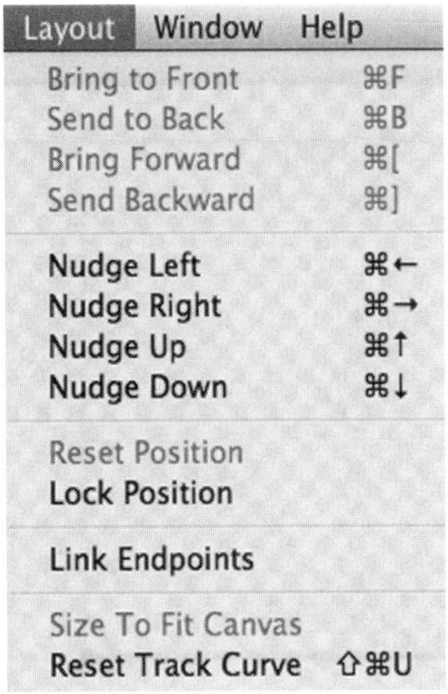

Layout	Window	Help
Bring to Front		⌘F
Send to Back		⌘B
Bring Forward		⌘[
Send Backward		⌘]
Nudge Left		⌘←
Nudge Right		⌘→
Nudge Up		⌘↑
Nudge Down		⌘↓
Reset Position		
Lock Position		
Link Endpoints		
Size To Fit Canvas		
Reset Track Curve		⇧⌘U

FIGURE 11.28 The *Layout* dropdown menu.

The *Nudge* functions of this menu allow you to gently move text or graphics around the screen with a few keyboard strokes. If you don't like how you have placed your title over its background, just highlight the text and use these commands to move it up, down, left and/or right. Once you find a position you like, you can then use *Lock Position* to prevent any further accidental shifts.

Window dropdown menu

As we saw earlier in this chapter, when we discussed how to reset the default window arrangement for the application, this menu gives you control over which windows are visible, and how they are positioned on the screen. This menu is shown in Figure 11.29.

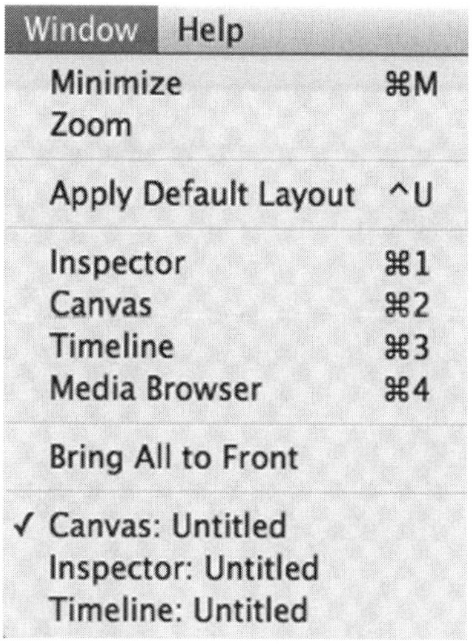

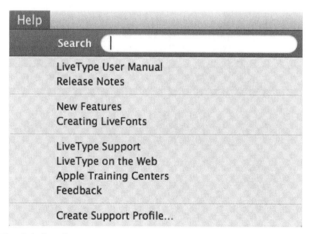

FIGURE 11.29 The *Window* dropdown menu.

Help dropdown menu

Finally, we have the *Help* dropdown menu, as shown in Figure 11.30, which is primarily useful for giving you access to the LiveType User Manual. Use the manual to look up answers to additional questions you may have.

FIGURE 11.30 The *Help* dropdown menu.

That's it for the basic interface. Let's set up a project now.

Setting Up a Project

First, let's go to the *Edit* dropdown menu and select *Project Properties*, as shown in Figure 11.31. The menu that pops up, as shown in Figure 11.32, allows you to choose the video format that matches the format of the FCE project to which you will export these titles. If this is the first time that you have opened LiveType, the default *Preset* at the top will read *CCIR 601 NTSC 40:27*. Let's discuss what that means.

Simply put, standard digital video has a pixel aspect ratio of 720:480, but displays at 640:480 (the analog aspect ratio). This default setting (actually 720:486) more or less matches the standard NTSC setting in which we have been editing the

Edit	View	Mark	Track	Lay
Undo				⌘Z
Redo				⇧⌘Z
Cut				⌘X
Copy				⌘C
Cut Keyframe				⇧⌘X
Copy Keyframe				⇧⌘C
Paste				⌘V
Delete				
Select All				⌘A
Select None				⇧⌘A
Select Previous				⌘<
Select Next				⌘>
Project Properties...				⌘0
Spelling				▶
Special Characters...				⌥⌘T

FIGURE 11.31 Select *Project Properties* from the *Edit* dropdown menu.

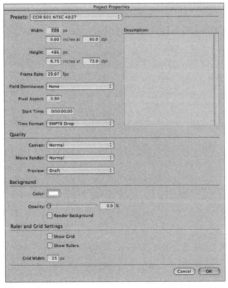

FIGURE 11.32 The *Project Properties* menu.

Nail Polish files, as shown in Figure 11.33. If you were editing in a different format, however, then you would click on the *Presets* pop-up menu, up top, as shown in Figure 11.34, and choose the format that best fits your project.

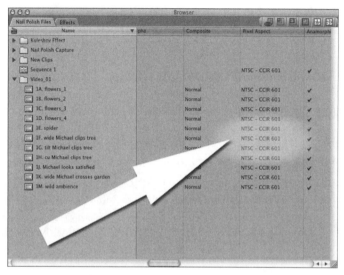

FIGURE 11.33 In FCE, you can find the *Pixel Aspect* of your project in the Browser.

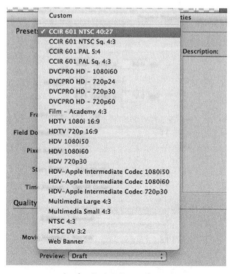

FIGURE 11.34 The *Presets* pop-up menu in the *Project Properties* menu.

There is no way, in standard DV, to easily create widescreen anamorphic titles in LiveType. Since you probably aren't going to be working much in standard DV anymore (or, at least, not for much longer), and the other presets match their format's aspect ratios perfectly, this shouldn't be a big problem. The reason why standard DV is different is because the anamorphic squeeze is artificially imposed on a square-ish format. In the HD formats, the rectangular widescreen aspect ratio is built in.

We will create widescreen DV titles in this chapter, however, since that is our *Nail Polish* format. But Apple has a solution, which they describe on their support site.[1] Choose the *NTSC DV 3:2* preset, as shown in Figure 11.35. Then change the *Pixel Aspect* in the upper half of the *Project Properties* menu to *1.19*, as shown in Figure 11.36 (compare to Figure 11.04). Click *OK*, and you'll notice how the *Canvas* window has changed to an aspect ratio now, as shown in Figure 11.37. If you want LiveType to remember these settings until you change them again, regardless of whether or not you quit the program, go up to the *LiveType* dropdown menu and select *Remember Settings*, as shown in Figure 11.38. We are now ready to start designing a title.

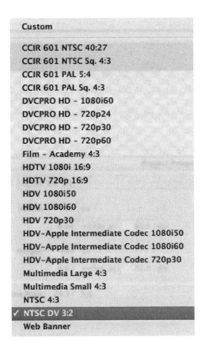

FIGURE 11.35 Choose *NTSC DV 3:2* from the *Presets* pop-up menu.

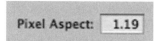

FIGURE 11.36 Type *1.19* in the *Pixel Aspect* field.

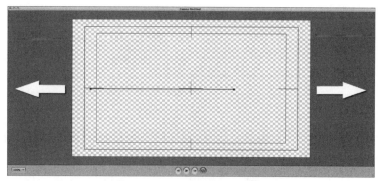

FIGURE 11.37 The Canvas changes to a widescreen aspect ratio.

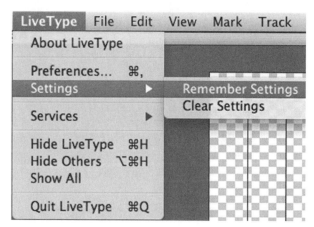

FIGURE 11.38 Select *Remember Settings* from the *LiveType* dropdown menu.

Designing Your Title

Even the most basic white-on-black title card will look better if created through LiveType than in FCE. That's because FCE is not a graphics program; it's an editing program. It is not designed to make striking titles or motion graphics. It can do an adequate job with them, but if you can master some basic skills in LiveType, then you will be able to generate more professional-looking titles.

To that end, click in the Inspector, make sure the *Text* tab is selected, and type your text, as shown in Figure 11.39. As you type, the text appears simultaneously in the Canvas, as shown in Figure 11.40. The Canvas will always show white text over a checkerboard-patterned background, by default. The checkerboard represents the alpha channel, or layer of transparency. If we add an actual background graphic, which we will do soon, the checkerboard will disappear and be replaced by that background.

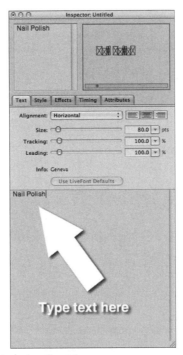

FIGURE 11.39 Type your text in the Inspector.

FIGURE 11.40 The text then appears in the Canvas.

Next, look down at the Timeline. We now have a 2-second piece of media, in Track 01 (the only track so far), with a red render line over it, as shown in Figure 11.41. You can change the length of the media, as we will soon see.

FIGURE 11.41 The text appears as media in the Timeline.

Notice how, in the Canvas, the words *Nail Polish* are not centered. That's because, when we changed the format and aspect ratio of the project, that blue line in the Canvas – also called a *Track* – did not change its size, and shifted over in the screen, off-center. This is easy to fix.

Click in the center of the blue track line, and all the letters of *Nail Polish* will be highlighted. Drag the line over to the right until it is centered, as shown in Figure 11.42, and let go. The green title safe lines are very helpful for this, so you should leave them on, and always keep your text within their boundaries.

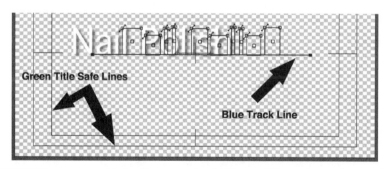

FIGURE 11.42 Center your text in the Canvas, moving the blue track line, and using the green title safe lines as your guide.

Next, let's change the default font. Go into the Media Browser and click on the *Fonts* tab. Choose a new font, like Arial Black, as shown in Figure 11.43. Click on the *Apply* button at the bottom, rather than on the *Apply To New Track* button, which would create a new track in the timeline, with text-as-yet-to-be-typed, and leave the words *Nail Polish* in the original track, unchanged.

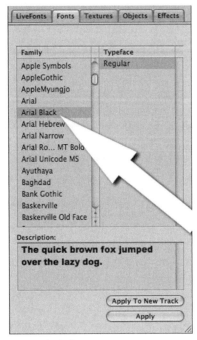

FIGURE 11.43 Change the font to Arial Black.

Now look back at the Canvas. As shown in Figure 11.44, the letters of *Nail Polish* are chunky and wider than before, per the new font's characteristics. By default, LiveType applies a gentle drop shadow on the text, helping to make it stand out if you lay it over an image or piece of video. You could tweak these settings if you wanted, by going to the *Style* tab of the Inspector, but we're not ready to do that yet.

FIGURE 11.44 The new font is shown in the Canvas.

Next, let's change the length of this title. You could do this in the *Timing* tab of the Inspector, but let's try an easier way. Grab the end of the clip in the Timeline and drag right, as shown in Figure 11.45, stopping at the *Out* point, which, by default, is at 6 seconds. If you want to see more of the Timeline than just these 6 seconds, you can use the same *command* key + *minus* key combination as in FCE to zoom out. (or you could use the *View* menu). This will only let you zoom out so much, however.

Grab the edge of the text media, and drag right to lengthen

FIGURE 11.45 Grab the edge of your title and drag right to lengthen.

To see even more of your Timeline, you need to drag the actual *Out* point further to the right, as shown in Figure 11.46 (you can also drag it to the left to make your title shorter). Once you have extended that *Out* point, you will be able to zoom out even more. Every time you make the viewable area of the Timeline longer, you are able to zoom out further. When it comes time to export your LiveType movie, or import it into FCE, however, only the parts within the *In* and *Out* points will be visible. By default, the start of the Timeline is the *In* point, but that can change. Setting *In* and *Out* points is done in the same way as in FCE, by using the *I* key and the *O* key, or by going to the *Mark* menu.

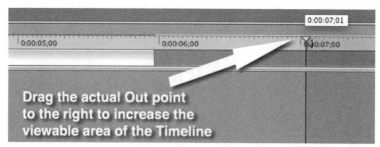
Drag the actual Out point to the right to increase the viewable area of the Timeline

FIGURE 11.46 To see more of the Timeline, drag the *Out* point to the right and then you will be able to zoom out further.

Let's undo our actions until we have a 6-second title again. If you play through the title, either by clicking on the recognizable play button at the bottom of the Canvas, as shown in Figure 11.47, or by clicking in the Timeline and pressing the spacebar, the playhead will move through the Timeline, turning the red line to green, as shown in Figure 11.48. If you have *Loop Playback* selected, which is the rightmost button of the transport controls at the bottom of the Canvas, as shown in Figure 11.49, next to the play button, then the playhead will keep on playing through your title, over and over again, until you stop it. This can be useful when you are creating more elaborate titles and need to see the action a number of times. You don't have to play through the red line before exporting; it's only useful to be able to see motion effects as they appear in real time.

FIGURE 11.47 The play button in the Canvas.

FIGURE 11.48 As you play through the title, the red line turns to green.

FIGURE 11.49 The *Loop Playback* button.

Now let's go ahead and export this simple title card.

Exporting Your Title Directly to FCE

The simplest way to export a LiveType title directly to FCE is to simply save the LiveType project in the same folder as your FCE project. Let's do that now. Go to the *File* menu and select *Save*, as shown in Figure 11.50, or just press the *command* key + the *S* key. Choose your location and give your file a name, such as *Nail Polish Title 1*.

File
Edit
View
Mark
Track
Layout
New ⌘N
Open Template... ⇧⌘O
Open... ⌘O
Open Recent ▶
Close Window ⌘W
Close Project ⇧⌘W
Save ⌘S
Save As... ⇧⌘S
Place... ⌘I
Place Background Movie... ⇧⌘I
Export Movie... ⌥⌘E
Export Frame... ⇧⌘E
Render Movie... ⌘R
Render Preview ▶
FontMaker...

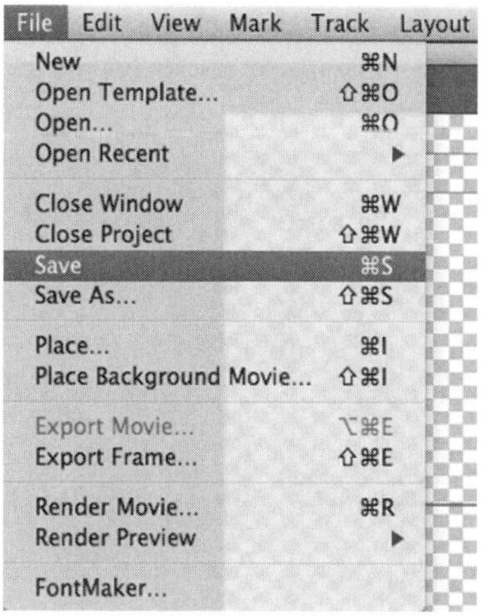

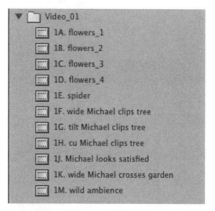

FIGURE 11.50 Choose *Save* from the *File* menu.

Many people are confused by the difference between the Save *and* Save Project As... *functions. You can use either one when you save your project for the first time. Thereafter, for that same project, just use Save, and your changes will be safeguarded. Use* Save Project As... *only if you want to save a new version of your project with a new name, perhaps to use it as a template for a new project.*

TIP

Now that our project is saved, we need to open up our *Nail Polish* FCE project. If, in that project, you still have all of the extra HD footage that you imported during our exercises in Chapter 10, you can delete it, as we only need the actual *Nail Polish* footage from the *Video_01* Bin, as shown in Figure 11.51. Within this FCE project, we now need to go to the *File* menu and select *Import Files*, as shown in Figure 11.52. Find the LiveType project – which should be easy to find

Video_01
1A. flowers_1
1B. flowers_2
1C. flowers_3
1D. flowers_4
1E. spider
1F. wide Michael clips tree
1G. tilt Michael clips tree
1H. cu Michael clips tree
1J. Michael looks satisfied
1K. wide Michael crosses garden
1M. wild ambience

FIGURE 11.51 We only need our original *Nail Polish* footage for these exercises.

since you saved it to the same folder as the FCE files – and select it as the file to import. It will then appear in your Browser, as shown in Figure 11.53. Remember how we had to create a custom pixel aspect ratio to create an NTSC DV widescreen title in LiveType? The final part of that equation is to scroll over in the FCE Browser to the *Anamorphic* column and select that option for this file, as shown in Figure 11.54.

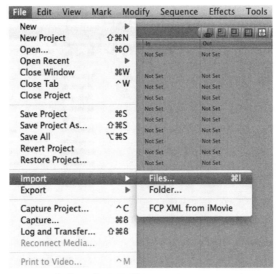

FIGURE 11.52 Choose *Import Files* from the FCE *File* menu.

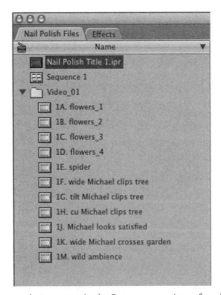

FIGURE 11.53 The LiveType project appears in the Browser as a piece of media.

FIGURE 11.54 Check the *Anamorphic* column.

As long as you are working on your own computer, or on a computer that has the same version of LiveType that you do, this is all you have to do to import a title from LiveType into FCE. Just save it, and then import it. Final Cut Express will treat it like a self-contained piece of media. You can just drag it down to the Timeline as you would any other clip, as shown in Figure 11.55. And, if you make any changes to the original LiveType project, they will immediately be reflected in the FCE project, since the files are automatically linked.

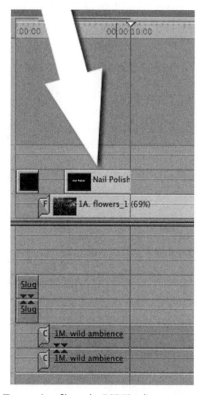

FIGURE 11.55 Drag the LiveType project file to the FCE Timeline as you would any other media files.

There are a few other ways to export. Let's look at them, briefly.

Exporting a LiveType File as a Self-Contained Movie File

Let's say you are working on a computer at school or work, which has LiveType, and you want to take your new credits home with you to finish your movie. The only problem is, you don't have LiveType at home. Or, perhaps, you're a PC user who edits on Adobe Premiere, and you want to be able to import your work as a QuickTime *.mov* file. Whatever your reason, there may be a time when you want to export your LiveType file as a self-contained movie file.

If that is the case, then once you have finished editing your title within LiveType, go up to the *File* menu and select *Render Movie*, as shown in Figure 11.56. The *Save* pop-up menu appears, as shown in Figure 11.57. Look at the bottom of the screen, and you will see two options, to *Render Background* and to *Render Only Between In/Out Points*, as shown in Figure 11.58. The bottom option should be clear. If you uncheck it, everything in the Timeline is exported, which you may not want. The top option lets the program know whether or not you want there to be a background or an alpha channel (that layer of transparency). If the box remains unchecked, then the text, or any objects placed in a non-background track (which we will discuss soon), appears over black, unless you drag the title over another clip, in which case that clip shows through the title. If the box is checked, then any background textures you have added in LiveType are

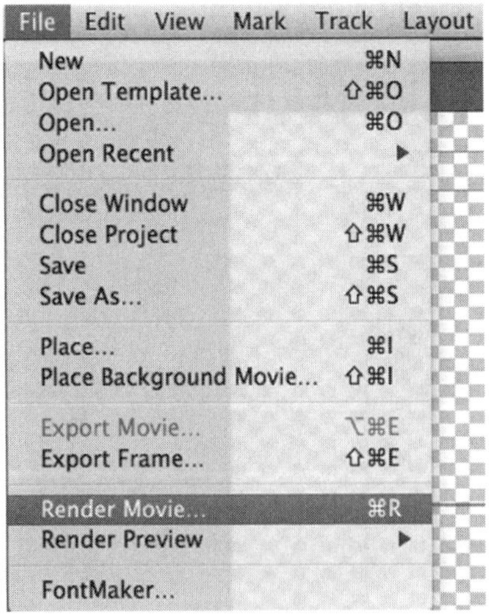

FIGURE 11.56 Select *Render Movie* from the LiveType *File* menu.

exported with the title. So if you want a background, check this box. If you want an alpha channel, leave it unchecked.

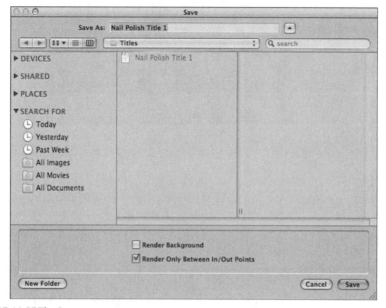

FIGURE 11.57 The *Save* menu appears.

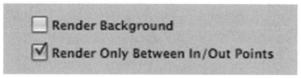

FIGURE 11.58 If you want an alpha channel, do not check *Render Background*.

Choose a file name that makes sense, and click on the *Save* button. Another window will appear, which is our rendered – or exported – movie file, as shown in Figure 11.59. If you accidentally close this window, you can always reopen it by going to the *File* menu, since we know where we saved it. The file has been saved in the same video format to which LiveType is currently set. You can import it into FCE, and that program will treat it just like any other *.mov* file. However, there is no longer a convenient direct link to the LiveType project, so making changes and updating the title in FCE becomes a little more cumbersome.

FIGURE 11.59 Once your title movie is rendered – or exported – it appears in a new window on top of your project.

If, for some reason, you want to export your title in a different format than the one to which you have set the project, then you can use the *Export Movie* function, as shown in Figure 11.60. This option is only highlighted and available, however, if you have first rendered your title as a self-contained movie. Once you select the option, the *Save exported file as...* menu appears, as shown in Figure 11.61. This is the same menu, with the same options, as the *QuickTime Conversion* menu in FCE, so you can refer back to that section in Chapter 10 for a refresher.

File	Edit	View	Mark	Track	Layout
New					⌘N
Open Template...					⇧⌘O
Open...					⌘O
Open Recent					▶
Close Window					⌘W
Close Project					⇧⌘W
Save					⌘S
Save As...					⇧⌘S
Place...					⌘I
Place Background Movie...					⇧⌘I
Export Movie...					⌥⌘E
Export Frame...					⇧⌘E
Render Movie...					⌘R
Render Preview					▶
FontMaker...					

FIGURE 11.60 Choose *Export Movie* from the *File* menu.

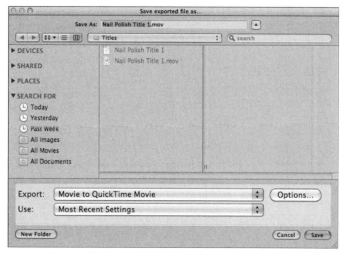

FIGURE 11.61 The *Save exported file as…* menu functions in the same way as the *QuickTime Conversion* menu in FCE.

The final export option you can use is the *Export Frame* function, also located in the *File* menu, as shown in Figure 11.62. This option lets you export a single frame – the image shown wherever the playhead is stopped in the Timeline. This is a convenient tool if you need to export a still image of a title card.

File	Edit	View	Mark	Track	Layout

New	⌘N
Open Template...	⇧⌘O
Open...	⌘O
Open Recent	▶
Close Window	⌘W
Close Project	⇧⌘W
Save	⌘S
Save As...	⇧⌘S
Place...	⌘I
Place Background Movie...	⇧⌘I
Export Movie...	⌥⌘E
Export Frame...	⇧⌘E
Render Movie...	⌘R
Render Preview	▶
FontMaker...	

FIGURE 11.62 The *Export Frame* option in the *File* menu.

Now it's time to make a much more elaborate title card, where we will explore a few more options.

LiveType Elements

All of the various media that we use in LiveType to create our titles, including fonts, LiveFonts, textures, objects, and/or effects, are called *elements*. How you put them together determines how your final product will look. You can use as many or as few elements as you like.

LiveFonts

Let's begin by saving our *Nail Polish Title 1* title as a new project entitled *Nail Polish Title 2*. Next, let's change our font, and choose a LiveFont to replace Arial Black. Go to the *LiveFont* tab of the Media Browser and choose something, such as *Script*, under the *Pro Series* category, as shown in Figure 11.63. Notice how the script is previewed in the pane up above, so you can clearly see what it looks like. Click on the *Apply* button.

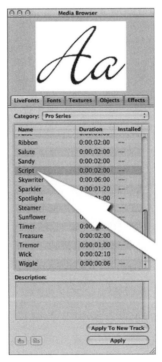

FIGURE 11.63 In the Media Browser, choose the *Script* LiveFont from the *Pro Series* category.

While we had a 6-second title, it is has now shrunk down to 2 seconds. Put the playhead at the start of the Timeline and press play. You should see, in 2 seconds, the *Script* LiveFont spell out *Nail Polish*, as shown in Figure 11.64, and then, when it's done, you should see the text disappear as the playhead continues for another 4 seconds. Drag the right edge of the clip in the Timeline to the *Out* point at 6 seconds, then put the playhead at the start again and press play. You should now see a much slower version of the same action, drawn out over the full length of the Timeline, but it doesn't look as good when it moves that slowly. It would be better if the text could spell itself out at the previous rate of 2 seconds, and then stay up, without disappearing, for another 4 seconds. Let's figure out how to do that.

FIGURE 11.64 *Nail Polish* spelled out in the *Script* LiveFont.

First, undo the 6-second extension we just created, so that we're back at a 2-second clip. Now go into the *Timing* tab of the Inspector, as shown in Figure 11.65. You can see that there are many options here. We'll try one of them, and you can experiment with the rest on your own.

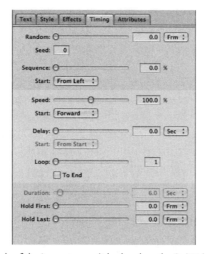

FIGURE 11.65 The *Timing* tab of the Inspector, as it looks when the *Script* LiveFont is selected.

At the bottom of the tab, notice the *Hold First* and *Hold Last* options. Some LiveFonts and effects start simple and then have something happen at the end, while the font we have chosen has its effect at the very beginning. Let's change, in the little pop-up menu to the right of *Hold Last*, the abbreviation *Frm* (frames) to *Sec* (seconds), and enter a value of 4 in the field next to it, as shown in Figure 11.66. Now the LiveFont will spell itself out for 2 seconds and then hold for 4 more seconds on the words themselves. The clip in the Timeline now shows a clear separation between the first half (the spelling) and the second half (the holding), as shown in Figure 11.67.

FIGURE 11.66 Enter a value of 4 seconds in the field next to *Hold Last*.

FIGURE 11.67 Now the text clip in the Timeline is divided into two parts – the spelling and the holding.

Textures

Now let's add a background. Go to the *Textures* tab in the Media Browser, and look through the many options, changing categories to see the full range of possibilities. After you have browsed for a while, choose *Phosphor*, under the *Smoke* category, as shown in Figure 11.68. This background will look interesting underneath our red LiveFont. Next, click on the *Apply To New Track* button, which we haven't used before. Your Timeline should now have a new track underneath the old one, as shown in Figure 11.69. Since the default length for this texture is only 4 seconds, we will have to make it longer if we want it to last as long as the text. Before we do that, however, hover over the horizontal bar in the center of the Timeline. A little yellow pop-up window will appear, as shown in Figure 11.70, to let us know that anything below this divider is officially a background. If you choose to render your title without rendering the background, then anything below this line will be left out.

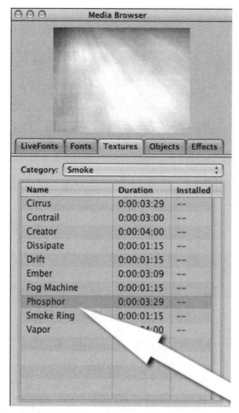

FIGURE 11.68 Choose the *Phosphor* texture under the *Smoke* category.

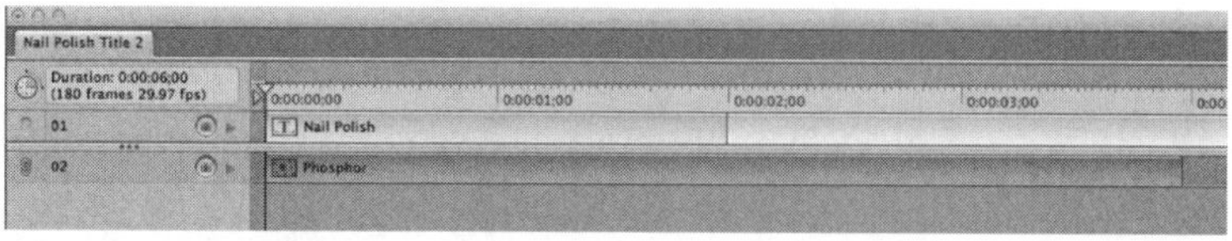

FIGURE 11.69 Click on the *Apply to New Track* button and the texture will appear in a new track in the Timeline.

Tracks below this separator are background tracks.

FIGURE 11.70 Hover over the separator to see what it is for.

Let's now lengthen the texture by dragging the right edge to the 6-second *Out* point marker. Then press play. We have successfully created an animated title with an animated background, as shown in Figure 11.71. Remember, if you don't like the position of the text in the screen, all you have to do is move that blue track bar to a new position.

FIGURE 11.71 Our new title, with text and background.

Objects

Now let's add an object to the mix. Go to the *Objects* tab in the Media Browser, and take a look at what's there. You'll see plenty of *lower thirds* possibilities, which could be useful if we were making a documentary. Since we're not doing that, let's go into the *Tech* category, and choose *Tech 04*, as shown in Figure 11.72. It's a very dynamic and striking animation. Click on the *Apply to New Track* button. Your Timeline will now have three tracks in it, as shown in Figure 11.73. Since the default length of the *Tech 04* object is 9 seconds, it extends 3 seconds beyond the *Out* point. Before we do anything else, go ahead and play the new title from the beginning to see how the object behaves and how the whole thing looks, as shown in Figure 11.74.

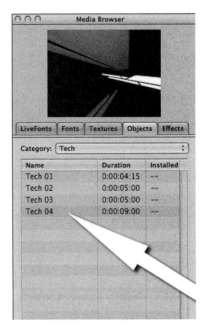

FIGURE 11.72 Choose the *Tech 04* object under the *Tech* category.

FIGURE 11.73 After you apply it to the Timeline, we see three tracks, one of which – the object – goes 3 seconds beyond our *Out* point.

FIGURE 11.74 Our new title, with text, object, and background.

If you were to drag the right edge of the object and pull left, so that the object were now only 6 seconds long, fitting within the *In* and *Out* points, the animated motion would happen faster than it does currently. You can decide whether you like that better or not.

Now, before adding an effect, let's first add another text track, with a regular, non-animated font. Go back to the *Fonts* tab in the Media Browser, and this time choose something other than Arial Black, such as *Papyrus*, as shown in Figure 11.75. Then click on the *Apply To New Track* button, and a new track will appear in the Timeline. There's nothing in it, because first we have to type something. If you go to the Inspector window, you'll see a blank box, under the *Text* tab. Let's type *a film by me* in that field, as shown in Figure 11.76. As soon as we do that, a 2-second text clip appears in the new track, positioned wherever the playhead was when we typed the text (in this case, it was at the beginning of the Timeline), as shown in Figure 11.77.

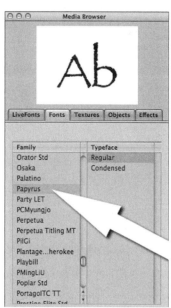
FIGURE 11.75 Choose *Papyrus* as the new font for our new text track.

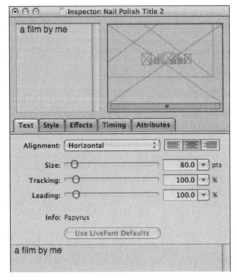

FIGURE 11.76 Type *a film by me* in the *Text* tab.

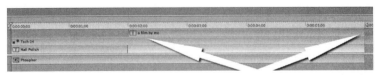

FIGURE 11.77 After we type the text, a new 2-second clip appears in our new track.

Let's not keep the new text at the beginning of the Timeline, however. Grab it with your mouse and slide it over to the *Out* point, then extend the left side to the 2-second mark, so that the text starts at 2 seconds and runs for 4 seconds, as shown in Figure 11.78. If we place the playhead towards the end of the Timeline, we can see a glimpse of what the final result will look like, as shown in Figure 11.79.

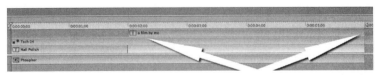

FIGURE 11.78 Grab the new text with your mouse and slide it over to the *Out* point, then extend the left side to the 2-second mark.

FIGURE 11.79 This is what our new title looks like.

Effects

Now that we have a simple non-animated text track, let's add an effect. Go to the *Effects* tab in the Media Browser, look under the *Glows* category, and choose *Experience*, as shown in Figure 11.80. Before you click *Apply*, however, make sure that the right track in the Timeline is highlighted. The color of a highlighted track's clip will be darker than when it is *not* highlighted. If we select the top track, as shown in Figure 11.81, it appears as a deep goldenrod color, while it is a paler yellow when it is not selected, as shown in Figure 11.82.

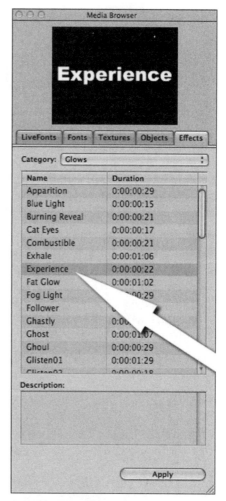

FIGURE 11.80 Choose *Experience*, under the *Glows* category.

FIGURE 11.81 When the top track is selected, it appears as a goldenrod color.

FIGURE 11.82 When the top track is deselected, it appears as a pale yellow color.

Select the top track and click *Apply*. Now the effect appears, attached to the top track in a subtrack, as shown in Figure 11.83. Two things determine the duration of the effect: its basic default length (in this case, 22 frames long), and the length of the clip to which it has been applied. Here, it appears to be about 1.5 seconds long. If you want it longer, you can extend it by grabbing the edge of the effect in the Timeline and dragging to the right, as shown in Figure 11.84. Not all effects look good when you shorten or lengthen them. Often the calculation that LiveType makes is, in fact, the best one. Undo the extension of the effect we just created, and watch how the glow looks in the Canvas.

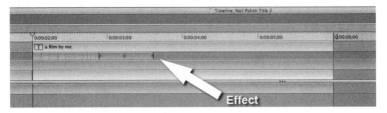

FIGURE 11.83 The effect appears in a subtrack, attached to the top text track.

FIGURE 11.84 You can lengthen the effect by extending its edge to the right.

Let's add one more effect. Go back to the *Effects* tab and choose *Fade In* from the *Fades* category, as shown in Figure 11.85. Make sure that the top track is selected, again, and click *Apply*; the fade now appears below the other effect in the Timeline, as shown in Figure 11.86. If you don't like the way this combination of effects look, you can extend them, or drag them right or left, until you find the look you want.

FIGURE 11.85 Choose *Fade In* from the *Fades* category.

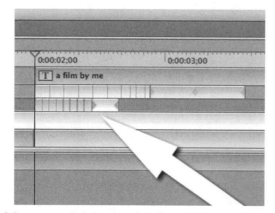

FIGURE 11.86 The fade now appears below the other effect in the Timeline.

If you do tweak the effects, or other element parameters, note that, each time you do, the render color switches, for the entire Timeline, from green back to red. The only way to make it green again is to play through the entire Timeline. It will then go back to red when you make another adjustment. Anytime you change anything, the whole piece must be recreated, but it usually doesn't take long to do.

Using the inspector to change parameters

Lastly, let's change a few of these elements, using the Inspector, to learn about a few more tools. Let's start by changing the LiveFont color. Highlight the LiveFont track in the Timeline and then go up to the Inspector and click on the *Attributes* tab. Look at the color box in the lower half, as shown in Figure 11.87. Even though our text is red, the box shows a purplish periwinkle color. That's the default display color in the box. Once we make a change to that color, our text will change, and that box will show the new color of our text.

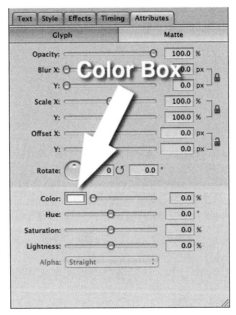

FIGURE 11.87 Open the *Attributes* tab in the Inspector and look at the color box.

Click on that box, and a new menu opens labeled *Colors*, as shown in Figure 11.88. If you have used other Mac applications that involve color adjustments, you may have come across this same menu, or one like it. Click anywhere in the circle, and use the slider on the right to make further adjustments. If you click on the other categories, above, you will find other ways to change the color. Choose a color that you like, and close the window. Now, in the Canvas, we can see the results of our color change, as shown in Figure 11.89.

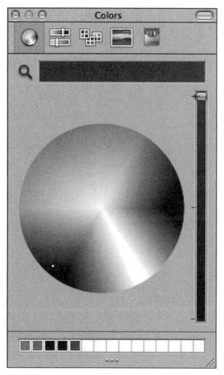

FIGURE 11.88 The *Colors* menu.

FIGURE 11.89 The *Nail Polish* text has changed color.

Next, let's make the drop shadow underneath the *a film by me* text more pronounced. Click on that track and go to the *Style* tab in the Inspector, as shown in Figure 11.90. Here, you have four categories – *Shadow, Glow, Outline,* and *Extrude* – all of which have many different controls, which you can explore on your own. For now, let's stay in the *Shadow* category and look at the parameters, as shown in Figure 11.91. The default *Opacity* for the shadow is *50%*. To make a darker drop shadow, change that to *100%*. Let's also move the shadow closer, horizontally, to the text, so that it's almost more of an outline, by changing the *Offset X* value to 2.4, as shown in Figure 11.91.

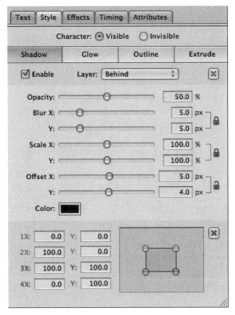

FIGURE 11.90 Go to the *Style* tab in the Inspector.

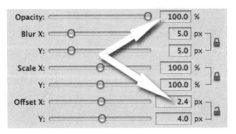

FIGURE 11.91 Change the *Opacity* and the *Offset X* under the *Shadow* category.

LiveType also lets you change the parameters of just part of a word – or just one letter – if you want to make eclectic titles. Let's highlight just the *me* of *a film by me*. Next, at the top of the *Text* tab, move the *Size* slider to around 206 points, as shown in Figure 11.92. Now look in the Canvas, and you'll see that the word *me* has been hugely expanded, as shown in Figure 11.93.

FIGURE 11.92 Go to the Style tab in the Inspector.

FIGURE 11.93 Change the *Opacity* and the *Offset X* under the *Shadow* category.

While titles such as this are fun, we also want to create some professional-looking credits. So, tundo what we just did, and then reduce the size of that entire text line, move it up a notch, and then move the *Nail Polish* line down, so that the floating object above it isn't quite as close, as shown in Figure 11.94. You know how to do all of this now – just highlight the tracks in the Timeline and then grab the blue track line in the Canvas and drag up or down.

FIGURE 11.94 We can rearrange the elements of our title to form a more professional composition.

Next, let's make adjustments to the object. Highlight that track in the Timeline and then go to the *Style* tab in the Inspector. Let's click in the *Enable* box for each of the four categories: *Shadow*, *Glow*, *Outline*, and *Extrusion*. Under the *Glow* category, go down to the *Color* box and choose a red color, as shown in Figure 11.95. If it's too red for you, tweak the opacity, at the top.

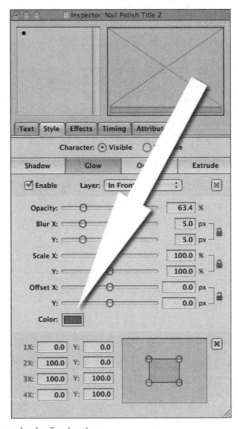

FIGURE 11.95 Choose a red color for the glow.

Next, under the *Outline* category, choose a white color for the outline, as shown in Figure 11.96. Keep everything else as is, and go to the *Extrusion* category.

Extrusion means to extend the sides of an object – to pull its edges one way or another – so that it looks somewhat three-dimensional. It's different than either an outline or a drop shadow. Think of the old Superman shield logo, and you'll understand extrusion. Choose a black color, as shown in Figure 11.97. After all of these changes, our object looks quite different, as shown in Figure 11.98.

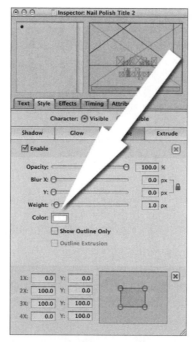

FIGURE 11.96 Choose a white color for the outline.

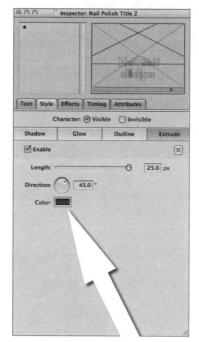

FIGURE 11.97 Choose a black color for the extrusion.

FIGURE 11.98 Now our object looks quite different.

Play through the full Timeline sequence. You will notice that the object, as its animation unfolds, covers the text, at times, as shown in Figure 11.99. That's because we created the LiveFont track first, and it sits underneath the object track in the Timeline. All we have to do is either move one of the tracks forward or backward, using the *Layout* dropdown menu, or just grab the LiveFont text track in the Timeline and drag up or down. Move the object track below our text tracks, and the object no longer covers the text as it plays, as shown in Figure 11.100.

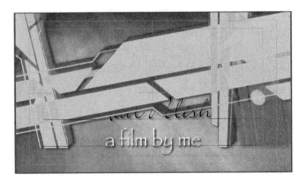

FIGURE 11.99 The object covers our text.

FIGURE 11.100 Move the object track below the text, and now the text covers the object.

Let's now change the color of the background. Click on the background track in the Timeline, go to the *Attributes* tab in the Inspector, click on the *Color* button, and choose the same red color that we chose for the object. Now there is some uniformity in our overall sequence, as shown in Figure 11.101.

FIGURE 11.101 After we change our background color to match our object, we have more uniformity.

You should now know enough about how things work to be able to experiment on your own, but let's examine one last tool. Highlight the non-LiveFont text track and then go to the *Textures* tab of the Media Browser. Select the *Timewarp* texture under the *Space* category, as shown in Figure 11.102. This is the same tab where we select backgrounds, such as the one we are currently using in our Timeline, but you can also use these to embed – or *matte* – a pattern into text and objects themselves. All you have to do is click on the *Apply to Matte* button at the bottom of the tab, which we discussed earlier, and this pattern will be embedded in the highlighted text or object. Click on that button now. The line *a film by me* is no longer white, but has a new (and animated) color scheme, as shown in Figure 11.103.

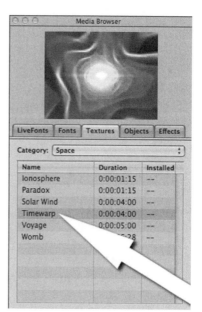

FIGURE 11.102 Select the *Timewarp* texture under the *Space* category.

FIGURE 11.103 After we click on *Apply to Matte*, the texture is embedded in the text.

Remember, you can turn your tracks on or off by clicking on the buttons on the left side of the Timeline, just like in FCE. You can do this to the effects as well. This way you don't lose your work if you just want to see how the sequence plays with or without something.

Viewing LiveType in FCE

Now we will import this new title into FCE, but save your work first, of course. We don't have to quit LiveType to import our file. Go back to FCE and import the *Nail Polish Title 2* project we just completed, as shown in Figure 11.104. Remember to check the *Anamorphic* column, as we did for *Nail Polish Title 1*. Then drag the title down to the Timeline, render it, and play it through, watching the sequence in the Canvas. You will see that the title plays perfectly, but without the background, as shown in Figure 11.105.

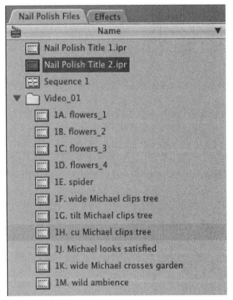

FIGURE 11.104 We import *Nail Polish Title 2* into our FCE project.

FIGURE 11.105 After we drag the title to the Timeline and render it, we see that the background is missing.

Just as when you use the *Render Movie* function, you have to tell LiveType to include the background outside of the LiveType application. In LiveType, go back to the *Project Properties* menu, found under the *Edit* dropdown menu. In the lower half of that menu is a box you need to check, labeled *Render Background*, as shown in Figure 11.106. Once you have checked it, go down to the Timeline in your LiveType project and play through the sequence one more time, so that it renders from red to green. If you don't complete this step, the change you just made will not be recognized when you go back to your FCE project.

FIGURE 11.106 Check in the *Render Background* box in the *Project Properties* menu.

Go back to FCE. Now the background is there, and you can add fades, or anything else you want, since it will behave like any other media clip. You have now seen firsthand how a LiveType project imported into FCE will update itself as you make changes in LiveType.

This was the last of our software-based chapters. Now we are ready to tackle some creative editing in the final four chapters of this book.

In this chapter, we learned about the basic interface of LiveType, the companion title-designing software that comes bundled with FCE. We started by examining each of the different windows and their respective tabs and categories. We then explored the dropdown menus to familiarize ourselves with the tools of the program. Along the way, we discussed the differences between regular, or static, fonts, and LiveFonts.

Before we created our first title, we first had to learn how to set up our project to match our expected output format. Since there is not a preset format for DV NTSC widescreen, we had to tweak some settings in the *Project Properties* menu.

The first title we designed was a static title card, and we used the simplicity of the design to become more comfortable with the interface. We then explored how to export it directly to FCE and how to export it as a self-contained movie. The former method just involves saving the LiveType project file and then importing that file into FCE, while the latter method is very similar to some of the ways we exported movies directly from FCE.

In the rest of the chapter, we learned about the *elements* included with the software and used textures, objects, and effects to create a title sequence. When we were done with our second, animated title we imported it into FCE and discovered the importance of making sure a title's background is exported with the title (unless the title uses an *alpha channel*, which we also discussed).

Now that we are done learning about the FCE and LiveType programs, let's go cut some Kuleshov Effect footage in Chapter 12, and put all of this technical knowledge into action.

1. What are the four windows in LiveType?

2. What are *elements*?

3. What is the difference between LiveFonts and regular system fonts?

4. What is the easiest and best way to import a LiveType title into FCE?

5. Why would you export a LiveType file as a self-contained movie?

DISCUSSION / ESSAY QUESTIONS

1. Why would you use LiveType, instead of the built-in FCE text generators or the Boris application?

2. What do you think would happen if you set the Project Properties in LiveType to a different setting than the format being used in FCE?

3. How elaborate should a title card or title sequence be?

4. Discuss the pros and cons of making credits in LiveType and then editing them together in FCE vs. bringing your movie into LiveType and timing your credits there.

Further Research

LiveType offers many options for creating title and credit sequences. To practice further, make a simple text track and then apply all of the different effects, in turn, to see how they work. Then try applying the different textures as mattes to that same text to see what you think of that option. Only then should you start exploring the various LiveFonts. Whatever you do, however, don't be afraid to experiment with all of the options, in various combinations, in LiveType.

You should also take a look at the work of some of the great titles designers of film history. Here are a few names to start you off:

- Saul Bass (1920–1996) – made titles for Alfred Hitchcock and Otto Preminger, among others

- Maurice Binder (1925–1991) – made titles for the James Bond films

- Kyle Cooper (1962–) – has made titles for many films in the last 20 years or so

Finally, explore some online resources on the history of titling.[2] Just search for *title design*. There is also a movie on the history of modern typography called *Helvetica* (Gary Hustwit, 2007).

References

1. http://support.apple.com/kb/HT1796
2. Here is a good website, among many choices, to get you started:
   http://www.artofthetitle.com/

CHAPTER 12

THE KULESHOV EFFECT

OVERVIEW AND LEARNING OBJECTIVES

In this chapter, you will:

- Review the basic editing principles discovered by Soviet filmmaker and theorist Lev Kuleshov in the early 1920s
- Create a Kuleshov Effect of your own using footage provided on the included DVD
- Adapt Kuleshov's principles to the 21st century
- Practice some basic filter correction on a few shots

What is the Kuleshov Effect?

In Chapter 1, we discussed both Lev Kuleshov and Sergei Eisenstein and their roles in film editing history. These were the young artists who found a film print of a famous Russian actor, shot before the 1917 Russian Revolution, and, from 1918–1921, in the middle of the chaos sweeping over their new country – the Soviet Union – worked with that footage enough times to develop several new theories of film editing. Sergei Eisenstein took these theories and codified them into a series of principles since known as Soviet Montage, compiled in the book *Film Form*.[1]

What, then, was Kuleshov's original experiment? If you remember (we discussed it in Chapter 1), the idea was simple: take a shot of an expressionless actor and cut from it to various other shots, then back to the original shot. An audience watching this sequence of shots will add expressions and emotions into the actor's "performance" that aren't there. In other words, editing makes the story. The juxtaposition of unrelated shots can, if carefully constructed, create meaning where there was none before.

We are now going to try that experiment ourselves. Even though editing theory and technique have advanced far beyond what either Kuleshov or Eisenstein envisioned, we will still learn something from their process. Sometimes going back to the basics is really the best way to start.

The Footage

We will work with four main shots, all shot for this book. One is of a man doing his best to show no emotion at all. The other three are an attractive woman, a bag of tortilla chips, and a cute dog. In the original experiment, the young filmmakers used slightly different shots to intercut into the shot of Ivan Mozzhukhin (the actor whose footage they found): a dead child in a coffin, a bowl of soup, and a woman lounging on a sofa. Here, we've changed the details a bit, but the idea is the same.

You will also have two extra shots, for context, if you want to use them. Since we are now in the 21st century, you may want to create an actual movie, once you have completed the exercise. Those shots will help, as will the simple music track you will find on the DVD, created in Apple's GarageBand® as a mood enhancer.

Getting Started

Let's create a new project for this chapter, so that we are, effectively, starting from scratch. Since we have already covered the FCE interface and the various tools, we will assume, from now on, that you understand how to make cuts and apply effects. If you need to remember how to do something we covered earlier, go back to one of the chapters on FCE for a refresher course.

Let's import the files we need. You will find them on the DVD in a folder marked *Video_02*. Import the full folder, and save your project as *Kuleshov Effect*. Set your scratch disks to the same folder on your hard drive where you have saved your project. When you're done, your new project's Browser should have just one default sequence, and one bin, labeled *Video_02*, as shown in Figure 12.1.

FIGURE 12.1 Our new *Kuleshov Effect* project has just one sequence and one bin, labeled *Video_02*.

All figures appear in color on the companion DVD.

There are six shots, as promised, plus one audio file. Let's double-click on each shot, in turn, to see it in the Viewer:

- Kuleshov_01 is the medium close-up of the man, as shown in Figure 12.2.

- Kuleshov_02 is the medium close-up of the woman, as shown in Figure 12.3.

- Kuleshov_03 is the shot of the bag of chips, as shown in Figure 12.4.

- Kuleshov_04 is the shot of the dog, as shown in Figure 12.5.

- Kuleshov_05 is a wide shot of the entire scene, as shown in Figure 12.6, starting before the entrance of the woman and the dog.

- Kuleshov_06 is a tighter shot of the same location, as shown in Figure 12.7.

There are some focus issues with this shot, but that will help learn how to use another filter when we try to fix it.

FIGURE 12.2 medium close-up of the man.

FIGURE 12.3 medium close-up of the woman.

FIGURE 12.4 Shot of the tortilla chips.

FIGURE 12.5 Shot of the dog.

FIGURE 12.6 Wide shot of the scene, for context.

FIGURE 12.7 Tighter shot of the same scene.

Now that we have our footage, let's start cutting. We can begin by adding two seconds of black slug at the beginning of the project, as a handle of blank, silent nothingness, from which the film will emerge. We will also add such a handle at the end of the film as well. All you need to do is find the slug generator (there are multiple places to find this, as you know from Chapter 9), create some slug, make it two seconds long, and drop it at the head of the Timeline, as shown in Figure 12.8. If you prefer 1 second of slug, or no slug at all, you can edit the sequence in your own way. When it comes time to export the film as a self-contained digital file, however, you will find that these handles make your work more professional.

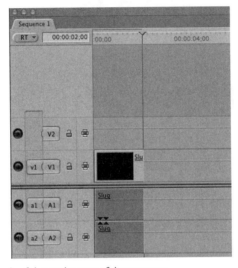

FIGURE 12.8 Two seconds of slug at the start of the sequence.

Next, take the first shot – *Kuleshov_01* – and drag it down to the Timeline, dropping it after the slug, as shown in Figure 12.9. This should work fine, except that there may be a green line at the top of the Timeline, which indicates that we need to render the file we just dragged there. This indicates that the *Kuleshov_01* video clip is not in the same format as our sequence. This makes sense, because we were just editing our *Nail Polish* files in the older NTSC DV format, while the Kuleshov clips were shot in HDV. Go to the Browser and scroll to the right until you see the video format columns, as shown in Figure 12.10, and you will see the discrepancy between the sequence and the clips. While it's possible that the FCE project settings have already been changed, for our purposes, we will assume that FCE is still set to the *DV/DVCPRO NTSC* format and needs changed.

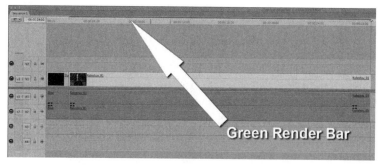

FIGURE 12.9 Drop *Kuleshov_01* after the slug – notice the green render bar at the top of the sequence.

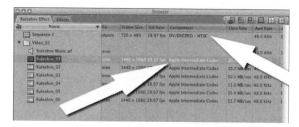

FIGURE 12.10 Your Browser shows you the differences in format between the NTSC sequence and the HDV clips.

To change the format, if you remember, you need to go to the *Easy Setup* menu, as shown in Figure 12.11, under the *FCE* dropdown menu. If you haven't changed anything, it will still be set to *DV-NTSC Anamorphic*. We want to change it to the same format as the footage, which, as you saw in the Browser, is *1440 × 1080* at *29.97fps*, which indicates that it's *HDV 1080i*. Let's select that format, then, as shown in Figure 12.12.

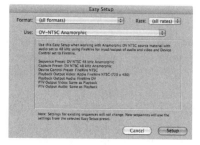

FIGURE 12.11 Go to the *Easy Setup* menu to change the project's format.

FIGURE 12.12 Choose *HDV-Apple Intermediate Codec 1080i60* as our new format.

This, however, does not change the format of the sequence that was already there. Go ahead and create a new sequence. This new sequence will have the correct format, as shown in Figure 12.13. Let's delete the old *Sequence 1* and rename this new sequence *Kuleshov Sequence*, as shown in Figure 12.14. You'll have to double-click on this sequence for the Timeline to reappear, since it will have disappeared when you deleted the old sequence. Once you are all set with the new sequence, you can re-drag a 2-second piece of slug down to the Timeline, and then re-drag the first Kuleshov shot. The green render bar should no longer be there, which means that we have solved our format issues.

FIGURE 12.13 Create a new sequence, and the format change will be reflected there.

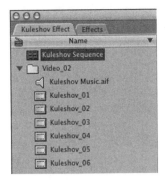

FIGURE 12.14 Rename the new sequence *Kuleshov Sequence*, and delete the old sequence.

There is a far easier way to reset the format of a sequence, but many beginning filmmakers find it confusing, at first. If you have new, blank sequence and you drag a piece of media to it, and that piece of media is in a different format than that of the sequence, then FCE will ask you, with a pop-up window, if you want to reset the sequence to match the clip settings, as shown in Figure 12.15. However, the catch is that there cannot be any other prior media in the sequence already. If there is, then FCE will assume that the sequence format is correct, and adapt the new clip to that format. The reason why FCE did not show us that window is because we had already dropped some slug in the sequence, and slug will always take on the format of the sequence to which it is dragged.

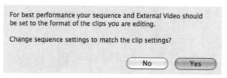

For best performance your sequence and External Video should be set to the format of the clips you are editing.

Change sequence settings to match the clip settings?

No   Yes

FIGURE 12.15 The pop-up window that asks you if you want to reset the sequence settings to match the clip settings.

Cutting Our Own Kuleshov Effect Experiment

The first shot, of the man – *Kuleshov_01* – is 27 seconds long. The man stares slightly to camera left. For modern viewers, someone staring straight at the camera would look as he if were engaging with us, the filmgoers, rather than with the woman, dog, or chips that are off-camera. Since he stares off to one side, we expect to soon see the object of his interest. The shot is slightly underexposed on the right side – as we discussed in Chapter 11 – but we will fix that once we are done with the actual editing.

Starting with the first shot

You can cut your own Kuleshov Effect scene in a variety of ways. For now, however, let's create three separate little vignettes, each separated by a title card, and then add a little extra scene at the end, using one of the wider shots. These will not be long vignettes and will each use only 15 seconds of *Kuleshov_01*. Those 15 seconds have to match every time – they need to be the *same* 15 seconds – otherwise the lesson of this experiment is lost. So first, let's choose the 15 seconds of *Kuleshov_01* we want to use.

We didn't have to drag the shot down to the Timeline to choose our 15 seconds, but there it is, so we'll double-click the shot from there, so that it appears in the Viewer. Even though it seems as if the man is doing the same thing for almost 30 seconds, let's quickly scroll through the shot, anyway, to see if there are some moments we like better than others. After all, the leaves moving behind the man, as well as the lighting, are different at different points in the shot.

Once you are done watching the shot, mark your *In* and *Out* points, as shown in Figure 12.16, making sure that you have exactly 15 seconds. In case you have forgotten, the length of the shot is shown in the *Timecode Duration* field, in the upper left of the Viewer, as shown in Figure 12.17. The actual timecode of the frame where your playhead is stopped is shown in the *Current Timecode* field, as shown in Figure 12.18.

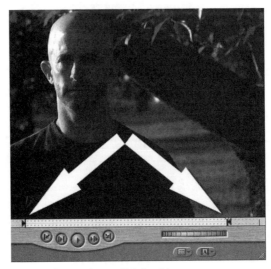

FIGURE 12.16 Mark your *In* and *Out* points on *Kuleshov_01*.

FIGURE 12.17 The *Timecode Duration* field in the upper left of the Viewer.

FIGURE 12.18 The *Current Timecode* field in the upper right of the Viewer.

Since we double-clicked the shot from within the Timeline, that clip is now shorter, and no longer directly follows the slug, as shown in Figure 12.19. We'll need to close the gap. You can either just slide the clip over, or place your playhead somewhere between the slug and the clip, and press the *control* key plus the *G* key. You'll find this option under the *Sequence* dropdown menu. Next, go back to the Viewer, which should still be showing the same shot (unless you double-clicked on something else), and place the playhead at a spot that divides the shot into a 10-second and 5-second section. Press the *M* key to set a marker at that spot, as shown in Figure 12.20. Since the

Viewer is showing us a clip that is in the Timeline, that marker should also show up in the Timeline as well, as shown in Figure 12.21. Select the *Razor Blade* tool and make a cut at that marker, as shown in Figure 12.22. We're done with *Kuleshov_01*, for now.

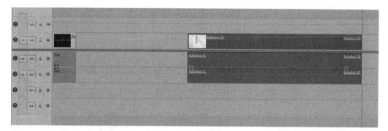

FIGURE 12.19 After we shorten the clip in the Viewer, it is also shortened in the Timeline, and we will need to close the gap.

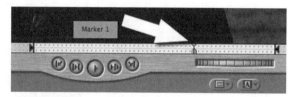

FIGURE 12.20 In the Viewer, place the playhead at a spot that divides the shot into a 10-second and 5-second section, and put a marker at that spot.

FIGURE 12.21 That marker appears in the Timeline as well.

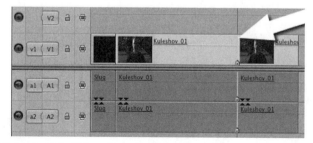

FIGURE 12.22 Using the *Razor Blade* tool, cut the clip at the marker.

Adding what "Kuleshov" sees. part 1

For each of the other shots, we need to find 5 seconds that we like. We'll only choose 5 seconds, as the emphasis in the Kuleshov experiment should be on the actor and on how cutting to different shots changes his "performance." So let's now look at *Kuleshov_02*, the shot of the woman. Instead of dragging it down to the Timeline first, let's double-click it directly from the Browser.

The moment where the actress turns her head is good, as it adds motion and interest to her shot. Since the shot of the man is so static, this makes a nice contrast. Let's choose 5 seconds that includes that motion, then, and set our *In* and *Out* points accordingly, as shown in Figure 12.23. We are now ready to drag the shot down to the Timeline. Let's place it directly over the second half of the *Kuleshov_01* shot, as shown in Figure 12.24. Since both clips are now 5 seconds long, it should be a perfect fit.

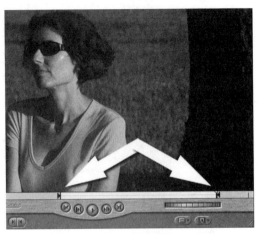

FIGURE 12.23 Set our *In* and *Out* points in *Kuleshov_02* to include the motion of the woman's head.

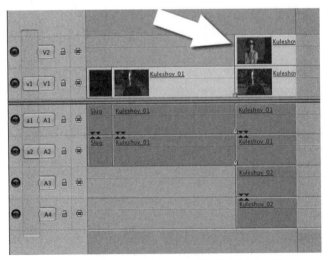

FIGURE 12.24 Drag this 5-second clip on top of the second half of *Kuleshov_01*.

Make sure *Snapping* is on, and drag the second half of the *Kuleshov_01* shot to the right, until it snaps at the edit point at the end of *Kuleshov_02*, as shown in Figure 12.25. You have now completed the rough cut of the first Kuleshov moment. Go ahead and watch it. You may notice that it doesn't play that well at the edit points. The audio – without correction – does not allow for good transitions between shots. We'll fix that when we are done with all three moments. For now, you can also turn off the volume on your computer for a moment, and just play through the sequence visually, as our Soviet friends did in the 1920s. Eventually, you may want to delete the sound entirely, although we will not do that in this chapter.

FIGURE 12.25 Drag the second half of the *Kuleshov_01* shot to the right, until it snaps at the edit point at the end of *Kuleshov_02*.

Let's move on. The next two Kuleshov scenes will be easier to do, as we are going to keep the exact same bit of *Kuleshov_01*, changing only the cutaway each time. The easiest way to do that is to select all three clips in the Timeline, as shown in Figure 12.26, then copy them, place the playhead at the last edit point in the Timeline, and paste those very same clips at that spot. You will then have two exact copies of the sequence of shots we created, side by side, as shown in Figure 12.27. Highlight the second copy of *Kuleshov_02* and press the delete key. We now have an open spot for the next cutaway, as shown in Figure 12.28.

FIGURE 12.26 Select all three clips in the Timeline.

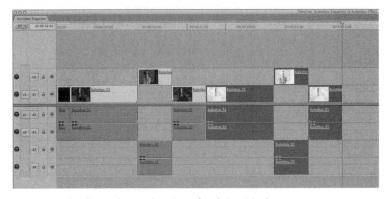

FIGURE 12.27 Copy the clips and paste them just after their originals.

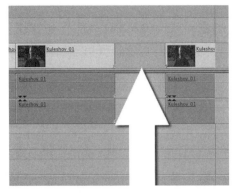

FIGURE 12.28 Delete the second copy of the *Kuleshov_02* shot to create a space for the next cutaway.

Adding what "Kuleshov" sees. part 2

That next shot will be *Kuleshov_03*, which is of the bag of tortilla chips. Double-click it from the Browser. Then, as we did with *Kuleshov_02*, set an *In* and *Out* point, choosing 5 seconds that you like. Drag it down to the Timeline, placing it in the spot we cleared when we deleted the second copy of *Kuleshov_02*. You have now completed the rough cut of the second Kuleshov moment. Take a moment to watch your work. Again, there are the same sound issues, but you can ignore them for now. Go ahead and copy this sequence of shots, and paste it after itself, as shown in Figure 12.29. This time, however, do not delete the second copy of *Kuleshov_03*. We will *overwrite* it when we drag our *Kuleshov_04* clip down to the Timeline.

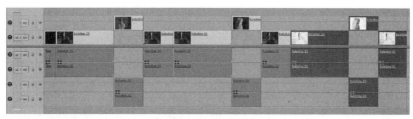

FIGURE 12.29 Copy the second sequence of clips and paste them after their originals.

Adding what "Kuleshov" sees. part 3

Double-click *Kuleshov_04* from the Browser, and make your 5-second selection. As we did with the actress, try to choose a moment where the dog turns her head, again for visual and dramatic interest. Once you're done, drag *Kuleshov_04* down to the Timeline, and drop it in the same space occupied by the second copy of *Kuleshov_03*, making sure that the arrow cursor is pointing down and not sideways (see Chapter 7). Since both clips should be 5 seconds long, *Kuleshov_04* should perfectly *overwrite* the copy of *Kuleshov_03*. We are now done with the rough cut of all three moments.

Fixing audio

We still have the sound issues. Again, you may want to just delete all of the sound, but for our purposes today, let's keep some of it, smoothing out the rough transitions.

Let's start by going to the upper right of our Timeline and deselecting *Linked Selection*, as shown in Figure 12.30. Once that is done, select the audio for the second and third shots in each shot Kuleshov scene, and delete it, as shown in Figure 12.31. Then, in each scene, grab the audio from the first part of *Kuleshov_01*, and drag it to the right, extending it to the end of that particular scene, as shown in Figure 12.32. This gets rid of all of the sound issues, as each scene now has just one piece of sound throughout.

FIGURE 12.30 Deselect Linked *Selection* in the Timeline.

After you make this adjustment, you will notice a little red box that appears in each sequence, in the second half of *Kuleshov_02*, marked with a *+05.00*. This box lets you know that the clip is 5 seconds out of synchronization with the audio below it. This makes sense, since there is now a 5-second offset between that image and the sound. FCE knows that the video and the audio belong to the same Master clip (both are from *Kuleshov_01*) and wants you to know that the video and audio do not match. Since all of the sound in this shot is being produced by off-camera activity, it doesn't matter.

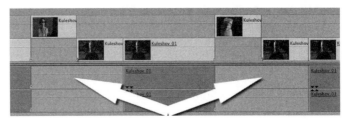

FIGURE 12.31 Delete the audio from the second and third shots in each Kuleshov scene.

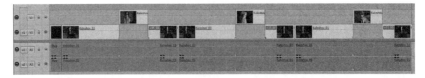

FIGURE 12.32 Extend the audio from the first half of *Kuleshov_01* in each scene.

Go ahead and watch each sequence of shots in turn now. What do you think? Since the audio now plays without any awkward break between shots, you can focus on the visuals. Do you think the experiment works? Hopefully, you do, and also see some of what Kuleshov discovered about the power of context.

Finetuning our experiment

Let's now fine-tune our segments. We need to separate each Kuleshov scene, and we can do that with a series of title cards. In Chapter 11, we covered LiveType, but let's use Boris now, for more practice with effects and generators within FCE. Boris, as we discussed before, is better than the basic *Text* generator. We'll use LiveType again later in this book.

As we did in Chapter 10, go to the *Effects* tab, then to *Video Generators*, then to *Boris*, and finally to *Title 3D*, as shown in Figure 12.33. Double-click that icon, then go to the *Controls* tab in the Viewer, click on the box that reads *Click for options*, and then, once the *Boris Title 3D* menu pops up, type the text for our first title card – *The Kuleshov Effect Take 1* – as shown in Figure 12.34. Boris, unlike the regular *Text* generator, allows you to change the font size of individual lines of text (or even of individual letters). You can also add underlining or italics, as we have done here, without applying it to the entire title.

FIGURE 12.33 To create our title card, go to the *Effects* tab, then to *Video Generators*, then to *Boris*, and finally to *Title 3D*.

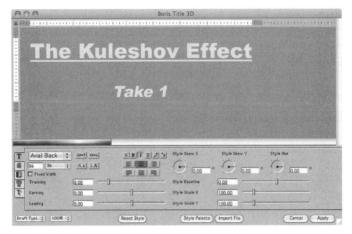

FIGURE 12.34 Type our first title in the *Boris Title 3D* menu.

Next, go back to the *Video* tab of the Viewer and change, in the *Timecode Duration* field, the default length of the card from 10 seconds to 5 seconds, as shown in Figure 12.35. With the fade-in dissolve that we will add, this will leave about 4 seconds of time to read the title, which should be enough. Once this is done, make sure the playhead is placed, in the Timeline, right after the slug, and drag your title to the Canvas, dropping it on the *Insert* button that pops up, as shown in Figure 12.36. It should drop nicely in front of the first shot, as shown in Figure 12.37.

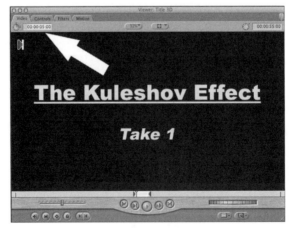

FIGURE 12.35 In the *Timecode Duration* field, change the default length of the card from 10 seconds to 5 seconds.

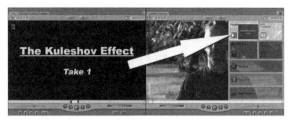

FIGURE 12.36 Drag your title to the Canvas, dropping it on the *Insert* button.

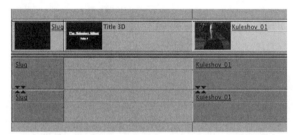

FIGURE 12.37 If you placed the playhead after the slug, the title should drop in just the right place.

A good rule of thumb for title cards, in terms of length, is to read them out loud to yourself as they play through on your screen. Speak slowly, to make sure that people of all ages and abilities would be able to accomplish the same task. If you reach the end of the title long before its end, then the title is too long. If you can't read all of the text in the time allotted, then the title is too short. There is no better way to time titles.

While the *Boris Title 3D* generator is still in the Viewer, click again in the *Controls* tab, on the *Click for options* button, and change *Take 1* to *Take 2*, as shown in Figure 12.38. Then place the playhead in the Timeline at the end of the first sequence and drag this new title to the Canvas, dropping it on the *Insert* button again. It should be placed perfectly before the second Kuleshov moment, as shown in Figure 12.39. Repeat this process one more time, replacing *Take 2* with *Take 3*, and you should have a Timeline with three Kuleshov sequences, each separated by a title card, as shown in Figure 12.40.

FIGURE 12.38 Change *Take 1* to *Take 2*.

FIGURE 12.39 Drop the new title before the second segment.

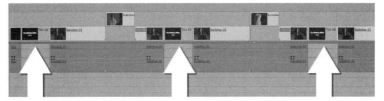

FIGURE 12.40 Repeat the process one more time, and you should have three titles, each before each scene.

Now let's add some video and audio fades to make it all flow more smoothly. Go to the *Video Transitions* bin of the *Effects* tab, as shown in Figure 12.41, for the video fades. For the audio fades, go to the *Audio Transitions* bin of the same *Effects* tab, as shown in Figure 12.42. Drag the effects, each in turn, down to the Timeline and drop them where you want them. Each fade is, by default, 1 second long. You can make it longer by double-clicking the fade in the Timeline, and then following instructions, or simply by dragging it one way or the other to make it shorter or longer. Let's keep the fades at their default length. When we are done, we should have a sequence with fades at the beginning and end of each title card, and at the beginning and end of each Kuleshov scene, as shown in Figure 12.43.

FIGURE 12.41 Go to the *Video Transitions* bin of the *Effects* tab for the video fades.

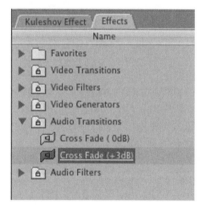

FIGURE 12.42 Go to the *Audio Transitions* bin of the *Effects* tab for the audio fades.

FIGURE 12.43 We should end up with a sequence that has fades at the beginning and end of each title card, and at the beginning and end of each Kuleshov scene.

The only thing left to do is to render the fades. They will play in real time, without rendering, but they'll look much better if we actually render them (the audio fades do not need to be rendered). Go up to the *Sequence* drop-down menu and select *Render All*, or press the *option* key and the *R* key, and you will see the pop-up render indicator letting you know how much time it will take, as shown in Figure 12.44. It should be just a few seconds, and then your entire Kuleshov movie is done.

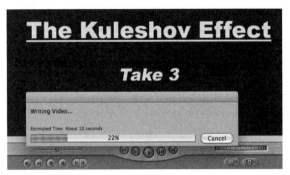

FIGURE 12.44 Press the *option* key and the *R* key, and your transitions will render quickly.

 ## Beyond the Kuleshov Effect – a Modern Addition

Let's take this experiment one step further. There is some footage that we have yet to use, plus that music file. The goal here is to cut an extra scene that will play, as *Take 4*, at the end of our Kuleshov movie. In this scene, we will use the same 15 seconds of the shot of the man, but add more context by using the wide shots. We'll layer the music underneath as an additional tool to affect the mood of the piece. Take a few minutes, then – however long you need – and watch *Kuleshov_05* and *Kuleshov_06*. When you are done, listen to the *Kuleshov Music* audio file (which was composed in Apple's Garage Band application).

On your own, cut the new scene, starting with *Kuleshov_05*, followed by the first 10 seconds of *Kuleshov_01*, followed by *Kuleshov_06*, followed by the final 5 seconds of *Kuleshov_01*. As before, in order for this exercise to be useful, you must use the exact same footage of *Kuleshov_01*. When you are done cutting the video clips, remove the original audio from the clips, and add the music underneath instead. Finally, add a new tile – *The Kuleshov Effect Take 4* – and apply the same kinds of transitions as before. Don't forget to place 2 seconds of slug at the end for a final handle. You should end up with a perfect conclusion to the other three scenes, as shown in Figure 12.45.

FIGURE 12.45 Cut *The Kuleshov Effect Take 4* segment, using the two wide shots and the music and a title card and transitions.

When you cut with music, it's a good idea to pay attention to the rhythm and beats within it. You can do this best by double-clicking the file and analyzing the audio waveform in the Viewer, marking certain beats, as shown in Figure 12.46. You can also easily apply a fade up or fade down this way using the *Pen* tool.

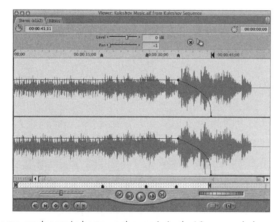

FIGURE 12.46 You can mark certain beats on the music in the Viewer, and also create a fade out with the *Pen* tool.

Music and other mood-inducing sounds can be helpful tools to affect the tone of a film, or even to affect an actor's performance. The music can't do the work you should have done through shooting, directing, and editing (i.e., to supply story), but it can be a good enhancer. In our final scene here, the music adds a new layer of meaning to the imagined performance of the man, taking Kuleshov's idea one step further.

Correcting Shots with Filters

We are almost done. We just need to correct the exposure issue in *Kuleshov_01* and the focus issue in *Kuleshov_06*. The best way to fix these kinds of problems, especially focus, is to avoid having them in the first place, by shooting your footage correctly. But mistakes of some kind are inevitable, and you should know how to deal with them.

Brightness and Contrast vs. Gamma

Let's start with *Kuleshov_01*. In the *Video Filters* bin, under *Effects*, is another bin labeled *Image Control*. Here you can find many ways to change and correct your image. Many people gravitate towards the *Brightness and Contrast* filter when their shots are too dark, but that's not actually the best filter to use, as it can very quickly make your shadow areas look milky and grainy. Instead, use the *Gamma Correction* filter, as shown in Figure 12.47, which takes a more nuanced approached to the color and exposure variables of your video clip. Gamma encoding is a digital function that helps control *luminance* – brightness – in a non-linear fashion. Drag the filter and drop it on the first *Kuleshov_01* clip in the Timeline, as shown in Figure 12.48.

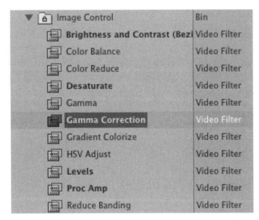

FIGURE 12.47 Use the *Gamma Correction* filter to brighten your shot, rather than the *Brightness and Contrast* filter.

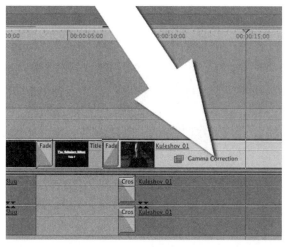

FIGURE 12.48 Drag the *Gamma Correction* filter to the first *Kuleshov_01* clip in the Timeline.

Next, double-click the shot from the Timeline, and go to the *Filters* tab in the Viewer, as shown in Figure 12.49. There is a slider there, with *1* as the default number (which is the uncorrected setting for your shot). If we look closely at the uncorrected version of *Kuleshov_01*, before we change the filter settings, we see that it is really dark on the right side, as shown in Figure 12.50. To watch the live process of adjustment to the shot, place the playhead in the Timeline over a part of *Kuleshov_01*, so we can see it in the Canvas. Make sure you have the brightness of your computer screen turned up enough – you wouldn't want to make corrections based on a dark screen.

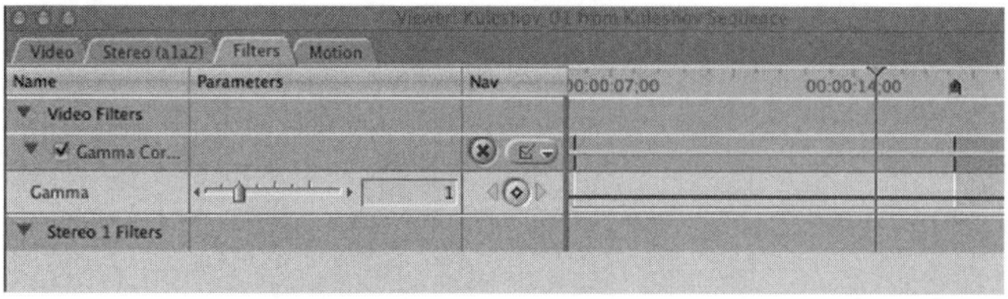

FIGURE 12.49 Go to the *Filters* tab in the Viewer to find the *Gamma Correction* filter after you drop it on the shot.

FIGURE 12.50 We can see, when we look closely, just how underexposed the *Kuleshov_01* clip is on the right side.

If you want to make real color or exposure adjustments, you should really invest in an external monitor, larger than your computer screen (unless you have a large HD monitor as your screen). If you are editing to and from tape, you can connect to the monitor through the tape deck or camera. If you are working on an HD project, recorded on to flash memory storage, you can connect the HD display directly to the computer. Regardless of how this is done, connecting a monitor that can accurately represent the colors and exposures of the format in which you are editing is very important. That's what those colors bars you see in the Video Generators bin are for: to match the colors that come out of FCE to the colors on your monitor.

It's also important to consider a high-quality sound system for your editing station, so you can accurately judge your final sound mix.

The way the *Gamma Correction* filter works is that the lower values of the gamma curve, below 1, make the shot lighter, while the values above 1 make it darker. Unlike with the *Brightness and Contrast* filter, you can brighten the image considerably while avoiding some of the issues with the milkiness of the shadows. However, it is still possible to go too far. For example, let's drag the slider down to a .53 value. If we look back at the shot now, as shown in Figure 12.51, it looks brighter and clearer, but also a little too grainy and milky. It's a better idea to stay somewhere in the .68 to .79 range. Put the slider at a .79 value, and you'll see that the shot looks brighter, as shown in Figure 12.52, but without that excessive washed-out look. Part of the man's face is still dark, but not as distractingly underexposed as in the original; the contrast between the two sides of the face actually looks good, adding shape to the shot.

FIGURE 12.51 With the *Gamma Correction* slider at *.53*, the shot looks too grainy and washed out.

FIGURE 12.52 With the *Gamma Correction* slider at *.79*, the shot looks brighter, but not too milky in the shadows.

Pasting Attributes

Now we want to take this filter setting and apply it to all of the other *Kuleshov_01* shots. You could highlight all of the other shots and then drag the filter down from the *Filters* tab in the Viewer and drop it on all of them simultaneously, or you could try something called the *Paste Attributes* method.

First, in the Timeline, highlight the *Kuleshov_01* clip to which we have already made a correction. Then, press the *command* key and the *C* key, or go to the *Edit* dropdown menu and select *Copy*. Next, highlight all of the *Kuleshov_01* clips in the Timeline that still need the correction. Then, press the *option* key and the *V* key (or go to the *Edit* menu again and select *Paste Attributes*). When you do that, the *Paste Attributes* pop-up menu appears, as shown in Figure 12.53. As you can see, there are many different attributes of the shot that might be available to paste, depending on what you have done to the shot you just copied. All we want to do is select *Filters*. Do that and click on *OK*. As soon as you do that, you will have just pasted the *Gamma Correction* filter – with the same settings – to all of the clips you highlighted.

FIGURE 12.53 The *Paste Attributes* pop-up menu.

Adding sharpness to a blurry shot

Finally, we will correct the blurriness in *Kuleshov_06*. It looks like the middle-ground of the shot is where the focus was set, rather than the foreground, as we can see in Figure 12.54. Mistakes like this happen all the time, especially if the shooter uses the LCD monitor on the camera, rather than the *diopter*, or eyepiece. There is no perfect fix for this issue, but we can at least make the shot look a little better.

FIGURE 12.54 *Kuleshov_06* looks like the focus was improperly set to the middle-ground of the shot, rather than to the foreground.

Go to the *Sharpen* bin of the *Video Filters* bin, and select the *Sharpen* filter, as shown in Figure 12.55. Drag this down to the *Kuleshov_06* shot in the Timeline. As before, make sure your Timeline playhead is positioned somewhere in the middle of that shot, and look at the Canvas. You will see that the default settings of the *Sharpen* filter add a lot of *video noise* – grain, texture, and pixels – to the shot, as shown in Figure 12.56. We will have to change the settings, as the result is not very attractive, and does not match the look of the rest of the scene.

FIGURE 12.55 Go to the *Sharpen bin* of the *Video Filters* bin, and select the *Sharpen* filter.

FIGURE 12.56 The default settings of the *Sharpen* filter add too much *video noise* to the shot.

Double-click the shot in the Timeline, and go to the *Filters* tab in the Viewer. The *Amount* slider is set to *100* (full strength) by default. As you drag it to the left, decreasing the value, you can watch how the appearance of the shot changes in the Canvas. Let's try a reduced value of *21*. This setting adds just enough noise to the shot to mask the bad focus in the foreground, as shown in Figure 12.57, but not enough to be distracting and look like we added a filter.

FIGURE 12.57 A *Sharpen* setting of *21* adds just enough noise to mask the bad focus, but not enough to look bad.

Checking your work before exporting

If you do not have an external video monitor attached to your computer in some way, the least you will want to do before exporting is to check the way your project looks when you increase the size of the viewing window. Your computer's monitor may not have great resolution, no matter what you do, or may have resolution that is not a good match for the video format in which you have been working, but enlarging the image is still a good way to check focus and other issues.

We can make the Canvas larger using two methods. First, you can drag the lower right corner of the Canvas window and then reposition that window on your screen to make it as large as you'd like it to be, as shown in Figure 12.58. Remember that, in order to put the arrangement of your windows back to the default settings, just press the *control* key and the *U key*, or go to the *Window* dropdown menu.

FIGURE 12.58 You can enlarge your Canvas by grabbing the lower-right corner and dragging; you can reposition the entire window by grabbing the center of the frame.

Secondly, you can go to the *View* dropdown menu, scroll down to *Video Out*, and select *Digital Cinema Desktop Preview – Main*, as shown in Figure 12.59. As soon as you do that, the entire computer screen will fill with your movie, at whatever point the playhead is positioned, and you can press the *spacebar* to play. When you are done viewing your film this way, just press the *esc* key at the upper-left corner of your keyboard.

FIGURE 12.59 To fill your entire monitor with your movie, go to the *View* dropdown menu, scroll down to *Video Out*, and select *Digital Cinema Desktop Preview – Main*.

ON DVD

We are now done editing the Kuleshov footage. You can view a completed version of all four scenes, in a row, on the companion DVD, where it is labeled *Kuleshov Effect Movie*. Unlike the actual footage, the completed film has been compressed to leave room on the DVD for the editable clips. It's in the same compressed format as the other completed films on the disc. Enjoy watching it and comparing it to your own work.

SUMMARY

In this chapter, we returned to the lessons of Lev Kuleshov and Sergei Eisenstein, and their radical notions – for the 1920s – of how editing two shots together creates a new, third meaning. They posited that the performance of an actor derives from the context in which the audience sees it, and that the editing drives the story. We used their arguments as the departure point for some experimentation of our own.

Using footage from the DVD that accompanies this text, shot in HDV 1080i format, we made three short Kuleshov-inspired scenes of our own. We worked with the same basic kinds of shots as Kuleshov did, including one of a main male actor and a series of different cutaways. As we cut, we practiced some very basic sound design principles, deleting bad audio and improving transitions between the better audio. We also practiced using the Boris title generator to create title cards used to separate one scene to the next.

When we were done with our three remakes of the different Kuleshov scenes, we used additional footage from the DVD to cut a more modern adaptation of Kuleshov's ideas, adding wider shots for greater context, and music for mood. The result was no less effective in proving how editing creates, or at the very least enhances, the emotional resonance of a story.

Finally, we took two shots – *Kuleshov_01* and *Kuleshov_06* – with significant shooting errors (exposure and focus) and used those errors to practice using filters. We discovered that the *Gamma Correction* filter is an excellent tool to correct – within limits – dark shots. We also saw that

SUMMARY

the *Sharpen* tool is an equally useful tool for correcting shots that have mild focus issues. Along the way, we learned how to use the *Paste Attributes* function to replicate filters on multiple clips at once.

In Chapter 13, we will start re-cutting *Nail Polish*. You will have access to the clips for the entire movie, and not just the first scene. You will first be required to cut the movie as a comedy and then, in subsequent chapters, as a drama and a thriller. These exercises will give you hands-on editing experience and will help you develop your editing skills. The lessons of this chapter should be especially useful as we try to change the mood and genre of *Nail Polish* with each new version.

REVIEW QUESTIONS: CHAPTER 12

1. Who were Lev Kuleshov and Sergei Eisenstein?

2. Describe the principle behind their experiments with the shot of Ivan Mozzhukhin.

3. What is one way that music can affect our reaction to a shot?

4. What is a good way to brighten a shot that is slightly dark?

5. How do you copy attributes, such as filters, from one shot to many other shots with just a few keyboard strokes?

1. After completing the work you did in this chapter, do you think the Kuleshov Effect is a good way to create an actor's performance?

2. What modern applications of the Kuleshov Effect have you seen in a recent film you liked?

3. Have you watched any films where the actor could have benefited from a less overt display of emotions and a more context-driven (i.e., Kuleshov-style) editing?

4. Who deserves more credit for a Best Actor Oscar™ – the actor, the director, or the editor? Or do they all deserve some credit? Explain.

Further Research

If you haven't done so already, cut your own version of these Kuleshov-inspired exercises. Screen them for friends and then ask them what they think of the man's performance in each case. Pay attention to their feedback.

Try shooting some of your own footage to create, from scratch, your own Kuleshov Effect film. If you want to make an exact copy of what Kuleshov did, you can find many versions of the original film on YouTube and other such sites. Remember that you need an attractive woman, a child's coffin, and a bowl of soup, if you want to remake it shot for shot. But that's not necessary to recreate the actual effect of the cutting, so shoot how, and what, you want.

If you think there are other shots in the footage we just cut that require correcting, or changing, apply some additional filters. It's good to experiment with them to see how they work.

Finally, there are some more films by Soviet contemporaries of Lev Kuleshov that you should watch. In Chapter 1, we recommended *Strike* (1925) and *Battleship Potemkin* (1925), both by Sergei Eisenstein. If you didn't watch them then, go ahead and do so now. They're fascinating, both artistically and historically.

If you want a Soviet montage comedy, try the short film *Chess Fever* (Vsevolod Pudovkin, 1925). It mixes real documentary film with staged fiction footage and is fun to watch. You can find it on a three-film DVD set entitled *Three Soviet Classics (Earth / The End of St. Petersburg / Chess Fever)*. The other two films in the set are worth watching as well. And finally, why not try a film by Kuleshov, himself: *By the Law* (1926). Sadly, as of this writing, it is only available on VHS tape. The good news is that that video tape also comes with *Chess Fever*.

Reference

1. Eisenstein, Sergei. *Film Form: Essays in Film Theory*. Ed. and Trans. by Jay Leyda. New York: Harcourt Brace & Co., 1949.

CHAPTER 13

NAIL POLISH – CUTTING FOR COMEDY

OVERVIEW AND LEARNING OBJECTIVES

In this chapter, you will:

- Review the mechanics of how to cut for comedy
- Import and examine all of the footage from *Nail Polish*
- Re-cut the entire movie, using picture and sound, to maximize the laughs
- Color correct a few shots using the *Color Correction* filter

What Makes a Comedy Funny?

In Chapter 3, we looked at how genre affects the editing process. Now is our chance to put those notions into practice. When we analyzed *Four Weddings and a Funeral*, we saw that the pacing of the cuts was integral to the humor. In the opening scene of that film, the editor and director created a fast-paced sequence that drew laughs from the suspense of the moment. In that sense, the film almost resembled a thriller, except that the payoff was funny, rather than scary.

What we are going to try and do in this chapter is figure out what, if anything, is humorous in the footage and story of *Nail Polish*, and focus on that aspect. If the comedy requires a slow pace, than that is how we will edit; if it requires a fast pace, then we will cut that way. Perhaps the pacing of certain moments will be neither fast nor slow, but what will be important is how we create the setup for the punch line. Every story has its own particular structure, and how that story plays to an audience depends on how well the director and editor understand that structure.

ON DVD On the DVD that accompanies this book, you will find the footage for the rest of *Nail Polish* in a folder labeled *Video_03*. The footage for the first scene, if you remember, lies in the folder *Video_01*. As you examine the footage, you will see that the individual clips are sometimes quite short. This is because what you are getting is *not* all of the uncut rough footage, but only the shots that were actually used to make the original film, with 1-second handles added at the start and end of each. This way you have some extra video to allow you to make different cuts, if you want, and it also allowed us to fit all of the footage on the DVD in the original NTSC DV format.

You will also find 28 audio files in a folder labeled *Nail Polish Sound*. These files have already been converted to the AIFF format. All of them come, copyright-free, from Apple's GarageBand program (as did the music we used in the Kuleshov Effect film). You are under no obligation to use them. They might help, however, in establishing different tones for the different genres in which we will be cutting. Some of the files are musical, while others are mood-inducing *accents*. If you want additional sound effects, open GarageBand on your own computer – if you have it – and see what it has to offer. You should know, however, that you cannot export music and effects as AIFF files from GarageBand.

NOTE *In Chapter 10 we went over how to convert audio files from MP3 or AAC formats into AIFF.*

Prepping for the New Cut

To begin, let's import all of the clips we will need. You should already have imported *Video_01*, back in Chapter 7 (and you should have saved a cut of the first scene, in Chapter 8). Now it's time to find the *Video_03* and *Nail Polish Sounds* folders and bring them into the project. Go ahead and do that now. Copy the folders to your hard drive, and then import them

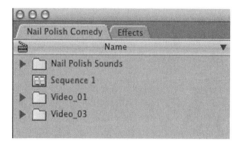

FIGURE 13.1 Our new *Nail Polish Comedy* project has three bins and one sequence.

into FCE. When you are done, save a copy of your project as *Nail Polish Comedy*. You should now have three bins and one sequence in your Browser, as shown in Figure 13.1. If you are starting from scratch, make sure that you carefully choose a location on your hard drive for all of these files, and do not forget to set your scratch disks.

All figures appear in color on the companion DVD.

ON DVD

Let's open up the *Nail Polish Sounds* bin, as shown in Figure 13.2. As you can see, we have many choices. As we review how *Nail Polish Comedy* was edited, and how you can recreate the film, yourself, we will choose different sounds for different genres. Feel free to use other sounds later.

Next, let's open up the *Video_03* bin. There are many clips here, perhaps too many to be shown, all at once, in your Browser. To expand the Browser viewing area, let's double-click the bin. This opens it up in a new pop-up window, as shown in Figure 13.3. Hopefully, your

FIGURE 13.2 In our *Nail Polish Sounds* bin, we have many audio files to choose from.

computer screen has a fine enough resolution to allow you to drag the corner of the bin so that you can see all of the files inside. If not, you can always just scroll through them. When you are done looking through this expanded window, click on the *control* key and the *W* key to close it (if you click on the *command* key and the *W* key, you will accidentally close the entire project).

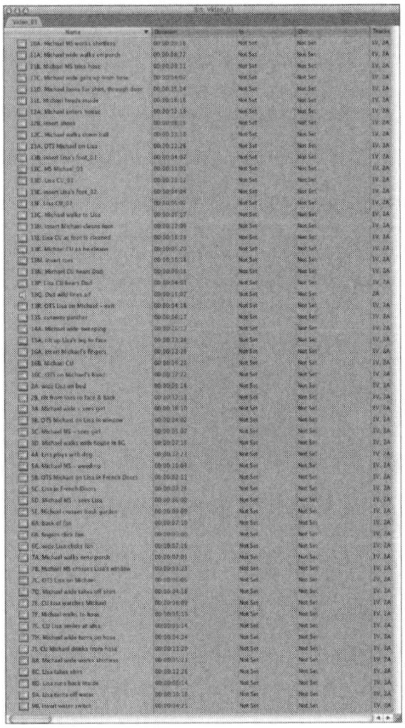

One minor issue in FCE is the way it handles consecutive numeration of files, as shown in Figure 13.4. If you have labeled the file names with numbers, the program lists all numbers that begin with a *"1"* first, followed by all numbers that begin with a *"2,"* etc. Look closely at the middle of the Browser window. After shot *16C*, we next have shot *2A*, and then the numbers go up in order after that. One solution would be to begin the numbers with a *"0,"* such as *"01A."* Another solution would be to begin your file names with a word that precedes the numbers, such as *Scene 1A* or *Shot 1A*; then the program would list everything in chronological order from 1 to 100, or higher.

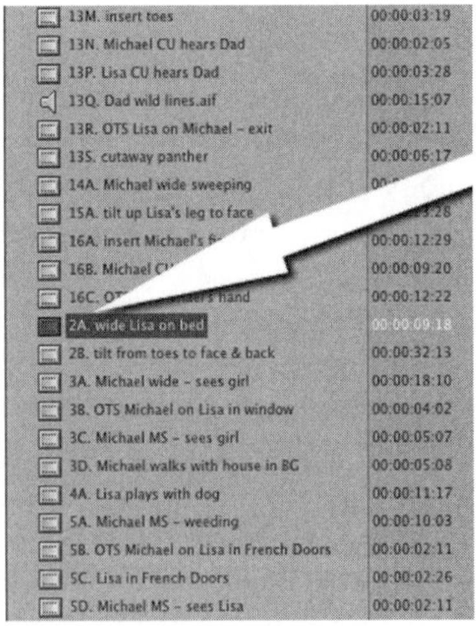

The key to successful editing, as we have discussed before, is careful organization. So let's create separate bins for each separate scene, and place all of the relevant footage for each scene in the appropriate bin. Since all of the shots are clearly labeled, this should be easy. When you are done with the clips from *Video_03*, you should end up with 15 new bins, labeled by scene, as shown in Figure 13.5.

FIGURE 13.3 The *Video_03* bin, which we have double-clicked on to open in a new Browser window, has all of the additional clips from *Nail Polish* not found in *Video_01*.

FIGURE 13.4 If your file names begin with a number, Final Cut Express will list them in order by the first digit, grouping all of the file names with a *"1"* together, before moving on to the file names with a *"2,"* etc.

To complete our reorganization of the Browser, let's re-label the *Video_01* bin as *Scene 1* and drag it to the *Video_03* bin. Next, re-label that bin as *Nail Polish Clips*, as shown in Figure 13.6. Some of this work may seem tedious, but never forget how important it is to know where to find what footage.

FIGURE 13.5 Organize the footage from *Video_03* by making a separate bin for each scene.

FIGURE 13.6 Re-label *Video_01* as *Scene 1*, place it in the *Video_03* bin, and then re-label that bin as *Nail Polish Clips*.

Now that this initial work is done, save the project, if you haven't done so already. It would be a shame to lose your work if the application quit unexpectedly. You should also save a master copy of the project, as it looks right now, using the *Save Project As …* function. You can use this master copy as your starting point for the versions of *Nail Polish* we will create in Chapters 14 and 15.

Many professional editors have developed the habit of constantly hitting the command *key and the* S *key (the keyboard shortcut for* Save*), and you should, too. You never know when a power outage might hit or the application might freeze, so get in the habit of saving frequently. Don't forget that you can also set your* Save a Copy Every _ Minutes *function to a number that makes sense for you – such as 5 minutes – in the FCE User Preferences, as we discussed at the end of Chapter 7.*

And now, before we start cutting, you should watch, if you haven't already, the full cut of the original *Nail Polish* movie. You will find it on the DVD as well. Unlike the footage, itself, the full movie is in a highly compressed format, to allow for more room on the DVD for the actual footage. The quality is still good, however. You should also re-read the script, which was included in Chapter 5.

You will also find, on the DVD, the versions of *Nail Polish* from each of these final three chapters (and they are also highly compressed). After watching the original cut of the film, watch the *Nail Polish As Comedy* version. It's half as long as the original movie, since the footage doesn't support a longer comedy. In the rest of the chapter, we will work backward from the intended result, as if the movie were already cut, analyzing the choices that led to this particular version. You can try and make your own project match the illustrations and descriptions ahead, or you can use the suggestions as a departure point for a radically different cut.

Nail Polish as Comedy

To put together a version of *Nail Polish* that is supposed to be funny, we need some help establishing the right comedic tone right at the start. One thing to always keep in mind while writing, directing, and/or editing a film is that your audience appreciates knowing what kind of film they are watching. If you succeed in creating a certain kind of atmosphere (of humor, of dread, of seriousness, etc.), then situations that might strike the audience members a certain way in a different setting, appear to them – in *your* setting – as a perfect fit for the general tone of the film. Before they realize something isn't *that* funny or scary, they're laughing or screaming, and that emotion is infectious. Again, context is everything.

Using music to set the tone

If you just watched the completed *Nail Polish As Comedy* film from the DVD, you heard the two different pieces of music that were used to set the tone of the film. Let's find them now, in the *Nail Polish Sounds* bin. They are *Dolce Vita* and *River Walk,* as shown in Figure 13.7. You may decide that you like different music, or no music at all, but let's stick with these for now.

FIGURE 13.7 Select *Dolce Vita* and *River Walk* from the *Nail Polish Sounds* bin.

Next, let's take a look at the Timeline for the completed film from the DVD, as shown in Figure 13.8. You can cut your version anyway you'd like, but we will look at what led to the film you just watched. In the Timeline, you can see that there is music at both the beginning and end of the film, and that *Dolce Vita* and *River Walk* alternate within those two sections. One piece of music is the theme for the girl, Lisa, and

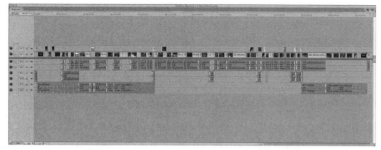

FIGURE 13.8 What the Timeline for *Nail Polish As Comedy* looked like when the film was completed.

the other is the theme for the boy, Michael. The two melodies are radically different, and the clash between them contributes to the humor.

Before this cut of *Nail Polish* was completed, two new items were added to the project, as shown in Figure 13.9: a sequence labeled *Color Correction* and a LiveType file labeled *Nail Polish Comedy.ipr* (*.ipr* is the file extension for LiveType). We will discuss these later, when we arrive at that part of the film.

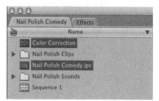

FIGURE 13.9 Before we are done, we will have to create a sequence for some color correction work and a title in LiveType.

The first 48 seconds

Now let's take a closer look at how the film was put together by analyzing smaller segments at a time. We can start with the beginning, up to the 48th second or so, as shown in Figure 13.10. Notice how there are markers in the *River Walk* music file, and how many of the video cuts fall where the markers are located. If you were to double-click on that file in the middle of the editing process, you would have seen, in the Viewer, the reason for the placement of the markers, as shown in Figure 13.11. When you cut with

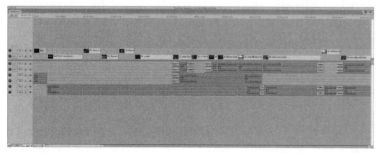

FIGURE 13.10 Look at the first 48 seconds of this cut of the film.

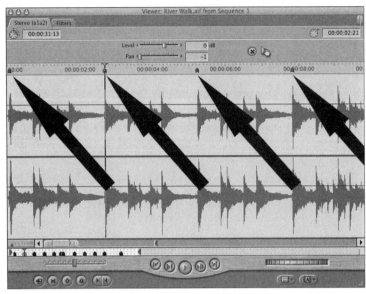

FIGURE 13.11 Place markers on the beat of your music.

music, it's good to keep the rhythm of the piece in mind when editing. Here, we have highlighted the downbeats, allowing some decisive cuts in this opening sequence. Always let the music speak to you, and take its particular qualities to heart.

We already cut, in Chapters 7 and 8, the first scene of *Nail Polish*, and so the first piece of music – *River Walk* – could be laid down directly underneath that previously edited opening. After marking the beats of the audio, you would want to then go through *Scene 1* and change the length of each clip to match the music. Since the music is the key to the humor, you would also delete the original sounds from the movie as well.

We also need a title for the very beginning, which you saw if you watched the completed film, and you may have noticed that the title card, as shown in Figure 13.12, replaced the original first shot. This title card was created in LiveType and is the *Nail Polish Comedy.ipr* file we mentioned earlier. As we discussed in Chapter 11, if you import a LiveType project directly into FCE, you can then easily go back and forth between the two applications. All you have to do to make quick changes to the title is to hold down the *control* key as you click on the file with your mouse (or right-click on it), and select *Open in Editor*, as shown in Figure 13.13.

FIGURE 13.12 The title card, labeled *Nail Polish as Comedy*.

Back in the Timeline, we spend 30 seconds setting up the arrival of the boy in the garden, before suddenly shifting indoors, using the abrupt transition from *River Walk* to *Dolce Vita* as a potentially funny moment. You might nevertheless want to apply a short audio dissolve, called a *cross fade*, between the two pieces of music, as shown in Figure 13.14, just to make the shift from the one to the other more natural (if abrupt). You might also want to leave some of the original sound from the scenes with Lisa, because her laughter (as she plays with the dog) adds a nice

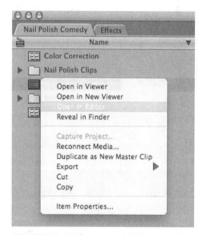

FIGURE 13.13 If you *control*-click or *right*-click on the *.ipr* file in the Browser, you can access the LiveType project by selecting *Open in Editor*.

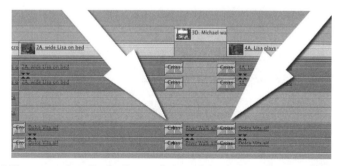

FIGURE 13.14 You can apply audio dissolves – called *cross fades* – between the two pieces of music.

touch. If you do that, you will probably want to lower the levels of the music to hear that original audio.

The first shot of Lisa that we see just shows her reading. After almost 9 seconds, the dog looks at Lisa's feet. With the jaunty sounds of *Dolce Vita* playing, this seems like a funny place to cut, so why not keep the shot running for that long. Since there is no coverage of this scene other than that shot, it makes sense to hold long enough to establish character and location, as we did with Michael.

After that, we go back outside, with a switch back to the original *River Walk* music, and a short 3-second shot of Michael crossing the garden in the opposite direction. And then back to Lisa, now playing with the dog. Again, her theme of *Dolce Vita* plays on the soundtrack.

We now have two clearly established locations and characters, each with a very different feel. We don't know how they relate to each other yet, but the contrast between the two situations moves the story along. In the original *Nail Polish*, we arrived at shot *4A. Lisa plays with dog* at a little over 2 minutes. In this version of the film, we get there in just under 45 seconds. This doesn't mean that comedies are always fast while dramas are always slow, but in this case the faster pace, combined with the music, helps us create the expectation of comedy (which is half the work).

Part 2 - The next 90 seconds

Let's now look at everything from 44 seconds to 1:32 (1 minute and 32 seconds), as shown in Figure 13.15. You can see, if you watch the film and look closely at the footage, that we begin to ignore the strict chronology of the shot labeling system at this point. We go from *4A* to *3A* to *6C* to *5A* (and then to *5B*, *5C*, and *5D*, back in sequence). To do this, you will have to familiarize yourself with the clips by watching all of them first. Remember that just because a shot is labeled as *3A. Michael wide - sees girl*, you don't

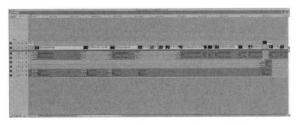

FIGURE 13.15 Now we are looking at the movie from 44 seconds to 1:32 (1 minute and 32 seconds).

have to use it as a moment when he sees Lisa, if you just use a portion of the shot where he is crossing the garden. The audience will never know what the original intention of that shot was; they'll just know it from the context in which you have placed it.

The rest of this section plays out in a very similar manner to that of the original *Nail Polish*, only a little faster. The order of events is the same, however. In sequence, Michael comes down to the porch, takes off his shirt, and Lisa watches him, having earlier spied him from a window.

Part 3 - 45 seconds of fast comedy pacing

In the next 45 seconds, from 1:32 to 2:16, everything is pretty much the same as the original film, except for a faster pace. Shots *9A* and *9B* follow *10A*, as shown in Figure 13.16, but otherwise we move forward in the script order. In shot *11B. Michael MS tries hose*, where Michael grabs the hose, the only audio for the shot has the director talking to the actor, so it's a good idea to remove that audio and replace it with our *1M. wild ambience* that served us well before. Again, you can use audio dissolves to minimize the aural impact of these cuts. You should always make sure you are using high-quality headphones, at the very least, or a well designed quasi-professional speaker system, in order to really hear how the audio sounds. Without this kind of setup, you may not hear the little audio "blips," where one audio changes into another, and so you won't be motivated to correct them. Never trust your computer's built-in speakers, as they are not professional enough for audio editing.

With this faster pace, which seems to be the right approach to making this particular footage work as a comedy, we reach the point where Michael is about to enter the house at about 2 minutes. In the original, we don't get to this point until approximately the 3-and-a-half minute mark. The bounciness of the music covers any continuity lapses that result from cutting this quickly, and we see only the information that is absolutely essential to understanding

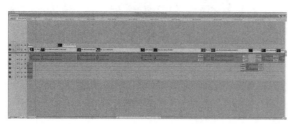

FIGURE 13.16 From 1:32 to 2:16, most everything is the same as the original script, but with a faster pace.

the plot. This more rapid pace also helps with a certain sense of expectation, essential to a good comedy (as it is to a good thriller). At a little past 2 minutes in the original film, we were still just getting to know both Michael and Lisa.

Part 4 - Michael meets Lisa

Let's now look at Michael's entrance into the house, and his first encounter with Lisa, from a little before 2:12 to about 3 minutes, as shown in Figure 13.17. This, again, follows the same basic structure as in the original film, but with significant bits missing: Michael looking under the table for his shirt; Michael taking off his shoes. While, in the original film, these were important to draw out the moments before the boy and girl meet, in this version they are neither funny or important as a setup for something funny.

There is also an added cutaway to Lisa as Michael calls out from the back entrance, as shown in Figure 13.18. This shot is actually from a later scene,

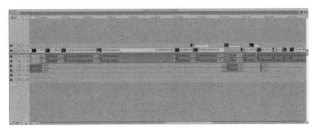

FIGURE 13.17 From 2:12 to 3:00, the cut follows the basic structure of the original, but with some significant pieces left out.

FIGURE 13.18 Shot 13D. *Lisa CU_01* is a good cutaway to use as Michael walks into the house, even though it is from a later scene.

but it works here to show Lisa smirking once she realizes that Michael has taken the bait. She has done something to relieve her boredom! Since that shot, *13D. Lisa CU_01*, came with audio that doesn't work here, you can simply place it on top of the shots from which you cut away (*12A & 12C*), and delete its original audio.

You will notice that Michael's walk down the hall is shorter, since we cut from his entrance into the hallway to his opening the door (from *12C* to *13A*). To help with that potentially abrupt cut, the sound from the end of *12C. Michael walks down hall* has been added underneath the audio of *13A. OTS Michael on Lisa*, with a long fade down, created with the *Pen* tool and clip overlays. Otherwise, there would be a major "blip" as we jump between the two shots.

When Michael gets to Lisa's room, there is a significant change from the original version of the film, The section of dialogue where Michael says "The water's out," has been removed. It's funnier to just have Michael enter, expecting one thing, only to have Lisa raise her foot to him and ask for assistance. In order to make it work, we have to use the audio from another shot to add a line from Lisa – "Please?" – underneath one of Michael's shots (*13G. Michael walks to Lisa*). Otherwise, her actions, while funny in a nonsensical way, are not logical. Our goal is to make a comedy where the plot makes some kind of sense.

When you watched both the original Nail Polish *and its adaptation,* Nail Polish As Comedy, *you may have noticed that the flow of action from shot to shot is fairly continuous. As we discussed in Chapter 2, cutting on action – or cutting on motion within the frame – is the best way to make your edits feel smooth. Since we are removing quite a bit of material from the original film to make this snappier version, we need to make sure that we cut, where appropriate and possible, from motion to motion. This applies even if we cut from a scene with just Michael to a scene with just Lisa. Try to enter their respective shots on some kind of movement.*

Color correcting white balance

Let's look at shot *12A. Michael enters house*, which comes after shot *11E. Michael heads inside* and before shot *12C. Michael walks downs hall*, as shown in Figure 13.19, with Lisa's cutaway as the bridge between these last

FIGURE 13.19 Let's take a look at shot *12A. Michael enters house*, so we can correct the improper white balance.

two shots. The *white balance* is a little off. This is because there were mixed light sources during the shoot, from both the sun and a tungsten light bulb indoors. This combination resulted in colors that look a little less than natural, particularly on Michael's skin. Let's take a look at how we can correct the shot.

When you shoot video, you have to white balance *the camera for a given lighting situation. This means that you adjust all of the colors of the spectrum by telling the camera sensors what white looks like in your current conditions. Usually, this is done by taking a white card, placing it in front of the lens – in the light in which you will be shooting – and pressing a white balance button. If you do this correctly, then all the colors in your shot will look normal. If you do this incorrectly, then the colors will be improperly balanced: the light from the sun, if not balanced, looks blue; the light from a tungsten lightbulb, if not balanced, looks orange; fluorescent lights look green.*

When we started exploring the finished *Nail Polish As Comedy* project, we noticed, in the Browser, a sequence labeled *Color Correction*. It can be much easier to work with a particular shot if you drop it in its own special sequence, especially with the *Color Corrector* filter. In this case, to fix the white balance issue, you could make a sequence with the shot to be fixed – *12A. Michael enters house* – and a set of *Bars and Tone*, as shown in Figure 13.20. You can find the *Bars and Tone* in the Video Generators.

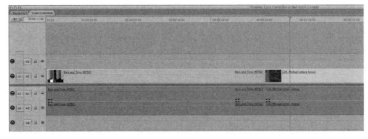

FIGURE 13.20 To best work with the *Color Corrector* filter, create a new sequence for the shot that needs to be corrected.

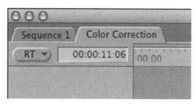

FIGURE 13.21 You can tell how many sequences are open by looking at the upper left of the Timeline.

After successfully dragging shot *12A* down to this new sequence, we would now need to find something that the application would read as true white, which is the equivalent of retroactively using a white card while shooting. The best thing would be to find a shot in this same scene in which there is a bit of white that is properly balanced. Shot *12A* is the only shot in this part of the hours, however, so that's where the *Bars and Tone* come in. In this new sequence, you should place the *Bars and Tone* at the head, and then place shot *12A* right after.

In the bin marked *Color Correction*, in the *Video Filters* bin under the *Effects* tab, you will find the *Color Corrector* filter, as shown in Figure 13.22. To correct the shot, drag this down and drop it on the clip. Then, double-click on that clip, and then click on the *Filters* tab in the Viewer. Click on the *Visual* button, as shown in Figure 13.23, which will bring you to the filter's color wheel, as shown in Figure 13.24.

FIGURE 13.22 You will find the *Color Corrector* filter in the bin marked *Color Correction*, in the *Video Filters* bin.

In the bottom right of this window is a little eyedrop tool, as shown in Figure 13.25. The *Color Corrector* filter works when you tell it what which color you want it to read as white. In this case, you would place the playhead in the Timeline over the bars and tone, so that they were visible in the Canvas, and then you would click on the eyedrop tool to activate it. Then you would go into the Canvas and click in the white section of the color bars, as shown in Figure 13.26. This action would tell the filter that *this* white is true white.

Then, after selecting your white, you would place the playhead, in the Timeline, over shot *12A*. To the left of the left color wheel is another eyedrop tool,

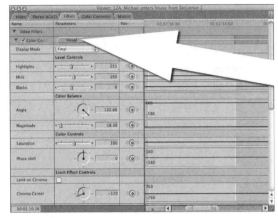

FIGURE 13.23 Click on the *Visual* button in the *Filters* tab.

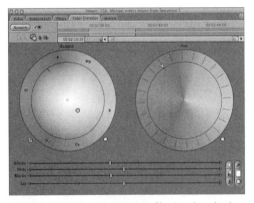

FIGURE 13.24 The *Color Corrector* filter's color wheel.

FIGURE 13.25 In the bottom right of the *Color Corrector* window is a little eyedrop tool.

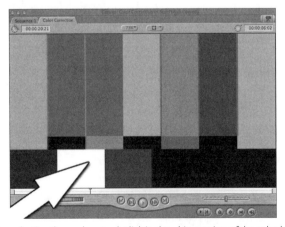

FIGURE 13.26 After selecting the eyedrop tool, click in the white section of the color bars – or in any area you wish to designate as true white for the upcoming correction.

as shown in Figure 13.27, and you would now click on it. To finish this process, you would go back into the Canvas and click to the left of Michael, on what was, originally, a white wall, as shown in Figure 13.28 (because of improper white balancing, that wall looked very yellow). If you had done everything properly up to this point, you would see, as soon as you clicked on that wall, the color balance of the entire shot shift and become more normal, as shown in Figure 13.29. Michael's skin tone will have improved remarkably, in fact.

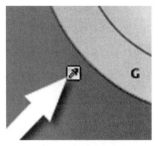

FIGURE 13.27 To the left of the left color wheel is another eyedrop tool.

FIGURE 13.28 After selecting this second eyedrop tool, go back into the Canvas and click to the left of Michael, on what was, originally, a white wall.

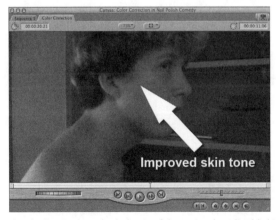

Improved skin tone

FIGURE 13.29 After this final step, the color balance of the entire shot should shift to a more normal appearance, improving Michael's skin tone.

ON DVD

In order to appreciate the color differences between shots, you will have to reference the color versions of the illustrations, included on the accompanying DVD.

In order for color correction like this to work, you need two things: a white that you trust as a true white and something in the incorrect shot that *should* look white. You could also have used a shot in the house that was properly white balanced, with its own white wall, instead of the color bars, but sometimes its easier to just use the bars and tone. You also don't need to make a separate sequence for color correction, but it often makes the task easier, as it isolates the elements with which you need to work. If you do work with a separate sequence, however, there is one more thing you need to do, which is drag the adjusted filter back to the original shot in the original sequence. You would go back to the *Filters* tab in the Viewer, and click on the *Sequence 1* tab in the Timeline. Then you would just grab the filter from the Viewer and drag it down to the as-yet-uncorrected version of shot *12A* in the main sequence, as shown in Figure 13.30. Now you would be done.

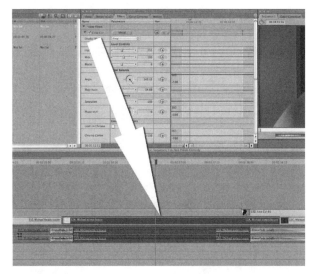

FIGURE 13.30 To finish the color correction, you still need to drag the corrected filter down to the uncorrected shot in the original sequence.

Part 5 - The final section and how it differs from the original

Let's look at the final section of the film now, from 2:55 to 4:06, as shown in Figure 13.31. Here, as in the beginning, some significant changes to the original cut of the movie have been made:

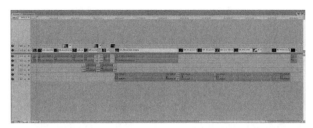

FIGURE 13.31 Let's look at the final section of the film, from 2:55 to 4:06.

- The lingering glances between Michael and Lisa as the application of the nail polish occurs have been removed

- The off-camera lines of dialogue of the father have been shortened

- The same two musical themes used at the start have been applied here, once Michael exits the house

- Instead of the entire slow tilt up from Lisa's foot to her face (*15A. tilt up Lisa's leg to face*), only the head and tail of that shot have been used so that we go directly from the toe with nail polish to her reaction.

- Finally, the ending has been changed, by using shot *3B. OTS Michael on Lisa in window* out of its original context. Instead of seeing Michael musing over his nail-polish-stained finger and then continuing with his work, we see him look up and see Lisa in the window once more. It's a final joke, implying that their interactions will continue in the same vein.

Color correcting different times of day

The only problem with this last strategy was that clips *16A* and *16B*, which precede the new position of shot *3B*, were shot at the end of the day, with a little sunlight left, while shot *3B* was shot more in the middle of the day. The quality of the light is not the same. In order for the shots to match in color, we would need to change either the shots from *Scene 16* or the shot from *Scene 3*. In this version of *Nail Polish As Comedy*, we changed shots *16A* and *16B*, making them look more like shot *3B*.

If we look at shot *16A*, as shown in Figure 13.32, and then compare it to shot *3B*, as shown in Figure 13.33, we see that it is darker, and with a

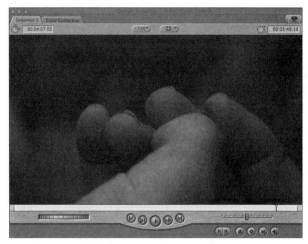

FIGURE 13.32 Shot 16A. insert Michael's fingers.

FIGURE 13.33 Shot 3B. OTS Michael on Lisa in window.

more muted set of colors than the other. To change this, we could drag the *Color Corrector* filter down to shot *16A*, double-clicked that shot, and go to the *Filters* tab in the Viewer. Rather than use the color wheels this time, since we aren't trying to match the shot to any particular white, just grab the *Magnitude* scrollbar under *Color Balance* and slide it to the right, as shown in Figure 13.34. A setting of *Magnitude 44* seems to make the color

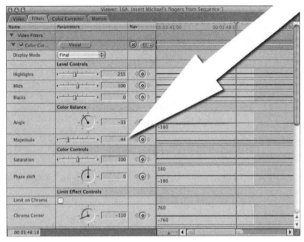

FIGURE 13.34 Under the *Filters* tab, after you have applied the *Color Corrector* filter, grab the *Magnitude* scrollbar under *Color Balance* and slide it until you find a setting that you like.

of *16A* looks more golden, as shown in Figure 13.35, better matching *3B*. If you like this setting, then you can copy and paste the filter to shot *16B* as well.

If you feel comfortable with these basic color correction techniques, there is one more shot we could fix. Shot *8C. Lisa takes shirt*, where Lisa takes Michael's shirt from the outside table, as shown in Figure 13.36, looks a

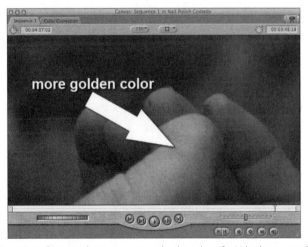

more golden color

FIGURE 13.35 A setting of *Magnitude 44* seems to make the color of *16A* looks more golden.

FIGURE 13.36 Shot *8C. Lisa takes shirt.*

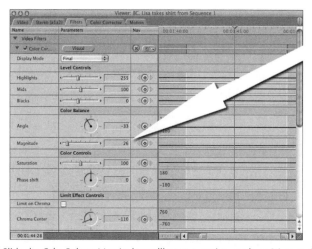

FIGURE 13.37 Slide the *Color Balance Magnitude* scrollbar to a setting, such as *26,* to make the colors of *8C* look less blue.

little too blue. Conveniently, there are some easy-to-select white areas on her skirt. But we may not need them. We could just drag the *Color Corrector* filter to that shot, and then slide the *Color Balance Magnitude* scrollbar to a setting, such as *26,* as shown in Figure 13.37, which makes the colors look less blue and more golden, as shown in Figure 13.38.

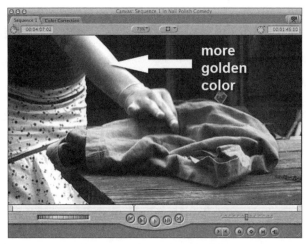

FIGURE 13.38 Shot 8C. *Lisa takes shirt*, corrected to look more golden.

That's it for color correcting. To finish, we could add an ending title, working with the beats of the music to make it match the rhythm. And then we could export the film as a self-contained movie file, as we learned how to do in Chapter 10.

Now that we have cut *Nail Polish* as a comedy, feel free to go back and re-edit your own version, making the changes that you think work best. In the next chapter, we will cut *Nail Polish* as a drama, and you will see that the challenges are quite different.

SUMMARY

In this chapter, we took the footage from the original cut of the short film *Nail Polish* and re-cut the film in a more comedic way. The way the film was conceived and shot did not necessarily support turning it into a full-fledged comedy, but we were able to change the tone and pacing in significant ways – making the film much faster – while still telling a clear story. While there is no single way to make a funny movie, we discovered that a change in rhythm worked well with the available material.

We began by analyzing the footage available on the accompanying DVD. All of the shots were labeled by scene number, but we had to import them and organize them in bins ourselves. We discovered a collection of audio files as well, only two of which we ended up using for this version of the film. Once we had finished organizing our footage and music, we saved an additional copy of the project in a safe location, to be used as our starting point in the remaining two chapters.

We then watched the finished *Nail Polish As Comedy* film from the DVD and began analyzing the choices made to arrive at that version, looking at each section in turn. While we did so, we reviewed the importance of music, how it can help set the tone of a film and how to set audio markers on the beats of that music. Using both the *Pen* tool and the built-in audio fades, we discussed audio dissolves between the clips and music for smoother transitions.

We also learned about a new filter – the *Color Corrector* – and practiced some basic color correction techniques. Some of the shots within the *Nail Polish* footage were not improperly white balanced, or didn't match other shots when we changed their original context, and this filter provided the simple means to fix that problem. While the exercises we performed didn't fully explore the full functionality of this filter, they were nevertheless effective. We are now ready to tackle the next cut of the film, and more.

1. How can you expand the Browser viewing area, so you can see more of the information therein?

2. How can you correct color errors in FCE, using a reference of true white?

3. What are two different ways to create audio dissolves?

4. How can you highlight the beats of a song, if you want to cut using the rhythm of the music?

5. Explain an issue in FCE with ascending numbers in file names.

DISCUSSION / ESSAY QUESTIONS

1. What makes us laugh in a comedy? How does editing help?

2. Discuss the role of music in one of your favorite films or TV shows. How important do you think it is to the storytelling, and why?

3. When you cut your own *Nail Polish as Comedy* film, what different choices did you make compared to those given in this chapter and why?

Further Research

If you haven't done so already, cut your own version of *Nail Polish as Comedy*. If you find other shots that need to be corrected, try using the *Color Corrector* filter on your own. You might also explore other filters to see how they affect the shots. You should also take the time to listen to the other music and audio files included on the DVD, so that you are familiar with them before we use them in the chapters ahead.

CHAPTER 14

NAIL POLISH – CUTTING FOR DRAMA

OVERVIEW AND LEARNING OBJECTIVES

In this chapter, you will:

- Review the mechanics of how to cut for drama
- Re-cut the entire movie, emphasizing the emotional connection between the characters
- Compare and contrast *Nail Polish As Comedy* to *Nail Polish As Drama*
- Duplicate the same color correction changes made in Chapter 13
- Practice basic sound design techniques

What Makes a Drama … Dramatic?

As we discussed in Chapter 3, a drama is a story in which meaningful subjects are tackled in a sincere manner, allowing the emotional life of the characters to be developed and explored. That's why we watch dramas, because we know that we will see a fully realized story inside of which fully realized characters live. Otherwise, we could just watch a movie like *Anchorman* (Adam McKay, 2004), in which no characters are developed and every situation serves as a setup for a joke. It's funny, but it's not a drama.

In the last chapter, we focused on making a comedy, doing the best we could with the footage we had. In this chapter, our task is easier, since *Nail Polish* was conceived as a drama (albeit one with a few comedic elements). We will start again, from scratch. Watch the original cut of the film on the accompanying DVD to re-orient yourself with the structure of the story.

You will also want to watch, also on the DVD, the film *Nail Polish As Drama*, to compare it to both the original film and, especially, *Nail Polish As Comedy*. Note the differences in tone and length between the comedy and the drama. The drama is 5:40 minutes long, while the comedy is just a little over 4 minutes. Music is used in a very different way in each. After watching these different versions of the movie, you should be ready to begin this chapter.

Where Do We Begin?

If you recall, at the beginning of Chapter 13, we went over the new materials – video clips and sounds – for these three different cuts, as well as the original cut of the first scene we had completed in earlier chapters. We imported the new files, organized them, and then saved a Master copy at that point. We will begin *this* chapter with that saved file. If you did not follow the sequence of actions in the last chapter, you may want to go back and read it now, as we will not revisit all of those same steps here. Open up that Master copy of the project and save it as *Nail Polish Drama*, as shown in Figure 14.1.

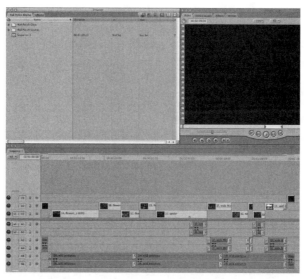

FIGURE 14.1 We begin this chapter from the saved copy of the file we created in Chapter 13, into which we had imported all of the *Nail Polish* clips and sounds.

All figures appear in color on the companion DVD.

As we did in Chapter 13, we will now work backward from the completed film – found on our DVD, that you hopefully just watched – *Nail Polish As Drama*. You have shown the end product, and we will now reconstruct it.

In your Browser, if you followed instructions last time, you should have 2 bins and 1 sequence, as shown in Figure 14.2. It's a good idea, since we will now have multiple projects that use the same footage, to rename this sequence something other than *Sequence 1*, in case we have multiple projects open at the same time. We could call it *Nail Polish Drama*. In order for us to see the dangers of *not* renaming the sequence, however, let's keep the generic name for now. Later in this chapter, we will discover, first-hand, why this is important.

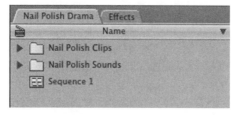

FIGURE 14.2 Our Browser has 2 bins and 1 sequence.

Let's start our process by making a new opening title in LiveType, as shown in Figure 14.3. For *Nail Polish As Comedy*, there were two effects used in that title: a fade and a glow (*Experience*), as shown in Figure 14.4. Since we want this title to look slightly different than the comedy title, let's choose a different glow effect (*Apparition*), as shown in Figure 14.5. Type your new text (*Nail Polish As Drama*) and save the LiveType project as *Nail Polish Drama*. Go back to your FCE project and import the newly created LiveType project. Make sure you follow the instructions we covered in Chapter 11 on how to create the right settings for an NTSC Anamorphic title. Don't forget that you'll still need to scroll through to the right column in the Browser and check the *Anamorphic* column, as shown in Figure 14.6. We are now ready to begin editing this new version of the film.

FIGURE 14.3 Let's make a new opening title in LiveType for this version of the film.

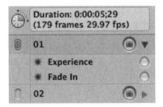

FIGURE 14.4 The title for the comedy used the glow effect entitled *Experience*.

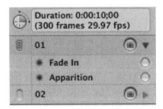

FIGURE 14.5 For the drama, let's use the *Apparition* glow effect.

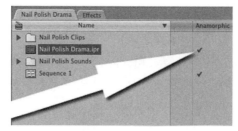

FIGURE 14.6 After following the instructions in Chapter 11 to properly format a widescreen NTSC title, you will still need to select the Anamorphic column in the Browser after you import the LiveType project into FCE.

Prepping *Nail Polish* for Drama

First things first. Let's look over the music in the *Nail Polish Sounds* bin to find a piece of audio that might help us set a more serious tone. In Chapter 13, we chose two musical numbers that contrasted nicely with each other, which helped to set up the comedy. Here, we need something different. Let's try *Synthetic Design*, which seems perfect for the opening. It conveys an interesting combination of melancholy and hope. To start our new cut, drag the LiveType title down to the Timeline, to track *V1*, after the slug, and then drag the music down, also dropping it just after the slug, in tracks *A7* and *A8*. We then apply, using the clip overlays and the *Pen* tool, a fade up to both the title and the music. If you still have a fade up on the first shot, *1A. flowers_1*, from your previous edits, remove that now. You should now see the first scene of *Nail Polish* with a new title and new opening soundtrack, as shown in Figure 14.7.

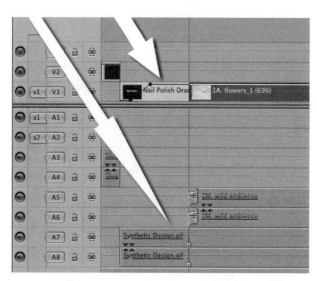

FIGURE 14.7 Our new opening scene of *Nail Polish* has a new title and a new piece of music.

In the opening of the comedy, we moved shot to shot through a series of straight cuts, with no dissolves or other transitions. In this version, let's try some dissolves, to see if they can help create a dreamier, more melancholy tone. In order for that to be possible, however, we need to have handles of unused footage at the head and tail of each shot. There has to be extra footage to dissolve from and to. Most of the shots we are using in the first scene are being used in their entirety, however. If we want to create dissolves, we need to double-click a shot – let's use the first one, *1A. flowers_1* – and then, in the Viewer, set an *In* point approximately 2 seconds after the head, as shown in Figure 14.8. After we do this, a gap will appear, on the Timeline, between the title and this first shot, as shown in Figure 14.9.

FIGURE 14.8 To create dissolves, we first need handles of extra footage, so set your *In* point after the head of the shot.

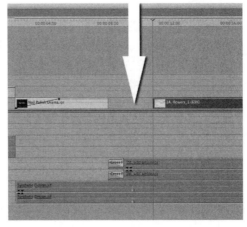

FIGURE 14.9 After we set this new *In* point, a gap opens up in the Timeline.

We also need a handle at the end of the title. To do this, go back to the LiveType project. If you remember, you can do this by control-clicking on the title itself in the Browser and selecting *Open in Editor*, as shown in Figure 14.10. Once in LiveType, you can drag the *Out* point of the sequence from 6 seconds to 10 seconds, for example, and move the text of *As Drama*, along with the effects, over to the right a bit more, as shown in Figure 14.11, to fit the rhythm of the new length of the title.

FIGURE 14.10 To access the LiveType project, control-click on the project in FCE's Browser and select *Open in Editor*.

FIGURE 14.11 In LiveType, change the length of the title by dragging the *Out* point of the sequence to the right and then reposition the other elements in the project, as needed.

After doing this, go back to FCE. The LiveType title should still be sitting in the sequence, where you left it, only it will have an extra 4 seconds of unseen and unused footage – a handle. Note, however, that when you make changes like this to a file that exists outside of FCE, the program will ask you to re-render the file, even if you had rendered it before the changes.

We can now apply a dissolve between the title and the first shot, as shown in Figure 14.12. In order to best adapt the footage to the new mood, we should

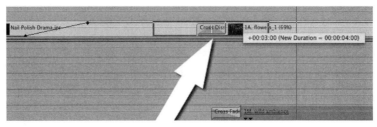

FIGURE 14.12 Now that we have handles of unused footage, we can apply a dissolve between the title and the first shot.

try a series of slow dissolves, so let's make this first one last 4 seconds. A slow opening, in this case, works best for the drama.

Now we need to re-cut the entire opening to match the new mood. If we are going to apply dissolves between all of the shots, however, they all need to have handles. You do this by setting *In* and *Out* points in the Viewer, for all of the shots in Scene 1. When you are done, if you are matching the comedy on the DVD, you will find that you have kept the shots in the same basic order as they were before, but shortened them to allow for the many dissolves, as shown in Figure 14.13. You will also remove the ambience that is there, since the music is overpowering, and we don't need any other sound.

FIGURE 14.13 After re-cutting the first scene, we should have the same shots as before, but with many dissolves between them.

Some of the dissolves, given how short these shots are, might even appear to almost overlap and touch, as shown in Figure 14.14. It's up to you to figure out the right length of each dissolve, and if you don't like having a new dissolve begin just as the previous one is completed, then drag the edges of the effect one way or the other until you are satisfied. Try to keep the dissolves long enough, however, to put the audience into an almost dreamlike state. One image should slowly morph into another, as shown in Figure 14.15, for a dramatic feel.

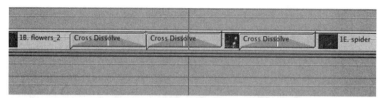

FIGURE 14.14 Some of the dissolves you apply, given how short the shots are, might appear to almost overlap and touch; you should make them as long or as short as you like.

FIGURE 14.15 Dissolves can help create a dreamy effect, as one image morphs slowly into another.

Cutting *Nail Polish* As Drama

Let's take a look at what the entire sequence for the completed Nail *Polish As Drama* film looked like before it was exported as the self-contained file you watched on the accompanying DVD. As shown in Figure 14.16, after the slow and dreamy opening, the story proceeds, without music, much as it does in the original cut of *Nail Polish*, although with greater economy of pacing. Then, at the end, there is a new piece of music – *Time Lapse* – that is similar to the first piece, but with a more hopeful sounding melody. This helps sell the idea that there has been some kind of change in the lives of these two young people. In a good story, after all, things happen, and people change, no matter how little. Otherwise, there is no reason for us to watch the story unfold.

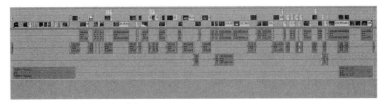

FIGURE 14.16 The entire sequence for the completed *Nail Polish As Drama* movie.

Part 1 - How the opening is different in the drama

You probably noticed, after watching the complete film, that there is another change in the opening, beyond the dissolves between shots. Toward the end of the scene in the garden, there is a fade to black before introducing Lisa, and then a fade up to her on the bed, as shown in Figure 14.17. The slow pace of the music – and the previous series of dissolves – made this seem like the right way to transition to Lisa. Since there is far less footage of her in the bedroom than of Michael in the garden, we need a way to fool the audience into feeling as if each character is getting equal treatment. In the comedy, we cut back and forth quickly. Here, we cut to her once, through a fade, before the music ends, and then hold on her for the full duration of the shot. This lends her moment of introduction a prominence to rival Michael's.

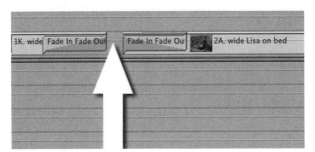

FIGURE 14.17 Toward the end of the scene in the garden, there is a fade to black before introducing Lisa and then a fade up to her on the bed.

Part 2 - How the next 30 seconds establish character

Let's look at how the next section, from 56 seconds to approximately 1:30, was put together. We continue with the further establishment of each character, up to the first sighting of Lisa by Michael. All is good, except for a mild audio issue. Since we are not using music under these scenes, as we did in the comedy, we discover that the sound of the fan's button, as Lisa clicks it on and off, creates an unpleasant crackle on the microphone. If we want to use this footage, we have to fix this problem.

To do so, first unlink the audio from the video for every clip with the fan. Then, every time there is a crackling sound, set markers to either side of it. Finally, cut out the crackle on the Timeline, using the *Razor Blade* tool. After all this, you will have removed the bad audio, leaving gaps that now need to be filled. On the track below each newly created gap, copy and paste a bit of sound from a different part of the same scene, as shown in Figure 14.18. Make sure you fade up and down at the head and tail of this new audio, using either the built-in fade effects or the *Pen* tool, so that we don't hear the sudden introduction of new sound. We performed these kinds of audio actions in Chapter 13, if you remember.

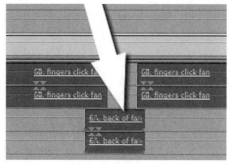

FIGURE 14.18 On the track below each newly created audio gap – created when you removed the crackle from the fan – copy and paste a bit of sound from a different part of the same scene.

If we double-click on the audio from which we removed the mistake, in shot *6B. fingers click fan*, we can see, quite obviously, that crackle, as shown in Figure 14.19. Just after the *Out* point, there is a large sound bump. It's not actually that loud. It doesn't push the audio meter into the red (which is called *over-modulating*), but it does sound like there is some kind of interference with the microphone, and so it had to be removed.

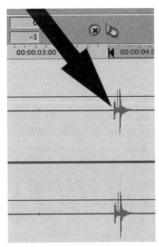

FIGURE 14.19 If we double-click on the audio from which we removed the mistake, in shot *6B. fingers click fan*, we see the crackle after the new *Out* point.

The audio that was used to fill in the gap was taken from shot *6A. back of fan*. Since it's from the same scene, the general ambience of the room matches. If we double-click *6A* now, we see very little sound in the part we are using, since good room tone does not register very high decibel levels. We also see the audio fades that were created, in this case, with the *Pen* tool, as shown in Figure 14.20.

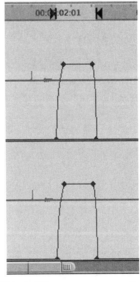

FIGURE 14.20 If we double-click *6A back of fan* now, we can see the audio fades that were created with the *Pen* tool.

The trick to fixing this audio problem is figuring out how to remove the crackle without removing all of the sound of the clicking button of the fan. There is a point, in *6B. fingers click fan*, just after the crackle, at which there is still the hint of a click. This is where we need to set our *In* point, as shown in Figure 14.21. If you play through this section in the completed *Nail Polish As Drama*, you can judge for yourself whether or not these series of sound edits work.

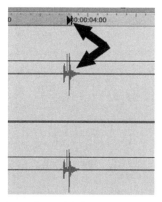

FIGURE 14.21 There is a point, in *6B. fingers click fan*, just after the crackle, at which there is still the hint of a click, and this is where we set our *In* point.

Part 3 - Similarities and differences in the next minute

The next section, from 1:30 to 2:30, has the same structure as the script and the original cut of the film. In the comedy, we kept one of the shots of Lisa in the window for the end of the film, as a final joke. Here, both shots are used as setup for the drama. When Lisa appears for the second time, in the French doors, the audio from that shot is too different from the audio of that shot of Michael, *5A. Michael MS - weeding* from which we cut. Fortunately, however, that particular shot of Michael is long enough to simply throw away the audio from the other shots in this mini-sequence – shots *5B*, *5C*, and *5D* – and place their video components directly on top of *5A*. We don't even have to remove that shot's video, since FCE can only show one video clip at a time, unless you play with the opacity of the shots. Whatever is on top is what we see. By keeping the audio of a single shot playing throughout this 4-shot sequence, as shown in Figure 14.22, we don't have to do any extra work with the sound levels and dissolves.

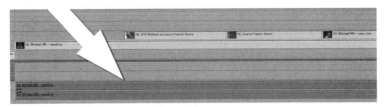

FIGURE 14.22 By keeping the audio of a single shot – *5A. Michael MS - weeding* – playing throughout this 4-shot sequence, we don't have to do any extra work with the sound levels and dissolves.

We can do something very similar in the sequence where Michael drinks from the hose. The shots on Lisa, as she watches Michael take off his shirt and turn on the hose, do not have usable audio, as they were filmed without a microphone. So, we should again simply place Lisa's shots on top of Michael's shots, as shown in Figure 14.23, thereby using his audio, instead of hers. It works nicely, and again saves us time.

FIGURE 14.23 In the sequence where Michael drinks from the hose, we need to replace Lisa's audio with audio from Michael's shots, and we can accomplish this by simply laying her shots on top of his, after first removing her sound.

Part 4 - The lead-up to Michael's entrance

The next sequence, from 2:30 to 3:45, takes us from Lisa turning off the water in the basement to Michael entering the house, as shown in Figure 14.24. Here, there are not many differences between this cut and the original film. You may notice, however, how the audio from *1M. wild ambience* has been placed underneath a number of other shots to fill in gaps between audio and/or smooth out transitions, as shown in Figure 14.25. There are, in addition, some audio fades, so that we don't notice the beginning and end of this extra ambience.

FIGURE 14.24 The sequence from 2:30 to 3:45 takes us from Lisa turning off the water in the basement to Michael entering the house.

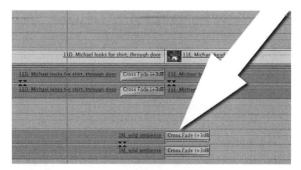

FIGURE 14.25 The audio from *1M. wild ambience* has been placed underneath a number of other shots to fill in gaps between audio and/or smooth out transitions.

There is one significant difference, however, in this section, between the drama and the comedy. Here, we see more of Michael from inside the French doors, which is the shot *11D. Michael looks for shirt, through door*, as shown in Figure 14.26. In the comedy, we did not see Michael kneeling. In the drama, we need to spend a little more time with him before he makes the decision to go inside, thereby building dramatic tension. He feels awkward because he has no shirt, and we need to emphasize that awkwardness.

FIGURE 14.26 In the drama, we see more of shot *11D. Michael looks for shirt*, where Michael is shown from inside the French doors to emphasize the awkwardness of the moment.

Part 5 - The final section and what makes the drama different

Finally, let's look at the last 2 minutes of the film, as shown in Figure 14.27. Structurally, this is also not that different from the original version of the film. The same things happen, in more or less the same order, but with a slightly different rhythmic pacing. The shot *12B. insert shoes*, which was left out of the comedy, has been re-inserted in the drama, as shown in Figure 14.28, to slow down the film at this point. At the end, we avoid using the slow pan and tilt up Lisa's leg, shot *15A. tilt up Lisa's leg to face* (which we didn't use in the comedy either), since it is too slow and lingering, almost voyeuristic, and that doesn't work here. Instead, we chop up the shot into an extreme close-up of the foot, as shown in Figure 14.29, and an extreme close-up of Lisa's mouth, as shown in Figure 14.30.

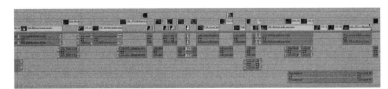

FIGURE 14.27 The last 2 minutes of *Nail Polish As Drama*.

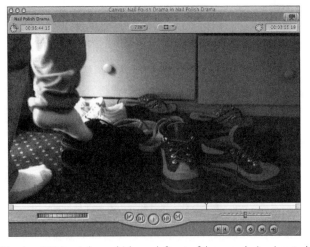

FIGURE 14.28 The shot *12B. insert shoes*, which was left out of the comedy, is reinserted in the drama.

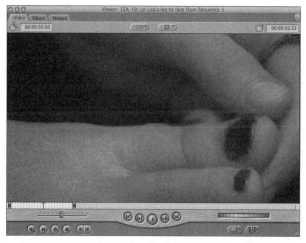

FIGURE 14.29 Shot *15A. tilt up Lisa's leg to face* is split up into an extreme close-up of the foot.

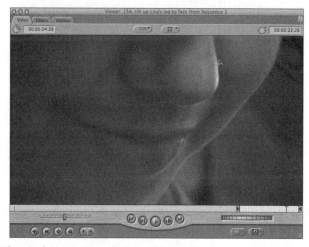

FIGURE 14.30 There is also an extreme close-up of the mouth.

The music *Time Lapse* ends the film, as we noted earlier, with a different tone than that with which it opened. It's a more hopeful melody. As we cut from Michael's close-up to his fingers, and then to his over-the-shoulders as he sweeps out of the camera's line of sight, this piece informs us of his thought process. We feel as if something transformative has happened to him.

Removing the boom from a shot

Before we finish with the film, however, we need to fix something in one of the shots we added to this version. If we look back at *12b. insert shoes*, we can see the boom in the frame, in the bottom-right corner, as shown in Figure 14.31. This is the kind of error that perhaps no one else would see, but we should fix it. While it would be unwise to zoom in much on any shot recorded in standard-definition video, as you would begin to see massive pixelation, a slight reframing zoom to crop out a boom microphone will not cause any noticeable change in picture quality. In high-definition video, you can get away with more zooming in, although you should still not overuse it.

FIGURE 14.31 In shot *12b. insert shoes*, we can see the boom in the frame, in the bottom-right corner.

To fix the shot, double-click on the shot in the Timeline, and then go to the *Motion* tab in the Viewer. In the top portion of the window, under *Basic Motion*, grab the slider to the right of *Scale*. You need to first make sure, before doing this, that your playhead, in the Timeline, is placed over the shot in question. Now, as you drag the slider, you can see at what point the boom is no longer in frame. In this case, that happens to be at 109% zoom, as shown in Figure 14.32. It's a good idea to always make sure there are no parts of the shot where the boom comes even more into frame, as boom operators can slip. Here, it looks good throughout.

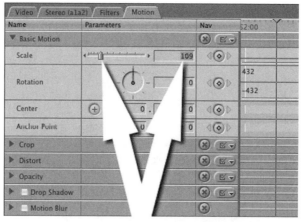

FIGURE 14.32 In the *Motion* tab of the Viewer, zoom in using the *Scale* slider until the boom is no longer visible.

Comparing the Drama to the Comedy

To see how *Nail Polish As Comedy* and *Nail Polish As Drama* compare, let's look at a scene from both cuts to see how long it is in each film. If you were working with your own two separate projects, it would be a simple matter to have both projects open at the same time. Each project would then appear as a different tab in the Browser, as shown in Figure 14.33. The problem that can arise when you open more than project at the same time is the one we discussed at the beginning of this chapter. If you keep the default name of your sequence as *Sequence 1* within each project, then it is easy to become confused in the Timeline window. This problem can be solved by simply naming your sequence something other than the default name of *Sequence 1*.

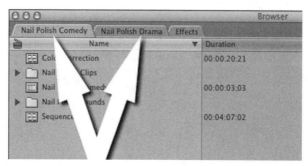

FIGURE 14.33 You can have multiple projects open at the same time.

If you don't rename your sequences, then you will have to find other ways to tell them apart. In this case, if we opened *Nail Polish As Comedy* after *Nail Polish As Drama* had already been opened, then the two sequences of the former project would appear, in the Timeline, after the one sequence from the latter project, as shown in Figure 14.34. To avoid any real chance of confusion, however, it is best to rename the sequences.

FIGURE 14.34 When you have multiple projects open, the sequences from each project will also appear simultaneously in the Timeline.

The scene we will compare is the one where Lisa and Michael meet, in the bedroom, when she asks him to paint her nail polish, since it's the climax of the movie. The easiest way to figure out the length of a particular moment in a sequence is to set an *In* and an *Out* point, in the Timeline, at the start and end of the scene you want, as shown in Figure 14.35. Make sure, since you have two open projects, that you have selected the correct sequence. After you do this, you can then go to the Canvas and look in the upper left, where the *Timecode Duration* field is located, to see the length of what lies between the *In* and *Out* points, as shown in Figure 14.36. Note that you will also see the *In* and *Out* points, as well, since the Canvas shows you what is in the Timeline. This scene, in *Nail Polish As Drama*, is 52:14 seconds long.

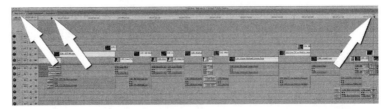

FIGURE 14.35 To figure out the length of a scene in a sequence, set an *In* and an *Out* point, in the Timeline, at the start and end of that scene, after first making sure you have the right sequence selected.

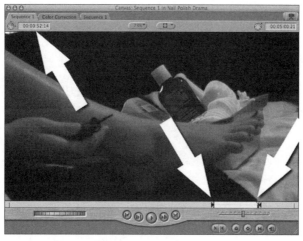

FIGURE 14.36 To see the length of what lies between the *In* and *Out* points in your sequence, go to the Canvas, and look in the *Timecode Duration field*.

Now we need to do the same thing for the comedy. The climactic scene, in *that* version, is only 33:02 seconds long, as shown in Figure 14.37. We can see, then, that the big moment in the drama is almost 20 seconds longer than the same moment in the comedy. Given what we have discussed about each genre, this should not come as a surprise. In the comedic cut, there is a greater focus on how the boredom of the girl leads to silliness. In the drama,

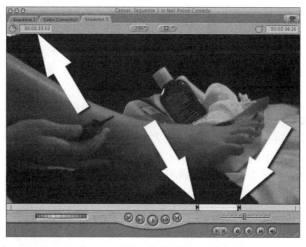

FIGURE 14.37 The same scene in the comedy is only 33:02 seconds long.

we focus more, instead, on establishing a meaningful relationship between the two characters. The extra time helps make that possible.

If you were to go through both of the cuts, in their entirety, you would not necessarily find that every moment in the comedy is shorter than every moment in the drama. In fact, the final section of the drama, after the bedroom scene – where we cut back and forth between Michael outside and Lisa inside – is actually a few seconds longer in the comedy. The way you cut a movie cannot always be defined by hard and fast rules. You have to find the pacing that your story, regardless of genre, requires. It is true, however, that the most dramatically important moments will probably be the ones that closely follow the conventions of genre pacing differences.

For the comedy, we are setting up a new story, in a way, since we end with Lisa appearing in the window again. In the drama, we are ending the story on a conclusive note. This significantly different approach to the ending of each film can help explain why the conclusion of the ostensibly faster paced film lasts longer than the more leisurely paced film.

Final Color Correction and Sound Design

In Chapter 13, we corrected two shots – *8C. Lisa takes shirt* and *12A. Michael enters house* – using the *Color Corrector* filter. Since we used these same two shots in this cut of the film, we need to do the same thing again. This time it can be done much more easily by simply dragging the filter on the previously corrected shot in the old project to the new project.

Go the sequence in the *Nail Polish As Comedy* project and find shot *8C*. Double-click it, then make sure you select the *Filters* tab in the Viewer. Next, click on the tab, in the Timeline, for the *Sequence 1* part of the *Nail Polish As Drama* project. Find shot *8C* in *this* sequence, and make sure you are zoomed in enough so that you can easily drop a filter on top of it. Then grab the *Color Corrector* from the Viewer and drag it down to the uncorrected *8C*, as shown in Figure 14.38. Do the same thing with shot *12A*, and you're done.

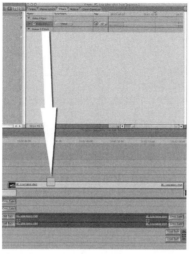

FIGURE 14.38 Drag the *Color Corrector* filter from the corrected shot in *Nail Polish As Comedy* to the uncorrected shot in *Nail Polish As Drama*.

At the end of the drama version of *Nail Polish*, we use the music *Time Lapse* to set the right tone of careful optimism. It doesn't, however, seem like it is enough. The shot under which it plays is *16C. OTS on Michael's hand*, as shown in Figure 14.39, which has its own audio of the methodical, monotonous sweeping sound of the broom. This really helps give Michael a sense of purpose (and drudgery). The moment with Lisa was meaningful, in some ways, because it broke up his boring and arduous day.

FIGURE 14.39 The shot under which *Time Lapse* plays is *16C. OTS on Michael's hand*, which has its own audio of the methodical, monotonous sweeping sound of the broom.

So, using the *Pen* tool and the clip overlays, it is a simple matter to gently raise the audio on the final shot (Michael sweeping) as we lower the sound of the music. As the hopeful music fades out, we are left with Michael, determinedly focused on his job. He has experienced a transformative moment, but life (and work) still goes on.

In this chapter, we edited a second version of *Nail Polish*, this time creating a drama, rather than a comedy. In doing so, we revisited some of the differences between genres that we explored in Chapter 3. While cutting *Nail Polish As Drama*, we examined rhythm and story and how they intersect.

We started from the version of the project we created in Chapter 13, and we discovered two new audio files, *Synthetic Design* and *Time Lapse*, which we used in place of the previous ones to create a new tone to the film. We also made a new simple title in LiveType.

As in Chapter 13, we went through the film section by section, comparing and contrasting it to the comedy, and discussing why different choices were needed to create greater emotional depth. Along the way, we discovered a need for shots and moments that had been ignored before. In one of these shots, we noticed a boom microphone in the frame and therefore reviewed how to zoom in on the shot to remove it.

When we were done, we had a film with a very different feel to it than the comedy. When we looked closely at the climactic scene, where Lisa asks Michael to apply nail polish to her toe, we saw that we had created a scene that was almost 20 seconds longer than its counterpart in the comedy. In making this comparison, we also discovered, on the technical side, that it is possible to have more than one project open at the same time. We explored how this fact can be helpful – as with the application of filters used in multiple projects – and how it can be confusing if we don't choose different names for the sequences in each project.

We ended our editing process by engaging in a very simple bit of sound design. By fading down the final music as we faded up the audio of Michael's broom, we concluded the film on a note of wistful, yet hopeful, melancholy. We are now ready to tackle the final cut of the film, in Chapter 15.

1. How do you open a LiveType project from within FCE?

2. If you have more than one project open at a time, how can you tell which open sequence belongs to which project?

3. How does FCE, in the Browser, present each open project?

4. How can you apply a filter from a previous project to a new project?

5. Why are handles essential to creating dissolves?

DISCUSSION / ESSAY QUESTIONS

1. How is a drama different than a comedy?

2. Is it possible for a film to fulfill the conventions of more than one genre? Can you give some examples?

3. When you cut your own *Nail Polish As Drama* film, what different choices did you make than those in this chapter and why?

Further Research

If you haven't done so already, cut your own version of *Nail Polish As Drama*. Take as long as you need. Remember that the creative process should never be rushed. On the other hand, don't agonize over every cut before you make it. Make your initial decisions quickly and rough out a structure. Then go back and spend more time watching and revising.

CHAPTER 15

NAIL POLISH –
CUTTING FOR
SUSPENSE

OVERVIEW AND LEARNING OBJECTIVES

In this chapter, you will:

- Review the mechanics of how to cut for suspense
- Re-cut the entire movie, emphasizing the footage – plus additional elements – that works to make the film a thriller
- Create a new motion graphics title in LiveType
- Learn how to *nest* one sequence within another

Nail Polish is not a Thriller

Nail Polish was written as a dramedy, a combination of a drama and a comedy. It was never intended to be re-cut as a thriller. The movie has moments of humor and moments of dramatic intensity. Can it support a complete reformulation as a scary suspense story? We'll find out.

There is, after all, a limit to how much the art of editing can affect the way we view certain shots, even taking the lessons of Kuleshov into account. Still, there is a way to take at least part of *Nail Polish*, add some unsettling sounds and music, and make the thriller idea work. In order to do so, however, we're going to have to set the tone right away. We'll also need to lose the final "nail polish" scene, where Michael paints Lisa's big toe nail, because that scene does not make for a scary ending. After watching *Nail Polish As Thriller* on the DVD (which you should do now), you might have better ideas about how to cut your own version.

In Chapter 14, we began our editing exercise from the point at which we had saved, in Chapter 13, all of the imported and organized *Nail Polish* footage from the DVD. Let's start from that same place now as well. If you need help getting to this point, refer back to the beginning of Chapter 13.

Prepping Nail Polish as Thriller

Once you have watched the completed new cut of *Nail Polish*, you will see how different it feels from either the comedy or the drama. There are also many similarities between those versions. The scenes appear to be in roughly the same order, with most, if not all, of the same shots used as in Chapters 13 and 14. As we did in those chapters, let's work backward, from each completed cut, looking at each section of the movie.

If you were to see the final project of *Nail Polish As Thriller* - the one used to cut the completed file on the DVD - you would see, in the Browser, the same two bins we used in the *Drama* cut, plus a new bin labeled *Nail Polish Thriller Sounds*, as shown in Figure 15.1. You would also see two sequences: one labeled *Final Droning Sound*; the other labeled *Nail Polish Thriller*. Our task now is to recreate the same project and the same film, using the same techniques.

FIGURE 15.1 Our new project includes the same two bins we used in the previous cut, plus a new bin labeled *Nail Polish Thriller Sounds.*

All figures appear in color on the companion DVD.

The *Nail Polish Thriller* sequence is the former *Sequence 1*, which has been given a new name to differentiate it from the sequence in the other projects (a renaming option which we discussed in Chapter 14), This way, if we open *Nail Polish Drama* or *Nail Polish Comedy* later in the editing process, to copy filters or work we did earlier, we will not be confused by the same sequence names. Finally, you will see a LiveType file, entitled *Nail Polish Thriller* (which is also the name under which this new FCE project was saved).

Let's look at what is in the *Nail Polish Thriller Sounds* bin. These are not new sounds, but come from the same audio collection we have been working with. Since this new cut requires a lot of sound work to help establish a scary mood, it makes sense to organize the music and effects that are most appropriate to a suspense film into their own bin. Many of these sounds are the ones with *Mystery* or *Suspense* in their names, not surprisingly. You can also always go to GarageBand, or any other application or CD you may have, and export different sounds for use in this film as well.

The *Final Droning Sound* sequence was created to house a series of repeated sounds. At approximately 2:40 minutes into the movie, you can hear a buzzing – or drone – that begins to slowly fade up, as an oppressive mood enhancer. This sound was placed into the master sequence as its own separate sequence, as shown in Figure 15.2, in a process known as *nesting*. If you click on that sequence-within-a-sequence, it will open up under a new tab in the Timeline, as shown in Figure 15.3. Inside of that sequence, you will see many copies of the sound clip *Texture and Ambience_169*. Since that sound clip is only 16 seconds long, many copies of it were combined into a sequence, with audio dissolves between them, to create the much longer droning sound that was needed.

NOTE

The reason some of the sounds included in this collection have awkward names such as Texture and Ambience_169 *is because those are their file names in Apple's GarageBand application. If you need to find these files later, you can look them up in GarageBand by name.*

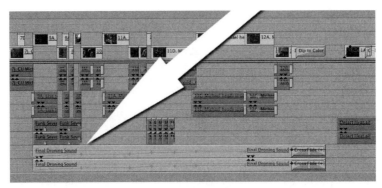

FIGURE 15.2 A series of sounds were combined in a separate sequence, and then that sequence was dropped into the Master sequence in a process known as *nesting*.

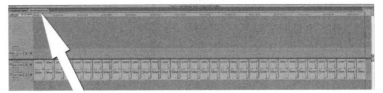

FIGURE 15.3 If you click on that sequence-within-a-sequence, it will open up under a new tab in the Timeline and show you multiple copies of the sound clip *Texture and Ambience_169*.

TIP

Nesting *is a very simple process where you place one sequence inside of another sequence. First, you make a sequence and cut whatever you want inside of it. Then, from the Browser, you drag the icon of that sequence down to the sequence inside of which you wish it to nest. Once you drop it in the master sequence, FCE will treat that other sequence as a self-contained clip. Any changes you subsequently make inside of that sequence will be reflected in the master sequence. The only potential problem is that, if you double-click the nested sequence, it opens in a new Timeline tab. If you wanted to apply a filter to it, and then make changes to the filter in the Viewer, you would have to do one of two things to have it open in the Viewer as a self-contained clip: you could either hold down the* option *key before double-clicking on it, or you could control-click on it, and select* Open in Viewer. *Nesting sequences in this way is a very convenient method to combine multiple items into single self-contained ones. Some editors cut feature films by nesting the sequences for each scene into one long master sequence.*

The title used at the beginning of *Nail Polish As Thriller* is noticeably different, and longer, than the titles used for the previous cuts. It plays for almost 18 seconds over the first piece of music, *Drone Whine*, as shown in Figure 15.4. This much fancier LiveType credit was needed, along with unsettling audio, to take the place of the scary footage that doesn't exist. It helps to establish a suspenseful tone. The title is comprised of one of the LiveType motion graphics backgrounds and many different effects applied to the text. Let's at how it was created.

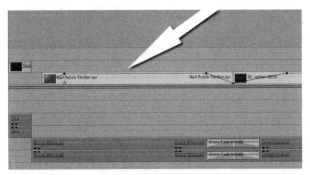

FIGURE 15.4 The title used at the beginning of *Nail Polish As Thriller* is noticeably different, and longer, than the titles used for the previous cuts, and plays for almost 18 seconds over the first piece of music, *Drone Whine.*

The Opening Title "Card"

The title "card" for the thriller is a bit more complicated than the last two titles, as shown in Figure 15.5. It consists of a moving background that has been tinted a different color than its default setting, and text that not only moves, but that has a moving graphic embedded – or *matted* – into the letters. All of these elements combined, coupled with the music, create a disturbing and dark introduction to the movie.

FIGURE 15.5 The title "card" for the thriller, as created in LiveType.

The moving background – or *texture* – is called *Womb* and can be found under the *Space* category, as shown in Figure 15.6. It's only about 7 seconds long, but if you apply it to your track, you can drag the edge, in the Timeline, to make it as long or as short as you want. This texture pulses and swirls, like a fiery black hole. It's also red, which might be a little too obvious (for blood), right at the start of the film, so we will need to change the color as well.

FIGURE 15.6 *Womb* is a texture that you can find under the *Space* category.

Another potential problem that this texture poses is that the whirling starburst lies at the center of the image, as shown in Figure 15.7, which might make it difficult to place text that can be easily read. Let's therefore move the starburst center to the upper-left corner of the screen to make room for the text. It's easy to do. After highlighting the background track to which you have applied the texture, go to the *Text* tab of the Inspector, as shown in Figure 15.8. Even though there is no actual text here, this is where you go to make size and position changes for any element in LiveType. Notice how the "text" is represented by a single black dot. This is how LiveType lets you know that there is something there (just not text, in this case). In the upper preview pane, you can see how there is

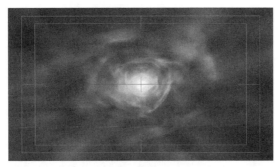

FIGURE 15.7 The whirling starburst of the *Womb* texture lies at the center of the image.

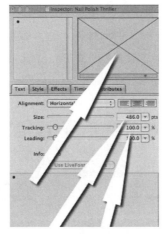

FIGURE 15.8 To change the position of any element in LiveType, go to the *Text* tab of the Inspector, where you see a diagram and alignment settings you can tweak.

a perfectly centered *X*-like configuration of lines. The default *Size* is listed as 486.0 points, and the *Tracking*, which determines the horizontal position of the background in the frame, is listed as *100%*. All we need to do now is adjust these settings. *Leading*, by the way, adjusts the spacing between separate lines of text in a text track, which does not apply to this situation.

For the *Nail Polish As Thriller* title, the size of the texture was increased, and it was repositioned on the left side of the screen as shown in Figure 15.9. To do this, the *Size* slider was moved to 759.6 points, which effectively pushed the starburst vertically up in the frame. Then the *Tracking* slider was moved to 140.4, moving the center to the left. Instead of a black hole, the texture now looks like a sun – or star – shining down on the rest of the image (and leaving room for the eventual text), as shown in Figure 15.10.

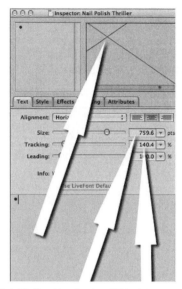

FIGURE 15.9 For the *Nail Polish As Thriller* title, the size of *Womb* texture was increased in size and moved over to the left.

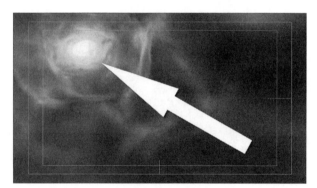

FIGURE 15.10 After being tweaked, the *Womb* texture now looks like a sun – or star – shining down on the rest of the image (and leaving room for the eventual text).

One way to change the color of a texture is to go to the *Style* tab, and then to the *Glow* option, where you check the *Enable* box and then, toward the bottom, click on the *Color* box, as shown in Figure 15.11. When the *Colors Menu* pops up, as shown in Figure 15.12, choose a color that you like, and then close that window. You will need to do one more thing, however, since this color will effectively cover the texture entirely: reduce the opacity of the glow. Go, then, to the *Opacity* slider and set it to something low enough to allow a decent amount of the original image to shine through, as shown in Figure 15.13. After all this, the finished image feels like there's a fog filter imposed on the texture, as shown in Figure 15.14.

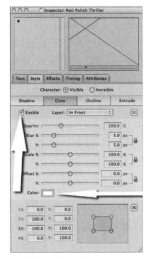

FIGURE 15.11 One way to change the color of a texture is to go to the *Style* tab, and then to the *Glow* option, where you check the *Enable* box and then, toward the bottom, click on the *Color* box.

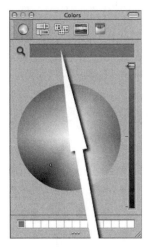

FIGURE 15.12 After the *Colors* menu pops up, choose a color that you like and then close that window.

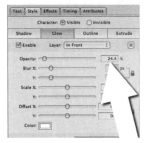

FIGURE 15.13 The glow color will hide the actual image unless you reset the *Opacity* slider to something low enough to allow a decent amount of the original image to shine through.

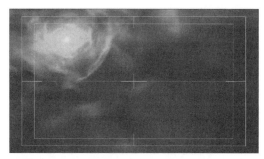

FIGURE 15.14 This method of changing the color of the texture makes it look as if there is some kind of fog filter on top of the image.

If you don't like how the superimposition of color looks on top of the texture, you can, in fact, simply change the color of the background texture. Under the *Attributes* tab of the Inspector, click on the *Glyph* category and then click on the *Color* box at the bottom and choose a color, as shown in Figure 15.15. This color will be applied to the texture directly, rather than being superimposed on top of it, and results in a very different look, as shown in Figure 15.16. Whatever you decide to do, you now have multiple methods of changing the color of a given texture.

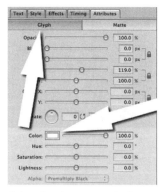

FIGURE 15.15 A more direct way of changing the texture color is to go to the *Attributes* tab of the Inspector, click on the *Glyph* category, and then click on the *Color* box at the bottom.

The text used in the title is *Arial Black*, as in the titles for the other two versions of the film. However, for *this* title card, you may have noticed that the text in the completed film is not white. That's because an additional texture was applied directly to the text itself as a matte. We briefly talked about this in our LiveType discussion in Chapter 12, but let's review it again here.

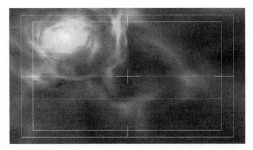

FIGURE 15.16 This method of changing the color tints the entire texture, rather than superimposing a block color on top of it.

In the Media Browser, choose a texture that you like. For this title, the *Contrail* texture, found under the *Smoke* category, as shown in Figure 15.17, was applied to the matte of the text. Make sure that your text track is highlighted in the Timeline, and then click on the *Apply to Matte* button. Now the text will no longer appear white, but will have the colors and movement of this smoky background, as shown in Figure 15.18. If you wanted, you could adjust the parameters of the texture even more by changing its scale and speed, under the *Matte* category of the *Attributes* tab, by moving the appropriate sliders, as shown in Figure 15.19. If you check the *Loop* box, the effect plays even more smoothly inside of your text, no matter how long you make that text in the Timeline.

FIGURE 15.17 The texture that was matted into the text for this title was *Contrail*, found under the *Smoke* category.

FIGURE 15.18 After this texture is applied, the text is no longer white, but has the colors and movement of this smoky background.

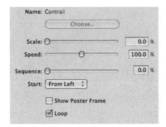

FIGURE 15.19 If you wanted, you could adjust the parameters of the texture within the text by changing the scale and speed of the effect, under the *Matte* category of the *Attributes* tab, by moving the appropriate sliders.

You can also set each text track – *Nail Polish* and *As Thriller* – to have the texture within move at different speeds, as was done for this title. It adds an extra layer of interest. Finally, you can also add a variety of fades in and out to each track, as shown in Figure 15.20, for even greater visual contrast.

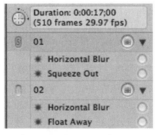

FIGURE 15.20 For even greater visual contrast between the two text tracks, you can add a variety of different fades in and out to each one.

Cutting Nail Polish as Thriller

After spending so much time on our opening title, we now need to come up with an audio accompaniment to match, to launch us into our suspenseful story.

In *Nail Polish As Thriller*, the audio clip *Drone Whine* was used in the beginning, as shown in Figure 15.21. This piece is an appropriately eerie companion to the swirling purple chaos created in LiveType, and the combination of picture and sound puts the viewer in the mood for something strange to happen. The audience is primed for suspense, and we don't have to work quite as hard to scare people. Again, context is everything.

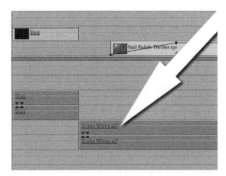

FIGURE 15.21 *Drone Whine* is the audio clip used in *Nail Polish As Thriller* to set the mood at the start.

Part 1 - How the opening title interacts with the footage

The entire opening sequence, minus the slug, lasts for 18 seconds. This may seem like a long time, but since the title is interesting, it actually doesn't feel that long. At the end of the LiveType credit, we fade to black, and then cross-fade *Drone Whine* into *Desert Heat*, using a slow 6-second dissolve (3 seconds on either side), as shown in Figure 15.22. And then, rather then go to the shots of the garden, as in the other two versions of *Nail Polish*, we fade up into the spider, so we go from dread (the purple black hole) to dread (the spider).

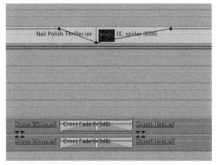

FIGURE 15.22 At the end of the LiveType credit, we fade to black, and then cross-fade *Drone Whine* into *Desert Heat*, using a slow 6-second dissolve (3 seconds on either side); we also fade up to *1E. spider*, rather than cutting to shots of the garden.

Notice how that shot – *1E. spider* – has been slowed to 60% of its original speed. This was done for three reasons: to build a feeling of dread, since the slow motion emphasizes the motion of the spider and makes it more eerie; to give viewers a shot of almost equal length to the opening title on which to let their gaze linger before beginning to cut faster from shot to shot; and, finally, it was done because the musical choice demanded something visually slow-paced, and the original shot was not quite long enough.

At about 35 seconds into the sequence, we cut shot *1E* in two, and make the second part move at regular speed again. We removed the sound from the slowed-down part, but we keep it in this original speed section, so we can hear Michael's entrance through the bushes. The rest of this introductory sequence, where Michael cuts the plant, is in the same order as in previous versions of *Nail Polish*. There are a few changes here and there, however, to the heads and tails of shots, making some slightly longer and some shorter.

For the introduction of Lisa's character, we can use one of the slow pan and tilt shots up her leg, from the toes to the face – shot *2B. tilt from toes to face & back* – that we discussed in Chapter 14. Keep in mind, however, that given the footage we have to work with, there is only one character in this film who can end up being the scarier and creepier character, and that is Lisa. This opening pan and tilt shot, combined with the eerie music, helps establish her as not only bored, but perhaps destructively so. If we fade to black from Michael's scene, and then, after a very brief pause, fade up from black to her, this dramatic pause can really heighten the mystery surrounding Lisa. It turns out that there is an explosive percussive cymbal sound in the music, right around the place where the pause between the two scenes occurs, as shown in Figure 15.23. This sound further emphasizes the evil

FIGURE 15.23 The pan and tilt up Lisa's leg is placed just after an explosive percussive cymbal sound in the music.

qualities we need to place on Lisa. If we then follow this shot with the wide shot we had used before, of Lisa on the bed with the dog, which looked innocent before, the scene now seems slightly strange and creepy.

Part 2 - Introducing character and fear

Looking at the next minute or so after Lisa's introduction, we see another fade to black, followed by a fade up on a single shot of Michael in the garden, before we cut back to Lisa playing with the fan knob. Since our goal in this version of *Nail Polish* is to make Lisa as potentially frightening as possible, we should really leave out the cute scene of her playing with the dog on the bed. For the fan scene, you could just copy the work we did for *Nail Polish as Drama*, since we discussed how to remove the bad sound on each click.

Using audio accents and filters

After this final setting of tone and introduction of character, it is time to show Lisa watching Michael. And here is where we can add some fun musical effects. There are two audio clips in our collection that are particularly suited to create the scary shocks that every suspense film needs: *Mystery Accents_04* and *Funk Seventies Rhodes*. Let's see how they might help the film.

These clips are both fairly short. *Mystery Accents_04* is a little over 2 seconds long, and *Funk Seventies Rhodes* is a little over 8 seconds long. To use them effectively, we need to repeat them or lengthen them in some way. It makes sense to repeat them, but we have to find a way to alter the sound with each repetition, perhaps by changing the pitch, so that they can be used like a progression of chords that rise or descend in quick succession. In Chapter 9, we looked, very briefly, at the *AUPitch* audio filter. Let's see how it can actually be used. The *AUPitch* filter is found in the *Apple* bin, which is inside the *Audio Filters* bin, under the *Effects* tab, as shown in Figure 15.24.

FIGURE 15.24 You will find the *AUPitch* filter in the *Apple* bin, inside the *Audio Filters* bin, under the *Effects* tab.

You will place the first *Mystery Accents_04* clip below the first video clip under which you want it to play, such as *3B. OTS Michael on Lisa in window*, as shown in Figure 15.25, so that the chord plays as we see Lisa watching

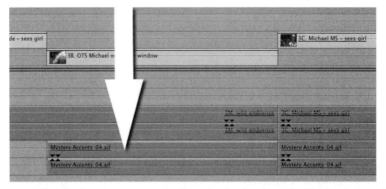

FIGURE 15.25 Place the first *Mystery Accents_04* clip under the shot *3B. OTS Michael on Lisa in window*.

Michael from the window in his OTS. The next *Mystery Accents_04* follows right afterwards, as we cut back to Michael's reaction.

To cut *Nail Polish As Thriller*, we raise the pitch of the first *Mystery Accents_04*. To do this, add the *AUPitch* filter and, through a process of experimentation, raise the pitch until it sounds like a good match with the clip that follows. In other words, place the two *Mystery Accents_04* clips side by side, after setting *In* and *Out* points on each one to get the timing just right, and then raise the pitch on the first clip until the two clips together form a nice melody. In *this* cut of *Nail Polish*, the pitch was raised to a numerical value of *200*, as shown in Figure 15.26. If you raise the value above *0*, the pitch rises; if below *0*, the pitch drops. Each time you change the pitch, you have to render the clip, otherwise, you will just hear a beeping sound.

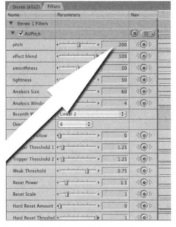

FIGURE 15.26 The pitch of the first *Mystery Accents_04* was raised to a numerical value of *200*.

At 2:10 minutes, which is when Lisa appears in the French doors, let's try the second audio clip effect – *Funk Seventies Rhodes* – which is a little longer, with multiple variations built into it, so it lends a slightly different feel to the moment. It is similar enough to *Mystery Accents_04*, however, that it sounds like it belongs in the same movie, while being different enough to keep the film's sound design from being too monotonous. Because this new clip is 8 seconds long, we do not need to alter the pitch for this first use of it.

Part 3 - Michael lured inside

Let's next consider the portion of the film that runs from 2:20 to 3:10 minutes. In this part of the movie, which, in terms of the shots used, is not that different from the comedy or the drama. Michael walks past Lisa's bedroom window, takes off his shirt, and drinks water from the garden hose. *Mystery Accents_04* is used again – three copies in a row, each with a different pitch, as shown in Figure 15.27 – when Michael crosses in front of Lisa's window, as part of the hopefully suspenseful and creepy sound design. Again, experiment with each clip to find the right pitch adjustment for the sequence.

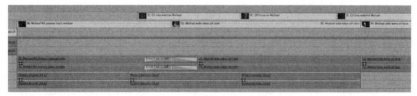

FIGURE 15.27 When Michael walks past Lisa's bedroom window, takes off his shirt, and drinks water from the garden hose, *Mystery Accents_04* is used again, with three copies in a row, each with a different pitch.

The first of the three *Mystery Accents_04* clips in this series is set at *200*, as before. The second is set to *500*, and the third one is set to *900*. As you change the pitch of a piece of audio, you might find that the sound becomes distorted when you adjust the pitch above *200*. The sound might become crackly and scratchy, as if playing on an old vinyl record. To correct this, you can adjust other settings in the filter, such as under the *Resynth Window* and *Overlap* pop-up menus, as shown in Figure 15.28, both of which affect the texture of the sound. Do not be afraid to make your own quick adjustments to filter settings, even if you do not know what everything means.

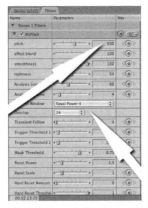

FIGURE 15.28 To correct sound distortion that results from pitch adjustment, you can adjust other settings in the filter, such as under the *Resynth Window* and *Overlap* pop-up menus.

A drone of dread

After Michael drinks from the hose, Lisa goes down to the basement to turn off the water, the better to lure Michael into the house, which in *this* version of the film will lead to something very bad. In addition to using *Funk Seventies Rhodes*, which is used again, twice in a row, with the first copy pitch-adjusted, there is an eerie drone sound that begins here, quietly, as shown in Figure 15.29, and gradually rises until the fateful climax of the film. The problem with using this drone sound – *Texture and Ambience_169* – is that it is fairly short. If you remember, at the beginning of this chapter we mentioned the nested sequence, entitled *Final Droning Sound*, into which multiple copies of *Texture and Ambience_169* (34 copies, to be exact) had been placed. The reason for this long nested sequence should now be pretty clear. We need a way to further bolster a sense of unease at this point in the film, and this droning sound is perfect.

FIGURE 15.29 As Lisa heads down the stairs to the basement, there is an eerie drone sound that begins, quietly, and gradually rises until the fateful climax of the film.

The one problem with this particular droning sound, *Texture and Ambience_169*, is that there is a noticeable audio "blip" in the middle of it, where the sound appears to drop out for a second. This is how it sounded in GarageBand, and the challenge, now, is to remove it in FCE. The best thing to do, then, is choose a short selection – that doesn't contain the "blip" – from within this audio clip by setting specific *In* and *Out* points, as shown in Figure 15.30. Then copy and paste this shorter version of the clip into a new sequence (which will become our *Final Droning Sound* sequence) enough times to create a sound long enough to last from the point where Lisa descends into the basement until the end of the film. We can then apply a 1-second dissolve between each copy of the clip, and the result will be a relatively smooth 2-minute audio file. We can then drag this sequence into our Master sequence – nesting it – and then, using clip overlays and the *Pen* tool, create a gradual rise in the audio level from the start of the drone, at 2:40, until the climactic final walk down the hallway, at 4:10.

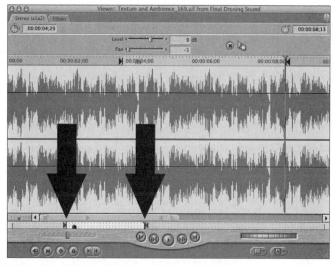

FIGURE 15.30 To isolate a section of *Texture and Ambience_169* that does not have an audio "blip," choose a short bit by setting specific *In* and *Out* points within the Viewer.

Part 4 - The power of ellipsis

As in all of the previous versions of the film, Lisa steals Michael's shirt, and Michael is unable to drink from the hose, as the water has been turned off. But now, because of the sound design and more careful presentation of Lisa (without any playfulness), the atmosphere is more sinister and the audience should be wondering if it is really such a good idea for Michael to go into the house.

Part of what helps make this new tone possible is the music. It is also the emphasis on different aspects of the characters, achieved through editing. For example, in part of the film – after the water has been turned off – there is a new shot that was used in neither the comedy or the drama: *8D. Lisa runs back inside.* This is where Lisa grabs Michael's shirt and then we see her from inside the door. It works here, since we don't want to tilt up to her smiling face, which is what happens if we let *8C. Lisa takes shirt* play as long as it did in the previous two versions. Instead, we want her to look very serious as she runs. This kind of change helps to sell the suspenseful nature of *Nail Polish As Thriller*.

Another change is noticeable as Michael discovers his shirt missing. *Mystery Accents_04* is used again – five times, and with pitch adjustment – but we also cut to a shot of Lisa watching Michael: *7E. CU Lisa watches Michael.* This shot is stolen directly from the scene where Michael first walks on to the porch. Here, a different portion of the same close-up is used to make it seem as if Lisa is constantly monitoring Michael's every move.

After this, Michael enters the house, in spite of our fears, takes off his shoes, and walks down the hall to Lisa's room. All the time, the sound of the droning – inspiring more and more dread, we hope – builds in intensity. Since we have no footage of anything bad actually happening to Michael, we need to create the illusion of disaster. One solution is to do two things to create some sort of climax: fade to red as Michael approaches Lisa's door and cross fade the *Final Droning Sound* sequence into the same *Drone Whine* with which we opened the film.

To fade to red, at the end of shot *12C. Michael walks down hall*, you can easily apply a *Dip to Color Dissolve*, as shown in Figure 15.31. Although we haven't used this transition before, you should know where to find it. Once you drop it at the end of the clip, double-click on it. Then, in the Viewer, you can choose a color, as shown in Figure 15.32. A blood-colored red would work best, since we are trying to create the illusion that Lisa has lured Michael to his death. Once you choose the color, the end of the shot will have a red filmy substance gradually overwhelm the image, as shown in Figure 15.33. If you drag the edge of the dissolve to make it fairly long, the slow pace of the red color overtaking Michael will be especially dramatic.

FIGURE 15.31 Fade to red, at the end of shot *12C. Michael walks down hall*, apply a *Dip to Color Dissolve*.

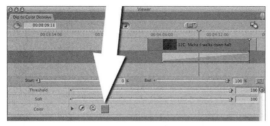

FIGURE 15.32 Double-click the transition and then choose a color in the Viewer.

FIGURE 15.33 The color you choose will gradually overwhelm the image over the course of the transition.

At the end of the *Dip to Color Dissolve*, we suddenly cut to black and to silence. This abrupt cut to nothing, at the end of the dread-filled walk, really sells the idea that something bad has happened to Michael. Then, at the end of an almost 4-second gap, the music *Desert Heat* starts up again, as shown in Figure 15.34, and, a little over 2 seconds after that, we fade up on shot *1A. flowers_1*. If the dramatic red "bloodbath" was the climax of the piece, now begins the ending.

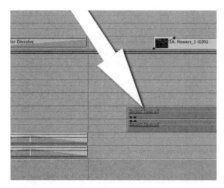

FIGURE 15.34 The music *Desert Heat* starts up again, after a brief pause, following the red *Dip to Color Dissolve*.

Comparing All Three Versions of the Film

Within the three different versions of *Nail Polish*, we have tried to maintain some musical continuity, so that the pieces felt as if they were part of a unified whole. This is why we return to *Desert Heat* at the end of this version. It is the same music, post-drone, with which we opened *Nail Polish As Thriller*. Here, the opening shots of the garden that were used in both the comedy and the drama are now used in the same sequence as in those films, only at the end. You could just open up *Nail Polish As Drama*, copy the opening shots, and paste them into this sequence. They work at this point in the film because they lend a creepy note to the fact that life in this location goes on, even if Michael does not. Finally, after cutting back to Lisa on her bed, we then cut to the same title we used at the opening and then fade to black.

To finish the project, wrap it all up by correcting the color of the same shots we corrected in earlier cuts of *Nail Polish*.

SUMMARY

In this final chapter, we cut our third and final version of *Nail Polish*. It was a little harder to do than the either the comedy or the drama, as the footage did not entirely support the exercise. Nevertheless, we put something together and created a suspenseful film.

We began by working in LiveType to make a motion graphics-based title card that we then imported into FCE to be placed on top of a very evocative audio clip. We needed to set a scary tone to the film right away, and these new elements helped us do so.

We reviewed the rest of the audio clips that come on the accompanying DVD, and isolated the sounds that best serve this kind of film, *Mystery Accents_04* and *Funk Seventies Rhodes* (the original file names from GarageBand were kept). We used these as helpful atmospheric accents to shape our scary story, applying the *AUPitch* audio filter to manipulate them even further. We also rearranged scenes and shots in new ways to move the plot in a surprising direction.

SUMMARY

Another sound we discovered was *Texture and Ambience_169*. We needed an especially long droning sound for the last part of the film, and this turned out to be the perfect audio clip for such a purpose. It wasn't a long enough clip, however, so we placed multiple copies of it inside a new sequence, and then *nested* that new sequence inside of the original master sequence. As a final climactic touch, as the drone ends, we placed a *Dip to Color Dissolve* on top of the shot of Michael walking down the hallway, making it appear that he is covered with red, indicating that he is, perhaps, walking to his doom. When we were done, we had a very different kind of film than either *Nail Polish As Comedy* or *Nail Polish As Drama*.

REVIEW QUESTIONS: CHAPTER 15

1. What are two ways that you can change the color of a background texture in LiveType?

2. How do you change the pitch of an audio clip, in FCE, and how do you fix any resulting audio distortion?

3. How do you matte a texture into text in LiveType?

4. What is *nesting*?

5. What is a *Dip to Color Dissolve*?

1. What challenges do you face when trying to cut a film in a genre for which it was not intended? What are some ways to surmount this challenge?

2. What role has music played in the three different versions of *Nail Polish*?

3. When you cut your own *Nail Polish As Thriller* film, what different choices did you make than those made in this and why?

Further Research

If you haven't done so already, cut your own version of *Nail Polish As Thriller*. If you haven't cut the other versions of the film, work on those, too. If you have any issues that come up as you edit, go back to the earlier chapters in this book and look up any information that you need to know. Everything that you need to know to edit basic (and not-so-basic) FCE projects can be found in this book.

CONCLUSION – FINAL THOUGHTS

So, What Does an Editor Do?

We began this book with a question: can you name a film editor? Even if you still cannot name any one particular film editor, you should now have, at the very least, a new appreciation for what a film editor does. You should also have emerged from this book with a good amount of actual how-to editing knowledge, from both a craft and a technology perspective. With Final Cut Express and LiveType, you should now be able to put together projects of some complexity.

There is too little appreciation in the world for the creative work of editors. Film editing is not just about taking footage from the director and putting it in order. It's about finding the story and setting the pace.

Choosing the Right Hard Drive

Depending on the available hard drive space on your computer, you may want to have a reliable external hard drive to store all of your media files and scratch disks. Actually, even if you have plenty of room on your computer, it is better to use an external drive as your main scratch disk, just in case your computer ever crashes. Hard drives die, too, however, so you should always have a second external drive to use for back-ups. It's expensive, but so is losing everything and having to start over.

Here are few things to keep in mind when choosing a hard drive (also remember that technology is changing all of the time, and you should stay current):

1. Make sure your hard drive has at least a triple-interface port (USB 2.0, Firewire 400, Firewire 800), and possibly a quad interface (eSata included). While Firewire 400 is being phased out, you'll appreciate being able to easily connect to such a port until it completely disappears.

2. Make sure your hard drive runs at 7200 rpm, rather than 5400 rpm (that's revolutions per minute). While flash drives are improving all of the time, they still can't match the capacity of old-school drive technology – yet – so you need to consider the speed of the components within.

3. Make sure your hard drive has at least 500GB of storage, if not 1TB (or even 2TB). Memory is inexpensive. Buy enough so that you don't run out of room.

4. Don't buy the cheapest drive available. Stick to tried and true brands, such as LaCie, G-Drives, or OWC Computing Mercury Drives. It's worth the few extra bucks.

5. Before loading your drive with files, reformat it in Mac OS Extended mode, rather than leaving it in the default MS-DOS mode that most drives come in. The latter mode poses serious issues for video editing on a Mac. If you don't know how to reformat, find someone who does, or read a Mac manual, such as the *Missing Manual*, by David Pogue, mentioned in Chapter 7.

To reformat your drive, you need to use the Disk Utility *application, which you can find in the* Utilities *folder of your* Applications *folder.*

6. If you need your drive to be readable on both Macs and PCs, partition it, making part of it PC-formatted (which will be readable on a Mac, anyway) and part of it Mac-formatted (which will not be readable on a PC).

Now go make movies.

APPENDIX

Answers to Odd-Numbered Review Questions

Chapter 1

1. Name the major figures in the invention of cinema. *Thomas Edison; Auguste and Louis Lumière.* When was the first public projection of a motion picture? *1895.*

3. Why is D.W. Griffith an important figure? *He is considered the "father of the close-up." His cinematic innovations, culminating in the controversial 195 film The Birth of a Nation, moved cinematic language forward by leaps and bounds.*

5. What is the 180° line? *It is an unseen line drawn through the middle of a scene being shot; if you stay on one side of it with the camera, then you will not confuse the viewer through errors in your cinematic geography.*

Chapter 2

1. List all of the different frame sizes of shots you can remember. *Close-Up, Medium Close-Up, Medium Shot, Medium Full Shot, Full Shot, Long Shot, and many more.*

3. How many different camera movements can you name? *Pan, Tilt, Tracking/Dolly, Handheld, and many more.*

5. What are the main issues you should consider before making a cut? *Is there a reason to cut at that particular spot? Does it serve the story to cut there, in that way?*

7. How does mise-en-scène affect editing? *Mise-en-scène, or blocking/staging, can function as in-camera editing: if you plan the shot well, you may predetermine where you should cut, or if you should cut at all/*

Chapter 3

1. Describe and discuss the three main film genres. *Drama - a generally serious and emotionally sincere rendition of a story. Comedy - a generally funny telling of a story, where the goal is to maximize the laughs. Thriller - a generally frightening and suspenseful version of a story, where the goal is to scare the audience as much as possible.*

3. What is the most important role of a drama? *To serve the emotional complexity of the narrative and the emotional needs of the character.*

5. What is the most important role of a thriller? *To scare the audience in as suspenseful a way as possible.*

Chapter 4

1. Define "documentary film." *A film that tells an ostensibly true story with real people, not actors.*

3. What was the first successful documentary feature? *Nanook of the North* (Robert Flaherty, 1922).

5. What is *Cinéma Vérité*? *This is a fly-on-the-wall style of telling a story, where the camera just records events, with no commentary from interviews or narration. It came from France in the late 1950s and early 1960s.*

Chapter 5

1. What is a short film vs. a feature film? *It depends on the venue and the country, but generally a short film is any film under an hour, while a feature film is over an hour in length.*

3. What kinds of short films exist today? *Commercials; Film Festival Entries; Promotional Videos; Many Webisodes or other online content; Films like the collection of shorts in* <u>Paris, je t'aime</u>*.*

5. What are some distribution options for short films today? *Film Festivals; Some cable outlets, such as IFC; Many Web sites.*

Chapter 6

1. What is an NLE system? *Non-linear editing systems are digital computer, like AVID or Final Cut Express, which let you manipulate your footage any way you want.*

3. When was the first NLE system invented? *1971.*

5. What are the main NLE programs available today? *AVID, Adobe Premiere, Final Cut Pro, Final Cut Express, and others.*

Chapter 7

1. What is a *scratch disk? The folder - designated by you - in which all of the media associated with your Final Cut Express project is stored.*

3. What is a keyboard shortcut key? *A key - or combination of keys - that, when pressed, performs a function found in a menu within a given application/*

5. What happens to the original source media that we manipulate in FCE? *Unless you go into the scratch disk and delete it, nothing happens to the source media, no matter how much you manipulate it.*

Chapter 8

1. What does *rendering* mean? *Creating an effect by creating a new piece of media that gets stored in your scratch disk.*

3. What are the tools on the Tool Palette that you have used so far? *Selection Tool, Razor Blade Tool, Pen Tool.*

5. What is a *keyframe*? *A point that you set in a given piece of media that, together with a second point, allows to create an animation within that media.*

Chapter 9

1. How do keyframes make animation possible? *Two keyframes in one media clip, if set to two different settings, cause the clip to change as it plays from keyframe point to the next. More than two keyframes will cause even more changes.*

3. What are the differences between the Roll, Ripple, Slip, and Slide tools? *They all allow you to affect the edit point between shots. The Roll Tool lets you slide back and forth over the edit point, changing the lengths of both shots as you do so. The Ripple Tool lets you do the same thing, but you only change the length of the shot on which you have clicked, while the length of the other shot remains the same. The Slip Tool lets you keep the length of the clip on which you have clicked the same, but displays different parts of the clip as you scroll through it (provided you have handles of extra footage). The Slide Tool lets you change the lengths of clips on either side of the clip on which you have clicked.*

5. How can you make titles? *By going to the Effects Tab and using the Text Generators inside the Text Bin inside the Video Generators Bin.*

Chapter 10

1. What is meant by *format* in the video world? *Format refers to the video compression, or codec, in which the footage is encoded. It also refers to frame rate and frame size.*

3. What are the different kinds of HD footage that FCE understands? *HDV, Apple Intermediate Codec, and AVCHD.*

5. How do you import music and photos into your project? *Just go to the File Menu and scroll down to Import.* What is AIFF? *Audio Interchange File Format, a high quality compression that is what most professional editing programs require for audio files.*

Chapter 11

1. What are the four windows in LiveType? *Canvas, Media Browser, Inspector, Timeline.*

3. What is the difference between LiveFonts and regular system fonts? *LiveFonts have previously created animations already within them, while system fonts are the same as what you would find in any other application on your computer. You can add animations to them, however.*

5. Why would you export a LiveType file as a self-contained movie? *If you wanted the animation to be a movie on its own, or for use in applications other than Final Cut.*

Chapter 12

1. Who were Lev Kuleshov and Sergei Eisenstein? *Two Russian* film pioneers of *the late 1910s and early 1920s, largely responsible for creating the art of editing. Kuleshov led a collective of young artists who discovered that the context of a shot within a sequence is more important than what is in the shot, itself. This discovery has since been labeled the "Kuleshov Effect." Eisenstein took these principles and made a highly influential film in 1925, The Battleship Potemkin.*

3. What is one way that music can affect our reaction to a shot? *Music changes the context of the shot; it affects our senses, making us see the shot in a different way.*

5. How do you copy attributes, such as filters, from one shot to many other shots with just a few keyboard strokes? *Command-C will copy the contents of a shot; Option-V, if you are clicked on a new shot, will offer you the chance to paste the attributes of your choice from the previous shot to the new shot.*

Chapter 13

1. How can you expand the Browser viewing area, so you can see more of the information therein? *Just grab the bottom right corner and drag.*

3. What are two different ways to create audio dissolves? *Use the built in fades inside the Audio Transitions Bin in eth Effects Tab; Use the Pen Tool and Clip Overlays.*

5. Explain an issue in FCE with ascending numbers in file names. *Unless you put an initial zero at the beginning of your numbering sequence, all of the numbers starting with "1" will be grouped together, as will all of the numbers beginning with "2," etc.*

Chapter 14

1. How do you open a LiveType project from within FCE? *Control-click - or right-click - on it and select "Open in Editor" from the pop-up menu that appears.*

3. How does FCE, in the Browser, present each open project? *As a separate tab.*

5. Why are handles essential to creating dissolves? *Without that extra "unseen" footage, there is nothing to dissolve from. A dissolve needs material from which to fade in.*

Chapter 15

1. What are two ways that you can change the color of a background texture in LiveType? *You can go to the Style Tab in the Inspector and change the color of the Glow; you can also go to the Attributes Tab of the Inspector and click on the color box under the Glyph category.*

3. How do you matte a texture into text in LiveType? *In the Media Browser, select a texture that you like, then highlight the text in the Timeline to which you wish to matte this texture, and then, in the Media Browser, click on "Apple to Matte."*

5. What is a *Dip to Color Dissolve*? *This causes your clip to fade out to, or fade in from, the color of your choice, rather than the default black.*

INDEX